SYMMETRY BREAKING IN SYNTAX

In this illuminating new theory of grammar, Hubert Haider demonstrates that there is a basic asymmetry in the phrase structure of any language, whatever sentence structure it takes. Moreover, he argues that understanding this asymmetry is the key to understanding the grammatical causality underlying a broad range of core syntactic phenomena. Until now, Germanic languages have been seen to fall into two distinct classes: those which take an object-verb sentence structure (OV) or a verb-object one (VO). However, by examining the nature of this universal underlying asymmetry, Hubert Haider reveals a third syntactic type: 'Type III'. In particular, he employs the third type to explore the cognitive evolution of grammar which gave rise to the structural asymmetry and its typological implications. *Symmetry Breaking in Syntax* will appeal to academic researchers and graduate students involved in comparative and theoretical syntax and the cognitive evolution of grammar.

HUBERT HAIDER is Professor of linguistics at the University of Salzburg. He specializes in the theory of syntax, comparative syntax and syntax and the brain. His previous publications include *The Syntax of German* (Cambridge University Press, 2010).

CAMBRIDGE STUDIES IN LINGUISTICS

General Editors: P. AUSTIN, J. BRESNAN, B. COMRIE,
S. CRAIN, W. DRESSLER, C. J. EWEN, R. LASS,
D. LIGHTFOOT, K. RICE, I. ROBERTS, S. ROMAINE,
N. V. SMITH

Symmetry Breaking in Syntax

In this series

106. SHARON INKELAS and CHERYL ZOLL: *Reduplication: doubling in morphology*
107. SUSAN EDWARDS: *Fluent aphasia*
108. BARBARA DANCYGIER and EVE SWEETSER: *Mental spaces in grammar: conditional constructions*
109. HEW BAERMAN, DUNSTAN BROWN and GREVILLE G. CORBETT: *The syntax–morphology interface: a study of syncretism*
110. MARCUS TOMALIN: *Linguistics and the formal sciences: the origins of generative grammar*
111. SAMUEL D. EPSTEIN and T. DANIEL SEELY: *Derivations in minimalism*
112. PAUL DE LACY: *Markedness: reduction and preservation in phonology*
113. YEHUDA N. FALK: *Subjects and their properties*
114. P. H. MATTHEWS: *Syntactic relations: a critical survey*
115. MARK C. BAKER: *The syntax of agreement and concord*
116. GILLIAN CATRIONA RAMCHAND: *Verb meaning and the lexicon: a first phase syntax*
117. PIETER MUYSKEN: *Functional categories*
118. JUAN URIAGEREKA: *Syntactic anchors: on semantic structuring*
119. D. ROBERT LADD: *Intonational phonology, second edition*
120. LEONARD H. BABBY: *The syntax of argument structure*
121. B. ELAN DRESHER: *The contrastive hierarchy in phonology*
122. DAVID ADGER, DANIEL HARBOUR and LAUREL J. WATKINS: *Mirrors and microparameters: phrase structure beyond free word order*
123. NIINA NING ZHANG: *Coordination in syntax*
124. NEIL SMITH: *Acquiring phonology*
125. NINA TOPINTZI: *Onsets: suprasegmental and prosodic behaviour*
126. CEDRIC BOECKX, NORBERT HORNSTEIN and JAIRO NUNES: *Control as movement*
127. MICHAEL ISRAEL: *The grammar of polarity: pragmatics, sensitivity and the logic of scales*
128. M. RITA MANZINI and LEONARDO M. SAVOIA: *Grammatical categories: variation in romance languages*
129. BARBARA CITKO: *Symmetry in syntax: merge, move and labels*
130. RACHEL WALKER: *Vowel patterns in language*
131. MARY DALRYMPLE and IRINA NIKOLAEVA: *Objects and information structure*
132. JERROLD M. SADOCK: *The modular architecture of grammar*
133. DUNSTAN BROWN and ANDREW HIPPISLEY: *Network morphology: a defaults-based theory of word structure*
134. BETTELOU LOS, CORRIEN BLOM, GEERT BOOIJ, MARION ELENBAAS and ANS VAN KEMENADE: *Morphosyntactic change: a comparative study of particles and prefixes*
135. STEPHEN CRAIN: *The emergence of meaning*
136. HUBERT HAIDER: *Symmetry breaking in syntax*

Earlier issues not listed are also available

SYMMETRY BREAKING IN SYNTAX

HUBERT HAIDER
University of Salzburg

CAMBRIDGE UNIVERSITY PRESS
Cambridge, New York, Melbourne, Madrid, Cape Town,
Singapore, São Paulo, Delhi, Mexico City

Cambridge University Press
The Edinburgh Building, Cambridge CB2 8RU, UK

Published in the United States of America by Cambridge University Press, New York

www.cambridge.org
Information on this title: www.cambridge.org/9781107017757

© Hubert Haider 2013

This publication is in copyright. Subject to statutory exception
and to the provisions of relevant collective licensing agreements,
no reproduction of any part may take place without the written
permission of Cambridge University Press.

First published 2013

Printed and bound in the United Kingdom by the MPG Books Group

A catalogue record for this publication is available from the British Library

Library of Congress Cataloguing in Publication data
Haider, Hubert.
  Symmetry breaking in syntax / Hubert Haider.
    p. cm.
  Includes bibliographical references and index.
  ISBN 978-1-107-01775-7
  1. Germanic languages–Syntax. 2. German language–Syntax. 3. Parallelism
  (Linguistics) 4. Germanic languages–Grammar, Comparative.
  5. German language–Grammar, Comparative. 6. Generative grammar. I. Title.
  PD361.H36 2012
  435–dc23   2012026427

ISBN 978-1-107-01775-7 Hardback

Cambridge University Press has no responsibility for the persistence or
accuracy of URLs for external or third-party internet websites referred to in
this publication, and does not guarantee that any content on such websites is,
or will remain, accurate or appropriate.

Contents

	Preface	*page* ix
	List of abbreviations	xvi
1	What breaks the symmetry in syntactic structuring	1
2	Linearizations are public, structures are private	20
3	BBC – asymmetry in phrase structuring	40
4	The cross-linguistic impact of the BBC	65
5	The Germanic OV/VO split	97
6	Adverbial positions in VO and in OV	136
7	Elements of the third kind – resultative predicates and particles in OV and VO	173
8	Asymmetry in nominal structures – word and phrase structure	190
9	BBC or LCA? – fact finding and evaluation	211
	Bibliography	250
	Index	263

Preface

This volume puts forward a good deal of the harvest of twenty years' occupation with verb–object/object–verb (VO/OV) as a main syntactic divide across languages. The enterprise got going in 1991, when I gradually became conscious of the fact that syntactic structures are universally asymmetric.[1] Languages share a uniform syntactic asymmetry. Their phrase structures are *right-branching*. Left-branching projections are not employed.

This volume contains only part of the harvest, though. The other part has already been published in 2010. Although the title of the publication *The Syntax of German* tells that the volume has a pre-assigned focus on German, it is nevertheless a book on the OV/VO-dependent syntactic properties, illustrated mainly with data from German, in comparison with English and other Germanic languages. Half of the itemized agenda below is covered there, namely the structuring of the verb phrase (VP) in OV and VO, the clause structure of SVO and SOV, VO-triggered constraints on wh-movement, scrambling, extraposition and verb clustering.

At the beginning back in 1991 stood a conjecture, viz. the *'basic branching conjecture'*. In the following years, I kept on investigating various domains of the right-branching hypothesis and its consequences for:

- *A-bar movement*   Haider (2004a, 2005, 2010a: ch.3)
- *adjuncts* (adverbials and attributes)   Haider (2000a, 2002, 2004b)

---

[1] I remember a friend and colleague of mine at the University of Stuttgart at this time, Werner Frey, asking me why in a German NP, a PP-contained anaphor may be bound by a preceding genitive, although the genitive would not c-command the anaphor in a left-branching NP structure. All of a sudden I realized that the German NP, just like the English VP, had been mistaken as left-branching for a long time. They are right-branching. The next step was generalizing the basic hypothesis (i.e. universality of right-branching) to any complex phrase and to study the effects of the head-initial vs. head-final architecture. The first international presentation of this idea was on 9 December 1991, at the *Conference for Lexical Specification and Lexical Insertion* at Utrecht University (published in Haider (1992) and in the conference proceedings that appeared in 2000).

- distribution of arguments in phrases and clauses   Haider (1992, 1993, 1997c, 2010a: ch.4)
- *extraposition* (no movement to the right)   Haider (1995a, 1997a, 2010a: ch.5)
- *functional* projections, functional subjects   Haider (1993, 2005, 2010a: ch.2)
- secondary *predicates*, including particles   Haider (1997b)
- the deduction of OV and VO   Haider (2000b, 2005, 2010a: ch.1)
- the discovery of a third type, viz. Type III   Haider (2005, 2010a: ch.4.4, 2010b)
- the *evolution* of grammars   Haider (1998, 1999, 2001a)
- the Germanic *diachrony* of OV and VO   Haider (2005, 2010b)
- the *typological* implications   Haider (1997d)
- *verb clustering* and clause union in OV   Haider (2003, 2010a: ch.7)
- *word* structure   Haider (2001b)

After two decades of continuous investigation into these matters, I feel justified in renaming the 'basic branching *conjecture*' and dare to construe the acronym BBC henceforth as the 'basic branching *constraint*' of universal grammar (UG). The capacious network of diverse but interdependent analyses that support each other has become tight enough so that my confidence in the basic soundness of the approach has grown proportionally.

Additional backing comes from the comparison with competing models, when it turns out that straightforward major predictions of the BBC and PDI (Principle of Directional Identification) model necessitate complex and ad hoc measures in other models. I learnt that what these models understand as universal syntactic properties have been tailored too tightly to SVO languages. After all, these theories were built almost exclusively on SVO data. OV data had to be 'squeezed' in. Obviously, it should not come as a surprise if an SOV grammar does not fit neatly into a 'universal' model that has inadvertently been designed for SVO. Typically, a patch-up strategy is used for deriving OV from VO. As a result, either the SOV grammar or the underlying grammar theory perceptibly suffers from collateral damage and invites additional ad hoc remedies.

What we deserve is a grammar theory that elevates the standpoint above the narrow horizon of VO languages. VO is not more basic than OV, and vice versa. In fact, there is no language type that is 'more basic' and could serve as the source for the derivation of all other types.² But there are structural invariants that are basic, and they determine the grammar of any type of languages.

One of these invariants is a universal constraint on structure building: syntactic structures are invariably right-branching, contrary to naive apprehension. This constraint in combination with the directionality *parameter* for the identification relation between heads and dependants (PDI) defines a system space that provides room for OV, VO and a type that has not received the appreciation it deserves yet, namely the *Type III*. It went unnoticed because these languages are still misinterpreted as atypical VO languages. This book describes the system space and its empirical reflections in diverse domains of the grammar, synchronically and diachronically (Germanic OV/VO split).

Even if syntactic structures are perfectly described, they are not fully understood as long as they are characterized in isolation.³ It is an underestimated commonplace that syntactic structures are put to use in language processing (production and reception). They are put to use and they have an adaptive design for the conditions of usage. A functionalist typically interprets this in a *form-follows-function* perspective. This perspective is misleading, however (Haider 1998, 2001a). Adaptive design in language is not functionalist design, viz. the design of the invisible hand of a tool maker. In Chapters 1 and 2 it is argued that adaptivity in language is the result of an ongoing process of evolution. It is '*cognitive*' evolution and it shares the basic principles of evolution with *biological*, neo-Darwinian evolution, without sharing the substrate. Biological evolution is selection on the genome level; cognitive evolution is selection on the level (of the format) of mental representations. They are subject to the substance-neutral conditions of evolutionary processes for reproductive systems, based on variation and selection.

The (cognitive) *co-evolution* of the structuring system (as a dimension management system) with the systems that utilize it (acquisition, parsing and production systems) is ultimately responsible for the basic asymmetries (and for *symmetry breaking*). Already in 1881, Darwin had seen the point of the close parallel between the descent of species and the diachronic development of

---

[2] But there is always a language that is mistaken as a model language. From the time of the mediaeval grammarians (e.g. the Modistae) until the nineteenth century, the model language was Latin. Today it is English.

[3] Syntax cannot be explained with reference to syntax only, unless you (mis-)treat it as a purely Platonic object. This would be much like the situation of the Englishman in the Chinese room, in John Searle's ingenious Chinese room thought experiment. The contexts of use are an essential part of the understanding of a system that is continuously put to use.

languages in the context of a theory of evolution (Darwin 1871, vol. I: 59).[4] Linguists of those days, however, were concerned with a different aspect of the impact of language on the theory of biological evolution. From the beginning, the fact that there is a language-gifted species was seen as a serious challenge for Darwinian evolution,[5] but apparently no one took up Darwin's own linguistic point during the past 130 years. His point was and still is that the process of evolution is substance neutral. Genetic evolution is just one possible instantiation of evolution. Another possible instantiation is cognitive evolution. Structures of human languages owe their adaptivity to *cognitive* evolution, just like the adaptivity of organisms is a result of *biological* evolution. All it requires is variation and selection. The selector in the cognitive evolution of grammars is the processing brain and its constraints on information processing. Functionalists (e.g. Croft 2009) assume that the selector is the society (and its 'needs'). This seems to be a misguided idea, however. Selection, unlike (social) engineering, is not driven by future purposes. *Variation* is driven by social factors but constrained by the nature of possible grammars (Wilson and Henry 1995). The nature of possible grammars is determined by the language-processing brain. This is the source of selection and it is the locus of the reproduction of grammars, too.

Here are the topics of the following nine chapters in a nutshell

Chapter 1 prepares the scene and presents the subject matter, namely *symmetry breaking*, as a fundamental property of syntactic structures and of grammars of human languages that determine these structures. For ease of reference, part of the chapter is a synopsis of the issues relevant for symmetry breaking that have already been covered in Haider (2010a).

Chapter 2 focuses on *cognitive selection* as the key for understanding the universal conditions on grammars in determining the structural architecture of complex phrases. The recipient side is the selector and the ultimate source of symmetry breaking. BBC as a principle of UG guarantees that core grammars

---

[4] Charles Darwin (1871: 59) had already appreciated the parallel between the evolution of languages and biological evolution: 'The formation of different languages and of distinct species, and the proofs that both have been developed through a gradual process, are curiously parallel.'

[5] 'Language is the Rubicon which divides man from beast, and no animal will ever cross it ... The science of language will yet enable us to withstand the extreme theories of the Darwinians, and to draw a hard and fast line between man and brute.' (Friedrich Max Müller's lectures: 'The theoretical stage, and the origin of language', delivered at the Royal Institution of Great Britain in April, May and June, 1861. Published 1862 in: *Lectures on the Science of Language*. London: Longman, Green, Longman and Roberts).

provide data structures that are parser friendly, as an economical solution to the problem of limited resources on the recipient side. This should not be read as a *functionalist* commitment, however. It is *adaptation by cognitive selection*, that is, a substance-neutral application of the Darwinian principles of evolution, applied to the selection of the cognitive representations of grammar systems.

Chapter 3 is an updated and amended version of work from the birth days of the BBC in 1991. The first three subsections present the originally surveyed empirical evidence for a principle that was presented as a conjecture at that time. Section 3.5 defends the BBC against apparent counterevidence from Slavic languages. The defence is turned into an argument for recognizing Slavic languages as Type III languages. The concluding section lists additional evidence that investigations since then have brought to light, plus a summary of the consequences of the BBC in combination with the PDI.

Chapter 4 deals with the BBC on the *typological* scale. Its focus is, on the one hand, on *missing types and structures*, as a consequence of the BBC, and on the other hand, on the exposition of the predictions of the BBC in a cross-linguistic and typological perspective. It argues for more fine-grained standards of investigating data adduced for broad typological generalizations.

Chapter 5 proposes a solution for a long-standing diachronic puzzle, namely the split into VO and OV types in the development of the Germanic language family. The solution is based on the insight that the PDI offers room for the existence of a *third* type, namely a type with *flexible* directionality, in addition to the strictly head-final (OV) and the strictly head-initial (VO) options. The Germanic split, which contrasts with the uniform development towards VO in the Romance family (arising from the Type III language Latin), is argued to follow from the coincidence of the development of the V2-property (fronting the finite verb) and the change from the third type to a type with fixed directionality.

The basic change in the diachronic development of the Germanic languages (and the Romance languages, too) is a change from *flexible* to *rigid* directionality of identification. In principle, the implementation of rigid directionality based on a predecessor language with flexible directionality provides a choice between two equally well-suited instantiations, and each of these options has found its adopters, as usual. As a consequence, one group of Germanic languages has ended up as OV, and the other group has become VO. A crucial ingredient for the balanced availability of the choice was the simultaneous emergence of the V2-property of Germanic languages.

Chapters 6 and 7 concentrate on particular empirical domains and their PDI-triggered grammatical properties. Chapter 6 describes the characteristic *distribution of adverbials* in OV and VO, respectively, as a consequence of the PDI. This requirement triggers *compactness* and thereby reduces the available positions for adverbials in VO. The grammar of *secondary predicates* (*result predication*) in the light of the BBC and the PDI is the subject of Chapter 7. The stranding pattern of result predicates in VO is immediate evidence for a shell structure in VO and its absence in OV.

Chapter 8 is devoted to nominal structures. First, it demonstrates that the BBC applies not only to syntactic structures at the phrase level but to the *word structure* as well. A restriction on recursive compounding that discriminates between the frequent head-final and the highly restricted head-initial word structures provides direct support for the BBC. Second, the properties of NPs as head-initial phrases in German are shown to coincide with the properties for head-initial phrases attested for English and other strictly head-initial languages. Third, the nominalization of verb clusters is shown to provide direct evidence for base-generating the typical verbal clusters of clauses based on head-final VPs, rather than deriving them.

Chapter 9, finally, compares in detail the BBC model with the LCA (linear correspondence axiom) model of Kayne (1994) and subsequent work. The comparison focuses on their relative success in accounting for the OV/VO correlates in particular, and the issue of symmetry breaking in general. The two explanations are in a complementarity relation: the LCA model derives OV from VO by massive *phrasal movement*, while the BBC model frames the account in terms of alternatively available *head positions*. Both approaches share the conviction that syntactic structures are principally right-branching. The chapter presents arguments for the empirical as well as theoretical (in-)adequacy of each of the competing models, with a superior record for the BBC, not surprisingly.

This volume, together with the volume from 2010, draws a coherent picture of syntactic structures as it emerges when a lot of pieces of a puzzle have been put together successfully (for a small but essential area of a vast empirical terrain).

Final remark: The majority of the chapters are organized as self-supporting parts. This brings about an inevitable amount of overlap. Instead of being too often redirected to other parts of the book while you are reading a chapter (in the paper version), you may occasionally encounter data and arguments already familiar to you from a chapter you consulted before. No chapter has been published before in its present form and with its present content, but of course, the book integrates the outcomes of previously published investigations.

Acknowledgements: This volume has benefited greatly from the time and efforts two anonymous reviewers invested into the draft version. I am very grateful for their questions, suggestions, critical remarks and their constructive reading. In the hopefully unlikely but unavoidable case – Murphy's law! – that you nevertheless encounter blunders, you have to blame it on, and tell it to, the author, of course.

Finally, I want to thank the Cambridge University Press production team of this volume for their proficient professional patronage and their congenial cooperation.

Abbreviations

ACC	accusative
ANS	Algemene Nederlandse Spraakkunst (grammar of standard Dutch); abbreviation for the title of Geerts *et al.* (1984) or Haeseryn *et al.* (1997)
BBC	basic branching constraint
BG	Burzio's generalization
C.PR	complex predicate
CED	condition on extraction domains
CL	clitic
COMP	complementizer (position); C°
DAT	dative
DIR	directive
DO	direct object
DS	deep structure (= syntactic representation before any transformation has applied)
ECP	Empty Category Principle
EIC	(Principle of) Early Immediate Constituents (see Hawkins 1994)
EPP	Extended Projection Principle $=_{def.}$ *'clauses have subjects'* (Chomsky 1982: 9–10)
F°	functional head (cover term for any category of functional head)
FEM	feminine
FIN	finite
FUT	future
GEN	genitive
I°	functional head for inflection features
IC	immediate constituent
INF	infinite
INTRANS	intransitive

IO	indirect object
IPP	*infinitivus pro participio*, Latin for 'infinitive instead of participle', in German: *Ersatzinfinitiv*
LCA	linear correspondence axiom (Kayne 1994)
LF	logical form
LOC	locative
MASC	masculine
ME	Middle English
MLC	Minimal Link Condition
NEUT	neutrum, neuter
NOM	nominative
OBJ	object
OE	Old English
OV	type of language with a head-final VP, that is, 'object–verb' order
P&P	Principles and Parameters Model (Chomsky 1981)
Part	participle
PASS	passive
PDI	Principle of Directional Identification
PF	phonetic form
PO	prepositional object
POSS	possessive
PRO	silent subject in clausal infinitival constructions
PRT	particle
RC	relative clause
REFL	reflexive
RES	resultative
S.CL	small clause
SF	semantic form (i.e. a syntactic representation as interface to conceptual structures)
SUBJ	subject
TRANS	transitive
Type III	third word-order type (= type with *underspecified* canonical directionality)
T3	Type III
UG	Universal Grammar
V°	category of the lexical element 'verb', as the head of the VP; zero-level (= terminal) category in terms of phrase structure

V'	category of sub-tree of a verb phrase that is neither the zero-level category V° nor the phrase-level category VP
VC	verb cluster
VO	type of language with head-initial VP, that is, 'verb–object' order
XP	phrase of an arbitrary category (*x* serves as a variable for the head category)

1 *What breaks the symmetry in syntactic structuring*

1.1 The asymmetry of syntax

Let us refer to syntactic structures as *symmetric* if for a class of (sub-)trees [A B], there is a corresponding class of (sub-)trees that differ only with respect to the order of their immediate sub-constituents, i.e. [B A], within a given language, or cross-linguistically. In this sense, the attested language *structures* are asymmetric.[1] This means that the *inverse order* of a well-formed sequence of phrases in a complex phrase structure is in general not a well-formed sequence, neither cross-linguistically nor within a single language. In terms of phrase-structure trees, a symmetric organization of syntactic structuring as a cross-linguistic property would entail that there is a *mirror image* of a given *structure* as a well-formed structure at least in some other language. Compare, for instance, a German VP and its English counterpart, as in (1a,b):

(1)   a. *give* the reader a hint
       b. dem Leser einen Hinweis *geben*
          the reader$_{DAT}$ a hint$_{ACC}$ give
       c. [$_{VP}$ [$_{V'}$ V° DP] DP]   (Chomsky 1981: 171)
       d. [DP [DP V°]$_{V'}$]$_{VP}$

Until the mid-eighties, before Barss and Lasnik (1986), (1a,b) and (1c,d), respectively, were assumed to betray mirror-image structures. The two nominal complements in (1a,b) are first combined with the head and then with the resulting intermediate projection. Head-*initial* structures were deemed to integrate the complements on positions *following* the head (1c), while head-*final* structures were seen as the result of integrating the complements in positions *preceding* the head.

---

[1] For a non-empty set *M* and a relation $R \subseteq M \times M$: R is *asymmetric* $=_{def.} \forall x,y \in M: xRy \Rightarrow \neg(yRx)$.

Later, starting with Barss and Lasnik (1986) and Larson (1988) and subsequent work, and contrary to Baker (2003: 350), syntacticians came to know that (1c) is *empirically* inadequate for English double-object structures in particular, and for double-object constructions with head-initial VPs in general. Unfortunately, this has not spread to typologists yet.[2] But, why is left-branching (1c) excluded on *theoretical* grounds? What is it that makes the symmetric siblings unavailable for the grammars of human language? In other words, the theory has to provide for *symmetry breaking*.

Particularly clear cases of a basic asymmetry are found at the *sentence periphery*. There are quite a few languages – e.g. Germanic languages (except English), Kashmiri, Romansh in Switzerland; see Holmberg (2012) for an up-to-date report – with a *V-second* property (= V-movement + phrasal movement to a clause-initial functional projection), but there are no languages with a *V-penultimate* property. This would be the mirror image of the V2-structure: the finite verb would move to a clause-final functional head, and a single phrase would move to the clause-final spec position of this very head.

The clause-initial phrase in the V2-structure is the result of A'-movement to a clause-initial spec position. This position provides alternative accommodation for various kinds of elements, neither of which has a mirror-image counterpart in other languages.

There are languages that move *question phrases* to the clause-initial position, both in main and in embedded clauses. There are no languages, however, that move these items to a right-hand *spec* position.[3] Analogously, neither *relative* nor *comparative* clauses show movement of phrases to the right. And finally, there is no language with a *clause-final expletive*, as a counterpart to the (Germanic) clause-initial expletives in V2-declaratives. This is a clear case of asymmetry, even if it has not been fully appreciated yet.

As for apparent rightward movement, there are numerous proposals for *extraposition* as an instance of A'-movement to the right, but proponents of these accounts remain silent on the grammatical causality of the profound syntactic differences between the alleged A'-movement to a clause-final position and the well-established cases of A'-movement to the clause-initial position

---

[2] Until now, typologists have tended (see, for instance, Dryer 2009: 185) to equivocate *head-initial/final* with *left-/right-branching*, without presenting any substantive syntactic evidence at all for this alleged correlation between word order and structure. The correlation between word order and structure is merely presupposed or stipulated and not substantiated by appropriate syntactic analyses that are sensitive for and predictive of structural differences.

[3] There are languages with clause-final wh-positions (see Chapter 3). But these are clause-final focus positions in a cleft construction, not the result of movement.

(see Haider 2010a: ch.5). Extraposition as A′-movement would violate several core constraints on A′-movement.[4]

The overall asymmetry puzzle struck me first in 1991 when I was asked why anaphor binding within a German NP apparently violates the c-command constraint under the assumption – until then unquestioned – that a head-initial phrase like the German NP is left-branching.[5] If the PP that contains the reflexive in (2a), or the bound pronoun in (2b), were indeed higher in the structure than their respective binders, the result should be a weak-crossover violation. But there is no detectable violation, and moreover the 'correctly' inverted order is deviant, contrary to expectations:

(2) a. die Wut [des Mannes^i [auf sich^i]]
 the fury the man's at himself
 'the man's^i fury against himself^i'
 b. die Zerlegung [jeglicher^i Substanz [in ihre^i Bestandteile]]
 the dismantling (of) each^i substance$_{GEN}$ into its^i components
 'the dismantling (of) each^i substance$_{GEN}$ into its^i components'

The same considerations apply to English VPs, as discussed by Barss and Lasnik (1986). And the solution is the same, too: both head-initial and head-final projections are structured in the same way, namely right-branching only. This universal property of phrase structures has been dubbed the BBC (*basic branching constraint*) in Haider (1992/2000).

(3) BBC =$_{def.}$ The structural build-up (*merger*) of phrases (and their functional extensions) is universally *right-branching*.[6]

If a phrase α is merged to a phrase β,[7] the resulting structure is [$_β^n$ α β]. Hence, merger produces *right-branching structures only*. Left-branching merger structures *[$_β^n$ β α] are universally ruled out.[8] The result is an *asymmetry* property for phrase

---

[4] Extraposition patently violates the core constraints of A′-movement (namely: no extraction out of a subject phrase, no extraction out of an NP inside a definite DP, no extraction out of an adverbial phrase).

[5] Thanks to Werner Frey, my colleague at the University of Stuttgart at this time, for this stimulating question.

[6] 'Right-branching' =$_{def.}$ a structure is right-branching iff the node on the projection line follows the node attached to the projection line. In other words, the branching node on the projection line is on the right-hand side.

[7] 'Merge α with β' =$_{def.}$ combine α with β into a phrase structure [$_γ$ α β], where γ is a projection of either α or β.

[8] This premise applies to (internal) merger. The BBC remains silent on the question as to whether there could be a transformational source of left-branching structures, as, for instance, adjunction to the right by movement to the right. Extraposition might appear as a prima facie candidate, but its properties (see Haider 2010a: ch.5) do not support this conjecture.

structures (4). The curly brackets in the bottom line of the structures in (4) are to signify that the branching restriction is independent of the linearization restriction of head and complement, that is, head-final or head-initial order. The linearization follows from the directionality parameter for identification by a head.

(4) a. **right**-branching b. **left**-branching

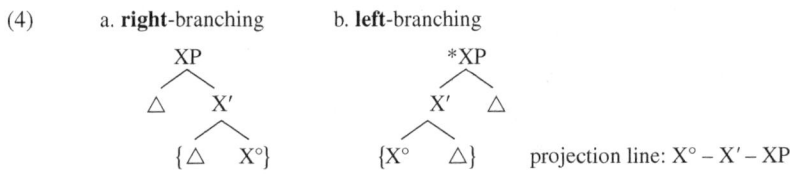

projection line: X° – X' – XP

The BBC in combination with an identification requirement (5) between the head and its dependants produces a rich set of implications that cover a significant portion of the syntactic differences between head-initial and head-final phrases and clauses. The identification requirement is characterized as follows:

(5) *Directional Identification*: merged positions in the projection of the head of a phrase need to be properly identified by the head under *canonical directionality*.

Canonical directionality is the basic parametric factor that produces head-final or head-initial structures, respectively.[9] The constraint is formulated under (6):

(6) *Principle of Directional Identification (PDI)*: a merged phrase P must be properly identified.
Def.: A merged phrase P is *properly identified* by the *head* of the host phrase h° iff
(i) P is in the canonical directionality domain of h°, and
(ii) P and (an extension of) h° *minimally, mutually c-command* each other.[10]
(Extension of h° $=_{def.}$ projection of h° [-maximal])

The BBC and the PDI in combination immediately cover and explain a wide range of properties of head-initial vs. head-final structures. For details see Chapter 3.[11] Here is a summary of the main consequences:

---

[9] The idea that directionality is a relevant parametric factor is not a new one. It has been discussed since the advent of the Principles and Parameters (P&P) Model. (e.g. Koopman 1984; Travis 1984, 1989; Frazier 1985) and has been revived in the Minimalist Program (e.g. Saito and Fukui 1998).

[10] This subsumes any submaximal projection of a head, including the trivial projection, that is, the head itself.

[11] The *binary branching* property of phrase structures immediately follows from (6ii), once the relation is strengthened to *uniqueness*, that is, if identification is strengthened to biuniqueness: the head or its projection *uniquely* identifies the dependent element and for any dependent

Corollary 1: OV languages (i.e. phrases with a head-final organization) are the straightforward instantiations of the BBC in combination with the PDI, because the canonical directionality is in harmony with the branching direction for head-final phrases.

Corollary 2: Head-*initial* organization (VO) is necessarily more complex because of shell structures, but it has an advantage for processing. It presents the head early (preferred for bottom-up processing).

Corollary 3: Both OV and VO are each *necessarily* not fully optimal for the conditions of usage, that is, for the processing of grammatical structures when parsing them (see also Chapter 2):
(i) OV has the *simpler* structure, but the head is presented *late*;
(ii) VO has a more *complex* structure, but the head is presented *early*.

From the processing point of view, each of the two options has its unavoidable price. Hence it must not come as a surprise that we find them implemented in approximately the same percentage of languages. There is no unique way of organizing phrase structure such that it is optimal for the *simultaneous* application of *bottom-up* and of *top-down* strategies. OV and VO are the best approximations.

In addition, OV and VO are *not complementary*. There is a *third* option (*Type III*), namely the option of *underspecified* canonical directionality. The diachronically attested stages of Indo-European languages (and many present-day languages, as e.g. Slavic ones) are of Type III (see Chapter 3, section 3.5, and Chapter 5). The diachronic Germanic word-order split (North Germanic languages became VO; most West Germanic languages became OV) finds its explanation as a change from underspecified (i.e. Type III) to specified directionality. This change had two possible alternative outcomes, namely OV and VO. These options found their implementations.[12]

1.2 Symmetry breaking – adaptation for *time* and *dimension* management

The exclusion of left-branching structures is the result of symmetry breaking. This contrasts with the fact that there are *apparently symmetric* linearization

element there is not more than a single identifier. In an n-ary projection, the identifier would minimally c-command – and be c-commanded (by) – more than a single item.

[12] The fact that this happened only in the Germanic family is not accidental. Romance languages started from the Type III Latin and each language ended up as a VO language. It was the V2-property of the Germanic languages that became the key property for opening alternative channels for the change from underspecified to specified directionality (see Chapter 5).

6   *Symmetry Breaking in Syntax*

patterns. The German examples in (7) *appear* to be symmetric in their linear order, since either the head precedes the complement, or the complement precedes the head.

(7) a. [P DP]$_{PP}$ wegen$_{P°}$ des Geldes$_{GEN}$ – (for the) sake (of) the money
    b. [DP P]$_{PP}$ des Geldes$_{GEN}$ wegen$_{P°}$ – (for) the money's sake
    c. [PP V]$_{VP}$ auf jemanden$_{ACC}$ warten$_{V°}$ – for someone wait
    d. [V PP]$_{VP?}$ warten$_{V°}$ auf jemanden$_{ACC}$ – wait for someone
    e. [PP A]$_{AP}$ mit jemandem$_{DAT}$ unzufrieden$_{A°}$ – with someone incontent
    f. [A PP]$_{AP?}$ unzufrieden$_{A°}$ mit jemandem$_{DAT}$ – incontent with someone

However, a little knowledge about German syntax suffices for destroying the symmetry suspicion: a pre- and postposition such as *wegen* is the rare exception in German, and the other examples are secondary patterns. The phrase-final PP in (7d,f) is in an extraposed position. Symmetric patterns are rare for a given *language*, and so they are *cross-linguistically*, apparent mirror-image examples of the kind in (8a,b) notwithstanding.

(8) a. walk along the river
    b. den Fluss entlang gehen   German
       the river along walk
    c. be content with this
    d. damit zufrieden sein   German
       this-with content be

Again, this cross-linguistic symmetry – English is serializing in one direction, German in the other – is merely incidental but not representative. A representative case is illustrated in (9). The order in complex head-initial phrases compared to the order in complex head-final ones is identical, modulo the opposite positioning of the *head*. There is no mirror-image order otherwise (Haider 1992). An exemplary piece of evidence for the shared c-command property is the binding effect between quantifier and the bound variable in the form of a pronoun.

(9) a. dass sie *jedem^i ein Paket an seine^i Privatadresse* schicken werden
       that they everybody a parcel to his private address send will   German
    b. omdat *ze iedereen^i een pakje naar zijn^i privaatadres* zullen opsturen
       that they everybody a parcel to his private address will send   Dutch
    c. that they will send *everybody^i a parcel to his^i home address*
    d. at de forklarede *hver deltager^i problemet på hans^i eget sprog*   Danish
       that they explained every participant problem-DEF in his own language

This invariance property follows immediately from the BBC and the PDI. The BBC accounts for the universal right-branching structure and the PDI accounts for the positioning of the head on the phrasal periphery (preceding or following the dependent elements, respectively). The argument structure of the verbs guarantees that the ranking of the arguments determined by the lexical argument structure of the head is mapped onto the syntactic structure. In sum, this accounts for the invariant cross-linguistic order of the dependent elements, with the conclusion that the source of asymmetry is the BBC.

Why should natural languages embody the BBC as a restriction on their core grammar? The answer must be sought in the *cognitive evolution* of grammars. Languages, just like species, are subject to evolution. In the case of grammars it is *cognitive* evolution rather than *biological* evolution.[13] Evolution is adaptation by selection out of a pool of variants. For languages, the selector is the (child's) processing brain that has to acquire the grammar of a given language by merely being exposed to the language. Like in biological evolution, the winner is the variant that 'infests' more brains than the other competing variants. The winning variant multiplies itself more often. And just like in biological evolution, the emergent result is an *adaptive* quality. See also Haider (forthcoming).

What is the adaptive quality of a right-branching architecture that is not embodied in a left-branching architecture? The adaptive quality, as in biological evolution, is a quality that becomes operative in the environment of the system/organism. The environment of grammars is *language processing*. Grammar is the system that the brain employs for language processing, either in reception or in production. What is the adaptive advantage of *right*-branching over *left*-branching, then? It is the greater ease for time and dimension management.

Processing time is a limited resource (Haider 1997e) and right-branching structures offer a significant advantage for *dimension management* under *time* limitations. Grammar is a dimension management system. It is the algorithm that we employ when we map one-dimensional arrays (PF) onto at least two-dimensional box-in-box structures (SF), and vice versa.

Syntax is (in part) an algorithm that projects at least two-dimensional structures onto one-dimensional arrays (i.e. the phonetic/phonological representation) of terminals (in reception) and compresses two-dimensional structures to one-dimensional strings of terminals (in production). It thereby bridges a

---

[13] A grammar is a self-reproducing cognitive system. It is a cognitive virus. The language learning brain gets 'infected' by a given grammar variant in the course of language acquisition. The acquired grammar then determines the language which is the basis for spreading this grammar to other brains.

dimension gap. It enables the mapping of the one-dimensional representations (strings) of phonetic/phonological structure to the at least two-dimensional hierarchical box-in-box structure of semantic representations, back and forth. The dimension mismatch is an unavoidable consequence of the respective interfaces. Sound structures are organized along the time axis (linear organization), conceptual representations are timeless, hierarchically organized complex structures (hierarchical, box-in-box organization).

The receptive side is the crucial filter. It is the input side for language acquisition and it is the side with the limited resource in language use, namely the processing time span. This is the selector for cognitive evolution. Any data structure that can be processed more effectively will have an advantage over a structure that incurs higher processing costs. The production side, on the other hand, is under no time pressure, but the perception side is. As a speaker, I may consume as much time as I need for the production of an expression. But, as a listener, I am dependent. I have to finish the processing of a given expression while the next utterance is coming in. Otherwise my processing channels will get jammed.

Given the resource limitation, this amounts to a constant selection mechanism for an organization of data structures that saves processing time. The data-to-parser fit is optimal if the parser – a left-corner parser – can *simultaneously* operate bottom up and top down, that is, with immediate and continuous data processing (bottom up) plus immediate *grammar guidance* (top-down information on possible structures). This clearly favours right-branching structures (10b) over left-branching ones (10a):

(10) a. [[[[h° X] Y] Z]$_{HP}$ ...]   left-branching
      b. [... [Z [Y [X h°]]]$_{HP}$]   right-branching

The bracket notation in (10) already demonstrates the disadvantage of (10a): the parser has to *guess* how many brackets need to be opened. Without look-ahead, the parser cannot possibly know how deeply embedded the phrase is. So, the cost is frequent backtracking.

(10b) does not involve this disadvantage at all. For every phrase under construction, its mother node is necessarily the *immediately* dominating node. This is the optimal architecture for simultaneously combining top-down information (associated with the dominating phrasal nodes) and bottom-up information, provided by the terminals that are parsed at any given moment.

On top of this, there is involved a third facet. This is the lexically stored syntactic information associated with the head of the phrase. Early availability of this information is advantageous for predictions in parsing. (10b), however, is head-final, because of the BBC (as a reflex of the advantage of right-branching) and the fact that phrases are endocentric: a phrase is a head plus its dependants, and the structural build-up starts with the head. Hence the head is in the most deeply embedded position. Improving this suboptimal situation is the source of VO structures, but this improvement is costly to a certain extent.

Presenting the head of a phrase earlier incurs costs in a BBC-constrained system. The cost is the more complex structure as a result of the mismatch of the canonical directionality and right-branching. Head-initial structures induce a shell structure. Consequently, a head-final structure on the one hand, and a head-initial organization on the other, are equivalent, that is, equally costly or equally cheap outcomes of *cognitive selection* for parser friendliness, otherwise one of the two types would have vastly outnumbered the other in the course of grammar change over the past millennia.

1.3   Head first or head last – costs and gains

SOV and SVO are the most widely attested basic serialization types for natural languages. This means that a grammar variant that produces one of these two serialization types is more often superior to its competitors and therefore it is reproduced more often in language acquisition. Why does one of these two types not outperform the other, or, even stronger, why are not *all* languages of only *one* of these types? A satisfactory answer must be able to locate cost and gain characteristics that each of these types fulfils equally well. Here is a sketch of the answer.

OV is harmonic with the BBC. The canonical directionality of OV is identical with the directionality imposed by the BBC. As a consequence, phrases are head-final. The result is a strict OV language. But, if the early presentation of the head is an advantage for the parser, the head-final property of the OV type is a disadvantage at the same time. Compensation for this disadvantage has its costs, however. Early presentation of the head requires a *more complicated* structure, namely a shell structure (11).

(11)   [... [Z [V_j [Y [e_i X]]]]]

The head position is in the deepest position with the required directionality in (11). This is the only position that obeys the BBC and the PDI in each of the two directionality settings. The position of the two other dependants, namely Y and Z, is on a left branch according to the BBC, and therefore not in the directionality domain of the lower head, if its canonical directionality is to the right. Hence, the PDI is not fulfilled. The solution is the re-instantiation of the head. This produces the shell structure in (11). A simple count of the closing brackets in (11) and (10b) shows that (11) is more complex than (10b). This is the cost factor: either a simpler structure, with head *last* as 'disadvantage', or head *first*, but with a complex structure as 'disadvantage'. Structural complexity is the price for the advantage of an early presentation of the head, and late presentation of the head is the unavoidable disadvantage for the structurally simple head-final architecture.

If the verb in (11) moves even across Z, the result is the VSO order. In SOV, the subject is merged as the highest local argument in the VP, but in this position, it is not within the directionality domain of the head, and hence it is not directionally identified. It needs a c-commanding head for its identification. This is the source of the *obligatory functional subject* position in VO (viz. Chomsky's EPP property). The functional head that selects the VP identifies the position of Z in (12a). It may attract the finite verb, and its spec accommodates the raised subject. SOV, in comparison, does not need any of these measures. The objects and the subject are merged *within the same* directionality domain (12b). Each dependant is on the canonical side, identified by the head or one of its projections.

(12) a. $[_{Spec-F°} \ldots [F° \rightarrow [Z [V_i \rightarrow [Y [e_i \rightarrow X]]]]]]$
      b. $[Z \leftarrow [_{V'} Y \leftarrow [_{V'} X \leftarrow V°]]]_{VP}$

The special treatment of the subject introduces a specific set of asymmetries into VO that are alien to OV, namely the structural asymmetry between the VP-internal objects and the VP-external subject. In the VO-biased literature on grammar theory, this property has mistakenly been elevated to the status of a universal (cf. Chomsky's EPP). It is a universal, but only of the VO clause structure.

1.4 The OV/VO syndrome

The interaction between the BBC (3) and the PDI (6), with its parametric option for the canonical directionality, is the source of an intricate set of syntactic properties that predict and cover systematic differences between head-final (OV) and head-initial (VO) phrases and clauses. Here is a non-exhaustive list of ten syntactic properties that are differentiated by the head-initial vs. head-final property of syntactic phrases in general and VO vs. OV in particular:

(13) a. Complex head-initial structures require a *shell structure*; head-final structures do not.
      b. Head-initial structures are *compact*, head-final ones are not.

c. The *rigid serialization* of head-initial structures is a corollary of compactness, and the *'free' word order* ('scrambling') in head-final phrases is a corollary of the absence of compactness.
d. Clauses of the SVO type require *a functional subject position*, SOV-type clauses do not.[14]
e. *Subject expletives* for the structural subject position in SVO, as well as *quirky subjects* in SVO are a corollary of (13d). They are absent in OV.
f. *Subject–object asymmetries* with extraction constructions in VO and their absence in OV are a corollary of (13d) and of (13a).[15]
g. Head-initial structures display an *edge effect* for adjoined phrases, head-final structures do not.
h. In word formation, *head-initial* compounds are infrequent and *not recursive*, head-final ones are frequent and recursive.
i. The lower/higher position of the *negation particle* of clausal negation in OV and VO is a function of its domain requirement, respectively.
j. The particle positions (for verbal particles) in between two objects are positive indicators of the VO shell structure.

In addition, the symmetry-breaking condition in UG that is the causal factor for the existence of the BBC is at the same time the cause for a ban on a particular class of recursive structures in head-final phrases:

(14)   It accounts for the *obligatoriness of verb clustering* in clauses with a head-final VP (and its absence in clauses with a head-initial VP).

The derivation of (13) and (14) from BBC (3) in combination with PDI (6) is informally described in Haider (2010a: ch.1). It has been developed over the years, starting with Haider (1992/2000). Chapter 3 contains the original arguments in a slightly updated version and amended with a section that provides the derivation of the properties listed in (13) and (14), not all of which had been considered in the original paper. Here is an overview of the explanation of the properties listed in (13) condensed into a nutshell.

---

[14] Chomsky (1982: 9–10) suggests the EPP (= Extended Projection Principle) as a principle that requires a clause to have a subject. When the P&P Model was in vogue (1981: 40), Chomsky was cautious enough to restrict the EPP to 'English and similar languages'. Later, it was elevated to universal force. See Alexiadou and Anagnostopoulou (1998) for a differentiation in terms of feature-checking routines.

[15] Note, importantly, that this does NOT mean that there are no differences at all between extractions out of subjects vs. objects in OV. There are *parsing*-triggered differences (front vs. rear) and there are intervening factors such as the 'bridge verb' effect, whose effect is *argument specific*. This means that a bridge verb relation may apply to its object, but not to its subject. Hence, if experiments yield differences, this does not contradict the claim, as long as the trigger has not been proven to be the very structural difference (see Haider 2010a: 90–2, 39–42).

The PDI requires *minimal mutual* c-command. In (11), this is implemented as a chain property. Because of the minimality requirement, no *interveners* are tolerated. This is the source of *compactness* of head-initial structures. Scrambling is a derivational source for producing interveners, namely the scrambled phrases. Hence, invariant order is the result of the absence of scrambling, and this, in turn, is the effect of the compactness property.

The need for a *functional subject position* becomes obvious once we look at (12a). The functional head is the identifier for the top argument position in the pre-head position in the VP of an SVO-type clause. Since this argument position is not in the directionality domain of its verbal head, it needs a functional head as external identifier. A functional *head* goes together with a *spec*. This spec position is the functional subject position in SVO.[16] It is the trigger for a *subject expletive* in case an argument is not available (see the passive of intransitive verbs in Scandinavian languages). If this spec position is not the exclusive location for nominative, a non-nominative argument may raise to this position. This is the *quirky subject* phenomenon of Icelandic.

Extraction constructions are sensitive to the location of the extraction site. For arguments, the extraction site must be a position within the phrase of the head whose argument the containing phrase is. (13d) triggers an immediate difference between SVO and SOV. SVO subjects and objects are in different domains; the SOV subject remains in its original domain, together with the objects, namely within the VP. Hence, in SOV, extraction processes treat the subject and the objects on a par, but in SVO, a subject–object asymmetry arises. This is the source of the so-called 'subject condition' ($=_{def.}$ the structural subject is an opaque domain for extraction) as part of the syntactic conditions on extraction domains.[17]

The *edge effect* (Haider 2004b) is a property of head-*initial* phrases. It is a consequence of the directionality mismatch between the BBC and the canonical directionality in head-initial phrases. It is typical for adjunction to head-initial projections.

---

[16] What is called EPP (= every clause has a structural subject) in Generative Grammar is the obligatory realization of this spec position in SVO. V1-languages (i.e. SVO languages that front the finite verb, as, for instance, Welsh) front only the verb, but do not lexicalize the spec position. Hence it is hard to decide between two competing analyses: either the spec position remains empty or the spec position is absent in these structures.

[17] CED = *condition on extraction domains* (Huang 1982): *unselected* domains are opaque. This applies to the functional subject position ('subject condition') as well as to adverbials ('adjunct condition').

(15) a. He has [(*much more*) carefully (**than anyone else*)] analyzed it
 b. He has [(*much less*) often (**than I* (*thought*))] rehearsed it
 c. Er hat es [*sehr viel* sorfältiger *als jeder andere*] analysiert (= a)
 d. Er hat es [*viel weniger* oft (*als ich* (*dachte*))] geprobt (= b)
 e. als niemand *luider* (*dan Jan*) kan roepen   Dutch
   'if no one louder than Jan can shout'
 f. omdat ik het *veel sneller* (*dan Jan* (*denkt*)) in een zakje kan inpakken
   'since I it much faster (than Jan (thinks)) in a little-bag can pack up'

Descriptively, the *edge effect* is the reflex of a constraint against post-head material in a phrase that serves as an adjunct to a head-initial constituent. Material is allowed on the left but not on the right-hand side of the head of the preverbal adverbial phrase. Note, first, that this effect must not be mistaken as a restriction that discriminates between 'simple' and 'phrasal adverbials', since the simple ones may be extended by pre-modifiers.[18] Second, this constraint is not an *adjacency* constraint for the head of the VP- and the adverbial phrase, as (16a,b) illustrates, and it is not restricted to comparative constructions but to any not strictly head-final adjunct (16c,d). This is confirmed by the analogous constraint for adnominal attribute illustrated in (17).

(16) a. Surely, he has [(more) *often* (*than anyone else*)] *rudely* criticized her
 b. She had *less often* (*than I had expected*) *nearly* failed an exam at the first time
 c. They *probably never* have seen a real politician
           (example from Baker 1991: 309)
 d. *They [*with high probability*] [*at no occasion*] have seen a real politician

The edge effect for adverbials is the direct counterpart of the *edge effect of prenominal attributes* in the N-projection. (17c) is the example corresponding to (15). Note that there is an edge effect for *adnominal attributes* in German but not for *preverbal adverbials*, since NPs are head-initial but VPs are head-*final* projections. Hence, the edge effect is not a language-specific phenomenon but a *projection-specific* one, depending on the canonical directionality of the head.

(17) a. eine [viel größere (**als ich dachte*)] Summe
   'a much bigger (*than I thought) sum'
 b. ein [unzufriedener (**damit*)] Syntaktiker
   'an unsatisfied (*it-with) syntactician'

---

[18] Bouchard's (1995: 409) account in terms of 'simple vs. phrasal' is too restricted. He claims that preverbal adverbials in English or French are head-adjoined to the verbal head and therefore 'simple'. This cannot be entirely correct since the adverbial may be phrasal, as the examples show, since they allow pre-head modification.

c. ein [viel schöneres (*als ich dachte)] (*neues*) Haus
'a [much-more beautiful (*than I thought)] (new) house'

The theoretical relevance of the edge-effect phenomenon is obvious: edge effects are unknown for phrases in *spec positions*, as e.g. phrases in Spec-C or Spec-I. So, an adjunction analysis of adverbials is compatible with an edge effect, but a Spec-F analysis of adverbials is not.[19] Analogously, prenominal attributes are adjuncts, and not specs of an agreement head or any other functional head.

The theoretical side of this effect is not yet fully understood. It appears as if the phrase the adjunct is adjoined to is selected by the head of the adjunct as an (improper) complement. In this case, the adjacency property would be an immediate consequence.

(18) a. has [much more *rudely* [criticized her]$_{VP}$] (than I thought)
      b. a [much *higher* [pile of papers]$_{NP}$] (than I thought)

Since the explanation of the phenomenon is not the prime concern here – whatever explanation may turn out to be the adequate one, it is sufficient that the phenomenon is in a clear correlation with head-initial phrases only – I shall leave it open for the time being (see Chapter 6, subsection 6.2.2, for a proposal of an explanation).

The branching constraint applies to any recursively built structure, that is, to phrase structure as well as *word structure*. Heads in the verb structure are final heads, and in the rare cases of *initial* heads, the structural build-up is restricted to the trivial size of a two-member structure, as an immediate consequence of the branching constraint. This is the topic of Chapter 8, which deals with head-initial compounding in Romance languages.

Clausal negation is a scope-sensitive phenomenon. The scope of negation is the set of proposition-situating devices, such as tense and mood. These features are normally spelled out on a finite verb. Hence (the base position of) the finite verb must be in the scope domain of negation. This domain is the c-command domain of negation. Therefore it is not surprising that in SVO, the negation particle precedes the VP. It should be surprising, however, that syntacticians take this as sufficient reason for elevating the SVO pattern to the rank of a universal generalization. In SOV, the negation particle is found in a much lower position:

---

[19] Note that the ban against sentential and prepositional phrases as preverbal adverbials (that is adverbials between the position of the finite auxiliary and the left edge of the VP) is also an aspect of the edge effect because clauses and PPs are left-headed. So their complement blocks adjacency between the phrasal head and the point of attachment.

(19)   Da hat wohl wer was *nicht* ganz kapiert
        There has PRT someone something *not* completely understood

Intentionally, the arguments in (19) have been instantiated as indefinite pronouns (in the form of wh-pronouns) since these are known to be inert for scrambling. The negation particle nevertheless follows. It is preferred in *the lowest position* provided that it guarantees scope over the finite verb. Another option for SOV is suffixing negation to the finite verb, as in Japanese. The low position of negation is facilitated by the absence of compactness in head-final structures (see Chapter 6, §6.2.1).

Finally, the *stranding of verbal particles* in the pertinent languages (as e.g. in English, Norwegian, Icelandic) provides immediate evidence for verb positions. Particles normally do not move but they may be stranded. In V2-OV languages, stranding is a consequence of fronting the finite verb. In VO languages there is a second source of stranding, namely the formation of the shell structure necessitated by the inverse directionality.

In English, but also in Norwegian (and other Scandinavian varieties), particles may be serialized in various patterns. One variant is the V-adjacent variant. In this variant and in all other variants (including the stranding variant by V2) the particle follows. This is a robust difference between OV and VO. In OV, the particle precedes and is adjacent to the verb (except for the stranding variant by V2, where it is adjacent to the trace of the fronted verb). The second robust difference is the fact that there are VO languages with non-adjacent particle positions in the VP (20a–c), but there is no OV language with a particle position that is not adjacent to the verb or its trace. Moreover, in VO, a particle does not follow the objects in a double-object construction (20d), but in OV this is the only licit position.

(20)   a. The secretary sent the stockholders *out* a notice   (Jacobson 1987: 32)
        b. Valerie packed her daughter *up* a lunch   (Dehé 2002: 3)
        c. Susan poured the man *out* a drink
        d. *Valerie packed her daughter a lunch *up*

The intermediate particle position in (20a–c) is a stranding position in the VP-shell, that is, the position is a position of the verbal head whose surface position is higher up. A satisfactory account must cover the following generalizations: *first*, the cross-linguistic generalization that particles precede in OV but follow in VO, and that only in VO may particles intervene between objects (19). *Second*, unlike adverbials, particles do not violate the compactness requirement of head-initial phrases. Unlike adverbials, they intervene between objects (20). *Third*, in double-object constructions, a particle must not end up in a clause-final position, although it may be clause-final in a simple transitive construction.[20] Here is the solution:

(21) a. ... [$_{VP}$ V°(*+particle*) DP$_1$ [e$_{V°}$ (*+particle*) DP$_2$]]]   SVO
     b. ... [$_{VP}$ DP$_1$ [DP$_2$ (particle+) V°]]]   SOV

In the VP-shell structure (21a), there are two verb positions, hence there are two particle positions. In the OV structure (21b), there is a single verb position, hence there is a single particle position.

Eventually, the *obligatoriness of verb clustering* (14) is an OV property. In Germanic OV languages, clustering becomes visible in the variation of the serialization patterns of clause-final verbs: all Germanic OV languages allow/require verb-order variation, but no VO language (Germanic or not) tolerates verb-order variation. In OV languages without V-movement (e.g. East Asian languages), clustering has no serialization effect. It betrays itself only in 'transparency' effects of allegedly cascading, centre-embedded V-projections. However, there are no centre-embedded V-projections that are transparent in these languages. In fact, there are no centre-embedded V-projections at all in these clauses, but only V-clusters. The clustering effects in German are described in full detail in Haider (2010a: ch.7, §7.4). For the sake of illustration, let me choose a single property that has not been adduced so often. It was considered first by Bartos (2004) in the discussion of clustering in Hungarian.[21] In German, as well as in many other languages, an infinitival verb may be nominalized. In German, this converts a final head (V in the VP) into an initial head (N in the NP):

(22) a. [Nachrichten$_{ACC}$ [auf dem Handy *empfangen*]]$_{VP}$
        messages   on the cell-phone receive
     b. das [*Empfangen* von/der Nachrichten auf dem Handy]$_{NP}$
        the receive(ing) of/the messages$_{GEN}$ on the cell-phone
     c. [Deadlines [verstreichen lassen müssen]]$_{VP}$
     d. das Verstreichenlassenmüssen$_{N°}$ der/von Deadlines
        the expire-let-must the/of deadlines

---

[20] The example '*He poured the whisky *slowly* out' (Dehé 2002: 38) is misleading. As shown in (i), 'out' can function like a PP pro-form, since it may be modified by 'right' (den Dikken 1992). The example in (ii) supports the correlation: if what looks like a particle can be modified, it is not treated as particle but as a PP pro-form. If, on the other hand, it cannot be modified, it must be a particle and then a compactness effect shows as in (ii).

(i) I poured it right out.
(ii) The strike was called (*right /*finally) off

[21] Hungarian is not SOV, but a Type III language (see Chapter 5 and Chapter 3, §3.5). These languages comprise OV patterns as a proper subset. Hence, they allow clustering.

e. *the lett(ing) expire of deadlines – *the need(ing) let expire (of) deadlines
f. das Gehenlassenmüssen$_{N°}$
the go-let-must ('the obligation to let so. go')
g. dass sie uns [[gehen lassen]$_{V°}$ müssen]$_{V°}$
that they us [go let must] ('that they have to let us go')

Note, first, that the object in the nominalized construction is post-nominal and marked with genitive (22b), which is the required case for adnominal complements. In the VP, it is preverbal and marked accusative (22a). This is a clear indication that the verbal head has been converted into a nominal one.

The nominalized clusters in (22d,f) surely must appear bizarre to speakers of VO languages since they are not only absent but entirely impossible in these languages. Nominalization as a word-formation process[22] operates on X° categories. Clusters are complex V° categories (= head-to-head adjunctions of verbs) and therefore they are predicted to participate in these nominalization operations. For the competing view – complex embedded V-projections – this phenomenon is embarrassing since it is unexpected and virtually underivable. For details see Chapter 8.

1.5 Counterproposals – symmetry claims

Recently, symmetry of syntax has been a topic of two monographs. Both works share the focus on the alleged symmetry of *merge* in the Minimalist Program. Liao (2011: 8,161) favours the idea that there is a core system of syntax that is symmetric (in the algebraic sense of symmetry)[23] with primitive syntactic relations as Cartesian products of their basics. Symmetry breaking is regarded as an interface effect: a concrete phrase structure is regarded as a unique pattern generated by some way of departure from the inherent symmetry. Citko (2011) ventures to demonstrate that it is *possible* to find linguistic data in support

---

[22] Deverbal nominalization must not be confounded with *phrasal conversion*, as in the case of a determiner selecting a VP, as in (i):

(i) dieses dauernde [alle Deadlines unbekümmert verstreichen lassen]$_{VP}$
this constant [all deadlines casually pass-by let]

Here, the full VP structure is selected like an NP, but the internal structure is that of a VP, with a preverbal accusative object, rather than a post-nominal genitive object, as in an NP headed by a deverbal N.

[23] Symmetry may be a property of a relation, a function, a graph, a geometric object or of (the output of) a system. In physics, 'symmetry' is the term for invariance under specified groups of rotations, reflections, etc.

of the claim that *merge*, *move* and *labelling* (i.e. syntactic categorization) are basically symmetric, that is, ambi-directional. The strain of this endeavour has perhaps blurred the awareness of the basic question, namely the question as to why finding clearly symmetric properties in cross-linguistic syntax is so arduous and why asymmetry prevails.

As for *merge*, it is hard to see what would be the advantage of treating it as a symmetric function.[24] Take, for instance, the merger of a head with its complement. The verb determines the resulting VP, and the DP merged with a verb does not yield a DP with an 'associated' verb. The relation is patently asymmetric, not merely as an interface effect, but simply because of asymmetric selection relations. The potential *symmetry* of *merge* as a *graph property*, on the other hand, is trivial. It is an unavoidable property of combinatorics when two subgraphs are to be joined and *linearized*. The crucial point is not the potential symmetry as an abstract system potential but the actual asymmetry in phrase structure.

What both authors seem to take for granted is that *merge* may be justly regarded as an ontological (neuro-cognitive?) reality, rather than a theoretical construct whose existence awaits attesting at a reasonable level of plausibility. Whatever properties are associated with *merge* in theory need to be substantiated by clear-cut empirical facts. If these facts warrant a model with surprising (a)symmetry properties, this may stimulate research on alternatives for the internal make-up of the system. The hypothetical-speculative approach – 'let us assume that *merge* exists with properties we ascribe to it, and certain properties that can be deduced' – is obviously premature. How could you be sure that you are talking about facts and not fiction, as long as all you have is a programmatic idea applied to selected data samples from a single language type (English and other VO languages) that covers merely portions[25] of the grammar of English and closely related languages?

Finally, drawing close parallels to symmetry notions in physics (Liao 2011: 4–7) is more sophomoric than revealing. Language acquisition and the resulting mental capacities for language processing are rooted in a neuro-biological

---

[24] A symmetric function of n variables is one whose value at any n-tuple of arguments is the same as its value at any permutation of that n-tuple.

[25] It is an undeniable quality of the Minimalist Program that even after almost two decades, its coverage is but a minor subset of the coverage of the Principles and Parameters Program, and that core results of the P&P system have to be ignored because they have not been integrated. The Minimalist Program remains silent on what had been the central issue of grammar theory before, namely the theory of constraints on derivations (notably what has been subsumed under *conditions on extraction domains*).

system with a long evolutionary history. Biological systems typically do not *function* symmetrically since they are not *isolated* (closed), but *open*, in systems theory terms. They are, and need to be, constantly fed with energy, and they are constantly changing, and the change is directional (mainly because of the dissipative nature of the changes, whose stochastic quality is characterized by the second law of thermodynamics). A cell that has died does not regain its prior state and become alive again, and a fertilized egg that has been poached cannot be reintegrated and successfully hatched, and a suffix that has got lost in the course of morpho-phonological reduction is never re-established. It is far from evident that it is more likely that linguistic processes are symmetric rather than asymmetric. Symmetry per se is not a more likely or preferred quality of systems. In the context of linguistic structures and their derivations, there is no a-priori reason for simply presupposing it.

2 Linearizations are public, structures are private

The two main issues of this chapter are the *adaptive quality* of symmetry breaking and the primacy *of linearization* in a theory of syntax. Functionality of syntactic structuring is undeniable. It is not the toolmaker's functionality of functionalism, however. It is the effect of evolutionary adaptation as a result of variation plus selection. This is not biological evolution but evolution on the level of cognitively represented structures. Like *biological* evolution (cf. Mayr 1991), *cognitive* evolution[1] produces adaptive structures as a consequence of 'grammar *mutation*' plus *selection* from the pool of mutations.[2] The selecting environment is the entirety of first-language acquiring and processing brains and their enhancement by an improved parser–grammar congruence. The following claims will be explicated and defended:

- *Linearization* is a grammatical property with epistemological priority.
- Syntactic structures *rest on linearizations.*
- Right-branching structures guarantee optimal *grammar–parser congruence.*
- The adaptive properties of grammars are a product of *cognitive* selection.
- The BBC is part of what constitutes UG.[3]

---

[1] The principles of Darwinian evolution are substance neutral. See also Dennet (2002). This had been understood and emphasized already by Darwin himself (1871: 59), when he discussed the innovation and survival of lexical entries (words): 'The formation of different languages and of distinct species, and the proofs that both have been developed through a gradual process, are curiously parallel' and 'The survival or preservation of certain favoured words in the struggle for existence is natural selection.'

[2] In Darwinian parlance, *cognitive evolution* is the mental territory where the 'struggle for the survival of the fittest gràmmar' takes place. It is the territory of the mental activities in acquisition, production and reception of language.

[3] The hypothesis that phrase structure systems are fundamentally asymmetric was presented first at the Conference for Lexical Specification and Lexical Insertion at Utrecht University (9 December 1991: 'On the structure of argument structure, – and its projection') and published in Haider (1992). In the conference presentation, the hypothesis was worded as follows: *every basic projection is right-branching (UG).* The conference volume took its time to make its way to the public (2000).

2.1 How grammars go public

The structure computation system for linear arrays that is embodied as a major syntactic component of the grammar of a human language is the product of *cognitive* evolution, that is, its properties are a result of the interaction of variation and (cognitive) selection. Like *biological* evolution, *cognitive* evolution is an interactive process of mutation and gradual adaptation by *blind* selection.[4]

The process of mutation is *grammar change* nourished by *variation*. Today, grammatical *mutation* is fed by several external sources. Here is a non-exhaustive list of contemporary contributing factors: multilingual language contacts, imperfect bilingualism in a superimposed language or dialect (e.g. the present-day situation of English in India, or French in Africa), and group preferences for grammatical differentiation (especially in the lexicon) as a means of maintaining group membership (see Donohue and Wichmann 2009). Nowadays, grammatical mutations get their chance only in linguistic biotopes without normalization by schooling and writing conventions. In the past millennia, grammar mutations had a better chance of survival because there were no privileged, strongly protected variants (i.e. 'standard' languages).

Learnable grammars are grammars whose productions can be analyzed efficiently and effectively by the learner's processing resources. Their properties can be assembled efficiently by being exposed to the productions because the learner can rely on the support of cognitive dispositions. We traditionally refer to their present stage as the human language faculty (modelled in the various approaches towards a theory of UG).[5]

The main source of *selection* is the acquisition process. Only those grammars survive and spread that are able to successfully infest children's brains. The central task for the learner is filtering out the grammar of a given language. It cannot be ingested or copied; it must be reconstructed from the language input the learner receives. The input, however, does not fully determine the grammar (cf. 'Plato's problem', viz. the underdetermination[6] of a grammar by

---

[4] 'Blind' means that evolution is neither goal-directed nor random. It is driven by the non-random and non-directed process of selection. Selection is local, hence not goal-directed, and it is non-random since it selects a variant according to its local adaptivity.

[5] The difference between a species-specific linguistic disposition and the general problem-solving capacities becomes evident in two cases. The first case is that of the approximately 2–3% of children that lack this disposition from the beginning. They are said to suffer from SLI (specific language impairment). The second case is L2-acquisition that starts after the critical phase of approximately seven years of age.

[6] The major problem is not so much a *scarcity* in terms of data types or tokens. The crucial problem is the fact that the necessarily *finite* set of data a learner encounters can be made compatible with a vast number of different grammars. The empirical fact that the interim grammars of

any finite subset of productions). A given finite set of linguistic input can be integrated in any grammar: either it fits, or the interim grammar will be modified by the learner in order to make the input fit. The process of getting an easy fit is a process that feeds variation, and eventually guarantees easily learnable grammars as a consequence of evolutionary adaptation.

There are two simple facts with a non-trivial implication. The *first fact* is that grammars are *learnable*, but the grammar as a system of knowledge of a given individual is *inaccessible* to the learner him/herself, as well as to other individuals (as e.g. us linguists). The criterion of learnability is a trivial fact because an *unlearnable* mutation of a grammar created by a single individual's brain would not spread. The general implication is this: if components of a grammar that must be learned are not learnable from the *productions* of the grammar they are not learnable at all. The productions have the form of linearizations, in other words, concatenations of terminals. So, the grammar of a language must be learned from *linearizations* to a large extent.[7] This signifies the epistemological priority of linearization.

The grammar that I have in my head is *private*. It is inaccessible to you. Only its productions can I make public by uttering or writing something. Currently you are exposed to productions of my brain's non-native grammar of English that is surely different from the grammar of readers whose primary linguistic input has been English. Every time you perceive formal deviances in my writing you may guess how my L2-grammar differs from your L1-grammar, but you would not have a direct way of inspecting my grammar, no matter how intensely you interviewed or scanned me, nor do I have any direct way of inspecting my grammar either.

The *second* obvious fact is that grammars are *put to use*. They are used for processing higher-than-one-dimensionally structured entities (i.e. phrase structures) through a one-dimensionally constrained channel (i.e. phonetic forms). In production, the grammar is an algorithm for mapping a hierarchically organized configuration, that is, an at-least-two-dimensional object with a box-in-box architecture, onto a linear array. In simple words, a structure is linearized. In reception, the structure compressed into the linear array is unfolded back again into its hierarchical organization. In other words, grammars are algorithms for

---

L1-learners all converge at a shared single grammar is the fact that calls for an explanation (see also Berwick *et al.* 2011).

[7] Linearization is not only the surface property of phrase structures. It applies to word structure as well. Hence, even morpho-syntax (esp. inflection) involves linearization. This is seen best in agglutinating languages or in polysynthetic ones.

compressing and unfolding complex structures into, or out of, linear arrays. The *linearization* is the target of the algorithm in each of the two perspectives.

The non-trivial implication is that *linearizations* are not only the epistemologically primary objects; their patterns are also the primary objects for understanding the design of the grammars of human languages. The grammar of a human language is a product of steps of cognitive evolution that lead to an efficient solution for the problem of *dimension management* (compressing or unfolding) required by the channels of transmission.

The present-day languages' grammars are each a particular solution out of many possible solutions within the system capacity of the human language faculty. Learning the grammar of a specific language is compiling a knowledge system that guarantees these effects, given input from the individual language. This knowledge system must not be confounded with the actual processing activity, however. The actual activity is parsing or generating, but parsing or production is grounded immediately in the compiled grammar, and the grammar is constrained by UG. What we call UG is the *grammar formation capacity* provided by our brains. It is the network of brain resources that have been recruited for language processing. Their limits are at the same time the limits of possible grammars.

Let me emphasize a curious trait of the field: present-day structuralist grammar theories, in particular members of the Generative Grammar family, tend to undervalue the fact that grammars are put to use.[8] The interface conditions between a knowledge system (grammar) and its conditions of application (reception and production processes) are on hardly anybody's agenda. Functionalist approaches, on the other hand, emphasize the functionality and do not appreciate the fact that the overall architecture of grammars is not determined by the conditions of usage, just like the architecture of wings or fins is not *determined* (but only selected) by the environmental conditions. A given architecture has been gradually adapted to the environmental conditions in a gradual process of variation and selection. The proper understanding of the full picture presupposes three components, viz. a system with a-priori given structures, variability of the system and selection. The evolutionary result is a system with adaptive properties.

---

[8] Even if functional motivations are undervalued in Generative Grammar, they have never been questioned, as Newmeyer (2001: 103) argues: 'Surely there are significant connections between structure and function; this is not and has never been in doubt' (Chomsky 1975: 56).

2.2 Grammars are friendly to the parser – by chance and necessity

Grammar development, that is, grammar change, is a continuous process over many generations of users. Let us focus on an arbitrary single step. Assume that in the piecemeal cognitive evolution of grammars, there is a choice between two analyses for a given set of linearizations ('construction'), one of which is more 'friendly' to the mental parser than the other. Each analysis is part of a different grammar variant. The outcome is easy to predict. The friendly grammar will win; the less friendly one is ignored and avoided. This is so because a grammar is learned from linearizations, and linearizations have to be parsed before they can be analyzed by the learner's brain. An improved fit between mental parser and grammar is the predicted outcome of the evolutionary process. As in biological evolution, the adaptations in the evolution of a cognitive capacity are localistic, with collateral implications for the overall system. The existing grammars are the result of a linguistically a-priori system of brain resources plus cognitive mutation and selection, driven by the optimization of the grammar and parser fit.

What is a 'parser-friendly' grammar? A minimal standard of friendliness is compatibility, that is, the structures imposed onto a linearization by a given grammar do not impede parsing more than a competing grammar variant would. If this is the case, the more friendly grammar will win. The less friendly one will not find (as many) brains to nest in and hence will not get the chance to spread.

If I were a grammar, what should I offer to the mental parser in order to qualify as friendly? Resource-saving increase of economy will be appreciated (Haider 1997e). The mental parser has two limited, interdependent resources, namely *processing time*[9] and *buffer size*. If the structures that I as grammar provide for linearizations are bulky and time consuming for computing, the mental parser will be under unhappy pressure and make its superordinate 'grammatical mind' try to avoid them. So, I as a grammar better support the parser by handing in structures that can be *efficiently and effectively* read off the linearizations without demanding excessive buffer storage space.

The mental parser is fed with input that consists of arrays of terminals, that is, *heads* of phrases and their lexically accessible information. The task of the mental parser is to organize them into a hierarchical box-in-box structure, that

---

[9] Parsing is on-line. So the parser must be shadowing the production of the incoming signal. This imposes a continuous time pressure for following the ongoing utterance. Economy is projective economy (Haider 1997e).

is, a structure with phrases inside phrases. An effective parser must shadow the incoming utterances and start processing immediately, when the first item arrives. It cannot wait till the end of the array has been reached; otherwise the buffer will spill over. So, there is need for an effective *bottom-up strategy*, starting successfully at the beginning of an utterance. The grammar, on the other hand, provides general *top-down* information, that is, predictive information of how a phrase is possibly structured in the given language, without specific reference to any given specific array. This contributes a predictive power to parsing. These two components need to cooperate in an optimal way. This is the *criterion for 'parser friendliness'*:

- *Friendliness criterion*: a '*parser-friendly grammar*' is a grammar that provides the mental parser with structures that are optimal for the *simultaneous* application of top-down *and* bottom-up strategies.

Top down means immediate support by the grammar, bottom up means early decisions on the string-to-structure mapping process of an utterance based on input information. The friendly grammar is a grammar that guarantees the *simultaneous* applicability of the top-down *and* the bottom-up process *at the active node projected* in the parsing process.

The friendliness criterion combined with a left-corner parser is served perfectly by right-branching structures. The *left-corner strategy* (Abney and Johnson 1991; Stabler 1991, 1994; Resnik 1992; Schneider 1999) is the type of incremental parsing algorithm with a bottom-up component interacting continuously with a top-down component, and it is a plausible algorithm in terms of human sentence processing/parsing in many senses, as one of the reviewers of the draft version observed. (S)he raised the following point:

> If, independently of grammar, the human language performance system can employ this type of algorithm, then the importance of the friendliness criterion can be undermined, because independently from the grammar formalism, there can be an algorithm that can unfold a well-formed grammatical structure incrementally. Thus, as long as assuming such an algorithm is plausible, the grammar itself does not need to be 'friendly' to the parser.

The point is well taken. Parser and grammar are independent. The parser could be fed with *any kind* of data structures. The structure of the parser and the format of the data it is processing are independent.[10] The data do not determine the parser, and the parser cannot interfere with the data structures dictated by the grammar of the speaker who uses these structures.

---

[10] This, by the way, is an anti-functionalist aspect. The parser does not constrain a grammar.

But, and here comes the crucial aspect, some data structures are hard to parse and some are easy to parse for the given parser architecture. The hard ones are the left-branching ones; the easy structures are the right-branching ones. Synchronically, parser and grammar are independent systems. Diachronically, they are intimately related by (cognitive) co-evolution.[11]

From the point of view of the *cognitive evolution* of grammars, the outcome is predictable. The parser is part of the *selection* environment. Therefore, the cognitive evolution of grammars has favoured parser-friendly structures. Grammar change is adaptivity by selection. Since the parser is part of the selection environment, there will be a steady drift towards optimizing parser friendliness. The outcome we perceive as a property of UG: core grammars are subject to the BBC. It guarantees optimal fit between data structures and parser.

In the following section it will be argued that the prevalence of a particular type of asymmetry of syntactic structures (viz. right-branching) becomes understandable once one realizes that only grammars that enforce right-associative projections meet the requirement of friendliness to the parser. Symmetry breaking is an interface requirement between the linguistic knowledge systems (grammar) and the linguistic processing systems (parsing and production). Only when grammars are put to use does the issue of right- or left-branching become a crucial issue.

2.3   If top down plus bottom up, then *right-associative* structures

There are only two logically possible ways of organizing a *uniformly* binary branching structure, namely as a right- or as a left-associative structure (see (1a) and (1b) respectively): the phrase can be layered by merging with phrases that *precede* as in (1a) – right-associative[12] – or with phrases that *follow*, as in (1b) – left-associative. Is one of these two options friendlier to the mental parser than the other? There is an answer, and it is yes. It is (1a).

---

[11] This concept is not identical with Deacon's (1997: 44) concept of language–brain co-evolution. In his view, the human brain has been shaped by and for language and has become the brain of language, and language adapted and became the language for the brain. Parser–grammar co-evolution is the interdependent cognitive development of two mental capacities. One of them, the parser, is strongly dependent on the independently available brain resources that have been recruited for symbol processing. The grammar, however, is a product of cognitive evolution. There may be 'neural Darwinian processes' (Edelmann 1998), but I doubt whether the approximately 7,000 generations of *Homo sapiens* provide the time span that is necessary for substantive brain reorganizations geared by language–brain co-evolution.

[12] The nodes on the projection line of the phrase that results from merger follow their sister node, that is, they are on the right-hand side of a phrase merged with a node on the projection line of a phrase.

(1) a. [$_{XP}$ ZP [$_{X'}$YP [$_{x'}$... x°...]]]   right-associative = right-branching
     b. [$_{XP}$ [$_{x'}$ [$_{x'}$ ... x°...] YP] ZP]   left-associative = left-branching

Before going into the details of *friendliness*, let us take into consideration one more factor, namely the *position of the head* in the projection of a phrase. Phrases are *endocentric*, that is, an element in the foot position constitutes the head of the phrase, and the head is (normally)[13] peripheral, that is, it either precedes or it follows *all* its dependants. Two states of associativity (left or right) plus two possibilities for attaining a peripheral head (left or right) yields four possible projection structures, two of which are cancelled by endocentricity, namely the head-initial counterpart of (2a) and the head-final counterpart of (2b), for which the head would merge as the top element of the structure.

(2) a. ... [$_{HP}$ ZP [YP [XP [h°]]]]
     b. ... [$_{HP}$ [[[h°] XP] YP] ZP]

Which one of the two structures in (2) is the friendlier one? The answer is straightforward, though maybe not immediately evident. It is the structure (2a). Let us first examine why it is not (2b). At first glance, this structure might appear to be nearly optimal since its build-up seems to be congruent with an incremental production process that merges each new phrase with the previously built-up structure. This impression is misleading, however. The shadowing of the incremental procedure breaks down on the *recipient's* side. This becomes evident once we look at phrases with at least one embedded phrase, with both phrases structured in the manner of (2b)

Head-initial, *left*-associative structures cannot be merged in such a way that parsing could proceed strictly parallel with a merging process. This becomes immediately obvious once one simultaneously inspects the structure of a phrase and the structure of its dependants. Let us assume (2b) is instantiated as a complex VP with several arguments, as in (3a), one of whose DPs is expanded in (3b), as illustrated by the expression (3c).

(3) a. ... [$_{VP}$ [[[V°] XP] YP] ZP]
     b. ... [$_{VP}$ [[[V°] DP] [$_{DP}$ [$_{NP}$ N° PP]]] PP] ...
     c. ... send her reviews of her paper to her office (by email at noon)

The parser meets V° and merges it with the following pronoun to form a V'-phrase. The next element is a noun. This element, of course, cannot be merged immediately with V'. It is the head of a phrase that must be built up before its top node can be merged with the already existing V'. But the top

---

[13] If, in a given structure, the head is not peripheral (see the option in a Type III structure, Chapter 5), this is a structural variant out of a set that contains structures with the head in the peripheral position.

node is not the node that the parsed noun can be attached to *immediately*, since there may be encountered elements coming in that give rise to several nodes in between the already parsed phrase and its top node, due to right-associativity. What this illustrates is the simple insight that there cannot be a grammar that structures an utterance such that a left-to-right bottom-up production of a linear array is going to proceed strictly homomorphic with a simultaneous parsing procedure.

What is the unfriendly property of (2b), then? It is the fact that every time the parser needs to instantiate a new phrase it cannot decide in advance 'how many brackets will have to be opened', that is, how many layers there are in between the bottom of a phrase it starts with, any intermediate active node and the top node. This is a source of indeterminacy that is prone to end up in a series of backtracking moves revising the decision on what constitutes the top node of the given phrase. Imagine, finally, a complex clause. It will start with the verb of the matrix VP followed by the most deeply embedded phrase, for instance, an argument clause. This structure is the severe form of centre embedding. The most deeply embedded constituent is sandwiched by elements of the matrix clause, but the top-down support cannot apply because a decision on the node it should start from, namely the top node, has not yet been reached in the course of parsing.

Let us summarize the reasons that eliminate the *left*-associative structure (2b): The unfriendly property of (2b) is the fact that in a complex projection, the active node most often will not coincide with the top node. So, there is no immediate convergence of top-down and bottom-up information for most nodes. But this is the decisive property. A continuous supply of top-down information presupposes a structure that allows the parser to immediately identify the top node of a projection once it reaches the boundary of this very projection. This is the case in *right*-associative structures (2a).

The superiority of (2a) rests on the fact that (2a) has itself a 'left-to-right' top-down structure. Proceeding to the right in a phrase is proceeding towards the bottom of the phrase. This reduces backtracking because the first node of a new phrase encountered by the parser proceeding with the processing of an array is necessarily the top node, irrespective of the complexity of the phrase: the parser can safely postulate the top node (or the top node of a sub-phrase) and thereby start with a combined top-down and bottom-up procedure for the simple reason that the complexity of the phrase does not influence the decision on the top node (of the phrase or a sub-constituent of it). The more complex a phrase is the more layers of embedding it has, but this decision is not due at the *beginning* of a phrase. The layers are added in a downward direction as a function of the input, that is, as a function of the bottom-up information.

The decision of the parser for structures like (2a) is always a *local* decision: is the next element the head of the projection I am parsing? If yes, I am finished with this projection; if no, I instantiate a new intermediate projection node as a new active node. This node will be the *top node* of whatever material still waits to be integrated in the phrase that is currently being processed. The upshot of this explication should be the insight that phrase structures have to be right-branching in order to qualify as parser friendly.

In the above considerations, the initial or final position of the head did not play a specific role, but it matters, of course. The head is a highly contentful source of mainly lexically stored grammatical information that is relevant for decisions on the structuring of a phrase. This is the topic of the following section.

2.4 OV and VO – the two ways of compromising for the benefit of the parser

The early presentation of the head of a phrase to the parser is another act of friendliness because it provides information for predictions about where to expect which elements in the rest of the phrase. This aspect would per se favour head-initial projections over head-final ones. 'Unfortunately', a right-branching projection with the head in the foot position is necessarily a head-*final* projection. In a binary projection of a lexical head, each argument to be projected requires a separate layer of projection. For functional projections, with their simple spec–head–complement structure, this problem does not arise. Since binary branching leaves room for a single complement only, the head in the foot position can *precede* only a single complement. If, as in complex head-initial lexical projections, there is more than one argument, the head cannot be both in the foot position and precede the argumental complements in a right-associative structure. The solution entails a complication.

If a head is to precede more than one complement it must be higher in the structure than its dependants. This higher position is not a foot position, however. So this structure is not admitted as a *base* structure. But it is admissible as a derived structure. This is the source of the complexity of head-initial structures, usually referred to as the VP-shell of VO structures. The shell structure of complex VPs is an immediate result of combining the *three* factors that determine a head-initial complex projection: phrases are *projections* (viz.

endocentric = head at the foot position = merger starts with the head of the phrase), phrases are *right-associative* and the head *precedes* (in VO).

In other words, VO is the result of implementing two apparently conflicting demands, namely the necessity for the verb to function as the *head* in the *foot position* of the projection, on the one hand, and the parser-friendly property of presenting the head early while obeying the left-associativity restriction, on the other.[14]

In grammar-theoretic terms this is translated into a *parametric* option for the head, namely, the licensing direction, with *anterograde* licensing (i.e. licensing to the right, rather than to the left as in head-final projections) or *retrograde* licensing. Being in a foot position, a head that licenses to the right would license only the complement sister to its right (see the lowest V-projection in 4). The solution is the *iteration* of the basic projection scheme, namely the head–complement pattern: in (4), a VP with three phrases merged with the V-projection; this scheme is instantiated three times. Viewed from this perspective, the necessity for a *VP-shell* structure of the head-initial VP, and in fact for any complex head-initial projection, immediately follows from the associativity constraint (BBC).

If, as in (4), the basic projection scheme is reiterated x-many times, there are x-many head positions, but there is only a *single* lexical head. So, the structure will be well formed only if the head positions are co-indexed, which is equivalent to the formation of a head-movement chain. This is the *raison d'être* for the shell structures in VO clause structures.[15]

(4)

$$\begin{array}{c} \boxed{VP} \\ \triangle \quad V' \\ V_i^0 \rightarrow VP \\ \triangle \quad V' \\ V_i^0 \rightarrow \triangle \end{array}$$

---

[14] A less effective way of solving this problem is a V2-grammar. Independently of OV or VO, the finite verb is presented as early as possible, but in many cases this verb is not the main verb, but a grammatically less informative auxiliary or quasi-auxiliary. V2 is a relatively rare 'invention' (see Holmberg in press).

[15] The position to the left of the top V'-node – the clause-internal subject – is characteristic of SVO. If the verb were to move further on to a higher shell above the subject, the result would be VSO.

Head-final projections (see 5) meet the three above-mentioned criteria for a well-formed projection (endocentric, right-associative, directional licensing) right away: the head and its projection nodes license to the left. The head stays in the rightmost and thereby deepest position. All nodes are attached to the left of their sister node on the projection line. (6) is the projection excluded by the associativity constraint.

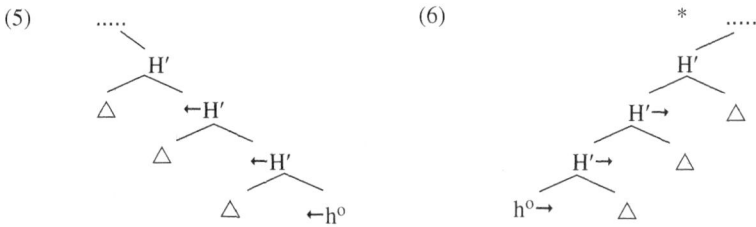

(4) illustrates the shell structure of a VP, but it is in fact representative of any complex head-initial lexical projection. A complex head-initial N-structure (see the example in (7b) and its structure in (8)) will have the corresponding shell structure within the N-projection.

(7)   a. dass ... [$_{VP}$ der Mann^i [gegen sich^i [wütet]]
    b. das [$_{NP}$ Wüten$_j$ [des Mannes^i [e$_j$ gegen sich^i]]]
    c. that the man$_j^i$ [$_{VP}$ e$_j$ rages against himself^i]
    d. Karls^i [$_{NP}$ Wut auf sich^i]
       Karl's fury at himself

German and Dutch are languages with mixed directionality. V and A are retrograde, N and P are anterograde licensers. Since verbs can be easily converted into nouns by means of the nominalized infinitive construction, as the pair (7a) and (7b) illustrates, the directionality effects on projecting the lexically specified argument requirements onto a syntactic structure can be checked on corresponding minimal pairs of V- and N-projections (details in Chapter 8). The c-command relations between the binders and the dependent anaphors are alike in (7a–c). (7c) is the SVO solution, while the verbal counterpart of (7b) would be a VSO-structure, with the head preceding all of its arguments. The SVO-like solution is (7d). In German the pre-head genitive position in the DP is more restricted than in English. It is open for proper nouns but not for NPs in general.

A complex, head-initial NP (8) has the same kind of shell structure as a complex head-initial VP since they are subject to the same kind of grammatical triggers for structure (see Chapter 8, on the comparison of VP- and NP-syntax, with minimal-pair structures; viz. with verbs and deverbal nouns as heads, respectively).

(8) ..... $\boxed{NP}$

$$N_j^0 \rightarrow NP'$$

$$\triangle \quad N'$$

$$V_i^0 \rightarrow \triangle$$

2.5 When performance meets UG, does form follow function?

What is the empirically adequate and theoretically satisfactory explanation for a parser-friendly asymmetry principle (BBC)? Generally, we find (see the history of biology) two competing attempts, an immediately *performance-related* account[16] and a *system's* account. The former account represents the *functionalist* perspective. In this view, the structures we find in natural languages are formed by the users according to their needs of processing, and hence they are the way they are used for. The latter account posits that the grammars that determine the structures are subject to independent general constraints, and therefore the structures are the way they are. The adaptive properties, if recognized, are explained as evolutionary-formed properties (adaptation by biological or cognitive evolution).

The obvious question to ask is this: is the asymmetry in the phrase structures of human languages due to a *performance* restriction in the linguistic phenotype (that is, the acquisition and use of the grammar of a given language), or is it a *constitutive* property of human grammars, that is, a property of the human language faculty, viz. of UG? In other words, does performance restrict grammars or is the grammar organized in such a way that it happens to enhance performance?

This alternative is immediately reminiscent of a classical issue in biology: does the phenotype adapt to the environment and pass this adaptation on to the descendants, as Lamarck believed, or are the astounding adaptations the result of arbitrary mutation plus blind selection, as Darwin argued? Grammar is adaptive, but not in the functionalist, Lamarckian style.

---

[16] This is the outdated Lamarckian position. It posits a 'need' or 'drive' to change, directed to meet an organism's needs.

I shall argue for an evolutionary account of adaptation and, in particular, I shall argue that this is a case of adaptation by *cognitive* selection. It is the same mechanism as Darwin characterized on the genetic level of organisms (viz. variation plus selection), but unlike biological evolution it is not substance-bound. Its pool of variants is a set of sets of mentally representable 'grammars', and its selector is the environment of language acquisition and processing provided by the human brain. This is the biotope in which grammar variants 'struggle for life' (Haider 1999).

Languages are organized the way they are organized because our brain provides effective processing mechanisms for certain data structures. When processing capacities were recruited for language processing in the evolutionary history of the cognitive capacity that we call the human language faculty, this was the recruiting of already existing processing mechanisms for novel tasks (exaptation; Haider 1991). In the course of the evolution of *Homo sapiens*, the time span was too short for the brain to develop completely new processing devices specialized for language processing. So, the language faculty has a-priori properties. It has not been designed for language. Language is parasitic on already existing production and processing architectures. The recruited brain capacities on our way to the language-gifted *Homo sapiens* could not have been pre-adapted for the processing of recursive symbol structures with high complexity.

As a consequence, the structures we find in human languages are those that have turned out to be effectively and efficiently processable given the *available* resources. They passed the cognitive selection processes. In the retrospect perspective, the specific ensemble of processing structures of the human brain available for processing language structures is a matter of chance. In a slightly different species it could differ significantly, but the fact that the constraints imposed by these processing capacities are respected by the grammars of human languages is a matter of necessity. In sum, the processing system does not determine the grammar system, but it determines the history of adaptation towards a better fit.

Let me sketch an argument: given a formal property P of phrase structures (e.g. lack of *right-associativity*), one is tempted to ask: 'What is the explanation for P?'

- Answer A: Grammars embody P because P makes processing certain structures easier (*performance-driven, functionalist*).
- Answer B, step 1: Grammars embody P because this is the reflex of a domain-specific cognitive capacity we call the human language faculty (*system driven*).

Step 2: Structures that meet P are easier to process since there exists a processing capacity in the human language capacity for P.

Step 3: Evolution selects grammars that enforce P. The adaptive quality of grammars with the property P is a consequence of *selection-driven adaptivity by cognitive evolution*.

How can we distinguish between A and B? We study the scope of P. If P is mandatory and discrete, answer B is appropriate. If P is preferential and gradient, answer A is likely to be justified. Here is a case for P: phrase structures are (right-associatively) asymmetric. Answer A: asymmetric structures are preferred for ease of processing, and P is preferential. Answer B: asymmetric phrase structures reflect a constructional invariant of phrase structures that is discrete and imperative.

So, the question translates into an issue of grammar theory: why are grammars the way they are? The answer must be framed in terms of cognitive capacities and selection: the grammar guarantees easily processable data structures because ease of processing is one of the selection properties in the history of the cognitive evolution of the human language faculty: it is the receptive aspect (*string-to-structure mapping*), and not the perspective of generation (*combinatorics of elementary units*), that is the decisive factor, both in on-line usage, in the course of grammar acquisition, and in an evolutionary perspective.

It is a truism that the language-specific variables of a grammar enter the head of the learner only if the data they are instantiated in are processable. The learner is a cognitive filter that selects. So, first of all, the cognitive constitution of the learner determines what is a possible grammar.

Second, the learner is a recipient. The on-line task of the learner, and in fact any listener, is to map a one-dimensional array of terminals (= phonetic form) onto an at-least-two-dimensional representation, namely *semantic form*. The capacities of the cognitive filter are reflected in its product, the compiled rule system called grammar, and ultimately in the productions of the grammar.

In sum, there is no denying that grammars have an adaptive design. The explanation of this fact is controversial, however. For a functionalist, grammars are *mental tools*, whose form is supposed to follow from the various functions that the toolmakers have in mind for their tools.[17] The competing view is one

---

[17] Unfortunately, functionalist accounts are more interested in construing functional needs they see embodied in specific constructions, and neglect too often the many obviously dysfunctional aspects of grammars. Grammars set limits, and these limits cannot be transgressed, even if they may be dysfunctional for specific needs of communication (Haider 1998). English, for instance, forbids double questions that are allowed by German or Japanese:

that sees adaptivity as the result of an evolutionary process of variation and selection in the cognitive evolution of grammars. There is no toolmaker, and there is no intended design, since any process of cognitive evolution is blind. Adaptivity is the result of the 'survival' of certain grammar properties and the loss of others in the competition for acquisition.

Hawkins is a superb advocate of a short-cut, functionalist account: 'Many fundamental and abstract structural properties of grammars can be explained by simple considerations of processing ease. In other words, grammars are in large measure performance driven' (Hawkins 1994: 409). The central principle of processing ease is the EIC-measure (the Principle of Early Immediate Constituents): *the human parser prefers linear orders that maximize the IC-to-non-IC ratios of constituent recognition domains* (Hawkins 1994: 77).

The EIC-measure is first of all a descriptive measure for distribution patterns across languages. Second, it is a hypothesis that the parser is responsible for the distribution described by the EIC. And third, it ascribes a preference, not an absolute constraint. There is no threshold EIC-value imprinted in our brains that would trigger categorial decisions.

The merely preferential quality under the final authority of grammar is easy to demonstrate, for instance, if a language with a clause-initial subject position (9a) is compared with one in which subjects can be postponed. (9b) is a possible serialization in Italian but not in English: the IC-to-non-IC ratio in (9b) is in general much higher than that in (9a), simply because the subject is a locus of clausal embedding, as in (9a), and a postponed subject removes the material out of the constituent recognition domain: the relative clause is recognized in the clause-final position, so the rest does not enter the IC-to-non-IC ratio, if the subject with the clause is postponed.

(9) a. [The man [(that) she [gave [the valuable camera to]]]] ran away
English order
b. Ran away [the man [(that) she [gave [the valuable camera to]]]]
Italian order

However, subject postponing is not a general option for SVO languages, nor is extraposition a general option for any OV language. In German (10), relative clauses may be extraposed and this greatly enhances the processability, especially when there is an additional embedded clause (10e). But the relative participial

(i) Wer hat weshalb protestiert?
who has why protested
(ii) *Who has protested why?

Is German 'more functional' than English if it allows questions (i) that are illicit in English (ii)?

construction (10b) cannot be extraposed, no matter how complex it is (10f). Despite the fact that (10b) has a much more inferior ratio than the extraposed version (10d) would have (see Hawkins 1994: 272), extraposition is strictly banned.

(10)   a. Ich habe [den Mann [der an dieser Krankheit leidet]$_{RC}$] bedauert
(*extraposable*)
          I have the man who from this disease suffers pitied
    b. Ich habe [den [an dieser Krankheit leidenden]$_{RC}$ Mann] bedauert
(*non-extraposable*)
          I have the from this disease suffering man pitied
    c. Ich habe [den Mann] bedauert [der an dieser Krankheit leidet]$_{RC}$
    d. *Ich habe [den Mann] bedauert [an dieser Krankheit leidenden]$_{RC}$
    e. Ich habe [den Mann [der an dieser Krankheit [für die es keine Behandlung gibt] leidet]$_{RC}$] bedauert
          I have [the man [who from this disease [for which there is no treatment] suffers] pitied]
    f. Ich habe [den [an dieser Krankheit, für die es keine Behandlung gibt, leidenden]$_{RC}$ Mann] bedauert
          I have [the [from this disease for which there is no treatment suffering] man] pitied

The counterexample for the *non-discrete* and non-mandatory nature of the EIC-based prediction – the EIC covers statistical tendencies but not the imperative restrictions that hold within an individual language – is the edge effect (Haider 2000a) found with adjunctions to head-initial constituents: the head of the constituent adjoined to a head-initial constituent must be adjacent to the node to which the constituent is adjoined. The 'size' of the adjoined constituent does not matter.

(11)   a. He has [(*much more*) carefully (**than anyone else*)] analysed it
    b. He has [(*much less*) often (**than I (thought)*))] rehearsed it
    c. He has [(*much more*) carefully analysed it (*than anyone else*)]

Adverbial phrases in between the finite auxiliary and the VP may be complex but they must be head-final. This is not language specific but correlates with the headedness of a given phrase: the edge effect is found with head-initial target phrases only. In German, noun phrases are head-initial, VPs are head-final, and, as expected, the edge effect is found with prenominal attributes (13) but not with preverbal adverbials (12).

(12)   a. Er hat es [*sehr viel* sorgfältiger *als jeder andere*] analysiert
    b. Er hat es [*viel weniger* oft *als ich (dachte)*] geprobt
    c. als niemand [*luider (dan Jan (denkt))*] kan roepen   Dutch
       'if noone louder than Jan (thinks) can shout'

(13) a. eine [viel größere (*als ich dachte*)] Summe
'a much bigger (than I thought) sum'
b. eine [viel größere Summe (*als ich dachte*)]
'a much bigger sum than I thought'

The contrast between the distribution in (12) and (13) is not just a preference. In (13) and (11), *only* the extraposed variant is acceptable. The other variant is strongly deviant, no matter how minimal the intervening constituent is. For (12), improving the EIC-ratio by extraposition is possible but optional. There is no strong incentive for extraposition in (12), though.

What all these examples are meant to show is that the EIC does not overrule grammatical principles. Hence, a strong interpretation of EIC as a principle that ought to explain *abstract structural properties of grammars* would not be appropriate, and Hawkins does not maintain it as a mandatory and discrete constraint. The BBC, however, is a strict principle of grammar. Hence, a comparison between the EIC and the BBC is instructive for the issue under discussion.

The BBC is a constraint on admissible data structures. First of all, it reduces the search space of the parser, since the parser 'knows' which structure to expect for lexical projections and their functional extension. Moreover, BBC-constrained structures facilitate on-line parsing by reducing backtracking because in the right-associative structure precedence coincides with c-command: the preceding element is higher in the structure than the co-constituent. In particular, the leftmost sub-constituent of a constituent is dominated by the mother node of the constituent:

(14) a. ... [α_P X [Y [...]]]
b. ... [α_P[[...] Y] X]

Assume the parser proceeds to the constituent αP. In (14a), the parser will be able to project a new phrase node immediately when the first element of the constituent is reached. It can project the mother node for X without the risk of backtracking. In (14b), however, once the first item of the new constituent is reached, the parser would have to guess how many brackets it has to postulate, but the parser cannot decide the actual number of brackets before the end of the phrase has been reached. The BBC eliminates these problems by eliminating structures such as (14b). It is guaranteed by virtue of the BBC that complexity is a function of embedding and that dominance relations are preserved (for a more detailed discussion of parsing advantages for right-associative phrase structures see also Phillips (1995)).

The BBC predicts that head-initial structures are more complex than head-final ones (see (4) vs. (5) above). The higher degree of structural complexity, however, is compensated. Head-initial phrases are immediately identifiable because the first and highest element is the head. Thus, identification of the mother node of a phrase and identification of the category of the node are achieved simultaneously.

Therefore, if the BBC is a constraint of UG, the phrase structures of natural languages embody a property favoured by an incremental parser. We could imagine a different UG, let us call it UG', with left-associative structures instead of right-associative ones. The structures admitted by UG' would be as constrained as those of UG, but they would lack the advantage for incremental parsing. Assume that our *Homo sapiens* brain is in principle able to alternatively implement the *knowledge* system of a human grammar in terms of UG as well as in terms of UG'. The conditions of putting this system to use in on-line language processing would select structures of UG-constrained grammars, rather than UG'-constrained ones. This is to say that the cognitive evolution would be biased towards UG.

In this perspective, parsing considerations play the decisive role in the *evolutionary* perspective of the human language faculty rather than in the *phenotypic* situation. Languages are as they are because UG is as it is. And UG is as it is because it happens to be the formal reflex of a system for compiling grammars that has once and for ever emerged in the human brain's development. The grammars of the languages of today indirectly reflect their cognitive selection history just like the biological condition of an individual indirectly reflects the evolutionary history of its biological selection.

The adaptive qualities of the phenotype could be partly described from a purely functionalist perspective but this would nevertheless miss the essential point. The function is not the cause. In biology, this is a truism.[18] In the field of cognitive science and in linguistics in particular, it is time for this to become a truism as well: there is linguistic structure, and there are linguistic functions, and structures enable and restrict functions, but they are not determined by them (Haider 2001a). The function cannot determine the structure unless for artefacts. If a functionalist takes languages to be artefacts, s/he should be worried by the fact that the alleged toolmakers do not understand the alleged

---

[18] In order to understand the adaptive properties of wings, the consideration of their functions is helpful, but their evolutionary history may be entirely different. Wings were 'invented' independently at least four times, namely by pterosauria (pterosaurs), aves (birds), chiroptera (bats) and insects, with a different history of advantages, such as thermo-regulation, locomotion, sexual attraction, etc.

artefacts. The evolutionary account covers both the adaptivity and the analytic inaccessibility.

2.6 Summary

To a high extent, grammars of human languages display an adaptive design for the processing of the linguistic structures they determine. The adaptive quality is due to a set of properties that make these structures effectively and efficiently processable. Effective processing is the result of optimally combining top-down (= grammar-driven) and bottom-up (= input-driven) routines. This favours right-associative structures.

It is argued that the adaptive property of grammars is the effect of *cognitive co-evolution* between the recruiting of brain resources for language processing and the organization of grammars. Adaptivity is the result of a Darwinian evolution process in terms of variation and selection, not on the level of biological structures,[19] though, but on the level of domain-specific cognitive structures. As a result, the ensemble of domain-specific brain resources that constitute UG determines grammars that in turn determine effectively and efficiently processable linguistic structures.

---

[19] See Bierwisch (2000) for a detailed discussion of the conundra and paradoxes of attempts to explain the emergence of language as a *direct* product of biological evolution.

3 BBC – asymmetry in phrase structuring

3.1 Introduction

This chapter returns to the very starting point of the investigations on symmetry breaking in the early nineties.[1] Section 3.2 briefly revisits the core *evidence* for uniform right-branching structures from double-object constructions and the associated parameterization that yields head-initial vs. head-final phrase structures. Section 3.3 concentrates on Larson's original analysis that led to the assumption of shell structures, its ad hoc complications, and its straightforward derivation for head-initial phrases from the BBC. Section 3.4 revisits implications of the BBC for the distribution of particles and the positive evidence from English and Scandinavian languages. Section 3.5 defends the claim that scrambling is a phenomenon of head-final phrases against alleged counterevidence from Slavic. Independent evidence strongly supports the claim that Slavic languages are Type III languages. Section 3.6 summarizes the axioms and implications of the BBC and PDI (Principle of Directional Identification) system.

This chapter's focus is on an invariant property of phrase structures, namely their asymmetric organization. It compares head-initial and head-final projections, and mainly investigates two questions. *First*, what is the grammatical causality for the shell structures of complex, head-*initial* projections (see VP-shells in (αc)) and what accounts for the absence of shell structures in head-final phrases? *Second*, why is the right-associative, layered structure of head-*final* projections (see αa) not cross-linguistically mirrored by a left-associative structure in head-*initial* projections (see αb)?

---

[1] The bulk of this chapter (Sections 3.1 and 3.2, except 3.2.2) is entirely retro(spective) and merely terminologically and deictically updated. It recycles a paper (Haider 1995b) based on Haider (1992), which had been turned down by *Linguistic Inquiry* (*LI*) in 1993 ('The basic branching conjecture'). This paper had not been distributed before it became part of an article collection ('Studies on economy and derivation') in 1995 in a working paper series (*Working Papers of the SFB 340*, #70, Univ. Stuttgart, Univ. Tübingen and IBM Heidelberg). By then it had nevertheless already found its way into the text and the bibliography of an *LI* paper (on a phenomenon that figured prominently in the rejected paper) and an MIT Press monograph of the same year.

(α) a. [$_{VP}$ IO [DO [PP V°]]]   German (= head-final)
     b. *[$_{VP}$ [[V° PP] DO] IO]   'Mirror' English
     c. [$_{VP}$ V$_i$° [IO [[$_{V°}$ e]$_i$ [DO[[$_{V°}$ e]$_i$ PP]]]]   English (= head-initial, with V-shells)

The OV/VO issue has been clarified in terms of head-chaining (see αc) triggered by the parameterized property of directional identification (see PDI, (6) in Chapter 2). The incongruence between the directionality requirements of the BBC and that of the PDI for head-*initial* structures necessitates a structure with re-instantiated head positions for each argument position. Since there is only one lexical head, the additional positions are positions created by means of head-chaining. The formation of a head-chain is a grammatical necessity. It is an unavoidable consequence of a specific setting of the directionality parameter value for head-*initial* phrases and the universal restriction on projection structure, the BBC, that enforces right-associative structures, that is, structures with merger on the left-hand side. The result is the shell structure of head-initial phrases.

3.2   The structure of complex lexical projections

3.2.1   The facts

There is a fact, easy to check and yet as puzzling as it is simple (that had not been fully appreciated in the early nineties). The VP-internal basic serialization patterns of non-verbal elements are cross-linguistically invariant. A particularly perspicuous case is the pattern of double-object constructions with a directional PP. Both in OV and in VO languages, the order is the one indicated in (1). Examples from two languages of each type are provided under (2).

(1)   ... IO – DO – PP$_{(directional/resultative)}$ ...

(2)   a. dass sie *jedem^i ein Paket an seine^i Privatadresse* schicken
           werden   German
           that they everyone a package to his home address send will
        b. omdat *ze iedereen^i een packje naar hem^i thuis* zullen opsturen   Dutch
        c. that they will send *everybody$_i$ a package to his$_i$ home address*
        d. at de forklarede *hver deltager^i problemet på hans^i eget sprog*   Danish
           that they explained every participant the problem in his own language

The crucial property is this: the position of the *verbal head*, whether preceding or following, does not interfere with the relative order of the serialization patterns. If parametric headedness variation were in fact a symmetric property, we would expect VO structures to *mirror* the structure and serialization of the OV structure, as illustrated under (3). The head-initial mirror-image structure of (3a), namely (3b), does not exist. (3c), the counterpart of (3a) with the verb on the opposite edge of the VP is structured – inappropriately, as has become clear – in a way that has been taken for an appropriate English VP structure for quite some time. Its head-final mirror-image structure (3d) does not exist either. (3d) is a possible result of scrambling for (3a), though.

(3) a. [IO [DO [PP V]]] (e.g. German)   c.*[[[V IO] DO] PP][2]
     b. *[[[V PP] DO] IO]   d.*[PP [DO [IO V]]]

It is remarkable on the one hand that (3b) is not found as the VO-analogue of (3a), and it should come as a surprise on the other hand, that the relevant branching structure of (1) is uniform, both in OV[3] and VO systems. Binding of a variable as illustrated in (2) and other grammatical phenomena sensitive to c-command[4] point to the conclusion that the branching structure for OV and VO VPs must be the same. It is *right*-branching. Larson (1988) had realized the immediate consequence of some empirical facts noted by Barss and Lasnik (1986): if structures are binary branching, (3c) cannot be the empirically adequate branching structure for a sequence like in (1).

There is ample evidence, both cross-categorially *within* a language such as German, and *cross-linguistically*, that points to the same conclusion, namely, that head-initial and head-final projections are *each right*-branching. The binding patterns that require c-command between the binder and the bindee uniformly follow a right-branching structure. This is shown by the Icelandic example in (4), as well as the Danish sentences in (5) and the Swedish data in (6):

(4) a. Sjórinn svipti hanni^i [manni sínum^i]   Icelandic
        the-sea deprived her$_{ACC}$ [husband her[+$_{REFL}$]]$_{DAT}$
        the sea deprived her^i of her^i husband
     b. *Sjórinn svipti [konu sína^i] manninum^i
        the sea deprived wife$_{ACC}$ his[+$_{REFL}$] the-man$_{DAT}$
        the sea deprived his^i wife of the man^i

---

[2] Until the mid eighties, a *left-branching* structure [[V DP] DP] was considered a plausible phrase structure for a binary-branching VP in English. Chomsky (1981: 171) explicitly assigned this structure to 'John [[gave Bill] a book]'.

[3] Arguments for IO–DO base order in Japanese are provided by Hoji (1985) and Yatsushiro (2000).

[4] These phenomena, reviewed in Larson (1988, 1990), include A-binding, superiority and negative polarity items. In each case, the preceding element is the binder. Since the binder must c-command, the preceding element is the c-commanding one. This is possible only in a right-associative VP, not in a left-associatively layered one.

c. *Sjórinn svipti manninum^i [gömlu konu sína^i ...]
   the sea deprived of the man^i [his^i old wife ...]
   (Zaenen, Maling and Thráinnson 1985: 468)

Sentence (4b) is ungrammatical, because the antecedent does not c-command the reflexive. Reordering, for instance by means of heavy NP-shift, as in (4c), does not improve the acceptability. This is evidence for a structure-dependent relation rather than a merely precedence-dependent one.

(5) a. Jag gav honom^i sin^i hund   Danish
       I gave him his$_{REFL}$ dog
    b. *Jag gav sin^i ägare hunden^i
       I gave his$_{REFL}$ owner the dog   (Herslund 1986)

The Danish data correspond with the Icelandic facts. If binding requires c-command, the preceding NP must be in a higher position than the NP that follows it. Falk (1990: 57) presents parallel data from Swedish:

(6) a. Jag skickade flickan^i till sin^i dagmamma   Swedish
       I sent the girl to her$_{REFL}$ nanny
    b. *Jag sickade sin^i klänning till henne^i
       I sent her$_{REFL}$ dress to her

The resulting structure for a V-final VP is (7a). Although (7b) would capture the desired configuration with respect to the position of the complements, it cannot be the adequate structure assignment for a V-initial VP. The offending property of (7b) is obvious. It violates the endocentricity condition of X'-projections, since the head appears at the top of the projection line, and not at the bottom, and so the structure (4b) contains headless sub-projections.

(7) a. [IO [DO [PP V]]]   (=3a)
    b. *[V [IO [DO [PP]]]]

Head-initial N-projections pose the very same problem. In German, the V-projection is head-final but the N-projection is head-initial. Nevertheless, the serialization of the arguments is identical. If headedness and the resulting configuration were symmetric, the realization in head-initial projections should be the mirror image of head-final projections (cf. 8). This is not the case. Moreover, there is evidence that precedence goes together with c-command (cf. 9). The head noun in (8c,d) is the nominalized verb of (8a,b). This guarantees that the argument structure of the noun is in a direct relation to the argument structure of the verb.

(8) a. [diese Rechte] [auf jemand anderen] übertragen   German
       these rights on someone else confer

b. auf jemand anderen$_i$ diese Rechte e$_i$ übertragen (scrambled)
c. das Übertragen [von diesen Rechten]/[dieser$_{GEN}$ Rechte] [auf jemand anderen]
   the confer(ing) of these rights on someone else
d. *das Übertragen [auf jemand anderen]$_i$ [von diesen Rechten]/ [dieser$_{GEN}$ Rechte] e$_i$

The variation between (8b) and (8a) is the familiar contrast between a base order and a scrambled one. In head-*initial* constituents, phrase-internal scrambling is ungrammatical. This accounts for the ungrammaticality of (8d). In (8c,d), the head is an infinitive used as a noun, as a general option in German. NPs are head-initial, VPs are head-final.

It is an open question as to why head-initial projections should not allow scrambling to the right, as a mirror image of scrambling to the left in head-final structures. The answer will become clear in the course of the discussion.

The binding relations in the examples under (9) and (10) illustrate that the argument next to the head is in a position c-commanding the PP following it.[5] Hence the argument next to the head cannot be the sister of the head.

(9)   die Stolz [des Mannes^i [auf sich^i]]^6 German
      the pride the man's at himself
      'the man's$_i$ proudness of himself$_i$'

(10) die Zerlegung [jeglicher^i Substanz [in ihre^i Bestandteile]]
      'the dismantling (of) each^i substance$_{GEN}$ into its^i components'

The examples in (11) confirm the existence of a c-command requirement between the genitive and the PP on the evidence of variable binding. Evidence of a similar kind should be available for any language with head-initial N-projections. A Polish example is given in (11a), an Italian one in (11b).[7]

(11) a. Podróz Janka^i do swoich^i rodziców   Polish
         trip John$_{GEN}$ to self$_{POSS}$ parents$_{GEN}$
         John's^i trip to his^i parents
      b. l'aggressività di Gianni^i contro se stesso^i Italian
         the aggressivity of Gianni^i against himself^i

The examples in (11a,b) are structurally parallel to (10). The NP between the head noun and the PP can act as an antecedent for a reflexive in the PP. Hence

---

[5] The brackets merely indicate which phrase is more deeply embedded. The precise structure will be specified later.

[6] The observation that binding relations within an N-projection are at variance with the standard assumption of layering from left to right, is Werner Frey's original observation, which he communicated to me.

[7] The Polish example has been approved by Barbara Rozwadowska (p.c.); the Italian example by Livia Tonelli (p.c.).

there must be a c-command relationship. This c-command relationship is predictable under the BBC as a constraint on merger.

German is a handy language for checking cross-categorial patterns because the V-projection is head-*final* while the N-projection is head-*initial*. As emphasized in the introductory section, the serialization of the arguments is identical in both structures (cf. 8, above). Both anaphoric binding (cf. 9, above) and quantifier-variable binding (10, above) are parallel to the pattern found in V-projections: the preceding element c-commands the NP that follows:

(12) a. [jedes^i Argument [[in sein^i Gegenteil] verkehren]   German
        [every argument [[into its opposite] turn]
     b. ?in sein$^{?i}$ Gegenteil$_j$ [jedes^i Argument [e$_j$ verkehren]]

(12b) is a scrambled structure. It is marginal because directional or resultative PPs do not easily move clause internally in German (except under focus fronting). (12a) reflects a base order. This is confirmed by clause-internal scrambling (see 13a vs. 13b) and coordination (14) patterns.

(13) a. Circe hat die Seefahrer in Schweine verwandelt   German
        Circe has the seafarers into pigs transformed
     b. ??/* Circe hat in Schweine die Seefahrer verwandelt
        Circe has transformed into pigs the seafarers

(13) is by the same token evidence for the layered structure of the VP. This is confirmed independently by VP-coordination. In (14), the left edge of the disjuncts is clearly marked by the two coordinating elements. The PP is a close complement of the verb, as the contrast between (14a) and (14b) signals.

(14) a. jeden Baum [entweder [[*in Stücke hacken*] oder *schneiden*]
        each tree either into pieces chop or cut
     b. ?? jeden Baum [*in Stücke*] [entweder [*hacken* oder *schneiden*]]
        each tree into pieces either   chop or cut

The very same binding relations apply to N-projections, as in (15). Since the head of the N-projection in (15) is a nominalization of the verb in (12), it is safe to assume that they share the argument structure and that the base order determined by the argument structure will be the same. (15b) is primarily unacceptable because of scrambling, but the binding relation is deviant too.

(15) a. das Zerlegen jeder^i Uhr$_{GEN}$ in ihre^i Bestandteile
        the dismantling (of) each clock into its components
     b. *das Zerlegen [in ihre*^{i} Bestandteile]$_j$ jeder^i Uhr e$_j$

A comparison of (12a) and (15a), with respect to both the binding possibilities and the serialization of the arguments, points to the conclusion that head-initial projections and head-final ones do not differ in the internal branching configuration. They are invariantly right-branching structures.

3.2.2 The theoretical modelling

Larson (1988) presents an account of the so-called English dative alternation which is intended to capture the relevant branching properties of a double-object construction. He considers the V-position in (7b) a derived position. V has raised from a position adjacent to the most deeply embedded argument. His analysis is unnecessarily complicated, however. It invokes ad hoc assumptions (see the discussion below) and it does not arrive at a *principled* answer for the crucial question: what rules out the *left-branching* structure for an English VP and what enforces the right-branching one? His empirically motivated analysis does not provide a principled clarification for the non-existence of (3b).

Obviously, the right-branching VP in English must be the result of a UG restriction. But, as the theory stands (in the nineties), the correct branching configuration could not possibly be inferred from the data by the learner. We cannot reasonably assume that the highly indirect evidence that provoked Larson (1988) to formulate his analysis could trigger the proper structuring of the VP for a first-language learner.

The solution is much more direct and simple, fortunately: phrase structures are universally right-branching (due to the *basic branching conjecture*), as a basic property of UG.[8] The typological variation reduces to the directionality parameter. The shell structure is the solution for the following two (potentially conflicting) requirements under the regime of the BBC:

  (i) the head of the projection is in the foot position (i.e. the endocentricity effect of merging)
  (ii) the arguments of the head are identified *directionally*.

Identifying to the left (*regressive* identifying) triggers the OV structure, identifying to the right (*progressive* identifying) the VO structure. The following formulas (16) illustrate the structural difference between the two projection options. The corresponding trees are given in (17). The arrows indicate the directionality of identification by the head (or its projection).

---

[8] This is a familiar but slightly misleading way of putting it: the one-dimensional representation of a complex linguistic expression, that is, its linear order, should be characterized with respect to its primary ordering factor, namely the time vector: leftness means closer to the beginning and rightness closer to the end. Hence the claim of the universality of right-branching projections is a claim concerning the embedding: elements at the beginning of a *simple* projection are the least embedded elements. Of course, this does not preclude embeddings in complex constructions at the left.

(16)　　a. [XP₃ [XP₂ [XP₁ V°]]]]　　　　head-final
　　　　b. [vp XP₃[V°ᵢ [vp XP₂ [eᵢ XP₁]]]]　head-initial

(17)　a.

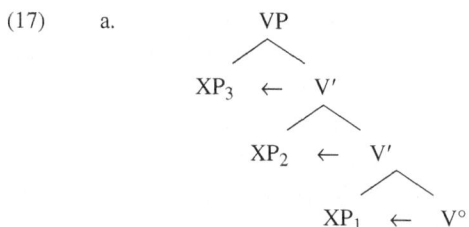

(17)　b.

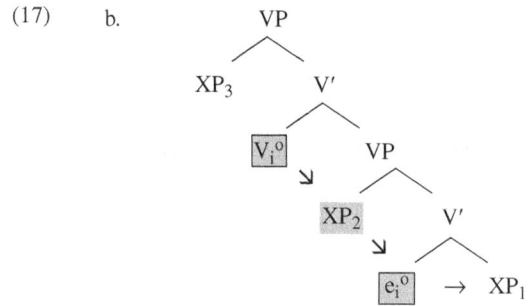

In (16a, 17a), the head is in the foot position, the projection is right-associative and each argument is in the directionality domain of the head and local to the head or one of its projections. (16b, 17b), too, is right-associative and has a head in the foot position of the chain. But, due to the progressive directionality, there is merely one argument position within the directionality domain of the head, namely XP₁ as the sister of the verb. All other positions are higher up, on the left. So, the verb must be re-instantiated as a head in order to provide the possibility of licensing the second argument (XP₂ in 16b) directionally. The result is a V-projection with two V-positions but a single lexical V. So the positions must be treated as positions of a single lexical head. *The outcome is a VP-shell structure with a head-chain.*

The top shell provides an additional argument position (XP₃ in (16b) and (17b)). It is a position local to the head but not in its directionality domain. This is the so-called VP-spec position. An argument in this position can be discharged, but it cannot be directionally identified by the lexical head. So it needs *external licensing* (by a functional head). In the head-final projection (16a, 17a), however, all arguments are in the licensing *and* identification domains of the head.

V-movement of the Larsonian kind (or iterative internal merger in the terminology of the Minimalist Program) is triggered by the requirement that the syntactically active A-structure of a head be discharged completely. If the verb is a regressively licensing head, it is able to project and discharge its A-structure *in situ*, since all discharged positions are within its domain on the right-branching structure. If, however, the directionality is progressive, the head can merge with the first phrase *in situ*. Any other phrase it merges with requires the instantiation of a higher head position for directional licensing.

These considerations are not specific for V-projections. They apply to any complex head-initial structure, in particular to the N-projections discussed above. For ease of reference, the examples are repeated below as (18) together with their common phrase structure (19):

(18)   a. die [$_{NP}$ Stolz$_i$ [des Mannes^j [e$_i$ [auf sich^j]]]]
             the   pride   the man's   of himself
        b. die [$_{NP}$ Zerlegung$_i$ [jeglicher^j Substanz [e$_i$ [in ihre^j Bestandteile]]]]
            the decomposition (of) each substance$_{GEN}$ into its components

(19)

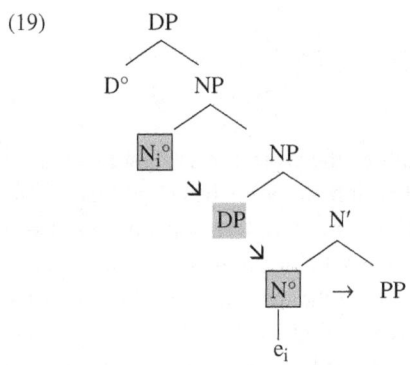

Note that the NP structure in (19) is congruent, modulo category labels, with a head-initial V-projection, as in 'decompose each substance into its components'. Head-initial N-projections consist of N-shells, just like head-initial V-projections consist of V-shells. There is no need to invoke 'light Ns' or 'light Vs' as currently assumed for post-Larsonian VP structures in the Minimalist Program. The shell structure is an inevitable by-product of the implementation of a progressively licensing head into an invariant right-branching projection format.

The interim summary so far is this:

(i) The parametric factor for head-initial and head-final structures is the *directionality* value for the licensing (by identification) directionality of the head (and its projections).
(ii) The position of a head of a projection is determined by the value of the licensing parameter. Regressively licensing heads remain in the foot position of the endocentric projections. The result is a head-final projection. Progressively licensing heads must be re-instantiated ('internally merged'). The result is a shell structure for head-initial projections.
(iii) The source of the OV/VO differences is the directionality of licensing in combination with the BBC and the endocentricity requirement (merger principle).[9]
(iv) The grammatical causality for the invariant linearization (e.g. IO – DO – PO) across OV and VO is the mapping of the hierarchically organized lexical A-structure onto a uniform right-branching syntactic projection skeleton (constrained by the BBC).
(v) (not discussed here, but relevant) The specified directionality value of the head extends to its projection nodes (uniform directionality). If the value is unspecified, the result is a Type III structure. For a detailed explication of Type III, see Chapter 5, §5.3.

3.3 On double-objects – Larson's odyssey on his way to right-branching structures

It is instructive to analyse how Larson tried to integrate the evidence uncovered by Barss and Lasnik (1986). His approach is highly conservative. He starts with the left-branching structure assigned to double-object constructions in those days and derives step by step a right-branching surface structure.

3.3.1 Data covered, theory missing

In his case study on English double-object constructions, Larson (1988, 1990) proposes a derivational solution to the empirical challenge of the Barss and Lasnik (1986) data. These data indicate that the c-command relations reflect a uniform left-to-right organization of phrases.[10] In the English double-object construction, according to Larson, a left-branching VP is *transformed* into a

---

[9] For arguments against an approach that derives OV from VO by extensive evacuation and movement of the VP see the final chapter.
[10] Barss and Lasnik (1986: 347f.) drew attention to the fact that phenomena sensitive for c-command are in conflict with left-branching structures. Relations such as binding, superiority and negative polarity licensing cannot be accounted for with these structures.

right-branching one by means of two movements (head movement *plus* raising of the direct object) and subsequent structure pruning. The trigger for the derived V-position is characterized as the result of a global rule: it is the need of case assignment to the arguments in the higher VP-shell (Larson 1988: 343). The particular linearization is the result of the *U*niformity of *T*heta *A*ssignment *H*ypothesis (UTAH: Baker 1988: 46)[11] applied to the VP-shell structure (Larson 1990: 601).

According to Larson (1988), the D-structures corresponding to (20a,b) are (21a,b), respectively. Note that they are left-branching (21b). The D-structures in (21) are supposed (Larson 1990: 602) to meet a relativized version of Baker's UTAH.[12]

(20) a. (XP) sent$_i$ a letter e$_i$ to Mary
      b. (XP) sent$_j$ Mary$_j$ e$_i$ e$_j$ a letter

(21) a. [$_{VP}$ [$_{V'}$ e [$_{VP}$ a letter [$_{V'}$ send to Mary]]]]   (Larson 1988: 342)
      b. [$_{VP}$ [$_{V'}$ e [$_{VP}$ e [$_{V'}$ [$_V$ send Mary] a letter]]]]   (Larson 1988: 353)

There are at least three undesirable aspects involved in this account: (i) it suffers from a high degree of arbitrariness, (ii) it does not provide an explanatorily adequate account for the trigger of V-raising and NP-movement, and (iii) it involves unnecessary and theoretically undesirable technical devices (arbitrary branching and the need of reanalysis).

First of all, it seems arbitrary to *not* place the direct object, *a letter*, into an identical DS-configuration in (21a) and (21b), if one assumes that UTAH (relativized or not) dictates the mapping from θ-structure to syntactic structure. Consequently, either (21a) would have to be replaced by (22a), or (22b) should replace (21b).

(22) a. [$_{VP}$ [$_{V'}$ e [$_{VP}$ e [$_{V'}$ [$_{V'}$ send to Mary] a letter]]]]
      b. [$_{VP}$ [$_{V'}$ e [$_{VP}$ a letter [$_{V'}$ send Mary]]]]

(i)   a. I showed John$_i$ himself$_i$ in the mirror
      b. *I showed himself$_i$ John$_i$ in the mirror
(ii) a. I gave nobody anything
      b. *I gave anybody nothing
(iii) a. I showed every$_i$ friend of mine his photograph
      b. *I showed its$_i$ trainer every$_i$ lion
(iv) a. *Which book$_i$ did <u>who</u> buy e$_i$?
      b. *Which book$_i$ did you give <u>who</u> e$_i$?

[11] 'Identical thematic relationships between items are represented by identical structural relationships between those items at the level of D-structure. (In order to make this fully formal one would need, among other things, a more exact theory of theta-roles than we now have; I will leave it at a rather intuitive level.)' Baker 1988: 46f.
[12] Relativized UTAH (Larson 1990: 601): 'Identical thematic relationships are represented by identical *relative* hierarchical relations between items at D-structure.'

In order to save (22a) under a Minimalist approach (Chomsky 1992), the DP, *a letter*, would have to move to a case position or the structure would crash. The spec position of the VP in (22a), which corresponds to the alleged D-structure position of the NP, *the letter*, in (21a), is not a case position unless the verb moves. But, according to Larson's view, V-movement is triggered by the altruistic goal of case assignment. Therefore we end up in a stalemate situation: the NP cannot move unless the verb moves, and the verb does not move unless the NP moves.[13]

Obviously, V-movement in (22b) yields an ungrammatical sentence (see 23). This result seems to be unavoidable in Larson's own system as well: it is unclear why the sister of the verb in the basic position, viz. *Mary* in (21b), should move to Spec-V in the derivation of (21b) from (21b), rather than the sister of V'. One would expect, given the adjacency requirement for case assignment, that the non-adjacent NP, that is, the phrase *the letter*, ought to move in (21b). Of course, this would result in the ungrammatical sentence (23):

(23)   * John sent$_j$ a letter$_i$ e$_j$ Mary e$_j$ e$_i$

Evidently, this sentence cannot be ruled out by appealing to the (relativized) UTAH, because the DS-configuration (21b) satisfies it. Larson (1988: 359f.) assumes that after movement of the inner NP, namely *Mary* in (21b), the V'-projection is optionally reanalyzed as V and that it thereby turns into a case assigner for *a letter*. This is both ad hoc and unsatisfactory. Obviously, the target position of NP-movement must be a case position; otherwise the moved NP *Mary* in (21b) would be caseless. Hence there are two case positions, in principle, namely the target position and the V-adjacent base position. So, (23) should be an optimal derivation.

Next, we have to ask ourselves what licenses the kind of structure Larson suggests. First of all, it is unclear, as already noted by Speas (1990: 79), what could license empty heads in the D-structure, not related to any lexical item. Under his perspective, the *empirical raison d'être* of the VP structure is its utility for performing V- and NP-movement on it. Theoretically, it is motivated by the single-complement hypothesis (Larson 1988: 380). This motivation, however, is insufficient. One has to ask oneself why the core grammar of English contains and requires structures like (21) rather than the structure indicated in (3b) or (3c), repeated for the sake of convenience under (24):

[13] I am arguing strictly within Larson's frame of reference, that is, the phrase-internal structure of a projection. If the derived V-position is considered to be an external spec position and the arguments are placed in the corresponding spec positions, we are no longer concerned with the projection structure of lexical heads.

(24) a. [[[V PP] DO] IO] (=3b)
b. [[[V IO] DO] PP] (=3c)

The 'single-complement hypothesis' itself is in need of clarification because it seems to apply only to head-initial projections. In non-scrambled head-final V-projections of e.g. Dutch or German, the verbal head occupies its base position despite the occurrence of more than one complement. So, there remains a question to be answered: what rules out (24a) or (24b) as the analogous structure of Dutch or German V-projection, modulo head placement?

Finally, Larson's analysis is not constrained enough (admitting both left- and right-branching) and it invokes the theoretically ill-renowned device of reanalysis. In his account, the internal branching structure of an English V-projection allows right-branching and left-branching sub-trees that may be 'recategorized' (= reanalyzed): in (25a), the V' dominating the D-structure positions is left-branching, but the higher V's are consistently right-branching. Reanalysis (i.e. recategorization of V' as V° (cf. Larson 1988: 359f.)) is needed to readjust the licensing relation between the NP *the letter* and a V° position.

(25) a. [$_{VP}$ [$_{V'}$ e [$_{VP}$ e [$_{V'}$ [$_{V'}$ send Mary] a letter]]]] (Larson 1988: 353)
b. [$_{VP}$ [$_{V'}$ e [$_{VP}$ Mary$_i$ [$_{V'}$ [V° send e$_i$] a letter]]]] (Larson 1988: 359)

In (25b), the most deeply embedded V' is reanalyzed as V° in order to turn it into a possible case assigner for the NP *the letter*. There seems to be no independently motivated reason why a branching node could turn into a head category and perform the duties of a head. Moreover, a structure like (25b) runs into immediate conflicts if chain formation meets an anaphoric dependency:

(26) a. I showed John and Bill each other/themselves (Jackendoff 1990: 431)
b. John and Bill$_i$ have not been [shown$_j$ e$_i$ [[e$_j$ e$_i$] each other$_i$/themselves$_i$]]

In (26b), there are four co-indexed NP-positions: [*John and Bill*] locally c-commands its trace of the passive NP-movement, this trace locally c-commands the anaphoric NP, which in turn locally c-commands the VP-internal trace of the dative movement. Hence, under relativized minimality (Rizzi 1990), a minimality conflict arises. The anaphor is the closest co-indexed potential A-binder.

The gist of this brief appraisal of Larson's position is the insight that it suffers from a lack of independent theoretical underpinning. Irrespective of its empirical merits or deficits, the particular choice of structure assignments and derivational steps is at best sufficient, but arbitrary. Any other weakly equivalent account would be justified on the same grounds. Second, it is unnecessarily complex. It invokes an intricate derivational machinery (head movement plus phrasal movement plus reanalysis). Head movement would be enough, as the BBC account demonstrates. Third, it fails to capture the systematic differences between head-final and head-initial structures.

3.3.2 Theory uncovered and data covered

The shell structure of today's Minimalist Program is right-branching. Larson's derivations had started out with a left-branching VP as base configuration. The original conception of the VP-shell involved a problem: the verb had to move, but there was no VP-internal target position available. Hence, a suitable position had to be *intrinsically* motivated by reference to some hitherto apparently neglected function. This was the birth of 'little-*v*'.[14] It was neither backed by a universal conception of phrase structure that would explain the existence of VP-shells,[15] nor does it generalize to head-initial phrases in general.

The Minimalist Program strives to produce an intrinsic motivation for the 'second' V-position in the VP. The primary 'task' ascribed to it is assigning a theta role to the external argument and case to the direct object. This is as unexpected a coupling of properties as it is in 'Burzio's generalization'.[16] Horvath and Siloni (2002: 109) emphasize that this heterogeneous task assignment to 'little-*v*' introduces a unique, conceptually strange kind of head into the Minimalist theory that is on the one hand *functional* and on the other hand a *θ-assigner* for the external argument. θ-roles are addresses for arguments in the lexical argument structure of a given lexical head. Non-lexical functional heads do not assign θ-roles since they do not provide lexical-conceptual content.

It is evident that the lexical-conceptual structure of the verbal head specifies the θ-role of the external argument. In (27a), 'cure' or 'surprise' is compatible with an animate (= agent) or inanimate causation. 'Recognize' in (27b) would be incompatible with an inanimate subject. So, 'little-*v*' has no 'authority' in assigning either an agent or a causer role. It could only act as a *transmitter* of the theta relation, not as its source.

---

[14] Chomsky (2008: 142): '*v** is the functional head associated with full argument structure, transitive and experiencer constructions, and is one of several choices for v, which may furthermore be the element determining that the selected root is verbal.' Note that this characterization does not contemplate the possibility that 'little-*v*' is merely an emergent structural by-product of head-initial phrase structuring.

[15] Kayne's antisymmetry system would not predict a 'little-*v*'. It has to be 'invented' as a functional head position.

[16] 'Little-*v*' does not – contrary to what is frequently claimed – explain Burzio's generalization, since the original formulation ('no case for the object, if no theta-role for the subject') is empirically inadequate anyway (see Haider 2000c). The empirically adequate generalization is this: no *structural* case for the *object*, unless structural case has been assigned to the *subject*.

(27) a. The doctor/the treatment has *cured/surprised* the patient (unintentionally)
b. A stray bullet/a sniper has *killed/recognized* the president
(unintentionally)

An argument in support of the theta-assigning function of 'little-*v*' has been seen in the lack of idioms in English in which the subject is part of the idiom. What this discussion overlooks entirely is a fact known since the nineties. Subject idioms are rare in VO languages but not in OV languages (see Haider 1993: 173), as illustrated in (28), for an obvious and immediately relevant reason:

(28) a. Gestern hat meine Kollegen$_{ACC}$ [*der Hafer*$_{NOM}$ *gestochen*][17]
yesterday has my colleagues the barley tickled
(the barley tickles so. = so. gets jaunty)
b. Fast hätte den Mann$_{ACC}$ [*der Schlag*$_{NOM}$ *getroffen*]
almost had the man the stroke hit
(the stroke hits so. = so. has a (heart) attack)
c. Wo hat den Mann$_{ACC}$ [der Schuh$_{NOM}$ gedrückt]?
where has the man the shoe pressed?
(the shoe presses so. = so. gets worried)

The reason is this: the idiomatic parts are *locally contiguous* parts within the VP. This is a reflex of their status as fully lexicalized units. In OV, the subject does not have to leave its VP-internal base position and may stay in its VP-internal position. The lack of subject idioms in VO is but a reflex of the fact that subjects are obligatorily raised out of the VP in English. This would destroy the lexical unit and the idiomatic reading. It is well known from the incompatibility of passivization with the idiomatic reading (29) that movement out of the domain of the base position disrupts the idiomatic reading. Obviously, if fronting the object to the VP-external subject position disrupts the idiom and thereby the idiomatic reading, the same applies to primary subjects in English. An idiomatic reading cannot arise.[18] In German, and in any other OV language, however, the subject does not leave the VP and hence it is available for idiom formation.

---

[17] The bracketed part can be topicalized by VP topicalization:

i. [Der Hafer gestochen] hat meine Kollegen
the barley$_{NOM}$ tickled has my colleague$_{ACC}$

[18] Note that the VP-*internal* V-chain does not interfere with idiomatic readings. Actually, it accounts for apparently discontinuous idioms in English: *give* sb. *a free hand*; *kick* sth. *into the long grass*; *send* sb. *to Coventry*; *take* sb. *to task*; *take* sb. *to the cleaners*; *take* sth. *into consideration*. The verb may form an idiomatic unit with the lower phrase and exclude the higher argument, because the trace of the verb and the lower constituent form a sub-constituent of the VP, as in: [*take*$_i$ [sth. [e$_i$ into consideration]$_{idiom}$]]$_{VP}$. In VO, the subject leaves the local domain, viz. the VP. This destroys the locality relation (for lexical storage as an idiom).

(29) a. The *bucket* was *kicked* by everyone   (no idiomatic reading)
      b. Your *leg* was *pulled* by me   (no idiomatic reading)

In general, what this discussion highlights is the lack of a principled *structural* motivation for the derivation of more than one verb position in the structure of a complex phrase that singles out head-*initial* phrases. The crucial question is this: what motivates the existence of 'little-*v*' for VO structures (30) and why is unequivocal evidence for 'little-*v*' completely absent in OV? If there is an intrinsic motivation, then 'little-*v*' must be a cross-linguistically present entity. However, if 'little-*v*' is an epiphenomenon of the structuring of head-initial phrases, it is predictably absent in OV.

(30)   [$_{vP}$ XP *v* [$_{VP}$ V YP]]

On top of this, the 'little-*v*' idea misses an important generalization. Whatever *intrinsic* property of *verbal* projections is assumed for motivating the existence of 'little-*v*' is unlikely to provide an answer for the existence of what would have to be called 'little-*n*' in the structure of complex head-initial *nominal* phrases (31a). In particular, an NP does not need a theta-assigner for its external argument since there is no external argument. Nevertheless, the shell structure of complex head-initial NPs is the same type of shell structure as that of complex head-initial VPs (31b).

(31)   a. [$_{NP}$ *n* [XP [N° YP]]]
        b. [$_{NP}$ N$_i$ [XP [e$_i$ YP]]]

In sum, the heterogeneous character of the properties assigned to 'little-*v*' (functional head, but theta-assigner for an argument) is just the reflex of its ill-understood grammar-theoretic status within the Minimalist Program (MP). Given that the need for more than a single head position in complex head-initial phrases follows from entirely structural requirements (namely the BBC in combination with the PDI), any intrinsic motivation for something like a 'little-*v*' is likely to be spurious and non-contingent.

In the BBC perspective, 'little-*v*' is only one of the V-positions in the shell structure of complex head-initial VPs. Its absence in head-final VPs is predicted. The parallel structure for complex head-initial NPs has the very same motivation, and there is no *intrinsic* need for a 'little-*n*' either. This account is economic and homogeneous. The MP account is heterogeneous and contingent on other grammar systems (theta assignment, case assignment). The onus of proof therefore rests obviously on the MP's side, and a convincing proof is missing.

3.4 Stranded particles as indicators of V-positions in a VP-shell in VO

There is direct evidence for empty verb positions in the shell structure in VO languages (see Haider 2010a: ch.1). It comes from Germanic VO languages that allow stranding particles within the VP-shell structure. In English, but also in Scandinavian languages such as Norwegian or Icelandic, particles may be serialized in several variants (Haider 1997b: Ch.7). One variant is the V-adjacent variant. In this variant and in all other variants (including the stranding variant by V2) the particle immediately follows the verb. This is a robust difference between OV and VO. In OV, the particle precedes and it is adjacent to the verb (except when stranded by V2).

The second robust difference is the fact that there are VO languages with non-adjacent particle positions in the VP (32), but there is no OV language with a particle position that is not adjacent to the canonical position of the verb. The examples in (32) are V2 clauses, but the split is also licit with the verb in its canonical VP-initial position, just like in English (33a,b).

(32)   a. Ég gerði nokkra bíla *upp*   Icelandic   (Rögnvaldsson 1982: 60)
            'I fixed some cars up'
           b. Ég gerði *upp* nokkra bíla
            'I fixed up some cars'
           c. Han spiste tørrfisken *opp*   Norwegian   (Svenonius 1996: 55)
            He ate dry-fish-the up
           d. Han spiste *opp* tørrfisken.
            'He ate up the dried fish'

The decisive cases are double-object constructions with the particle in between the two objects, as in (33c–e). The position of the stranded particle is the verb position in the lower VP-shell. This position is the foot position of the V-chain in the shell structure of a head-initial VP. In the stranding variant, the particle is stranded in exactly this position (34a).

(33)   a. He sent a message *out*
           b. He sent *out* a message
           c. The secretary sent them *out* a notice   (Jacobson 1987: 32)
           d. Valerie packed her (daughter) *up* a lunch   (Dehé 2002: 3)
           e. Susan poured the man *out* a drink   (Dehé 2002: 3)

A head-final VP, on the other hand, is a structure with a *single* verb position within the V-projection; hence there is only a single particle position, namely the position adjacent to the head (34b). There is no way for a particle to end up in between the two nominal objects in (34b).

(34) a. [$_{VP}$ Subject [V°$_i$ IO [e$_i$ DO]]][19]   head-initial VP
      b. [$_{VP}$ Subject [IO [DO V°]]]   head-final VP

In addition, the position of the particle relative to the verb is a direct indicator of the canonical directionality of the verb. The particle is directionally licensed by the head. In OV, without exception, the particle immediately *precedes* the verb, and in VO, the particle follows.[20]

(35) a. that he must give *up* the idea
      b. *that he must *up* give the idea
      c. dass er die Idee *auf*-geben muss   German
         that he the idea *up*-give must
      d. *dass er die Idee geben *auf* muss
         that he the idea give *up* must

If the 'little-*v*' were a *universal* grammatical entity, an OV language with particle stranding should strand the particle in the postverbal position when the verb steps left into the position of the 'little-*v*'. However, this kind of OV language has not been attested, and the probability that it ever will be attested is minuscule.

3.5 *Scrambling* is an OV phenomenon; Slavic languages are Type III languages

When a language permits scrambling, it is an OV language (see also Corver and Riemsdijk 1997).[21] *Unquestionable* VO languages do not scramble. This is an immediate consequence of the PDI, and, specifically, of the mutual, minimal c-command requirement that is responsible for the inverse compactness properties of head-initial and head-final phrases, respectively.

---

[19] Note that a particle in the clause-final position of a double-object construction is ungrammatical: no particle position without an adjacent verb position. There is no clause-final verb; hence there is no particle position.

   (i) *She handed the students the assignment *out*   (ii)*They made the president a liar *out*.

[20] As noted in Haider (2010a: 32), the particle positioning is reflected in word formation. Verb+particle can be nominalized as a whole (i) or the particle may be merged with the verb by a word-formation process (ii). In this case, the article precedes, since the word structure in general and compounds in particular are head-final in English.

   (i) the make *up*, the fall *out*, the sit *in*, the count *down*, spill *over* ...
   (ii) the *up*rising, the *out*put, the *in*come, the *down*pour, the *over*flow ...

   In OV languages, (ii) is the only option: der *Ab*fall, der *An*fall, der *Aus*fall, der *Ein*fall, der *Vor*fall, der Zufall ...

[21] Scrambling in the strict sense means reordering among *arguments* (see Haider 2010a: ch.4, §4.4). Scandinavian *object shift* is not scrambling, neither in terms of its phenomenology nor in terms of its grammatical conditions (see Haider 2010a: §4.4.1).

In a VO setting, VP-*internal* scrambling would produce an illicit intervener that violates minimal c-command between the verb and the XP in (36a). Scrambling to the left edge (36b), on the other hand, would target a position that is not identified by the verbal head, since this position is not within the canonical directionality domain.

(36)   a.* [$_{VP}$ **V°**$_j$ [*YP*$_i$ [XP [e$_j$ e$_i$]]]]   (VO: YP scrambled VP-internally)
        b * [$_{VP}$ *YP*$_i$ [$_{VP}$ **V°**$_j$ [XP [e$_j$ e$_i$]]]]   (VO: YP scrambled to the edge of VP)
        c.   [$_{VP}$ XP [*ZP*$_i$ [YP [e$_i$ **V°**]]]]   (OV: ZP scrambled VP-internally)
        d.   [$_{VP}$ *ZP*$_i$ [XP [YP [e$_i$ **V°**]]]]   (OV: ZP scrambled to the edge of VP)

In OV (36c,d), every phrase dominated by a node on the projection line of the VP is directionally identified by its sister node on the right-hand side. Therefore, minimality under mutual c-command is never at stake. Moreover, the left edge of the VP is within the canonical directionality domain of the head. These are the ingredients of a grammar setting that invites scrambling (cf. Haider 2010a, ch. 4, §4.4) for OV and rules it out for VO.

A strict correlation between the canonical directionality of the head and scrambling is confirmed by language-*internal* contrasts between head-final and head-initial phrases. In German, VPs and APs display scrambling variants, NPs don't. VPs and APs are head-final in German, NPs are head-initial.

Germanic VO languages do not scramble. *Slavic* languages, however, are likely to be cited as cases of alleged VO languages that permit scrambling. There is consensus that scrambling is typical for Slavic languages. Interestingly, in spite of the absence of comprehensive in-depth studies, it is widely consensual, too, that Slavic languages should be filed as VO languages. It is truly amazing, however, how small the empirical underpinning is for this assumption. It is more of a 'what-else' attitude, rather than a well-attested outcome of empirical investigations. Observed from an impartial vantage point, the Slavic word-order patterns are neither that of VO languages nor that of OV languages. Slavic languages are first-rate candidates for the status of Type III languages (see Chapter 5). This would not only explain their scrambling properties and downgrade data from Slavic languages as counterevidence for a claim pertaining to VO languages, it also explains a wide range of otherwise eccentric properties as regular Type III properties, none of which is a property of a VO language.

The following (non-exhaustive) list of word-order variants of a Russian clause is both typical for a Slavic language and atypical for a VO language (and an OV language as well). It is typical for a Type III language, however. Each of the variants is a possible Type III variant, but only a subset is compatible with OV or VO, respectively. Since present-day (Generative) grammar theory has predominantly been developed on the evidence from VO languages (English,

Scandinavian, Romance) and since it is a frequent pattern, it is not surprising that (37c), the SVO-congruent pattern among the Type III patterns, is routinely assumed to be the canonical variant.

(37) a. čto Maša Petru svoj dom *pokazyvaet*   Type III/SOV   Russian
that Mary$_{NOM}$ Peter$_{DAT}$ her home$_{ACC}$ *showed*
'that Mary showed Peter her home'
b. čto Maša Petru *pokazyvaet* svoj dom   only Type III
c. čto Maša *pokazyvaet* Petru svoj dom   Type III/SVO
d. čto svoj dom Maša *pokazyvaet* Petru   only Type III scrambling
e. čto svoj dom Petru Maša *pokazyvaet*   Type III/SOV scrambling
f. čto Maša svoj dom *pokazyvaet* Petru   only Type III scrambling

The *decisive* theoretical predictions have not been systematically checked thoroughly until now, however. Here is the first one: if (37a) is derived from (37c) by scrambling out of the VP across the verbal head, the scrambled items are predicted to be *opaque for extraction*. If, however, (37a) is a Type III base order, each argument is transparent for extraction. (38), a typical Type III serialization, with one object preceding and one object following the verb, clearly shows that preverbal phrases are not at all opaque for extraction. The wh-item is fronted and it is extracted out of an object phrase. *Opacity* is what the SVO analysis predicts, and this prediction is clearly wrong.

(38) a. *Jaki*$_i$ Grzegorz [e$_i$ *samochód*] kupił swojej żonie?   Polish
which$_i$ George [e$_i$ car]   bought his sister
'Which car did George buy for his sister?'
b. *Kakuju*$_i$ Igor [e$_i$ *mašinu*] kupil svoej žene?   Russian
which$_i$ Igor [e$_i$ car]   bought his sister

Some obvious and independent cases to be tested additionally are listed below (i–iv). In each case, the SVO-based prediction is the converse of the Type III-based one. The brief list of predictions for languages such as Polish or Russian (and other Slavic languages) is an invitation for a broader empirical assessment by native Slavic syntacticians. If a language is Type III rather than VO, it will have the following properties (among others; see Chapter 5, Appendix 5.1):

   (i) preverbal DPs in canonical order: *in situ* rather than derived behaviour (scope, binding)
   (ii) wh-movement with wh-subject *in situ*? – If yes, not VO
   (iii) edge effects for adverbials? – If no, not VO
   (iv) variability of auxiliary–verb order? – If yes, not VO.

If the language is VO, the preverbal DPs in (39) must be in derived positions. If the language is OV or Type III, they may be *in situ*. Hence, any indicator of an *in situ* position is an indicator for the Type III nature of the given language, and evidence against the VO estimate.

(39)   (…) Subject DP_i DP_j V (e_i e_j)

Scope is an indicator, for instance. In (39), if DP_j has to count as scrambled (in the VO assumption), it inevitably c-commands the trace of the scrambled DP_i, so it should get scope over DP_i. In Type III, the prediction is the opposite one. If DP_i < DP_j is a licit base order, then DP_j should not outscope DP_i. The prediction of the VO hypothesis is a scope asymmetry: in the preverbal position scope is ambiguous, but in the postverbal position scope follows the left–right order. Another indicator would be a phrase in the preverbal position that normally does not scramble. The empirically carefully bolstered assessment should be provided by native-speaking syntacticians. The properties (ii–iv), however, are easy to confirm even for a non-native.

Wh-in-situ is a source of evidence, since an *in situ* wh-*subject* is ill-formed in a Spec-F position (see Haider 2010a: 116–22). In Type III, and in OV, the subject may remain in its base position. Hence an *in situ* wh-subject is well formed just like any other argument as wh-phrase *in situ*. Relevant data are easy to locate in the literature (e.g. Stepanov and Tsai 2008: 613, 618).

(40)   a. Kto kogo videl?   Russian
           who whom saw
           'Who saw whom?'
        b. Kogo *kto* videl?
           whom who saw
        c. Ko je koga vidio?   Croatian, Serbian
           who is whom seen
           'Who saw whom?'
        d. Koga je *ko* vidio?
           whom is who seen

The edge effect is characteristic of head-*initial* structures and in particular of preverbal adverbials in VO. In OV and Type III, it is predictably absent. This is easy to check for any language. If the part of the VP following the bracketed constituent in the Russian example (41) were a head-initial VP, an edge effect would be inescapable. However, if this part is the lower portion of a Type III VP, the edge effect is predicted to be absent; and it is absent indeed (41).

(41)   V prošlom godu [gorazdo bol'še *čem Igor*] vyjgrala tol'ko maša
                                                                    Russian[22]

---

[22] Thanks to Imke Mendoza and Andrej Woltschanskiy from my neighbouring Slavic department for supply-on-demand of the Russian data and to Barbara and Grzegorz Dogil for the supply of the Polish examples.

in previous year [much more *than Igor*] won only Mary
'Last year, only Mary has much more won than Igor'

Auxiliary–verb order is another robust indicator. In any VO language, without exception, an auxiliary precedes the main verb in its canonical position. Whenever an auxiliary appears after the main verb (in its clause-internal position) this cannot be a VO clause. The following examples from Polish illustrate the variable order characteristics of Type III. Consequently, Polish cannot be filed as a VO language as long as this flat contradiction for assigning it to VO is not explained.

(42) a. We wtorek *poukładać musisz* w szafie   Polish
         on Tuesday (he/she) clean-up must in cupboard
      b. We wtorek *musisz poukładać* w szafie
         on Tuesday (he/she) must clean-up in cupboard
      c. Francuskiego *może* nauczyć sie własciwie każdy
         French can learn$_{(perf)}$ by-oneself actually everyone
      d. Francuskiego *nauczyć* sie może własciwie każdy
         French learn$_{(perf)}$ by-oneself can actually everyone

For the time being, these data shall suffice.[23] For a more detailed cross-Slavic survey on T3 properties, see Haider and Szucsich (forthcoming). They fully match the predictions for a Type III language and patently violate trustworthy VO characteristics. What they show at least is this: Slavic languages must not be classified as VO languages on the basis of nothing but a kind of 'what-else' argumentation since classification into either OV or VO is not a complementary classification. There is a third possibility. If Slavic languages are Type III languages – and the evidence points to this conclusion – they obviously cannot be employed for generalizations about VO languages.

3.6   In sum: the asymmetry theory that is behind syntactic symmetry breaking, in a nutshell

The following observations and generalizations characterize crucial aspects of the empirical setting of head-final versus head-initial structures.[24] They have

---

[23] It is truly amazing that these systematic and unexplained deviances from the VO patterns have been generously overlooked by those who base construction-specific arguments on the alleged VO status of Slavic languages.

[24] This (except for the final paragraph) is the abridged text of an abstract submitted to the 1997 Glow conference (Tromsö). In this chapter, only the observations 1, 3 and 4 are discussed. Observations 5 and 6 are discussed at length in Haider (2010a). As for the premises, premise 2 took its present shape fairly late: that *mutual* c-command is the key for understanding how an identical set of constraints produces two clearly different sets of properties modulo *directionality* is a more recent insight, communicated first in 2004 in a lecture at the University Marburg:

partially gone unnoticed for some time and then have resisted a theoretically straightforward and empirically adequate coverage:

- **Observation #1**: The 'unmarked' (canonical) *relative* order of arguments is identical in head-initial and head-final phrases, and the *relative embedding* is identical, too.
- **Observation #2**: Head-*initial* phrases are *compact*, head-*final* ones are clearly *not* (also true within a given hetero-directional language, such as Afrikaans, Dutch, Frisian or German, with head-*initial* NPs and head-*final* VPs). The following German example contrasts an infinitival VP (head-final) with an infinitival *nominal* construction (head-initial):
  (i) [Hunde (*während des Tages*) in einer Garage einsperren$_V°$]$_{VP}$
   dogs (*during the day*) in a garage in-lock
  (ii) das [Einsperren$_N°$ (**während des Tages*) von Hunden in einer Garage]$_{NP}$
   the in-lock(ing) (*during the day*) of dogs in a garage
- **Observation #3**: Word order in head-*initial phrases is strict*, but in head-*final* ones *it is variable (scrambling)*. The absence of scrambling in head-initial structures is a sub-instance of #2. The scrambled item is an intervener that violates compactness.
- **Observation #4**: Postverbal, *verb-distant* particles are licit only in head-initial V-phrases (with strandable particles). In head-final V-phrases, the particle of a particle verb always precedes the verb.
  (i) to *give* us *back* a coin
  (ii) ons een muntstuk *terug geven* Dutch
   us a coin back give
- **Observation #5**: A *functional* subject position is *obligatorily lexicalized* only in strictly head-*initial* clause structures ('EPP' property).
- Corollary i: *Expletive subject*s are *obligatory* in strictly head-initial clause structures and *absent* in clause structures with head-final VPs (notwithstanding the alleged expletive function of Dutch *er*).
- Corollary ii: Subjects are *transparent* for extraction in head-final clause structures, but *opaque* in head-initial ones. Head-*final* languages with obligatory subject expletives are predictably unattested.
- **Observation #6**: Languages with a head-*initial* VP and non-positional (i.e. relational) nominative checking allow for *quirky subjects*. A

'*Alle Sprachen sind gleich, nur mache sind gleicher*' (Nov.) and at the annual Austrian linguistics conference (Salzburg): '*Was es heißt, OV zu sein*' (Dec.).

quirky subject phenomenon cannot exist in clauses based on head-final VPs.[25]

These facts (O#1 to O#6) clearly discriminate OV and VO, and they follow immediately from the *directional* implementation of structural *licensing* for a merged item in an otherwise uniform and universal system, with the following minimal subset of premises P#1 to P#3 below. The observations O#1 to O#6 can be shown to directly follow as the composite result of the premises P#1 to P#3.

Theoretical premises

- Premise #1 (BBC): Merger is *universally* constrained: if YP is merged with X (X not an x° level category), the result is [YP X]$_{Xn}$. In other words, *the merged phrase precedes* and therefore the resulting phrase structures are universally *right-associative*.
- Premise #2: Structural licensing of the merged item is *strictly local*: in a well-formed structure, the merged item M and the (head of the) hosting item H *minimally c-command each other* (= MMCC = mutual, minimal c-command between M and H)
- Premise #3: The merged item M is *directionally identified* by (a projection of) the head of the hosting phrase H.[26]

The above observations immediately follow from these premises.

1. For head-*initial* phrases (43a), directionality of licensing is *not isomorphic* with the direction of merger, but for head-final ones (43b), it is. So, complex head-*initial* phrases require the re-instantiation of the (directionally licensing) head (producing a *shell structure*); head-final ones do not. Mutual c-command in (43a) is chain-based ($h_{i\,cc} \rightarrow YP_{\,cc} \rightarrow e_i$).

(43) a. **initial**: [XP [h°$_i$ → [$_{HP}$ YP [e$_{i°}$ → ZP]]]]
      b. **final**: [XP ← [$_{H'}$ YP ← [$_{H'}$ ZP ← **h°**]]]

The predicted shell structure for (43a) is necessary for O#2 to O#4: *compactness* is the effect of P#2 for shell structures. In (43a), the projection nodes are on the 'wrong' side, so a head-chain is required. This is the cause of the shell structure. Any intervener (adverbial, *scrambled* item) in (43a) destroys

---

[25] Example: Icelandic quirky subjects and VP-internal nominatives in passive.

[26] Note that P#3 is an 'amendment' to P#2. As a consequence of P#3, the head-initial vs. head-final option is the result of a single parameter. This parameter is the *directionality* parameter for *structural licensing* (progressive/regressive).

minimal mutual c-command either between the head and the complement or between the complement and the trace of the head. V-distant *particle positions* are V-positions in the shell structure with stranded particles. In (43b), however, there is always a sister relation between a phrase and a directional projection node of the head. It is the projection node that functions as licenser. Hence, there is no need for a shell structure or multiple $V°$-positions.

2. The *functional subject position* (O#5 and O#6) is a genuine SVO requirement (not VSO, not SOV): In SVO, the argument merged at the higher *edge of the VP* (the thematic subject; see 43a) is *local* to the head but without *directional* licence. So, a functional head is required for providing the *directional* licence. Its spec position is the EPP-trigger. In OV, all argument positions are within the directionality domain of the head, so there is no need for a functional licenser. Quirky subjects are predicted as follows: if nominative checking is not restricted to the functional spec position (but possible also in VP-internal positions), a non-nominative argument at the edge may raise to spec. By virtue of being the 'external' argument, it gains the subject properties of the external argument (that is: the properties of the phrase in the functional spec position of the external argument). In OV, this structure is not available.

3. When the directionality parameter is un(der)specified, the directionality of licensing is free. This is the situation that characterizes the Type III languages. They contain OV and VO patterns as admissible subsets, but there is a third subset of structures that are ungrammatical both in VO and OV. For details, see Chapter 5, §5.3.

4 The cross-linguistic impact of the BBC

4.1 Introduction

Linearization is a key property of syntactic expressions. In Generative Grammar, however, it tends to be treated as an epiphenomenon: the terminals ('numeration') are assembled ('merged') into a structure that is 'spelled out' and phonetically interpreted at the phonetics/phonology interface. The order of terminals, that is, the linearization, is a result of spell-out but has no independent significance in a derivation.

Let us assume counterfactually and just for the sake of demonstration that linearization is indeed merely the spell-out of a *hierarchical* organization, and that spell-out proceeds strictly top down, that is, '*higher* in structure' means '*earlier* in linear order'. Take, for instance, the linearization in (i). It could be the result of each of the structures in (ii) or (iii), and in fact any other structure variant with the same hierarchical organization, like, for instance, (iv). Any of these structures will yield the linear order (i), if spell-out linearizes the terminals in the prescribed manner that maps 'higher in structure' onto precedence. In other words, the structures in (ii) to (iv) are just notational variants with respect to the linearization of their terminals.

(i) A – B – C – D – E
(ii) [A [B [C [D [E]]]]]
(iii) [[[[[E] D] C] B] A]
(iv) [[[C [D [E]]] B] A]

What this illustrates is the following: the mapping of a hierarchical structure onto a linearization is a *function*, but not a unique one (i.e. neither surjective nor bijective), since there are several inputs for the same output. Conversely, the mapping relation of linearization onto structures would be a *one-to-many mapping*. This is at odds with the presumed organization of grammar as an algorithm that allows fast mappings between linearizations and structures (see Chapters 1 and 2).

Only if *directionality* is integrated as a basic feature of *grammar* do the mappings become bijective *functions* in most cases; that is, the mappings become unambiguous in both directions. The BBC requires more than merely asymmetric merger. It requires merger in a *specified* direction. Hence, the linearization in (i) is the linearization of the structure (ii), if grammars are constrained by the BBC, but not of either (iii) or (iv). This demonstrates the parser-friendly constraint imposed by the BBC plus directionality. It constrains the mapping of linearizations onto structures and vice versa.

In this chapter, the BBC-imposed properties *'earlier is higher'* and *'later is deeper'* are explored for their cross-linguistic empirical validity.[1] The BBC constrains the structural architecture and in doing so it constrains syntactic movement processes as well. Movement targets positions that are 'earlier' and thereby 'higher', instead of 'later' and thereby 'lower'. Here are typological generalizations that are corollaries of the BBC and will be investigated in the following sections.

> G1: If a language employs *V-movement* targeting the clausal edge, this movement targets a clause-*initial* position, but not a clause-*final* position (in other words: no head movement to the right, no clause-*final* functional head positions as targets of head movement).
>
> G2: If a language has *phrasal movement* (e.g. 'wh-movement'), this movement targets the clause-initial position. The converse – wh-movement targeting the clause-final position – does not exist. Apparent cases of wh-movement to the right will turn out to be base-generated cleft-like focus structures. As will be argued, there are no clause-final spec positions, and so there is no room for phrasal movement targeting clause-final positions ('extraposition' notwithstanding), and no room for clause-final expletives.
>
> G3: (Corollary of G1+ G2) There are languages with a *V2-property* (= V-movement + phrasal movement), but there are no languages with a *V-penultimate* property (as the mirror-image structure of V2).
>
> G4: If a language has *apparent movement* to the right (e.g. 'extraposition', 'scrambling' to the right), a rightward movement analysis is inadequate. This kind of alleged movement would violate robust restrictions of clear cases of movement. Neither extraposition nor 'scrambling to the right' is adequately characterized if analyzed as the result of movement.

[1] This chapter is an expanded, extensively revised and updated version of Haider (1997d). The paper originated from a contribution to the FAS inaugural symposium in Berlin, in March 1994.

G5: If a language has mandatory *expletive subjects* for otherwise subjectless clauses, the language is a VO language (without *pro-* or *topic-*drop). OV languages do not require subject expletives.

G6: If a language has *verb-order variation* in the simple clause between non-finite auxiliaries, quasi-auxiliaries, semi-lexical verbs and lexical verbs, this language is an OV language with V-movement. In VO languages, the *relative* order of verbs in the simple clause is always conserved.

This set of generalizations is not exhaustive. It merely lists several easy to identify properties of the clausal architecture that are consequences of a basic and general asymmetry, namely the exclusion of *left-branching* structuring.

4.2 BBC-geared structural invariants

The BBC is responsible for a fundamental asymmetry in the structural patterns of the grammar systems of human languages. It requires right-associative projections (in other words: phrases are merged to their target such that they precede their target) and forbids left-associative projections (in other words: derived positions must not follow the phrases they are merged with/attached to).

As a consequence, the patterns in (1) are admitted, the patterns in (2) and (3) are excluded. The patterns embrace base-generated lexical projections, their extensions by adjunctions (1d), as well as the functional architecture on the top of lexical projections. Whenever movement presupposes structural positions as targets (i.e. spec positions), the structural constraint is at the same time a constraint on movement because it rules out particular target areas. Analogously, movement to an adjoined position is constrained in the same way.

(1)   a. $[(XP) [F° [YP]]]$ spec–head–complement order of functional projections
         b. $[(XP) [h°_i [_{HP} \ldots e_i \ldots]]]$ head movement to a higher functional head only to the *left*
         c. $[XP_i [F° [_{HP} \ldots e_i \ldots]]]$ phrasal movement to a higher functional spec position only to the *left*
         d. $[ZP_i [XP [e_i V°]]]$ adjunction (by movement) to the *left*-hand side (*scrambling*)

The branching constraint rules out left-associative structures, both as projections of functional heads (2a), or as the functional extension of lexical heads (2b), as well as the result of adjunction (3). Functional extensions are projections in which a lexical head moves to a higher functional head position. The projection of this functional position is the functionally extended projection of the complement of the functional position. This will become important for the discussion of clause-final complementizers, below. A well-known instance of the functional extension of a V-projection is the raising of a verb to a functional head position, as in English V-to-'I' constructions. The patterns in (2) will be discussed in Section 4.3; the patterns listed in (3) will be the topic of Section 4.4.

(2)   a. * [[F° YP] *XP*], [[YP F°] *XP*]   functional spec position in a phrase-final position
        b. * [[[$_{HP}$ ... e_i ...] h°$_i$] (XP)]   head movement to the right

(3)   a. *... [[– e_i –] [XP$_i$]$_{Spec}$]...   wh-movement into a spec position on the right
        b. *... [[– e_i –] CP$_i$] ...   extraposition by movement to the right (adjunction)
        c. *... [[– e_i –] XP$_i$] ...   scrambling by movement to the right (adjunction)

Of course, (3b) does not imply that extraposition does not exist as a syntactic phenomenon. It merely implies that the *popular analysis* of extraposition as the result of movement to the right is inadequate (see also Haider 2010a: ch. 5).

4.3   Functional projections

Let us start the analysis with a closer look at the structure of functional projections. Generalizations G1 and G2 (and the corollary G3) are consequences of the BBC for extended projections. Functional heads targeted by head movement are heads that *precede* their complements. If there is a functional head following its complement, it is unavoidably a *lexical* functional head and therefore cannot be targeted by head movement.[2] Second, functional specs are initial specs only. These generalizations are corollaries of the BBC:

> Premise 1:   *Functional* extensions of lexical projections are uniformly right-branching (sub-instance of the BBC).
> Premise 2:   Directionality of complement licensing is parametric and specified as a property of (a *lexical* class of) heads.[3]

---

[2] A *lexical functional* head is a lexical item whose lexical category is that of a functional head, as, for instance, a lexical C° element (e.g. *that, dass, dat, que*, etc.).

[3] In the Germanic languages, even a lexical singularity for exceptional directionality is attested. There is a single measure word (*enough, genug, genoeg, nok* ...), that does not precede but *follows* (cf. *sufficiently* big vs. *big enough*). This exception has been conserved in all modern Germanic languages. It is truly surprising that an isolated lexical item has been spared by language change (which is expected to eliminate singular exceptions).

Premise 1, a sub-instance of the BBC that covers extended projections, rules out clause-final functional heads as targets of head movement, and it rules out clause-final specs. This fully covers G1–G3. A detailed discussion will follow.

Premise 2 is independent of the BBC. It is an axiom of the asymmetry model that covers the parametric property that is responsible for the head-initial versus the head-final organization of lexical projections. Importantly, it applies to functional heads as well, but only when they are instantiated with *lexical* elements of the category 'functional head', as, for instance, lexical complementizers, lexical questions markers, etc. As lexical elements, they can be associated with directionality information as part of their lexically specified set of properties.

The central axiom[4] is the branching constraint, illustrated in (4) by a V-projection embedded under a functional projection that conforms to the BBC. It requires lexical projections and their functional extensions to be right-branching. A *functional extension* of a lexical projection is a functional projection with the head of the lexical projection raised to the functional head position. For example, V-to-'I' turns the 'IP' into a *functional extension* of VP since the head of VP is moved to the head position of the IP. Note that this characterization applies to *functional* heads that are not lexicalized with a lexical functional head of the matching category. *Lexical* functional heads yield *lexical* extensions of a lexical projection.

What the BBC is meant to capture is the rigid right-branching structure *internal* to (functionally extended) projections of a lexical head. For the V-projection, for instance, this is the V-projection proper (i.e. the lexical projection) plus all of its *functional* extensions.

In (4), all non-top branching nodes on the V-projection line, that is, the V'-nodes, follow their sister node. On the F-projection line, the relevant node is F', and it follows its sister node, namely Spec-F. If the FP is a functional extension of VP (see below), the VP node in (4), being a right branch, meets the requirement of the BBC. The FP in (4) is representative of lexical projections with any number of functional projections above it. 'F' should be read as a variable for a functional head. The crucial structural difference between a head-initial and a head-final lexical projection will be explained below.

---

[4] The BBC is axiomatic in the following sense: if correct, it describes a universal property of data structures of human grammars. The property modelled by the BBC may be considered a primitive property of UG.

(4)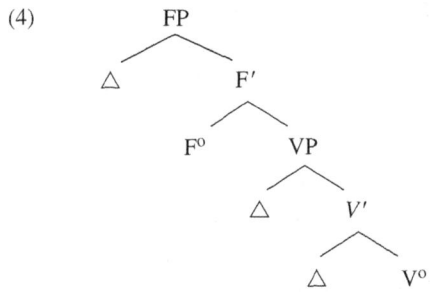

The BBC bans any left branch in a binary-branching projection that is a node on the projection line. As a consequence, *precedence* coincides with c-command: for any two nodes immediately dominated by a node of the same (extended) projection line, the node that precedes c-commands the nodes that follow, and the node that precedes is not a node on the (extended) projection line. This constraint eliminates left-associative projection structures as in (5).

(5a) violates the BBC, because F' precedes its sister node, the Spec-F node. In (5b), V'-precedes a VP-internal sister node and therefore violates the BBC. The BBC applies to lexical projections and their functional extensions in general. The VP in (5a) and (5b) is representative of any complex lexical, head-*initial* projection of any category (in particular also for the internal organization of head-initial NPs). The BBC does *not only* rule out base-generated right-associative structures like (5b), but any movement to the right, too, either as movement to a clause-final head or a clause-final spec position, because these positions would be illicit. Adjunction to the *right* (extraposition by movement) or scrambling to the right is ruled out as well.

(5)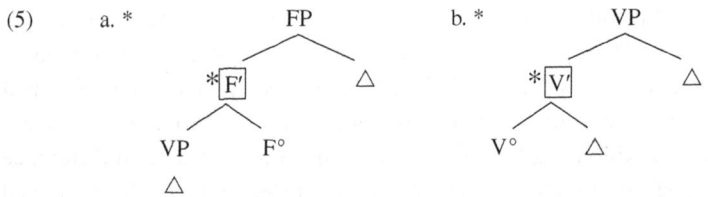

The phenomena discussed as *scrambling to the right* (see §4.4) are best analyzed as the result of V-movement to the left (cf. Haider 1997c, d; Mahajan 1997). Extraposition by movement to the right is an empirically inadequate analysis of extraposition. In Haider (1995a, 1997a and 2010a: ch.5), extraposition is analyzed partly in terms of V-movement to the left, partly in terms of the construal of base-generated structures.

Right-bound movement to a spec position as in (5a) and head movement to the right are banned as follows. If a functional projection is a functional extension of the projection of a lexical category, the BBC rules out functional heads to the right in general. In this case, the projection of the lexical category would be a left sister of the functional head and at the same time a node on the (functionally) extended projection line of $V°$, as a left branch. This is illustrated in (6a).

(6) a.   b.

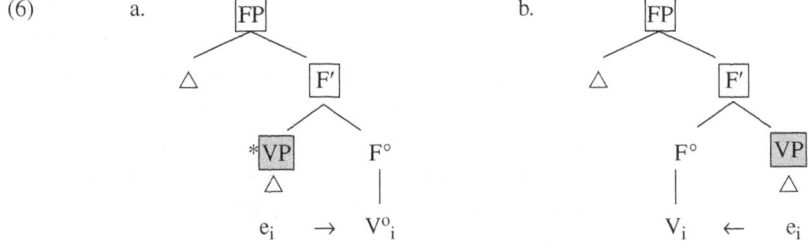

The VP node in (6a) is a top node in the V-projection, but simultaneously a node on the extended V-projection, whose top node is the FP. At this point, a clarification of *'functionally extended lexical projection'* is needed: a functional projection is a *functional extension of a lexical projection* if and only if the lexical content for the *non-lexical functional head* position is derived. One possibility is head movement, another possibility is feature attraction.[5] In both cases, the lexical head of the complement is the derived head of the functional projection.[6] Note that according to this definition, a projection of a *lexical* functional head (e.g. a lexical complementizer or a determiner) does not qualify as the *functional extension* of the complement of the functional head. In this case, the functional head is furnished with its own lexical content.[7] In (7a), the VP node is a node of its own extended projection; in (7b), the VP is

---

[5] Example: empty functional $C°$ in embedded wh-clauses. The empty $C°$-head is specified as [+wh] by spec–head agreement.

[6] Note that the excluded structures (5a) and (6a) have recently been extensively discussed under the heading FoF-constraint (Biberauer, Holmberg and Roberts 2009) for a head-initial VP and a clause-final functional head. This constraint is immediately covered by the BBC (see Appendix 5.2 in Chapter 5).

[7] Instances of head-final lexical functional heads are clause-final complementizers (as e.g. in Bengali; see §4.3.1), or the clause-final question marker *ma* in Chinese.

the selected complement of a lexical element, namely the lexical functional head Z in C°.

(7) a. *[$_{F'}$ [$_{VP}$ ... e_i ...] [V_i]$_{F°}$]
    b. [$_{C'}$ [$_{VP}$ ... V° ...] $Z_{C°}$]

With these provisos, the BBC rules out clause structures with movement to a clause-final functional head, but it does not rule out clause-final functional positions in general. It only rules out clause-final functional heads in a *functionally extended* projection. So, for example, a clause-final *lexical* complementizer as in (7b) does not violate the BBC, but 'I'-to-C to a clause-final empty C-position would be a breach of the BBC (7a). In (7b), the CP is not a functional extension of the complement VP. It is just a functional projection with a complement selected by a lexical C°-head. However, the BBC would rule out verb movement to the position of a clause-final functional head (even if it is alternatively realized by a lexical complementizer), as in (7a). In (7b), on the other hand, each node on the two projection lines is a node on a right branch. In sum, with respect to head movement, the BBC predicts the absence of head movement to a functional head on the right, but it does not rule out the existence of base-generated structures with lexical functional heads on the right. In the first case there is only a single extended projection line, in the second case there are two projections lines, whence the difference.

A test case for this prediction is the German or Dutch clause structure with clause-final finite verbs.[8] It is still a widely held assumption that the finite verb

---

[8] Corver's (1997: 350f.) proposal of A°-raising to a head-final AGR-position for the heads of AP-attributes of NPs is another empirical challenge for the BBC. It deserves a more in-depth reappraisal, but for the present purpose it may suffice to point out that there is clear evidence against A°-raising: the comparative phrase follows the head with the comparative morphology (see i and ii), and head-movement may strand the comparative phrase (see ii vs. iii):

(i) Ist er [schöner *als ich*]?   (ii) [Schöner *als ich*] ist er nicht
    is he more-beautiful than I?   more-beautiful than I is he not
(iii) Schöner$_i$ ist er nicht [e_i *als ich*]   (iv) *ein [[e_i *als ich*] schönerer$_i$] Mann
    more-beautiful is he not than I   a than I more beautiful man
(v) *ein schöner *als ich* Mann   (vi) ein schönerer Mann *als ich*

The ungrammaticality of (iv) is clear evidence against raising: according to Corver (1997: 361f.) only V-type adjectives raise overtly. But the pattern found with primary adjectives (see iv–vi) is identical with the patterns of secondary adjectives, that is, V-type adjectival participles (see vii–ix).

(vii) *ein *als dieser* störenderer Lärm   (viii) *ein störenderer *als dieser* Lärm
    a *than that-one* more-annoying noise
(ix) ein störenderer Lärm *als dieser*

in the clause-final position in Dutch or German is placed into a clause-final *functional* head position. If, on the other hand, this is ruled out by the BBC, the clause-final finite verb must be either *in situ*, or, if it is considered to be moved to a functional head position, this position must be to the left of the VP (see Zwart (1997) for Dutch, who derives this result within the framework of Kayne (1994)).[9] However, there is good evidence that the finite verb in German V-final constructions is indeed *in situ*, that is, in its base-generated position as the head of the VP (see Haider 1997a, 2010a: ch. 2, and § 4.3.2 of this chapter).

The following subsections will first examine cases of clause-final *lexical* complementizers (4.3.1) and then demonstrate that the assumption of clause-final functional heads that attract V-movement fails in confrontation with massive counterevidence (4.3.2).

4.3.1 Parameterized directionality of complement selection for lexical $C°$

Complementizer particles are elements of the lexicon. Therefore their lexical entry may provide lexically stored information for complement selection. In Dutch, for instance, the complementizers *dat* and *om* select a finite or a non-finite functional projection, respectively.

(8)   a. Ik probeerde [*om* [te winnen]]
           I tried   *for* to win
           'I tried to win'
    b. Ik denk [*dat* [ik zal winnen]]
           'I think that I shall win'

In addition to the syntactic features of the complement, the directionality of complement licensing is a property that is open for lexically geared parametric variation. The directionality value for complementizers may be language specific and it may even vary within the set of complementizer elements in a single language. An example is Bengali (data from Singh 1980; see also Bayer 1998: 245). Bengali is representative of a group of Eastern and South-eastern Aryan languages in this respect (Oriya, Assamese, Marathi, Dakkhini-Hindi).

Head-final clauses (9a) and head-initial ones (9b) differ in their distribution (see Bayer 1998: 259, 2001). Clauses with *clause-initial* complementizers

---

Raising of A° to an AGR-head would result in (vii), with stranding of the comparative phrase in a position preceding the raised A-head.

[9] In this case, the VP itself or its content has to be moved to the left as well; otherwise the finite verb would not end up as the clause-final element.

are obligatorily extraposed (see 9c). Sentential complements with clause-final complement marking, on the other hand, must not be extraposed (see 9d).

(9) a. chele-Ta [[or baba aS-be] *bole*] Sune-che
        boy-CL his father come-FUT3 COMP hear-PTS3
    b. chele-Ta Sune-che [*je* [or baba aS-be]]
        boy-CL hear-PAST that his father come-FUT
    c.*chele-Ta [*je* [or baba aS-be]] Sune-che
        boy-CL that his father come-FUT hear-PAST
    d.*chele-Ta Sune-che [[or baba aS-be] *bole*]
        boy-CL hear-PAST that his father come-FUT COMP

In his study on initial and final complementizers in Southern and Eastern Indo-Aryan languages, Bayer (1998) claims that the final complementizers are base-generated in the final position. He argues in detail against the hypothesis that these complementizers might happen to end up in the final position in the course of a derivation that moves the complement of C° to the left, thereby stranding the complementizer in a clause-final position.

Koopman (1984: §3.4.2) discusses the distribution of complementizers in Vata[10] and Gbadi. She notes that despite the presence of clause-*final* markers (Q-marker, complementizer, relativization-marker), wh-movement targets a sentence-*initial* position. This set of facts is additional counterevidence for a derivational account of clause-final complementizers: if C° was stranded, the moved complement of C° ought to be opaque for wh-extraction as the necessary leftward movement of the complement of C° would target either a functional spec position or an adjunction position. In each of these positions the moved phrase would turn into an extraction island, contrary to facts.

The theoretical implication of these facts is obvious: the distribution of lexical complementizers involves a directionality property. Even within one language, the directionality value for the set of complementizers need not be uniform. This is a variant property of lexical heads, known from languages with mixed directionality. In German, for instance, the majority of 'adpositions' are prepositions, but there are also a few postpositional forms.

(10) a. [Den Weg$_{ACC}$ entlang] pflanzten sie Tulpen
        the path along planted they tulips
        'along the path they planted tulips'
    b. [Entlang des Weges$_{GEN}$] pflanzten sie Tulpen
        along the path planted they tulips

---

[10] The clause-initial particle in Vata is *na*, the final one is *ka*. Clauses with initial C follow the selecting verb; clauses with clause-final C precede the verb. Koopman assumes that only the latter is a genuine complementizer.

The case difference between the postpositional and the prepositional usage of *entlang*, illustrated in (10), is an indicator of the different syntactic identity of *entlang* as postposition and as preposition.

German (and likewise all other Germanic OV languages) is an example of a language with mixed directionality. Lexical heads are partitioned into final ones (V°, A°) and initial ones (N°, P°), with a few exceptional specimens of final P°. All lexical functional heads (C°, D°) are head-initial. Japanese, on the other hand, is representative of a consistent head-final language. Lexical and lexical functional heads (e.g. complementizer particles, case particles) follow their complements.

(11) a. [[Hiroshi-ga Masao-o mita] ka dooka keisatsu-ni mitsuke-rare-na-katta]
[[Hiroshi Masao saw] *whether*] by the police not was found-out
(=*find+pass+neg+past*)
b. [[[Hiroshi-ga Masao-o mita] ka dooka keisatsu-ni mitsuke-rare-na-katta koto-ga]   kazoku-o shinpai saseta]
[[[H. saw M.] *whether*] by the police was not found-out] *that*-TOP] the family worry made]
'that it was not found out by the police whether H. saw M. made the whole family worry'

In sum, there is a difference between non-lexical functional heads and lexical (functional) heads: the latter have a directionality option (*initial/ final*), whereas the former are universally phrase-initial. This difference can be captured if directionality is considered a *lexically* specifiable property: for non-lexical heads, the directionality of complement licensing must follow from a system-internal property, because there is no lexical entry with a specifiable directionality feature. It follows from a structuring principle, namely the BBC. Lexical functional heads, on the other hand, are lexical elements and specifiable for head features. So it is expected that lexical functional heads, just like lexical heads of the major categories, are found either as initial or final heads, depending on the setting of the value for the directionality of complement licensing.

Note that the BBC does not rule out clause-final *lexical* functional heads, but is does rule out clause-final functional heads with secondary lexicalization, and thereby it rules out movement to (non-existing) clause-final specifiers, too. This captures the generalization that even in languages with clause-final complementizers, there are no clause-final specs. Movement does not target positions to the right. A case of apparent wh-movement to the right will be discussed below.

4.3.2 Clause-final functional heads in German and other Germanic OV languages?

In this section, evidence from two independent properties of grammar will be presented for the claim that the clause-final finite verb in a German or Dutch clause stays *in situ*, that is, it stays in the same position in which it would occur as a non-finite verb. In other words, it is *not* raised to a clause-final functional head position. Since these arguments have been expounded in full detail in Haider (2010a: ch. 2), this section will present them in a summary-like style.

The first piece of evidence is the fact that there are finite verbs which cannot undergo V-to-C movement. The result is corroborated by independent evidence from extraposition patterns. The evidence for finite verbs *in situ* is in fact two-fold. First, there are verbs that cannot be fronted to the V2-position because of a morphological peculiarity. Second, there are verbs that cannot be fronted for scope reasons. The fact that these verbs nevertheless can be used as finite verbs in the clause-final position is strong evidence against the assumption that finiteness requires head movement, as will be shown below.

As for the first set of data, the original observation goes back to Höhle (1991) and its relevance is discussed first in Haider (1993: 62f.): there are *finite* verbs in German that occur only in verb-*final* clauses in German, but not in V2- or V1-clauses (see 12). In other words, they do not move. If they were moveable, they could not be prevented from moving to the V2-position.

The verb class is fed by a productive process of word formation, namely particle+verb formation. If this option is applied twice, the result is an immobile verb. The reason is obvious. Particles of particle verbs are obligatorily stranded when the verb moves to the V2-position. But for verbs with two strandable particles, it is impossible to fulfil the stranding requirements for each of the two particles. If the verb moves and strands the closer particle, the other particle remains attached to the stranded particle (12b) and thus is not stranded itself. The distant particle could only be stranded if the verb moves together with the closer particle (12c), but in this case the unstranded particle violates the stranding requirement (see also Vikner 2001; Fortmann 2007). (12d) violates stranding for both particles. Consequently, any movement that requires stranding is impossible. This rules out V-to-'I' and subsequent movement to C, and it predicts (12a) to be ungrammatical.

(12) a. wenn du uns voranmeldest
if you us preregister (lit. *pre-on-register*)
b. *Du meldest$_i$ uns *voran*-e$_i$
you register us pre-on

c. *Du *an*meldest$_i$ uns *vor*-e$_i$
d. *Du *voran*meldest$_i$ uns e$_i$

The Dutch counterpart is a productive prefix corresponding to the English prefix *re-*, as in *rebuild*.[11] The Dutch prefix is inseparable, as (13a,b) illustrate. (13c,d) show that *opbouwen* is obligatorily split by V-to-C. In the combination with *her-*, however, V-to-C is blocked (14a,b). The restriction illustrated in (14) is representative of a large class of verbs with separable prefixes prefixed by *her-*.

(13) a. Hij *herbouwde*$_i$ het zeker niet e$_i$
       he re-built   it surely not
    b. *Hij *bouwde*$_i$ het zeker niet *her*-e$_i$
    c. Hij *bouwde*$_i$ het *op*-e$_i$
       he built   it up
    d. *Hij opbouwde$_i$ het e$_i$

(14) a. *Hij *bouwde*$_i$ het *herop*-e$_i$
       he built it re-up
    b. *Hij *heropbouwde*$_i$ het e$_i$
       he re-up-built it
    c. dat hij het *heropbouwde*
       that he it re-up-built

The grammatical causality of the exceptional behaviour in German and Dutch is easy to understand. The conflicting structural requirements – 'strand the particle' and simultaneously 'do not strand' – can be avoided only if the trigger of the conflict, namely movement, is avoided. The consequence is obvious, too: if finiteness requires V-to-'I', these verbs could not become finite. If, on the other hand, finite verbs can be checked for finiteness without (overt) V-to-'I', the verbs under discussion can occur in finite form, but they cannot undergo V-to-C because V-to-C implies overt movement. The empirical facts support the latter interpretation.[12]

The fact that the fronting of a finite verb to the top functional head of the clause is blocked implies that the given finite verb does not move at all (overtly) to a functional head that would serve as the intermediate head: once a finite verb in a V2 language is assumed to have moved to the functional head position that checks finiteness, there is no non-ad hoc way to block it from moving higher up to the V2-position.

Ad hoc restrictions blocking 'I'-to-C would miss the essential point, namely the fact that the blocking factor of the verbs in (12) and (13) is a factor of the morphological make-up of these verbs that becomes operative in contexts

---

[11] Henk van Riemsdijk (p.c.) made me aware of this phenomenon in 1991, at the 7th Comparative Germanic Syntax Conference in Stuttgart.

[12] Note that the fact that participle and infinitive formation is possible with these verbs (e.g. herop*ge*bouwd – re-up-built; herop*te*bouwen – re-up-to-build; voran*ge*meldet, voran*zu*melden) entails that movement to a functional head position is not involved: the pre- or infixed participle morpheme *–ge–* or the infinitival particle *te/zu* are morphological inflection elements and not independent functional heads (unlike the English 'to').

of movement triggered by finiteness. In the V-to-'I' analysis, the problem with these verbs becomes acute *before* 'I'-to-C. So, it cannot be captured as a restriction on 'I'-to-C.

The corresponding case of English, mentioned above, supports this conclusion: verbs that move to I° keep on moving to C° in the appropriate contexts. Verbs in I° cannot be exempted from moving to C° in contexts of obligatory 'I'-to-C movement. On the other hand, verbs that do not move to I, do not move to C in contexts of V-to-'I'-to-C. So, it is safe to conclude that a finite verb that does not move to C° does not move to I° in the first place, but that it stays in its position because it cannot be moved at all.

Let us turn to a *second, independent piece* of evidence: mandatory scope as a restriction on V-movement was discussed first in Haider (1995b) and (1997d). When a verb contains obligatorily scope-dependent material it must remain in the scope of the element it depends on. Obligatorily scope-dependent relations are characteristic of comparative and equative constructions.

The relation between the comparative phrase as the licensing element and the dependent *than*-phrase is subject to c-command on c-structure if the structure is complete, that is non-elliptic. A particularly revealing instance of this is the relation between a comparative adverbial and the verb as the target of comparison, and the telling contrast between Italian and English:

(15) a. The value has far more than merely tripled
b. The value far more than merely tripled

(16) a. Il valore si e molto *più* che solo *triplicato*   Italian
'the value itself has much more than only tripled'
b. *Il valore si *triplica*$_i$ molto *più* che solo e$_i$
'the value itself tripled much more than only'
c. *Il valore molto *più* che solo si *triplica*
'the value itself much more than only tripled'

The contrast between English and Italian reflects the well-established difference between the positions of the finite verbs in the respective clause structures. In English, the main verb does not leave its base VP position. In Italian, the finite verb appears in a functional head position c-commanding the VP. The adverbial comparative is an adjunct to VP and does not c-command the functional head. Hence (16b) is ungrammatical. (16c) is ungrammatical for a different reason: in order to arrive at the given word order, the finite verb must be either *in situ* or the whole VP must have been raised to the functional head position. Neither of these structures is grammatical. The finite verb cannot remain *in situ* in Italian and a functional head position cannot be the target of phrasal movement.

The German data parallel the Italian pattern in V2-contexts. V-movement destroys the scope relation and this relation is not reconstructed, otherwise (17b) would be grammatical.[13] It is not reconstructed because the target of the comparative operator is not the verb, but a part of it. The trace in (b) is the trace of the verb and not the trace of the target of the comparative.

(17)   a. Der Wert hat sich *weit mehr als bloß verdreifacht* in diesen Tagen
          the value has itself more than merely tripled in theses days
      b.*Der Wert *verdreifachte$_i$* sich weit *mehr als bloß* e_i in diesen Tagen
          the value tripled   itself   more than merely in these days

This example is representative of a broader class of constructions that also includes the equative construction.[14] As illustrated in (18), this construction shows the same pattern:

(18)   a. dass man alles *so gut wie verdreifachte dafür*
          that one everything as good as tripled there-for
          'that they as good as almost tripled everything for this'
      b. *Man ver*dreifachte$_i$* alles so gut *wie* e_i dafür

The example (18) shows clearly that the scope-bearing element is VP-internal. It follows an indefinite object that is interpreted as existentially bound. Existential binding of indefinites is possible only in VP-internal positions. Consequently, the finite verb must be VP-internal, hence *in situ*. If it were to rise to a clause-final functional head position, it would leave the scope domain of the operator element and would be predicted to be ungrammatical.

Note that the argument is independent of V-to-C movement. Any movement that fronts the verb across the scope-exerting element will crash. Hence, topicalization of the main verb, for instance, is expected to be ungrammatical, and the facts confirm this expectation. Topicalization is perfect (19a), but only if the comparative/equative tag is absent. (19c) is evidence that the ungrammaticality cannot be attributed to a kind of edge effect that forbids that the comparative or equative part ends up in sentence-final position. (19c) is as unacceptable as (19b).

---

[13] This contrasts with the reconstruction of scope under negation. In the following example, the fronted modal is in the scope of negation. Technically this is achieved by applying the scope computation to the head chain.

(i) Du sollst$_i$ nicht töten e_i – You shall$_i$ not e_i kill

[14] Note that a copy-theory of movement would make a different prediction. If the trace is not a copy but indeed an empty category the lack of reconstruction follows.

(19) a. Verdreifacht hat man alles
       tripled has one everything
    b. Verdreifacht hat man alles *{so gut wie / mehr als}
       tripled has one everything {as good as / more than}
    c. Verdreifacht hat man alles *{so gut wie / mehr als} was nicht mir gehörte
       tripled has one everything {as good as / more than} that not (to) me belonged

What is the conclusion? The conclusion is that there are particularly clear cases of counterevidence for overt V-to-'I' movement to a clause-*final* 'I'-position. So, if there is no overt movement to an alleged head position in a language in which finite verbs move overtly, this casts serious doubts on the existence of this position. Either this position does not exist at all, or this position is not targeted overtly. In the latter case it is at least pointless to insist that it must be a clause-*final* position.

Additional independent evidence against overt V-movement to the right can be found in extraposition constructions (first discussed in Haider 1990; see also Haider 2010a: ch. 2, §2.2.1). VP topicalization as in (20a) shows that the fronted VP may contain extraposed material. The order that would result if the fronted VP is reconstructed into its extraction site is ungrammatical, however (see 20b). The extraposed constituent must follow the finite verb (see 20c). This is inconsistent with a V-to-'I' analysis but it is compatible with an analysis without movement to a clause-final functional head:

(20) a. [Gesprochen *mit ihr*]$_{VP}$ hat er nicht mehr
       spoken   to her has he not any-more
    b.*dass er nicht mehr [gesprochen *mit ihr*]$_{VP}$ hat$_{I^0}$.
    c. dass er nicht mehr [gesprochen *hat*] *mit ihr*
       that he not any-longer [spoken has] with her

The facts discussed above are facets of a more general pattern: neither in German nor in Dutch, nor for other undisputed OV languages is there positive evidence for V-movement to the right comparable to the kind of evidence available for clause-internal verb movement to the left in VO. The pattern (21a) found in various forms with V-left has no counterpart for V-right (21b), for principled reasons, as I will argue below.

(21) a. ... [V$_i$ [XP [$_{VP}$ e$_i$ ...]]]   b. * ...[[[$_{VP}$ ... e$_i$] YP] V$_i$]

In sum, robust empirical evidence confirms that (21b) is justly ruled out. In particular, there is immediate evidence against verb movement to a clause-*final* functional head position in German or Dutch. Clause-final finite verbs in German and Dutch remain *in situ* with respect to an alleged clause-final functional head, just like the finite verbs in continental Scandinavian languages (see Holmberg and Platzack 1995) or the main verbs in English do, with respect to a preceding functional head. The grammatical causality is different, though. In Dutch and German the preconditions for movement would be fulfilled. The absence of head movement to the right is unexplained unless the head positions to be targeted do not exist.

4.4 The BBC and phrasal movement

Let us turn now to the discussion of G4 (i.e. the ban against any *phrasal movement* to the right). The BBC precludes any phrasal movement to the right simply because this would lead to left-associative projection structures: adjunction to the right is ruled out immediately. Substitution into a spec position to the right is not admitted either because this requires a functional head that opens up a left-associative extended projection: if the spec position is to the right, there must be a left sister constituent on the same projection line. But this constellation is ruled out by the BBC. So, the BBC does not only rule out intermediate rightward movement (as in the case discussed in §4.3.2 above) but it also precludes the existence of the mirror image of V2 languages ('V-penultimate languages'):

(22)   *[[[– e_j – e_i] V_i] XP_j]

The structure in (22) is the mirror image of a Germanic V2-structure. It is a V-penultimate structure with a right-hand spec position. Since (22) involves a left-associative extended projection it violates the BBC. No language of this type is known.

The ban against left-associative extended projections (i.e. the BBC) guarantees that a non-lexical functional head precedes its complement, and that the spec position of a functional projection precedes the functional head. The spec–head–complement order of functional projections is derivable from the BBC. The BBC eliminates three of the four ordering possibilities for projections consisting of a functional head, its complement and a spec position (23b,c,d):

(23)   a.   [Spec [head complement]]
        b.   * [Spec [[$_{complement...}$ e_i ...] head$_i$]]
        c.   * [[complement head] specifier]
        d.   * [[head complement] specifier]

One of the excluded structures is (22), with the derived head and the specifier on the right. The second is (23b), with a head at the right and the spec at the left. This order is ruled out when, as indicated, the functional projection is an extended projection. In an extended projection, the lexical head of the complement of the functional head is raised to the functional head position. The third and fourth items of (23) are ruled out by BBC as functional projections with the specifier at the right (23c,d).

Let us turn now to the illegal movement patterns listed at the beginning of this chapter. For ease of reference, they are repeated under (24). In fact, all these structures have been claimed to be represented in the data of some language. (24a) is still used as a standard analysis for extraposition. (24b) is argued for by Kenstowicz (1987) with data from Tangale, a Chadic language. (24c) would be the appropriate structure if scrambling could adjoin DPs on the right periphery, as Kural (1997) claims for Turkish. (24d) is one of the analyses (Rizzi 1982; Bonet 1990) for postverbal unergative subjects in Romance languages.

(24)   a. * ... [[– e_i –] CP_i] ...   extraposition by movement or adjunction to the right
        b. * ... [[– e_i –] XP_i]$_{CP}$ wh-movement to a right-hand spec position
        c. * ... [[[– e_i –] XP_i] ...] ...   scrambling by adjunction to the right
        d. * ... [pro_i – [[e_i –] NP_i]] ...   free subject inversion with the subject right-adjoined

Let us start with postverbal subjects. The branching constraint rules out analyses with the subject adjoined to the right (see 25), irrespective of base-generation or adjunction by movement (Rizzi 1982) or by movement to a right specifier of VP (Bonet 1990). The BBC requires a structure in which the postverbal subject is c-commanded by the object, that is, a VP-internal position for the postverbal subject.[15]

(25)   a. *[pro^i [I° [[VP] DP^i]]]   – adjunction to VP
        b. *[[[pro^i [I° [e_i [VP]]]] F] DP_i]   – movement to a postverbal functional spec

Evidence from variable binding and comparatives (Haider 1997a: §5.2, 2010a: ch. 5) is sufficient to cast doubt on adjunction analyses. In both cases, the postverbal subject would not meet the syntactic requirements for an adequate characterization of the data. Quantifier-variable binding (26), as well as the scope-sensitive relation in comparative construction (27), and the well-known lack of opacity effects for subject extraction ('that-*t*') support a BBC account,

---

[15] Ordóñez (1997) proposes the following analysis: a. The subject moves to a focus position. b. The object moves across the subject. c. The remnant TP moves to an even higher position. Since there is no straightforward, independent reason for the movement of the object and the remnant TP, I prefer for the time being a solution in terms of the reversal of discharge for the subject and have it generated in the deepest argument position.

that is, a structure assignment in which the postverbal subject position is in the c-command domain of an object position.

(26) a.?{Suo$_i$/il proprio$_i$} padre ha accompagnato ogni$_i$ bambino
  'his/the own father has accompanied every child'
 b. Ha accompagnato ogni$_i$ bambino {suo$_i$/il proprio$_i$} padre
  'has accompanied every child his/the own father'

The contrast in (26) is the familiar contrast between a properly bound variable and an improperly bound one. Q-binding requires c-command, so the postverbal subject in (26b) must be in the c-command domain of the object. This is incompatible with the structure resulting from base adjunction. A-movement analysis, on the other hand, would have to counterfactually predict a weak-crossover violation because the moved bindee would c-command both, its trace and the binder.

Data from comparatives match the patterns found above with variable binding. If a postponed subject were able to c-command the VP, a VP-internal comparative clause should be compatible with a postponed subject. The facts contradict this, however:

(27) a. Molte più persone hanno ballato [di quanto mi aspettassi]   Italian
  'More people have danced than I expected'
 b.*Hanno ballato e$_i$ [di quanto mi aspettassi] molte più persone$_i$

As predicted by the BBC, the postponed subject cannot license a comparative clause that precedes because it does not c-command it. If the postverbal subject were adjoined to VP it would c-command the comparative clause and (27b) would be well formed.

Wh-movement to the right would be an instance of either (23c) or (23d), if we abstract away from V-movement and allow for empty functional heads, a situation typically found with dependent wh-clauses. Kenstowicz (1987) claims that Tangale should be characterized as a language with wh-movement to the clause-final position and shows that in this SVO language, wh-subjects occur in the clause-final position. He does not discuss embedded clauses, however. The crucial case would be an embedded wh-clause or a relative clause with the relative phrase moved to a clause-final position. A closer look shows that the evidence is not compelling. What appears to be wh-movement to the right arguably is a base-generated cleft construction with a null copula.

Tuller (1992: 324) provides evidence that the Chadic languages have a clause-final focus position. Colarusso (1979) has shown that apparent wh-movement to the right in Circassian is a case of a cleft construction without copula. Since clefts introduce a clause-final focus position, Tangale would lend itself to an analogous analysis. The compelling case of wh-movement to the right is still missing. It would have to be an embedded wh-clause or a relative clause structure with wh-movement to the right, that is, clauses with a clause-final wh-pronoun. Structures of this type have not been attested, however (cf. Downing 1978).

Let us turn now to a potential case of *adjunction* to the right, namely so-called *rightward scrambling*. Scrambling to the left is a frequently observed phenomenon, both the clause-bound variant, as in German, and non-local variants, as in Japanese. The BBC forbids any scrambling to the right. Mahajan (1997) argues that what could be called scrambling to the right in Hindi should not be analyzed as scrambling. The adequate structure for the Hindi clause is a right-associative one, and postverbal arguments in Hindi result from V-movement to the left. In this view, Hindi combines XV and VX properties. It simply is a Type III language (see Chapter 3, §3.4 and Chapter 5).

Kural (1997: 504–5) claims that Turkish provides a genuine case *of scrambling to the right*, that is, adjunction to the right in non-embedded clauses. He bases his claim mainly on the scope interaction between the extraposed phrase and a non-extraposed object or subject. (28a) contrasts with (28b), where the object *üç kişi* (three people) is preverbal. But these data do not warrant the claim.

(28) a. Herkes dün ara-mış-ø [üç kişi]-yi
everyone$_{NOM}$ yesterday call$_{INDEF.PAST-3SG}$ three person$_{ACC}$
'Everyone called three people yesterday' (*group reading only*)
A group of three people received calls from everyone yesterday.
b. Herkes [üç kişi]-yi dün ara-mış-ø
everyone$_{NOM}$ three person$_{ACC}$ yesterday call$_{INDEF.PAST-3SG}$
'Everyone called three people yesterday' (*existential reading*)
Everyone called three arbitrary people yesterday.

Let us grant (for the sake of the argument) that a postverbal XP in Turkish is, as Kural assumes, adjoined high enough in the tree so that it c-commands the preceding phrases, and that c-command is a sufficient condition for scope taking. In this case the crucial reading for (28a) is not a group reading but the wide-scope reading of the numerical quantifier ('for each x of three, for every y: x called y'). The group reading is a reading without scope. The group reading is the result of construing the numerical DP as denoting an entity that is a set of three elements. This entity is the reference of the DP. So, the contrast between (28a) and (28b) does not prove Kural's point. 'Extraposed' postverbal quantifiers do not take scope, neither in Turkish nor in German.

A postverbal quantifier does not receive scope in German. In (29a), the scope effect is equivalent to sentence negation. In (30a), however, the postverbal position is incompatible with sentence negation. If the postverbal PP had scope over the (trace of) the finite verb, it should produce the same negation effect as in the preverbal position, but in (29b), the DP in the PP clearly cannot be interpreted as a negated quantifier:

(29)   a. Sie war *mit nichts* zufrieden
          she was with nothing content
          'she was not content with anything'
    b. Sie war zufrieden *mit nichts*
          she was content with nothing
          'she was content with(out) anything'

Since scoping judgements are notoriously subtle, let us check an independent piece of evidence, too. Effects of variable-binding violations (weak crossover) are less subtle.

(30)   a. Sie^j hat ihren$^{j/??i}$ Geburtstag mit allen Kolleginnen^i gefeiert, wenn es möglich war
          she has her/their birthday with all colleagues celebrated, if it possible was
          'whenever it was possible, she celebrated her/their birthday with all colleagues'
    b. Sie^j hat mit allen Kolleginnen^i ihren$^{j/i}$ Geburtstag gefeiert, wenn es möglich war
    c. Sie^j hat ihren$^{j/??i}$ Geburtstag gefeiert, mit allen Kolleginnen^i wenn es möglich war

The version with a postverbal quantifier (30c) does not have a natural reading with binding of the possessive by the quantifier. But this reading (i.e. the distributive reading) should be available, if c-command is sufficient for binding, and if a postverbal PP was in a c-commanding position. These data cast doubt on the strength of the Turkish data.

In Turkish, postverbal phrases are interpreted as background information in the discourse. Kural (1997: 499) maintains that 'material back-grounded in the discourse is placed in postverbal position, and it cannot be stressed or focused. A phrase is discourse-back-grounded if its denotation is part of the context assumed by the speaker and the listener in a given situation'. What this indicates is that the apparent scope effect in (28a) is not a scope effect at all, but merely the effect of the group reading of the phrase 'three people'. This is an *indefinite specific* reading of the postverbal phrase, triggered by virtue of belonging to the shared background information. Hence, the decision on the structural configuration of postverbal elements should not be based on scope relations of this sort, because they are not structure dependent.

A structure-dependent grammatical relation is the antecedent–anaphor relation. The antecedent must c-command the anaphor. Kural (1997: 506) notes that reciprocal anaphors may appear in the postverbal area (see 31) but cannot have wide scope. So he concludes that this situation 'leads to obligatory reconstruction'. This is a crucial but ad hoc assumption in his argumentation. Its theoretical status is questionable. If anaphors are reconstructed, why should scrambled phrases not be reconstructed as well? In undisputed cases of scrambling, like in German, anaphors cannot be scrambled because they do not reconstruct, as (32) illustrates. Why should only scrambled anaphors reconstruct in Turkish, and why not scrambled non-anaphors?

(31)   Herkes$_i$ dün aramiş birbirini$_i$
        'Everybody (=all) called each other yesterday'

The fact that *herkes* can be the antecedent of a reciprocal demonstrates in addition that it can denote a set of individuals. Hence, if subject and object are exchanged in (28a), the postverbal *herkes* would be interpreted in the group reading as denoting a specific group of individuals in the background information. The group reading interpretation of the object in (28a) or the subject in (28b) produces the desired effect: it is not in the scope of a quantified expression because it is not a scope-sensitive element. If this is correct, Kural's data do not prove his point.

If in clear cases of scrambling, like in German, reconstruction is not possible, it is safe to assume that this is not a language-specific property and that it applies to Turkish as well. Turkish, like Hindi, has Type III properties. What appears to be phrasal movement to the right is a consequence of V-movement to the left.

In (32b,d), the PP containing an anaphor bound by the object is scrambled across the object. In each case the result is ungrammatical. Binding by the c-commanding subject would yield a grammatical result. Obviously, anaphor binding is not reconstructed in German scrambling constructions. On the other hand, topicalization as an instance of wh-movement is reconstructed, as (32e) illustrates.

(32)   a. Beim Quadrieren muß man eine Zahl^i mit sich^i multiplizieren
           at squaring must one a number with itself multiply
           'When you square you must multiply a number with itself'
        b. *Beim Quadrieren muß man mit sich^i_j eine Zahl^i e$_j$ multiplizieren
        c. Sie hat die Hunde$_i$ aufeinander$_i$ gehetzt

she has the dogs at-each-other baited
   'She has baited the dogs against each other'
d. *Sie hat aufeinander$_i$ die Hunde$_i$ gehetzt
e. Aufeinander$_i^j$ hat sie die Hunde^j e$_i$ gehetzt

This completes the discussion of the two instances of phrasal movement to the right. Neither extraposition phenomena nor alleged cases of scrambling to the right challenge the validity of generalization G4, and thereby the validity of the BBC.

The generalizations G5 and G6, which will be the subject matter of the following sections, are generalizations that relate to the BBC in an indirect way. G5 is a consequence of the BBC plus the directionality requirement, and G6 is the ensuing effect of circumventing an otherwise unavoidable clash with the BBC for head-final structure, namely iterative central embedding of (extended) V-projections (producing lexically extended projections).

4.5 Expletive subjects

It is a simple and incontestable fact of German and Dutch, for instance, that they allow subjectless sentences (notably with the passive of an intransitive verb), and that the Germanic VO languages do not. They require an expletive, and if there is no suitable expletive available (as in English), the structure is not admitted (whence the missing passive for intransitives without subject in English). The reason is an indirect consequence of the BBC and the directionality constraint.

In SVO languages, as suggested already by the acronym S-V-O, the position of the subject is structurally unique. It is the only argument that *precedes* the verbal head, while all other arguments *follow*. In clause structure, the subject position is the spec of a functional head. The subject phrase is raised from its VP-internal pre-head base position into the obligatory surface position. The position is both an *obligatory structural position* and a position that is *obligatorily lexicalized*.[16] The head of the functional projection above the VP provides the directional identification of the VP-internal subject position, and introduces an obligatory spec position (see 35).

A good indicator of the syntactically mandatory subject position is a mandatory expletive. An expletive is semantically void. Its presence is owed to syntactic requirements only. The Scandinavian languages are good models for this

---

[16] In Generative terminology, this is referred to as the EPP property (EPP = Extended Projection Principle =$_{def.}$ clauses have (overt/covert) subjects (Chomsky 1981: 9–10)).

property. If an intransitive verb is used in the passive construction, the subject position is obligatorily lexicalized with an expletive.[17]

(33)   a. Ofte vart *det* telefonert   Norwegian
            often was *it* telephoned
         b. Ofte telefonere*s det*
            often telephones-PASS *it*
         c. Oft wurde (**es*) telephoniert   German
            often was (*it*) telephoned
         d. *Es* wurde oft telephoniert

(33a,b) illustrate the two syntactic options for passive in Scandinavian languages (see Åfarli 1992). One option (33a) is the familiar one, namely the combination of a participle plus a 'be'-type auxiliary. The other option is a passive affix (namely -*s*). This has developed from a middle construction with a cliticized reflexive. In both cases (33a,b), the subject position is obligatorily lexicalized with the expletive. The subject expletives of the Scandinavian languages are cognates of either the English 'there' or 'it'.

In strict OV languages, subject expletives are unknown. Passive in Japanese or Korean, for instance, produces subjectless clauses and the missing subject is not compensated by an expletive.

What is special about SVO in comparison to SOV with respect to the subject? It is the position of the subject argument in the VP structure. In OV, any argument of the verb is merged in the same directionality domain (34b). If the subject argument of an unergative verb is merged in the highest possible argument position in the VP, this position precedes the *verbal* head, both in VO and of course in OV. In VO, however, this position is not within the directionality domain of the head. In (34a), this is exemplified by a VP in an exceptional case-marking construction with a non-nominative subject. The subject of the VP precedes the verbal head 'precede', the object follows. In an OV structure, both the subject and the object precede the head.[18]

(34)   a. (let→) [$_{VP}$ the subject [$_{V'}$→ precede$_{V°}$ the object]]
         b. [$_{VP}$ das Subjekt [←$_{V'}$ dem Objekt vorangehen$_{V°}$]] (←lassen)[19]
            the subject$_{ACC}$ the object$_{DAT}$ precede le   (n.b. expository only)t

---

[17] English, once more, is an exception. It does not allow a passive of an intransitive simply because English lacks a syntactically adequate expletive. 'There' is always associated with a postverbal nominative and 'it' is associated with an extraposed clause.

[18] Note that the 'directionality defect' of the VP-internal subject position is a property of SVO. SOV and VSO systems do not have this 'defect'. In each case, the subject is *within* the directionality domain for the arguments.

[19] Be aware: German obligatorily applies verb clustering instead of VP complementation (see the following section). The structure is given here just for expository purposes.

Given the directionality premise,[20] the VP-internal subject position in an SVO clause is not in the canonical directionality domain of the head of the VP, but it is nevertheless in need of an identifying head with the *canonical licensing directionality*. This head is a functional head.[21] So, there must be a functional projection that selects the VP as a complement and satisfies the directional licensing requirement.

(35)　　[$_{FP}$ ... [$_{F'}$ F° → [$_{VP}$ DP [V° ...]]]]

Why does the subject raise to the functional spec position, and not merely the verb? Note that the base position of the subject DP in an SVO structure (35) is in the domain of its lexical head, but not in the directionality domain. So, a functional head F° is employed, but the VP-internal subject is not its sister. Hence, the functional head and the subject do not mutually c-command each other, and therefore the PDI requires suitable measures. In these structures, the PDI can be fulfilled in one of two ways.

One way is the *raising of the subject* to the spec position. The raised subject c-commands the functional head,[22] and the functional head c-commands the VP-internal subject position. This is what happens in the continental Scandinavian languages in embedded clauses, and in English clauses with a finite main verb: the subject is raised to spec, the verb stays *in situ*. Another option is raising the finite verb to the functional head position. The result is a V1-clause structure, as in Celtic languages (McCloskey 2005).[23]

(36)　　*Deir* siad gu-r *cheannaigh* agus gu-r *dhíol* siad na tithe　　　　　Irish
　　　　say they C-PAST *bought* and C-PAST *sold* they the horses
　　　　'They say that they bought and sold the horses'

---

[20] The *directionality premise* (PDI): positions in the projection of a phrasal head need to be identified under the *canonical directionality* of the head.

[21] Except for ECM constructions. In (30a), the lower subject is not functionally licensed because it is licensed already by the ECM verb that selects the VP.

[22] If nominative checking is not exclusively constrained to spec–head agreement but implemented in terms of an overt agreement relation, the raising requirement affects whatever is the highest argument in the V-projection. If this argument is not the nominative one, the result is a so-called *quirky subject construction* (see below), as in Icelandic. Note that this shows that the primary trigger of raising a subject is not nominative checking, but the minimal, mutual c-command requirement. This seems to be the grammatical source of the EPP property of non-pro-drop VO languages.

[23] McCloskey (1991: 259f.) explicitly points out that V1 is obligatory for finite clauses and in particular, that the fronting of the subject is ungrammatical. 'In non-finite clauses, however, VSO order is impossible; the subject is always phrase-initial in such clauses.' This contrast between finite and non-finite clauses is immediate evidence for the raising analysis of the finite verb.

The combination of both options is triggered when case checking and agreement are positional functions. In this case, both the subject and the finite verb are raised to their appropriate positions in the functional projection(s) above the VP.

In sum, the *functional subject* position of SVO languages is a direct consequence of the directionality 'defect' of the VP-internal subject position in SVO. An SOV clause structure does not suffer from this 'defect'; hence it arguably does not employ an obligatory functional subject position from the beginning.

Evidently, the functional layer above the VP in the VO architecture is not a 'just-on-demand' structure but a standard requirement for a VO clause structure. It is not merely triggered by the presence of a subject argument in need of licensing. It is an integral part of the clausal architecture of an SVO clause. The grammar principally provides the structural context for directionally licensing the preverbal, VP-internal subject position. Being a mandatory part of the structure, it must be 'interpreted', that is, receive a status in the derivation. Leaving it radically empty, both in the head and the spec position, would be ignoring the structure. The expletive is a way of syntactically interpreting the structure.

4.6 Verb order – 'messy' OV, 'tidy' VO?

The message of the section heading is illustrated in (37) and (38). In VO, the relative order of auxiliaries, semi-auxiliaries and the main verb is constant. In OV languages, order variation is a characteristic property (for languages with moveable verbs). This is true of all Germanic OV languages. Here are two representative cases, namely German (37) and Dutch (38):

(37)   a. dass er nichts gesehen haben *würde*   German
            that he nothing seen have would
            'that he would not have seen anything'
         b. dass er nichts gesehen *würde* haben
         c. dass er nichts *würde* gesehen haben
         d.*dass er nichts *würde* haben gesehen
         e. [Gesehen haben] würde er nichts

In German, only the finite verb changes place (37d). In Dutch, the position for a non-finite verb varies too, as in (38b,c). Dutch does not tolerate the 'German' order (37a), if more than two verbs are involved (38d).The cluster may even be topicalized (37e).

(38)   a. dat hij niets gezien *kan* hebben   Dutch (ANS 1984: 1,069)
            that he nothing seen have can

'that he cannot have seen anything'
b. dat hij niets *kan* gezien hebben
c. dat hij niets *kan* hebben gezien
d. *dat hij niets gezien hebben *kan*

What (37) and (38) illustrate is an effect of verb clustering. This phenomenon is discussed in full detail in Haider (2010a: ch.7, §7.5). It is an OV phenomenon. Verb clusters are by no means a peculiarity of Germanic OV languages. Sells (1990) discusses clustering properties for Japanese, and McCawley and Momoi (1986) for Korean. Han, Lidz and Musolino (2007) discuss transparency phenomena in Korean that are typical of the clause union effect that correlates with V-clustering. The peculiarity of Germanic OV languages is the fact that clustering is accompanied by verb-order variation in the cluster.[24] Why should UG provide or require clustering for OV grammars, but not for VO ones?

The UG 'motive' for granting clustering in an OV setting becomes evident once we look at the structures from the point of view of their processing implications. OV complementation produces *centre-embedding* structures, as in (39a); VO complementation does not (39b). Centre embedding is unavoidable in a BBC-constrained structure with the head-final choice. This would produce right-branching stacks of verbal projections.

Centre embedding is clearly an obstacle for parsing. This becomes evident if we look at the labelled bracketing structure in (39). In (39a), the parser has to guess the number of brackets to be opened in order to instantiate the root VP node. In the VO structure (39b), each of the VP complements is introduced by the head and immediately dominated by its phrase node. For the structure in (39b), the *least* embedded element *comes first*. In (39a), the *most deeply* embedded element comes first, followed in turn by the elements with a shallower embedding.

(39) a. [[[[... diese Strukturen verarbeiten]$_{VP}$ können]$_{VP}$ müssen]$_{VP}$ würde]$_{VP}$
these structures process be-able-to have-to would
'would have to be able to process these structures'
b. [$_{VP}$ could [$_{VP}$ have [$_{VP}$ been [$_{VP}$ processing these structures]]]]

---

[24] A correlating feature of this difference seems to be the following: all Germanic languages, except English, are V-movement languages (V2), with V-movement to a head-initial functional head. Japanese and Korean do not move verbs and they do not have overt head-initial functional heads. All Germanic OV languages show verb-order variation in the cluster, Japanese and Korean do not. We may conclude that verb-order variation in the cluster is absent if the verbs are immobile in the given language. This distinguishes strict OV from the Germanic OV languages.

By admitting clustering, UG provides grammatical means for circumventing *phrasal* centre embedding. Instead of projecting a cascade of centre-embedded VPs, a single VP is projected and the verbs are clustered (40a). The cluster is a syntactic structure resulting from head-to-head merger. It is the (complex) head of the VP. The structure above the cluster in (40a) is identical with the structure of a VP with a simple head (40b). Clustering avoids phrasal centre embedding and reduces the centre-embedding property to the strictly local area of the complex head, that is, the verb cluster. The clustering structure groups the verbs into a single, compact, head-to-head adjoined structure (40c). With this, the remaining centre-embedding domain becomes a local domain that does not involve recursive phrasal nodes.

Dutch grammar goes one step further. It allows to fully eliminate centre embedding in the cluster too, and to structure the cluster in a fully right-branching manner. The result is a mirror-image order for Dutch (40d) compared to German. (40d) is a cluster. It is as compact as the German cluster (40c).

(40) a. [… diese Strukturen [$_{V°\text{-cluster}}$ verarbeiten können müssen würde]$_{V°}$]$_{VP}$
these structures process be-able-to have-to would
'would have to be able to process these structures'

b. [… diese Strukturen [verarbeiten]$_{V°}$]$_{VP}$
these structures process
'process these structures'

c. [[[verarbeiten können]$_{V°}$ müssen]$_{V°}$ würde]$_{V°}$
process be-able-to have-to would
'would have to be able to process'

d. [zou [moeten [kunnen verwerken]$_{V°}$]$_{V°}$]$_{V°}$ Dutch
would have-to be-able-to process

Compactness is a key property of clustering. So-called restructuring constructions in Romance (especially in Italian) show transparency phenomena like the Germanic clustering constructions, but the verbs are not clustered. This becomes evident from the fact that adverbials may freely intervene.[25] This shows that the verbs are projecting their own VP and are not partners in a cluster. The transparency phenomena in Romance are explicable in terms of

---

[25] In Italian, but not in German or Dutch, the verbs in the 'restructuring' construction may sandwich 'cluster-foreign' material (Monachesi 1999), as, for instance, adverbials. The clitic *lo* in (a.) is the object of *comprare* and raised to the position of the matrix finite verb. This is one of the transparency effects characteristic of the restructuring construction:

a. Anna lo vuole (*immediatamente*) poter (*immediatamente*) comprare
Anna-CLIT-ACC wants (immediately) be-able-to (immediately) buy
b. dass es Anna kaufen (*aus Jux /*sofort) wollte
that it Anna buy (for fun / immediately) wanted

alternative sub-categorizations: an infinitival complement may either be a VP, and thus monoclausal, or an infinitival clause, and thus biclausal (see Roberts (1997) and Cinque (2004b), for a technical implementation in terms of the 'lexical' vs. 'functional' category of verbs).

Verb-*order variation* within or outside of the cluster is a by-product of clustering in languages with verb movement. It serves as a means of reducing the residual centre-embedding property in the cluster. Languages with inert verbs (such as Japanese or Korean) do not show this variation, but German and Dutch do.

In Dutch, the strictly head-final order is ruled out for clusters with more than two items, as illustrated in (38d), repeated here as (41). At least the finite verb must be reordered, but complete 'mirroring' is licit too.

(41)　　*dat hij niets *gezien hebben kan*　　　　　　　　　　　　　Dutch

In German, reordering is possible for auxiliaries that select auxiliaries (42b,c), but not for the auxiliary that selects the lexical verb (42d), which is the lowest selected element in the cluster (for details see Haider 2010a: ch.7).

(42)　　a.　dass er sie nicht *fragen können wird*
　　　　　　that he her not ask be-able-to-INF shall
　　　　　　'that he shall not be able to ask her'
　　　　b.　dass er sie nicht *wird* fragen *können*
　　　　c.　dass er sie nicht fragen *wird können*
　　　　d.　*dass er sie nicht *wird* fragen / *dass er sie nicht *wird* dürfen fragen
　　　　　　that he her not *shall* ask / that he her not *shall* be-allowed-to ask

In sum, clustering is a parser-friendly property. It massively reduces centre embedding. Clustering is not restricted to VP embedding. Even full clauses have an optional clustering variant (see Haider 2010a: ch.7, §7.5). This phenomenon is strong evidence for the evolutionary advantage of improving the grammar–parser fit. UG provides clustering as 'anti-dote' for the otherwise unavoidable higher complexity of centre embedding in OV clause structure.

4.7　Summary and typological implications

The BBC constrains the relation between structure and linearization. For any (extended) projection, precedence coincides with c-command for the immediate constituents of the projection. Since each constituent – if it is complex – is a phrasal projection, the BBC is a powerful constraint for the string-to-structure mapping algorithm. The BBC rules out any structures that contain a node on the projection line that precedes a node attached to it. Hence left-associative

94 Symmetry Breaking in Syntax

Table 4.1 *Syntactic structures predicted by the BBC*

a. right-associative *lexical* projections	$[\ldots [\ldots [_{X'} \ldots x°]]]_{XP}$
b. head-initial *functionally extended* projections	$[F° [\ldots]]_{FP}$
c. *spec* positions that *precede*	$[\text{Spec} [\ldots]]$
d. head *movement* to *initial* functional head position	$[x_i° [\ldots e_i \ldots]]$
e. phrasal *movement* to an *initial* spec position	$[XP_i [\ldots e_i \ldots]]$
f. an *expletive* in a *spec* position	$[\text{expletive} [x° \ldots]_{XP}]$
g. *adjunction* to the left	$[YP [\ldots]_{XP}]_{XP}$
h. word structure: *recursive* head-final compounds	$\#\#[z° [y° [x°]]]_X°\#\#$

structures or mixed structures with a right-sided roof are excluded (at least as base-generated structures).

Head-final and head-initial projections are subject to the same principles, modulo directionality and positioning of the head. For complex head-*initial* projections, a head-chain (shell structure) is the necessary consequence of the opposite orientation of the BBC and the canonical directionality of head-initial structures. The VX-XV parameter is the directionality parameter of identification. The cascade of the effects triggered by the BBC and the directionality parameter invite a typological assessment. As far as it is correct, it provides a model for a better understanding of the systematic differences between an OV and VO architecture of clause structure (see Chapter 9; Haider 2010a: ch.1). Table 4.1 summarizes the structures predicted by the BBC, and Table 4.2 lists the structures that are predicted not to exist in grammars of human languages because of the BBC.

The following structure is the combined result of the BBC with an anterograde directionality value for identification (PDI):

i. *shell structure* for complex head-initial phrases (SVO)	$[x_i° [YP [e_i [ZP \ldots]]]]_{XP}$
j. *shell structure* for complex head-initial phrases (VSO)	$[x_i° [YP_{SUBJ} [e_i [ZP \ldots]]]]_{XP}$

The PDI is also the source of the *edge effect* for adjuncts to head-initial phrases.

k. *edge effect* for adjunction to head-*initial* phrases	$[[\ldots z° (* \ldots)]_{ZP} [x°\ldots]_{XP}]_{XP}$

The edge effect is a consequence of adjunction to a phrase *outside* of the identification domain. Since adjunction is permitted only phrase-initially, the

Table 4.2 *Syntactic structures that are immediately incompatible with the BBC*

a. left-associative *lexical* projections	[[[x° [$_{x'}$ ...] ...]$_{XP}$
b. head-final *functionally extended* projections	[[...] F°][26]
c. *spec* positions that follow	[[...] Spec]
d. head *movement* to a final functional head position	[[... e$_i$ ...] x$_i$°]
e. phrasal *movement* to a final spec position	[[... e$_i$ ...] XP$_i$]
f. an *expletive* in a clause-final spec position	[[...] expletive]
g. *adjunction* to the right	[[...]$_{XP}$ YP]$_{XP}$
h. word structure: *recursive* head-initial compounds	##[[[x°] y°] z°]$_X$°##

edge effect concerns adjunction to head-initial phrases, but not to head-final ones. In the latter case, adjunction positions are within the domain and directionality of identification, which is retrograde for head-final phrases. As a consequence, head-initial phrases can be adjoined to head-initial phrases only if the adjunct phrase does not have a complement. This is what we see in English, both with adnominal attributes as well as with pre-VP adverbials.

Immediately related with the BBC but not directly covered in its originally defined version is the ban against centre embedding of sub-clausal verbal projections (i.e. VP, TP). This is the grammatical reason for the obligatory verb clustering in OV:

i. no centre-embedded *sub-clausal* verbal projections	[[...]$_{VP}$ V°]$_{VP}$

Full clauses may be embedded in German (43a), but Dutch, for instance, does not even allow centre-embedded infinitival clauses. Verb clustering (43b) is an alternative option also for a large class of infinitival complement clauses of control verbs (see Haider 2010a: ch.7, §7.5).

(43) a. Er hat [die Dokumente zu veröffentlichen]$_{CP}$ nicht versucht
       he has [the documents to publish] not tried
    b. [Zu veröffentlichen versucht]$_{VC}$ wurden die Dokumente nicht
       [to publish tried] were$_{3PL}$ the documents not
    c. [Die Dokumente zu veröffentlichen]$_{CP}$ wurde nicht versucht
       [the documents to publish] was$_{3SG}$ not tried

[26] A variant of this structure is licit, namely a structure with a *lexical* functional head. In this case, it is not a purely functional extension, but a head-complement structure, with a lexical functional head (cf. clauses with clause-final *lexical* complementizers; NPs with particles, as relation markers or definiteness markers).

In (43b), the verbal cluster is topicalized. The object of the infinitival verb is the passive subject. In the clausal infinitival construction, passive does not affect the case of the object of the embedded clause (43c).

The ban against left-associative structures (BBC) and the ban against centre-embedded verb projections are of the same nature but with different domains of application. The BBC constrains projections of any category. Clustering applies to verbal projections. Clustering can be subsumed under the BBC if we introduce the notion of '*lexical extension*' analogous and in addition to 'functional extension' and let the (BBC) apply to projections of any type of extension, functional or lexical.

Note that the V'° of (44) is typically either an auxiliary or a quasi-auxiliary verb (modal, causative verb ...). These are functional verbs.

(44)   *$[[... V^\circ]_{VP} V'^\circ]_{VP'}$

If VP' is defined as the *lexical extension* of VP, then the BBC rules out (44) because then VP is a right-branching sub-tree of the extended projection line of VP'. Auxiliaries and quasi-auxiliaries are plausible candidates for lexical functional verbs that give rise to lexical functional extensions.

There is only one verb class that apparently resists a simple integration under the heading of lexical functional verbs that give rise to lexically extended projections. This is the class of perception verbs (e.g. see, hear). They are obligatorily clustering, in German and Dutch, but normally categorized as main verbs. However, there is evidence that they function as evidentials, rather than full verbs, when they do not select a full CP.

In (45a), the perception must be direct and immediate, that is, I must see him. If (45b) is true, the perception may be indirect. I need not see him. It is enough that I see something that indicates that he is leaving.

(45)   a. Ich sehe$_i$ [ihn [weggehen e$_i$]$_{VC}$]$_{VP}$
           I see him leave
        b. Ich sehe, [dass er weggeht]$_{CP}$
           I see that he leaves
        c. Ich sah/hörte/*roch ihn wegfahren
           I saw/heared/smelled him away-drive

The fact that, cross-linguistically, perception verbs typically are used with the same construction that causative verbs are used with, points to their grammatical relatedness as quasi-auxiliaries.

In sum, subsuming the causality of V-clustering under the BBC completes and unifies the scope of this grammatical constraint as the grammatical embodiment of the parser friendliness of UG.

5 The Germanic OV/VO split

5.1 The puzzle

The puzzle is the diachronic syntactic split of the Germanic languages.[1] This is a singularity for languages in a contiguous area.[2] Other Indo-European language families such as the Romance or the Slavic families are homogeneous with respect to their word-order type. The basic clause structure of today's Germanic languages is either VO or OV, in the narrow sense,[3] with a single exception, namely Yiddish. This language will be shown to be a kind of Rosetta stone for understanding the diachronic syntactic process that led to the complementary word order split.

The North Germanic languages (Danish, Faroese, Icelandic, Norwegian, Swedish and all regional varieties) plus English, a *virtually* creolized Germanic language,[4] which acquired some of its exceptional properties[5] during the multilingual Anglo-Saxon Normanic-French period and the extensive contacts with Scandinavian varieties (Danish, Norwegian, esp. in the Danelaw districts;

---

[1] This chapter is an expanded version of Haider (2010b). The central idea – diachronic split as a consequence of the fixation of the (previously underspecified) parametric licensing directionality – was sketched for the first time in Haider (2005: §2.3).
[2] Note that the Germanic languages are languages of a connected geographic area with continuous contacts, and not languages in diaspora. During the time the split took place there can no longer be assumed to be any significant adstrate or substrate influence of non-Germanic languages.
[3] In the *narrow* sense, 'OV' should be read as 'head-final VP', 'VO' as 'head-initial VP'. In the *broad* sense, it means head-final for any phrase (OV) vs. head-initial for any phrase (VO). The Germanic OV languages are OV in the narrow sense. In addition, they are V2 languages, that is, in unembedded clauses, the finite verb is in a derived, clause-initial position. This property often masks the basic OV order.
[4] English is nevertheless/therefore (viz. all genuine Creole languages are VO) representative of a strict VO language: [*give* the reader a hint]$_{VP}$, [*conversion* of waste into fuel]$_{NP}$, [*into* fuel]$_{PP}$, [*unrelated* to German]$_{AP}$, [*the* book]$_{DP}$, [*that* this is so]$_{CP}$, [*to* [realize it]$_{VP}$]$_{IP}$ …
[5] It lacks the full 'mobility' of finite verbs and concomitantly the full V2-property of Germanic languages, and, in addition, it lacks suitable expletives for subjectless constructions, as, for instance, in the passive construction with intransitives. As for inflection morphology, it is the only language of Germanic origin that does not have infinitival inflection.

see Trips (2001)), are strict VO languages, in the sense that phrasal heads are head-initial without exceptions.

The West Germanic languages (Afrikaans, Dutch, Frisian, German, Letzeburgish, Swiss German and all other more local varieties) are languages with an OV sentence structure. In other words, the position of the *verbal* head is head-final. In the surface order, this property of the clause structure is partially masked by the pan-Germanic V2-property or by extraposition.[6] Each of these structural properties (OV vs. VO) triggers a cascade of syntactic consequences that constitutes the respective set of VO vs. OV characteristics (see Appendix 5.1 of this chapter).

The truly enigmatic quality of the present-day situation becomes evident once we address the potential grammatical causality of the split. It is obvious that the rise of VO (or OV, if the opposite perspective is entertained) cannot be the result of morphological decay or conservation, and in particular, the loss or conservation of case morphology in some languages. The reason is simple: first, there is no correlation between morphological decay on the one hand and VO order in the Germanic languages, and second, there is no correlation between the OV order and the diachronic conservation of a morphological case system. In each of the two groups, there are languages without a morphological case system just as well as languages with a rich inventory of morphological case markings.

It is true that the continental North Germanic languages lack case morphology, just like English. But this cannot be the trigger of the diachronic development. Icelandic and Faroese are strict VO languages, too, but their case system is even more differentiated and morphologically more explicit than in German. On the other hand, there are Germanic OV languages that have lost their case morphology (e.g. Afrikaans, Dutch), but not their OV properties. In sum, the OV/VO characteristics do not correlate with the deficit or surplus of grammatical morphology. With this in mind, the split of the Germanic language family obviously cannot be regarded as the effect of a drift geared by compensation for the loss of morphological (case) distinctions.[7]

---

[6] Clauses and PPs may be *extraposed*, that is, they may follow the clause-final verb position, but argumental NPs must not. Cross-categorially, the *Germanic OV languages* are languages with mixed headedness: VP and AP are head-final, but NP and PP and the functional heads are head-initial. Since a VP (or an AP in a copula construction) is the core phrase of a clause, the head-final property of the VP (or the AP) is the source of the OV properties of the clauses. The functional heads are head-initial (contrary to widely held beliefs; see Haider 2010a: ch.2).

[7] This fact does not exclude the nevertheless hard-to-prove possibility of a positive influence of the *decay* of the inflection system and the rise of *strict* word order. Strict word order is a by-product

We are left with a puzzle: the modern Germanic languages are syntactically clearly partitioned into VO and OV; the predecessor languages are arguably not, as far as we know, and among the experts of Indo-European studies it is uncontroversial that the development must have started within a single (proto-) dialect.

What was the situation before the split and how did the split come into being? The empirical side is sufficiently well investigated to the extent that it is safe to maintain that the predecessor languages (Old English, Old High German, Old Icelandic, etc.) are neither strict VO languages nor OV languages of the form we meet in the modern Germanic languages.

In principle, and disregarding the diachronic testimonies for the moment, the following three different scenarios are conceivable: the proto-language could have been (i), (ii) or (iii).

(i) SOV, with a split towards SVO
(innovation in the North Germanic dialects?)
(ii) SVO, with a split towards SOV
(innovation in the West Germanic dialects?)
(iii) 'XVX', with a split into OV and VO
(OV/VO as pan-Germanic innovation?)

In the *conservative-innovative* scenario, one of the two present-day groups would be the offspring of an innovative dialect, with the other group containing the descendants of the conservative dialect. This corresponds to the scenarios (i) or (ii). However, scenarios (i) and (ii) are very likely to be inadequate. First, as the corpora tell us, the attested languages are neither clearly SOV nor SVO. 'Clearly SOV' would entail that nominal arguments always precede the VP-final position of the verb, like in Dutch or German. This is not the case. 'Clearly SVO' would be the correct description only if the verb always precedes its objects, and if a dependent verb always follows the (auxiliary) verb it depends on. This is not the case either.

The third possibility, and this is the possibility defended in this chapter, is the possibility that the clause structure of the language(s) before the split was neither truly OV nor VO. What this entails for the theoretic side is that 'OV' and 'VO' do not partition languages into complementary sets. There must be at least a *third* option in general, and for the proto-language in particular.

The third option is this: word-order properties of a given language may appear like a blend of OV and VO properties. This impression is the effect

of head-initial structure. Kiparsky (1996) claims a direct correlation between the loss of morphology and the grammaticalization of head-initial phrase structure.

of a 'third-type' property, namely the option of an *underspecified* or *flexible* directionality property for verbal heads. In this case, the diachronic split is not a split segregating an innovative dialect from a conservative one; it is a split as the result of a syntactic change from underspecified/flexible to specified/rigid directionality. Rigid directionality inevitably produces either OV or VO. Both settings are innovative ones. There is no conservative continuation of a dialect with the pre-change setting (except for Yiddish).

The change from the flexible to the rigid setting of the directionality property of lexical heads involves a 'free' choice, much like tossing a coin. There are two ways of setting a rigid directionality value, namely as head-initial or head-final. Since there are two options offered by the grammar system, it should not come as a surprise that we see the rise of *two* (groups of) proto-dialects, each one implementing one of the two possible settings.

What the available text corpora show is the following: the Old Germanic languages were languages with a clause structure that was neither the clause structure of the presently attested Germanic VO type nor of the presently attested Germanic OV type. The old languages share syntactic properties that are found neither in the Germanic OV type nor in the VO type. They belong to a *third* type. This type is a hitherto unnoticed and unacknowledged member of the family that the other two types belong to. Here is the whole family:

(1)   a. directional identification '→': $[V^{\circ \rightarrow} \text{ XP YP}]$ VO
         b. directional identification '←': $[\text{... XP ...YP... } {^\leftarrow}V^{\circ}]$ OV
         c. un(der)specified identification: $[\text{... XP... } {^{(\leftarrow)}}V^{\circ(\rightarrow)} \text{ YP ...}]$ 'third' type

The set of three types in (1) is the result of the parametric differentiation of the directionality of licensing. Anterograde directionality produces VO (1a), retrograde directionality yields OV (1b). But, if the directionality value is *un(der)specified*, a combination of (1a,b) and (1c) becomes an option, too. Among its admissible surface orders, the third type comprises the patterns of (1a) and (1b), *plus* the pattern given under (1c), within the very same language. In other words, it looks as if a language of the third type simultaneously has properties of OV and of VO. But, and this is crucial, it also has a third word-order property that occurs neither in OV nor in VO, and it is this property that betrays this subtype. This is the order in (1c): the verb may be flanked by its nominal objects, with the objects in their *base* positions.

Thus, if it turns out to be true that the Germanic predecessor language was indeed of the third type, a change from underspecified towards *specified* directionality is a change with a forced choice. The third type changes either into (1a) or into (1b). Each type conserves a (complementary) subset of the surface orders, but, in addition, each type loses one special order variant, namely the X – V – X order (1c).

In this chapter, it will be argued that the split is indeed a split triggered by a change from un(der)specified directionality to specified directionality. This change produced (1a) and (1b) as the only possible, but alternative, continuations. Since each option is equally available, it is expected that each option has found its diachronic implementation and continuation. The equal availability was greatly enhanced and stimulated by the parallel development of the V2-property. This contributed to initiating the change and to masking the ongoing dialect split. Otherwise, the change would not have produced a heterogeneous language family.

Note that the set of basic syntactic differences between the two groups of modern Germanic languages is not an accidental set of syntactic properties. It is precisely the set of properties that is triggered by the converse setting of the directionality parameter, namely the characteristic properties of a head-final or a head-initial phrase structure (see Appendix 5.1 of this chapter).[8] The diachronic change from one type of phrase structuring (viz. the third type) to the respective other types was able to spread gradually since the third type produces a set of word-order patterns that could be easily partitioned into several subsets, each consistent and compatible with the parametric setting of the two different new grammar variants.

This is the situation as described by Andersen (1973) in terms of 'grammar' and 'via-rules': those variants that are not compatible with the individual's innovative grammar (in the course of language acquisition) are handled with correspondence rules that relate dialectal variants in the speech of others to one's own variant. This is a patch-up procedure for receptive use. In production, these patterns are avoided and thus not passed on in language acquisition.

Therefore, under the above auspices, it will be argued that the most plausible scenario is (iii): OV and VO Germanic languages should be regarded as 'entangled'[9] partners that are the result of a syntactic change that started with a language that was neither OV nor VO. Hence, what we need is a model language

---

[8] Examples for the accumulation of diverse changes are easy to list, as, for instance, in Romance languages. They are all VO, but with much cross-linguistic difference: most of them are pro-drop, but French is not. All of them are cliticizing, but only some of them admit clitic-doubling. All have infinitival morphology, but only Portuguese has agreement on the infinitival verb.

[9] This term is borrowed from physics (*entangled pairs*). In the present context, 'entangled partners' means that there are two grammar variants that result from a basic grammar variant, if there is a single (unspecified) parameter that, if fixed, admits only a single binary valuation. The alternative valuation of this parameter produces two complementary systems that differ only in the choice of one of the binary values of the parameter.

of the third type. Fortunately, this model language exists within the family of Germanic languages. It is Yiddish. This language, in its geolinguistic isolation among the Slavic languages, conserved the crucial syntactic trait of un(der)-specified directionality for a single language of Germanic origin.[10]

Apparently, the adstrate effect of third-type languages (Slavic) was necessary for conserving the third-type property in Yiddish. This points to a crucial connection between the change from the third type and the rise of the rigid V2-property. The role of V2 shows in the comparison with another Indo-European language family that developed out of a 'type-three' (T3) antecedent language. Latin was a language of the third type,[11] but all successor languages are rigid VO languages. Why is there no OV language among the Romance languages? Is this merely accidental? It is arguably not accidental since V2 turns out to be crucial for making OV accessible on a par with VO as the continuation of a type-three language that changes from flexible to fixed headedness.

The rise of V2 seems to have been a trigger for the change towards fixed directionality (i.e. the rise of VO and OV). When V2 got grammaticalized, the fronted finite verb had to be related to its base position. But in a T3 language, there are always several alternative positions for the verb in the VP. So, the identification of the base position of the V2-fronted verb had to cope with systematic structural ambiguities. Fixing the verb's directionality meant fixing the verb's VP base position and thereby removing the source of these ambiguities. In addition, V2 made sentences with a single verb string-identical both in the VO as well as in the OV setting. So, V2 opened a channel for the diachronic bifurcation of T3 changing into an OV and a VO dialect. V2 made the OV and the VO dialect indistinguishable for all sentences that contained only a single verb. This conjecture is supported by the fact that the change from Latin (a T3 language) to the Romance languages yielded VO languages only. There was no accessible way leading to OV.

---

[10] In fact, the West Slavic adstrate languages may have provided the type-conserving environment since these languages arguably belong to the third type, too. (Haider and Szucsich, forthcoming)

[11] (i)   OV: Caesar singulis legionibus singulos legatos et quaestorem *praefecit*
               [Caesar, Bell. Gall. 1,52]
   (ii) OVO: virtus [...] hominem *iungit* deo   [Cicero Acad. 2,139]
   (iii) VO: Nimirum *dabit* haec Thais mihi magnum malum   [Terentius Eun. 508 (3,3,2)].

Thanks to my colleague, and near-native speaker of Latin, Thomas Lindner, for providing the data for me. He informs me that (iii) is the least frequent pattern in classical Latin texts. Note that Terentius is a comedy writer who stages colloquial usages of Latin ('vulgar Latin').

5.2 Yiddish – a syntactic time capsule

Yiddish has not been filed and classified in either list of Germanic languages in the second and third paragraphs of this chapter although it is a continuation of a Middle High German dialect (whose lexicon has been enriched by Hebrew and Slavic import). The reason for this intentional neglect is easy to justify. Its classification in terms of OV and VO is controversial, and the controversy is unavoidable, since there is no straight solution. Yiddish is neither clearly OV nor clearly VO. The empirical basis of this controversy is at the same time the kind of independent evidence we are looking for. It is a lucky accident in the history of Germanic languages that this language still exists. It is the 'missing link' between the old Germanic languages and their 'middle' successors and the present-day languages. The syntactic factor that complicates the answer to the simple question – 'What word-order type is Yiddish, OV or VO?' – is the crucial factor at the core of the third type.

The innocent question is difficult just because it is ill posed. It is ill-posed because it presupposes that Yiddish is either OV or VO. Any answer that accepts this presupposition will necessarily become controversial, simply because the serialization properties of Yiddish do not fully match the order patterns of either English (as representative of VO) or German (as representative of Germanic OV). These circumstances have stimulated controversial claims that file Yiddish either as a strange VO language or as a strange OV language. In any case, it is assumed to be OV plus something else or VO plus something else. For Diesing (1997), it is VO with atypical movement of phrases to the left (*strange scrambling*), and for Geilfuß (1991), it is OV with atypical movement of nominal phrases to the right (*strange extraposition*). Here is an example for the word-order variation that led to the ambivalent categorizations. The three order variants in (2) are alternative, possible orders:

(2) a. [X Y V°]$_{VP}$ David hot [Rifken dos buch *gegebn*]
         David has Rifken the book given
     b. [V° X Y]$_{VP}$ David hot [*gegebn* Rifken dos buch]
         David has given Rifken the book
     c. [X V° Y]$_{VP}$ David hot [Rifken *gegebn* dos buch]
         David has Rifken given the book

The order in (2a) is – word by word – a perfect German order. (2b), as the gloss shows, yields a perfect English order, if you replace the lexemes by English ones. (2c), however, is ungrammatical both in English and in German. This is the order with the verb flanked by its objects, which is the signature order of the third type.

It is telling that the controversial claims share a core assumption, namely the assumption that the verb position is stable and that the non-verbal items are moved in order to arrive at the respective serialization variants. Diesing (1997) regards (2b) as the base order in the VP. Therefore (2c) and (2a) must be derived versions. The derivation involves a process of fronting of the object(s), which would be atypical for a VO language. In the OV approach (Geilfuß 1991), (2a) is taken to be the base order. The other variants are the result of atypical postponing of the nominal object(s).

Unfortunately, these ancillary processes are atypical in comparison with the properties of these movement operations in other (Germanic) languages. There is no independent evidence from unquestionable specimens of each of the two types (viz. OV and VO) that shows that these processes may exist at all in the given language type. There is no Germanic VO language that allows scrambling (viz. fronting of objects across the verb and across each other), and there is no Germanic OV language that admits the extraposition of nominal objects, except for 'heavy NP-shift'. The postverbal objects in Yiddish cannot be an instance of this kind of shift to the right of the verb in the clause-final position.

Vikner (2001) has argued in great detail that Yiddish shares the typical properties of Germanic OV languages and that it differs sufficiently from the properties of Germanic VO languages. The only blind spot in this picture is the word-order variation illustrated in (2). It simply does not fit (details in Haider 2005, §2.3).[12]

Once more: 'Who is right, the OV proponents or the VO proponents of Yiddish?' is an ill-posed question. Neither is right. Yiddish is neither VO nor OV; it is of the third type. The relation between the three order variants in (2) is not one in terms of movement of the objects or other VP-internal material. The solution is the insight that it is a property of the verb that is at stake. The verb may end up in different positions. Since the directionality is unspecified, it can be implemented freely, and this opens several possibilities of structure building.

(2a) is the result of the head-final option (viz. retrograde directionality), (2b) results from the head-initial option (viz. anterograde directionality), and (2c) combines both options, as illustrated in (3) :

---

[12] The OV properties discussed in Vikner (2001) comprise: order of verbs and auxiliaries; variation in the order of auxiliaries, particle–verb order; (lack of) agreement between an adjectival predicate and its subject. For a summary, see Haider and Rosengren (1998: §5.5), or Haider and Rosengren (2003: §6).

(3)   [X ⃖[V° ⃗Y]ᵥ']ᵥₚ   David hot [Rifken *gegebn* dos buch]
                            David has Rifken given the book

On the V' level in (3), the directionality is anterograde, and from there on it switches into the retrograde mode. It is this very switch in the directionality valuation that is responsible for the flanked position of the verb. In other words, the VP in (3) starts out like an English VP at the bottom and turns into a German-style VP at the next layer. Once more: the third type combines the directionality properties of VO and OV with a third order, namely (3), as natural options.

By historical accident, Yiddish has become a singularity among the modern languages of Germanic descent, but it is by no means a singular case cross-linguistically.[13] In the following section, the three types are briefly reconstructed in grammar-theoretic terms in order to demonstrate that the third type is a natural sibling of the two other types (viz. OV and VO).

5.3   OV, VO and the third kind

This section is but a sketch of the asymmetry theory, whose original version, as published in Haider (1992/2000), is laid out in Chapters 1 and 3 of this book.[14] A non-technical description of its present shape and impact plus additional empirical details can be found in Chapter 1 of Haider (2010a). Here is the gist of the matter. The following axioms determine the structural architecture of phrases.

The specific axioms of the asymmetry theory are A2 and A4. A1 is an axiom shared within many structuralist approaches to phrase structure, especially within Generative Grammar, and A3 has been under discussion since the advent of the Principles and Parameters Model of Chomsky, thirty years ago.

A1: Phrases are *binary* branching and *endocentric*[15]
A2: Phrases are layered to the *left* (i.e. *right-associative*): [X [Y [(...) h° (...)]]]   (BBC)

---

[13] Although this matter has not been investigated yet, there are quite a few candidates for the 'third type'. These are languages with 'free' word order for nominal arguments and variable verb positions. A prime candidate is the Slavic language family (see Chapter 3, §3.5). Hungarian seems to be a good candidate as well (T3 VP plus a functional roof: *topic* and *focus* as projections of functional heads).

[14] This section is repetitive if you have read Chapters 1 and 3. It is included since it is part of the paper the chapter is based on. For diachronically minded readers who start with this chapter, it provides the immediate theoretical background for the argumentation.

[15] Endocentricity means that a phrase contains a head position at its foot position. The head determines the category of the phrase and introduces lexically determined constraints like a specified argument grid.

A3: Phrasal heads are parametrically specifiable for a *canonical licensing directionality*

A4: The arguments of the head must be *properly* identified (PDI)
An argument A is properly identified by the head of phrase h°, iff
   a. A and h° (or an extension of h°, that is, a projection or a chain link of h°) *minimally mutually c-command each other*, and
   b. the position of A in the phrase of h° is in the canonical *domain* of h°.[16]

This set of axioms produces (most of) the corollaries that characterize the OV and the VO types, and the third type as well. Here are some core properties: a complex, head-initial VP has a *shell structure*; a complex head-final VP does not. A head-initial VP is *compact*; a head-final one is not. A head-initial VP requires a *functional licenser* for the subject (in the SVO type); a head-final VP does not. This is the grammatical source of the structural subject position in SVO and its absence in SOV. These properties are corollaries of A4 in structures constrained by A2. Let me illustrate these properties briefly.

In an OV setting such as German, the canonical licensing directionality is congruent with A2, namely 'to the left'. So, the structure of a head-final phrase like the VP is trivial. It is the direct result of binary layering, as illustrated in (4).

(4)   a. [etwas verzeihen]$_{VP}$
          something forgive
       b. [jemandem [etwas verzeihen]]$_{VP}$
          someone something forgive
       c. [*subject* [jemandem [etwas verzeihen]]]$_{VP}$
       d. [dass [jeder [jemandem [etwas verzeiht]]]$_{VP}$]
          that everyone someone something forgives

A4 is fulfilled in the following way: each argument minimally c-commands an extension of the head (namely its sister V'-node), and is minimally c-commanded by this extended head node in the canonical directionality. So, minimal, mutual c-command under canonical directionality is guaranteed.

The structural make-up for head-initial phrases is equally straightforward, but its resulting structure is more complex. The source of the apparent complication is the *converse* directionality requirements of layering (to the left) and the canonical directionality of the lexical heads (to the right). Here is the solution of the complication. At the bottom of the phrase (5a), things are simple. The next step (5b) introduces the complication. The second argument must be merged on

---

[16] The canonical domain for h° or a projection of h° is the c-command domain of h° or a projection of h° in the *specified canonical* direction.

The Germanic OV/VO split   107

the left, according to A2. However, this position is not in the canonical licensing domain since the head (and its extensions) licenses to the right. So, the head must be re-instantiated in the required position (5c). This is the point where the shell structure comes into being. There is only a single head verb. So, its surface position is co-indexed with its empty base position. The result is a relation that is non-distinct from a head-chain, that is, a chain as the result of V-movement.

(5)   a. [forgive something]
       b. [someone [forgive something]]
       c. [forgive [someone [forgive something]]]
       d. [*subject* [forgive [someone [forgive something]]]]
       e. [that [everybody [forgives [someone [forgive something]]]]]

Finally, the remaining argument phrase, viz. the subject, gets merged (5d). This is the point where VO languages diverge into SVO and VSO. In VSO, the verb is instantiated once more before the subject argument, in a second VP-shell. As a result, all arguments of the verb end up within the directional domain of the (fronted) verb. In SVO, on the other hand, the VP-internal subject is local to the verb, but not in its directionality domain. Directional licensing is 'delegated' to a functional head that selects the VP. The spec position of this functional head accommodates the raised subject. In other words, SVO employs a functional projection for licensing the subject, while VSO employs a second VP-shell.

Compactness is the result of A4 in VO. In (5c), 'forgive' minimally and canonically c-commands 'someone', and 'someone' minimally and canonically c-commands a chain link of 'forgive'. So, mutual minimal c-command in the canonical directionality is fulfilled. What would happen if an adverbial got squeezed in, either between 'forgive' and the object, or between the objects? The result would be ungrammatical, because the intervener disrupts the *minimal* c-command relation. This is the compactness property of a head-initial VP. Compactness is absent in OV, simply because minimal c-command always holds between the given phrase and its sister V-projection node on the right. Compactness is a consequence of the mismatch between A2 and the canonical directionality in VO. There is no mismatch in OV.

Compactness shows in the adjacency property of the verb and its object (6a), and in the adjacency of the objects (6b), and it shows in the absence of word-order variation (scrambling) as in (6c).

(6)   a. *[hug *gently* Mary]
       b. *[tell Mary *often* jokes]
       c. *[buy *the drink*$_{(i)}$ a friend (e_i)] – [buy a friend the drink]

d. [Maria *sanft* umarmen]
Mary gently hug
e. [Maria *oft* Witze erzählen]
Mary often jokes tells
f. [*den Drink* einem Freund bezahlen] – [*einem Freund* den Drink bezahlen]
the drink_ACC a friend_DAT buy   a friend the drink buy

Immediate and supporting evidence for the intermediate, empty verb position as in (5c) comes from particle constructions. English (like Norwegian or Icelandic) is a language with optional particle stranding. The stranded position must be a position on the chain of the re-instantiated verb since the particle is part of a complex lexeme consisting of the particle and the verb. The sentences (7a,b) illustrate this stranding position between the two objects.

(7) a. Valerie [packed_i [her daughter [e_i-*up* a lunch]]] Dehé (2002: 3)
     b. Valerie [poured_i [the man [e_i-*out* a drink]]]
     c. *Valerie [packed_i [her daughter [e_i *right up* a lunch]]]
     d. *Valerie [poured_i [the man [e_i *right out* a drink]]]

Particles of particle verbs are the only licit interveners between the objects in a double-object construction and this is so because they belong to the verb position. On the other hand, if a particle is modified, then it is a separate head unit and excluded from the verbal head position, as in (7c,d). Verbal particles are companions of the verb and therefore always adjacent to a verb position. If they are in a position distant from the verb, then they must have been stranded. In German and in Dutch, the position for a stranded particle is clause-final, and clause-final only.

(8) Susanne goss_i dem Mann ein Getränk *ein*-e_i
     Susanne poured the man a drink in

English and other VO languages that admit optional particle stranding (as e.g. Norwegian and Icelandic) display this sandwiched particle position. This very position between the two objects is an indicator of a verb position and for that reason it is independent evidence for the verb position entailed by the VP-shell analysis. Another piece of independent evidence is the simple fact that in an OV language, a verbal particle never appears between two objects.

(9) *Sie hat dem Mann *aus* ein Buch gehändigt
     she has the man out a book handed

Particles are not moved into positions distant from the verb. They are stranded. If a particle is not V-adjacent, the verb has moved and stranded the particle.

Finally, the subject is merged (5d). This is the characteristic property of an SVO language, in contrast to a VSO language. In VSO, the verb would be re-instantiated once more in order to have all the arguments in the canonical directionality domain. In an SVO language, the subject argument is merged VP-internally, but it is not in the canonical domain since it precedes the verb. Canonical licensing is delegated to a functional head, and the argument is raised to its spec position. This is the grammatical reason for the obligatory functional subject position in SVO clause structure.[17]

(10)   a. English$_i$ (has)$_{I°}$→ [e$_i$ [found its own way]]$_{VP}$
          b. [$_{IP}$ Susan$_j$ [$_I$° has → [$_{VP}$ e$_j$ [poured$_i$→ [the man [[e$_i$-*out*]→ a drink]]]]]
          c. let → [$_{VP}$ Susan [pour$_i$ [the man [e$_i$-*out* a drink]]]]

In (10a), the functional head, whether lexicalized or not, provides the canonical licensing for the VP-internal, preverbal subject position, and its spec position accommodates the surface subject. (10b) is an example with the pertinent details, both for the shell structure as well as for the surface positions of the subject and the verbs. (10c) illustrates the limited case of a (semi-lexical) verb selecting a VP. The causative verb provides the directional licensing (and the case) for the subject of the infinitival verb.

An immediate consequence of the need of functional licensing in SVO is the need of subject expletives. The functional projection is obligatory. It is the obligatory grammatical device for directional licensing. Spec–head agreement provides the identification of the subject argument. The EPP property (see fn. 17), in whatever grammatical construal, is satisfied by raising the subject. If there is no subject argument to be raised, the spec position is lexicalized by means of an expletive. This is true for VO languages, but it is not true for OV languages. German, for instance, does not admit an expletive in subjectless passive clauses (11b) while an expletive is mandatory in Scandinavian languages (11a). Similarly, an expletive is ungrammatical in German presentative constructions (11d), but obligatory in the Scandinavian counterparts (11c).

(11)   a. að */?(*Það*) hefur verið dansað   Icelandic
          that (expl) has been danced
          b. dass (*es) getanzt wurde   German
          that (it/there) danced was
          c. Í dag er *(*Það*) komin ein drongur   Faroese
          today is (expl) arrived a boy

---

[17] In the Chomskyan framework, this SVO property is elevated to the status of a universal property of clause structures, namely the EPP (= Extended Projection Principle = every clause has a subject (in a functional subject position)$_{HH}$).

d. Heute ist (*es) ein Junge gekommen   German
today is (expl) a boy arrived

Let us summarize: head-initial and head-final phrases differ in terms of the principles that determine their structural architecture *only* in the choice of the value for the canonical directionality. The systematic differences between head-initial and head-final structures are consequences of the interaction between the directionality valuation and the directionality-sensitive aspects of the universal axioms of structure building (A2, A3 and A4).

It is this interaction that produces the set of epiphenomenal differences between OV and VO. Complex head-initial structures are compact and require a shell structure.[18] Complex OV structures are neither compact nor would they require a shell structure. Moreover, the SVO architecture entails that the VP is the complement of a functional head that provides the directional licence for the VP-initial, VP-internal subject position. The functional spec position is the obligatory functional subject position in SVO languages.

As a summary of the brief exposition, (12) illustrates the deployment of arguments in a complex VP structure and their directional licensing relation. For the sake of a simple exposition, (12) just depicts the lower part of a VP. The subject argument is discharged in the triangled root part. The lexical argument variables are given in angle brackets. Cancelled letters denote already discharged arguments.

(12)   a. head-initial VP: b. head-final VP:

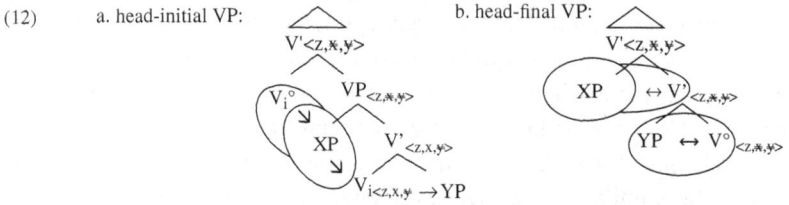

In (12a), the minimal, mutual c-command requirement under canonical directionality cannot be implemented as a sisterhood relation between the argument phrase and the extended verbal projection node (like in (12b)). Instead, it is implemented as a chain relation. This is so because of the mismatch between the canonical directionality and the universal directionality of merger. This very chain relation is the source of compactness. An adverb (13a), as well as a scrambled object (13b), would disrupt the *minimal* c-command relation. The

---

[18] The shell structure is by no means a peculiarity of complex, head-initial VPs. Complex, head-initial NPs have a shell structure, too, as shown already in Haider (1992/2000); see Chapter 2.

verb in (13a) would minimally c-command the adverb, but not the object. A scrambled object would produce the very same intervener effect.

(13) a. He showed (*voluntarily) the students (*secretly) the solution
 b. *He [showed$_j$ [the solution$_i$ [e$_j$ the students [e$_j$ e$_i$]]]]

This minimality-driven compactness property never shows in head-final VPs. In this case there is always a sister node as extended verbal head in the required directional licensing position, viz. following the licensee.

(14) a. Er hat [den Studenten [*freiwillig* [die Lösungen gezeigt]]]
 he has the students voluntarily the solutions shown
 b. Er hat [den Studenten [die Lösungen [*freiwillig* gezeigt]]]
 he has the students the solutions voluntarily shown
 c. Er hat [die Lösungen$_i$ [den Studenten [e$_i$ [*freiwillig* gezeigt]]]]
 he has the solutions the students voluntarily shown

How does Yiddish fit into this overall picture? Yiddish is representative of the third type. In this case, there is no *predetermined canonical* directionality. At each application, the directionality can be implemented in either of the two ways. Therefore, a VP may end up as head-final (15a), or as head-initial (15b), or in a *third manner* (15c).

(15) a. Max hot [Rifken [dos buch *gegebn*]]$_{VP}$
 Max has Rebecca the book given
 b. Max hot [*gegebn*$_i$ Rifken [e$_i$ dos buch]]$_{VP}$
 c. Max hot [Rifken [*gegebn* dos buch]]$_{VP}$

In the third manner, the verb combines with a direct object on its right (as in English), and then the construction proceeds like in a German VP, with the second argument merged on the left. The result is the position of the verb flanked by the two objects, which is the signature order of the third type. The three order variants admitted by a grammar of the third type contain the typical OV orders and the typical VO orders as subsets. It is this fact that explains why some researchers may regard one of these subsets as a base order. But, crucially, in a setting with a fixed directionality value, the flanked order would be ungrammatical. So, whatever subset is taken to be basic, the overall picture is invariably that of a strange specimen for the suspected type.

Here is the key to understanding the puzzle of the OV/VO split: the old Germanic languages are languages of the *third type*. The split is the direct result of a grammar change from *flexible/underspecified* directionality into *specified* directionality. 'Specified' means the choice of one of the binary values (either ← or →). The dialect split is the immediate consequence of the alternative implementation of the two complementary values. One valuation produces OV orders; the other value produces strict VO orders. The grammar change was apparently triggered or sustained by the nearly intractable verb-order variations fed by the mobility of the finite verb in Germanic languages (V2-property) and the concomitant VP-internal variations of the third type.

5.4 Old Germanic languages are of Type III

This subsection samples examples for the 'flanked' variant (i.e. OVO), which is characteristic of the third type, from Germanic languages. This serialization pattern is frequently attested in each of the older Germanic languages. Here are representative examples from Old English, Old High German and older Icelandic for the sake of illustration:

The following *Old English* data are quoted from Fischer *et al.* (2000: 51).

(16)   a. Se mæssepreost *sceal* [mannum [*bodian* þone soþan geleafan]]$_{VP}$
        the priest *must* [people [*preach* the true faith]] (*Ælet* 2 (Wulfstan1) 175)
    b. þæt hi [urum godum [*geoffrian magon* ðancwurðe onsægednysse]]
        that they our god *offer may* thankful offering (ÆCHom I, 38.592.31)
    c. Ac he sceal [þa sacfullan *gesibbian*]
        but he *must* the contenders *reconcile*   (*Ælet* 2 (Wulfstan1)188.256)
    d. Se *wolde* [*gelytlian* þone lyfigendan hælend]
        he *wanted humiliate* the living saviour   (*Ælet* 2 (Wulfstan1) 55.98)

(16a) and (16b) illustrate the flanked position of the verbs. The indirect object precedes, the direct object follows. (16c) and (16d) illustrate the head-final and the head-initial options, respectively. (16) represents the set of serialization variations for the non-finite verb in a grammar of the third type.

According to Fischer *et al.* (2000: 172), the development in the direction of a rigid VO organization took quite some time. It is still observable in the texts from the thirteenth to the fifteenth centuries. They point out that it is 'only after about 1300 that clauses with VO order begin to vastly outnumber those with OV order'.[19]

A reliable co-variant is the variation in the particle position. In VO, particles are postverbal, in OV, particles are preverbal. In the third type, both orders are licit, with preferences, though. The level of at least 85 per cent postverbal particles is not reached before the Middle English period. Pintzuk and Taylor (2006) present the following counts. The proportion of genuine OV orders (viz.

---

[19] They give, among others, the following late example of OV order, from Chaucer:
   (i) I may my persone and myn hous so *kepen* and *deffenden*
      'I can keep and defend myself and my house in such a way.'
                                               (Melibee 1334; Fischer *et al.* 2000: 163)

particle + verb) in clauses with a non-finite particle verb was 58.5% before 959 BC and gradually sank to 51.7% in texts of the period till 1150. Between 1150 and 1250, there was a rapid decline in the percentage, viz. to 29.7%. From 1350 onwards, the percentage had reached low enough a level, namely 4.3%, that it is safe to assume that the language had become a strict VO language.[20]

The examples from the *Old High German* text of *Notker* (see also Schallert 2006: 139, 172)[21] once more illustrate the three expected patterns of licit verb positioning, namely VP-final (17a), VP-initial (17b), and intermediate (17c,d):

(17) a. Úbe dû [dero érdo$_{DAT}$ [dînen sâmen$_{ACC}$ *beuúlehîst*]] (NB 47,4)
whether you [the earth [your seed give]]
b. áz sie [nîoman [*nenôti* des chóufes]] (NB 22,13)
that they [nobody NEG-urged the purchase$_{GEN}$
c. tánne sie [búrg-réht [*scûofen* demo líute]] (NB 64,13)
that they civil-right granted the people
d. Tisêr ûzero ordo […] mûoze [*duingen*$_i$ [mit sînero unuuendigi [e$_i$ [diu uuendigen ding]]]] (NB 217,20)
this external order must conquer with its infinity the finite things

Finally, specimens for each of the three positions are easy to find in *older Icelandic* texts as well (see Hróarsdóttir 2000). (18a) shows the verb in the intermediate position, (18b) has a head-final VP and in (18c) the verb is in the head-initial position of the VP.

(18) a. hafer Þu [Þinu lidi [*jatat* Þeim]]
have you [your help [promised them]]
b. Því eg get ekki [meiri liðsem [Þér *veitt*]]
there I can not [more help [you offer]]

---

[20] Example (ii) is from Ans van Kemenade and Geert Booij (originally presented at www.let.kun.nl/english/diachron.php. This site is presently not accessible.)

(ii) ær he *ut wolde faran* to gefeohte
before *he out wanted go* to fight ('before he wanted to go out to the fight') (*Or* 3.8.122.11)

Its interesting property is the stranded particle at the *beginning* of the cluster. This is a clear sign of cluster fronting. A verb would never strand a particle by moving to the right, unless in a cluster. This type of stranding can be observed in modern Dutch (Haider 2003):

(iii) dat hij het boek *op* had moeten hebben *geborgen*
that he the book up had must have saved
(iv) dat hij het boek *opgeborgen* had moeten hebben

In (iii) the cluster starts with a particle, whose verbal partner is on the right. In (iv) particle and verb are adjacent. In fact, there are other, cluster-internal positions too, for either stranding or joint appearance.

[21] In this Masters thesis, the diachronic situation of several old Germanic languages is scrutinized and successfully analyzed in terms of the 'third-type' hypothesis.

d. hefir hann [*ritað* sýslungum sínum bréf]
has he [written country-men his (a) letter]

Note that in (18a), the postverbal element is a pronoun. This cannot be a result of movement to the right since pronouns are fronted, not extraposed. So, (18a) and (18b) are minimal pairs, with pronouns immediately to the right or to the left of the verb.

In sum, the predicted properties of the third type show in texts of each of the diachronic predecessor languages of today's Germanic languages. The two main properties are the *variation* of the verb positions and the particular intermediate position of the verb: in each Germanic language, there has been variation in the positioning of the (non-finite) verbs. Arguments may precede, follow or occur on both sides simultaneously. It is the latter property that is the signature property of the third type.

5.5 A synoptic look at alternative accounts

An adequate account of diachronic syntactic change must take care of two issues at least. One is evidently the precise specification of what has changed in the grammar of a given language. The second and equally important issue is an adequate model of the change. It should provide a plausible and empirically testable answer for the following question at best: how does grammar theory gear the implementation of the change over time? This means that there must be a transition process from the old grammar setting to the new one and a period of co-existing variants in an interval of more than three generations of speakers.[22]

Languages do not change instantaneously, but grammars may. The change of grammar is not a change in the lifetime of an individual's mental grammar. It is a change that takes place when the grammar is acquired during language acquisition. A grammatical change has taken place whenever the grammar of a child (or the grammar acquired during second-language acquisition) differs from the grammar that generated the input. The grammar is hidden, the language is public (Chapter 2). Hence the true locus of change is analytically

---

[22] Generation 1 (G1) uses the 'old grammar'. A subset of Generation 2 fails to reproduce all aspects of the old grammar. All groups may employ 'via-rules' (see Andersen 1973). The innovative G2 uses the via-rules for processing those utterances produced by G1 and by the conservative G2 that are not admitted by the novel grammar of G2. Crucially, G2 speakers use via-rules only passively. So, G3, that is the offspring of the innovative G2 gets as input only G2-compatible expressions. As a consequence, the learners only embody the grammar of G2 in its steady setting. The drift towards the novel grammar gets momentum whenever the innovation proves to be 'advantageous'. What is advantageous is a property of the parser/generator-grammar interaction (see Chapter 2).

inaccessible (both for acquisition and for investigation). We can only infer it from a secondary source, viz. the linguistic expressions that are formed by speakers/writers having put to use the respective grammars.

English is one of the best-investigated human languages (if not *the* best-investigated one) and therefore a good candidate for reflections on the adequacy of various accounts that have been put forth. Each of the following three proposals, which will be discussed in passing, is representative of a particular strategy of explaining the particular changes in grammar that led from Old English (OE) to the SVO sentence organization in present-day English. A successful account of the diachrony of English has immediate implications for the understanding of the diachronic developments in other Germanic SVO languages. There are several options.

First, the observed variation may be the cumulative product of a bi-dialectal/bilingual situation. The idea of grammar competition has been proposed by Kroch (1994: 180): 'syntactic change proceeds via competition between grammatically incompatible options which substitute for one another in usage'. Pintzuk (1991, 2002) and Kroch and Taylor (2000) proposed an account along this line. Let me refer to it as the *competing-grammars model*. Pintzuk (1991, 2002), in particular, developed this idea into a specific claim: the speech community is assumed to have been 'bi-dialectal' = 'bilingual', and she assumes that OE had a 'double base': both the OV and the VO value of the relevant parameter were used, giving rise to two distinct grammars through the OE period. A change in this context is equivalent to the elimination of the competition between two incompatible but co-existing grammars by a dialectic synthesis.

A *second option* would be that the verb-order variation in OE may be a genuine grammatical one, if the grammar is taken to involve open parameters that allow VO and OV as *co-existing*, alternative settings. Let me call this the *(open-)parameter model*. To my (limited) knowledge, such a model has not been proposed explicitly. It would amount to Pintzuk's (1991, 1999) model with headedness variation in the VP and between VP and I°, implemented in a single grammar.

The *third possibility* is this: the variation could be the result of massive syntactic movements applied to otherwise regular (SVO) sentence structures. Let me call this the *excessive-movement model*.[23] This account is propagated by Roberts (1997) and Biberauer and Roberts (2005) in the framework of Kayne's (1994) theory, according to which human languages are SVO languages

---

[23] Actually, this is the opposite position to the by now classical model of van Kemenade (1987), who regarded OE as a regular (but not strict) OV language that has gradually changed into VO, with ample movement to the right during the time of transition.

universally. Under this hypothesis, a change towards SVO is the reduction of excessive movement in the course of which the 'regular' sentence structure that has been masked by the movement effects reappears.

The *competing-grammar hypothesis* takes the variation situation at face value and decomposes an apparently inconsistent set of patterns into two well-behaved subsets. For each of the sets there is a grammar (viz. one for SOV and one for SVO patterns), and the overall picture is characterized as the result of the co-existence of these two grammars (in the competence of the speakers). Some aspects of this strategy are problematic, though.

First of all, it does not offer a natural account for those patterns that are alien to each of the two grammars (in particular, the verb positions flanked by an object). Second, it amounts to the claim that speakers of the particular speech community must be regarded as *bilingual* in a very restricted sense. They have to be bilingual because the two alleged dialectal variants (OV, VO) are incompatible and cannot be subsumed under a single consistent grammar. But this is exactly the problem to be solved. The two grammars (viz. OV and VO grammar) are indeed incompatible since they embody the contrary setting of the directionality value. However, the alleged bi-dialectal variants appear within the texts of individual authors. So, an obvious question to ask is this: why should authors continuously switch and mix dialects in their writings? Wouldn't they primarily use their 'own' dialect variant and reserve the patterns of the other variant for communicating with speakers who prefer the 'other' variant? In the extreme case, the other dialect would be accessible only in a way characterized by Andersen (1973), namely, by via-rules.

The answer seems obvious. The writers did not mix anything, and they should not be accused of code switching. They merely used their native T3 grammar and the variation was an inherent property consistent with the grammar for this language.

For the competing-grammar hypothesis it seems to be difficult to provide a straightforward answer for the crucial question: why should the bilingual/bi-dialectal situation persist for centuries in a monolingual society? It is the persistence that poses the hard problem. Bi-dialectal differences are levelled in a speech community that is not forced into diglossia. Presently, the school system is a source of diglossia. Schooling enforces the standard variety as the L2 for dialect speakers. For OE and its development into Middle English (ME) it is difficult to claim that a diglossia situation was the source of the diverse verb patterns.[24]

---

[24] Lightfoot (1999) dubbed the competing-grammar hypothesis as a model with 'internalised diglossia'.

Finally, we have to zoom out for a moment and ask ourselves what the scenario that leads from OE via ME to modern English looks like in a comparative perspective. Where would the competing grammar situation of OE come from? Was it a 'VO virus' from French and Scandinavian language contacts that infected OE? The answer is most likely 'No', because *every* Germanic language of this time (Old High German till Middle High German, Old Icelandic till later stages, Middle Dutch, Old French, and so on) shares these properties.[25] It seems that independent of the theoretical merits of the grammar competition hypothesis, the grammar of OE and ME is not its best showcase.

The complex picture of word order in OE on its way to ME becomes much clearer once one contemplates the possibility of the *third type*. In such a language, apparent OV and VO patterns inevitably co-exist and, in addition, there is a pattern that occurs only in this type, namely the pattern with the intermediate position, that is, with the non-finite verb in between its objects. All these patterns are genuine patterns of this type and the divergence from either OV or VO is predicted and not exceptional at all.

The explanation for the diachronic development becomes simpler as well: the apparent bi-dialectal situation is but a mono-dialectal situation. The change from the third type to the VO type is a gradual one, like any internal change. In the Germanic languages, the changes are arguably invited as measures of simplification. The verb-order variability characteristic of the third type in combination with the rise of the V2-property produces a complex and structurally ambiguous set of distribution conditions for the verb.[26] The change from flexible to rigid headedness is a change that reduces the degrees of freedom in the grammar of order variation for the verbs. Concomitantly, parsing gets less complicated, but the change does not impede the syntactic power of the system.[27] Of course, this 'simplification' is the effect of filtering the input during language acquisition. The variation set was big enough so that there was

---

[25] Two properties are characteristic. One is the word-order 'variation' between the verb and its objects, namely {O – O – V, O – V – O, V – O – O}. The second property is the order between verb and auxiliary {O – V – Aux, O – Aux – V, Aux – V – O, *V – Aux – O*}. O – V – O (see 17c,d) and V – Aux – O (see 16b) are ruled out in OV and in VO languages. They are only found in Type III languages. Grammar competition between OV and VO would not cover them.

[26] Van Kemenade (1987: 177) already emphasized that the (underlying) order of OE was 'not easily retrievable from surface patterns' owing to the interaction of free parameter valuation, verb second and verb clustering.

[27] English has overdone this, obviously. It is the only Germanic language that forbids the movement of the lexical main verb. Thus, English lost (or never fully gained) the V2-property and had to 'invent' an ersatz candidate for contexts that require verb movement (viz. in main clause interrogatives): it is the only Germanic language that needs an expletive tense auxiliary (i.e. *do*-support).

a sufficiently large subset of the input that was compatible with a 'simpler' grammar, namely a grammar with a specified value for directionality instead of an un(der)specified one. Importantly, the tokens of this subset of patterns were still compatible with the old grammar. This is the basis for co-existence and for a steady development.

An account close to the spirit of the third-type hypothesis would be the *open-parameter* hypothesis. Here is a version of this hypothesis, which focuses on the directionality value of V° and I° (as in Pintzuk 1999). The attractive feature is this: V° and I° are freely valued for head-initial or head-final directionality. This produces four patterns:

(19)   a. O V Aux   I-final,   V-final
        b. Aux V O   I-initial,   V-initial
        c. Aux O V   I-initial,   V-final
        d. *V O Aux   I-final,   V-initial   (see Appendix 5.2)

But Kiparsky (1996) pointed out that the system potential provided by the combinatorics of the directionality feature for V° and I° (head-final, head-initial) as in (19) is too powerful. It predicts an unattested order (19d). This order is neither attested at any stage of English, nor in any other Germanic language. This option should show as a word-order pattern with non-finite verbs preceding the objects and the finite auxiliary verb following the objects.

It is not so much this systematic gap that seriously undermines the free valuation thesis, since there is an independent reason for the missing pattern, namely the BBC (see Appendix 5.2). Why is (19d) unattested? The straightforward answer is this: the VP would be a left branch in a functionally extended projection of the VP. This is exactly what is ruled out by the BBC (see Appendix 5.1 of this chapter and Haider 2010a: ch.7). Neither a head-initial nor a head-final VP may be merged with a head-*final* functional head. Functional projections targeted by head movement are universally head-*initial*.

The real problem for this approach is the pattern with the sandwiched V-position in between two objects. It follows from neither combination of possible directionality values for V° and I°. If extraposition is invoked this cannot be regarded as an acceptable source of this word order since argumental DPs are not extraposable in Germanic languages. It would merely be an ad hoc measure for covering the unexpected pattern.

In this context another issue needs to be raised: there are more ordering options than just those predicted by the free valuation for I° and V°, namely those in (20). And here comes the crucial point. All these variants of (19), that is, the free valuation variants, except (19d), and the additional variants (20), are found in Yiddish. With Yiddish as a model language, there is a source of independent, synchronic evidence provided by speakers (instead of corpora of extinct languages) for investigating the grammar of a third-type language. All we have to do is to show that the co-existing distribution patterns for verbs are also patterns attested in Yiddish.

Note that in VO languages, the serialization of verbs is strict; there is no variation in the order between main verbs, auxiliaries and semi-auxiliaries. The order is always (20c)

(20)   a. O V Aux   standard OV order (=19a)
        b. O Aux V   OV order as order variant in the verbal cluster
        c. *Aux V O*   VO order
        d. V Aux O   third-type order, with the verbs fronted as a cluster

Let us now briefly look at Yiddish. The following examples are listed in Vikner (2001: 66). Marked orders are indicated by '%'. The unmarked orders are those in which the *finite* verb *precedes* the indefinite object. (21f), by the way, would be the instantiation of (19d).

(21)   a. %az Jonas a hoyz koyfn vil   O V Aux
        b. az Jonas vil koyfn a hoyz   Aux V O
        c. az Jonas vil a hoyz koyfn   Aux O V
        d. %az Jonas a hoyz vil koyfn   O Aux V
        e. %az Jonas koyfn vil a hoyz   V Aux O
        f. *az Jonas koyfn a hoyz vil   *V O Aux

The marked orders in Yiddish are in fact marked or even ungrammatical orders in Germanic OV languages, but only in those Germanic OV languages that admit fully inverted base orders of the verbs in the verbal cluster, as in Dutch, in contrast with German. (22c) is an unmarked order, but the corresponding order in Dutch (22b) is ungrammatical.

(22)   a. dat Jan een huis zal (moeten) kopen   Dutch
        b. *dat Jan een huis kopen (moeten) zal   Dutch
        c. dass Jan ein Haus kaufen müssen wird   German
        d. *dass Jan ein Haus wird müssen kaufen   German

The Old English patterns for verb positions are closely parallel to the patterns found in Yiddish, and therefore they invite a parallel account (Haider and Rosengren 2003): like Yiddish, OE is a language with flexible directionality for $V°$. It admits OV patterns (in combination with verb clustering and cluster-internal order variation like in Dutch, which is inevitable for the OV setting), it provides VO patterns, like in any Germanic VO language, and – crucially – it shows the patterns of the 'third type', namely those triggered by the hybrid valuation of directionality.[28] The third-type structures combine VO and OV properties. Here is a *non-exhaustive* list of options:

(23)   a. $[V^{\circ} \rightarrow O]$ VO; T3
        b. $[O \leftarrow [V^{\circ} \rightarrow O]]$ T3
        c. $[S \leftarrow [O \leftarrow [V^{\circ} \rightarrow O]]]$ T3
        d. $[S \leftarrow [V_i^{\circ} \rightarrow [O [e_i O]]]]_{VP}$ T3
        e. $[S_j [V_i^{\circ} \rightarrow [e_j [e_i O]]]_{VP}]_{FP}$ VO

(23c) and (23d) start out as 'VO'. (23b) is the step with the switch to 'OV' and it continues like an OV structure, resulting in (23c). If the switch is implemented after the second step (23d), the result looks like a VO structure (23e), with an important difference, however. The subject stays in its VP-internal position and does not have to move to the functional spec position of the functional head that selects the VP. (23e) is the case of the genuine VO setting. It is exemplified by Icelandic.

If, in a third-type language, a VP is structured in the OV way, the collateral OV properties come into being, too. An important collateral property is the obligatory occurrence of verb clusters in place of centre-embedded VP complements. Since in OV languages with verb movement, the verbal clustering goes hand in hand with order variation, this is a second source of order variation in the languages of the third type.

In sum, there are three grammatical sources that feed the alternative position of verbs in a third-type Germanic language: first, there are the verb positions as a function of the directionality implementation (VP-final for the OV option, VP-intermediate for the switch option and VP-initial for the VO option). Second, if the head-final version is implemented for a given sentence, verb clustering is mandatory and this opens another source of variation. This is the order variation within the verb cluster.[29] Third, and finally, Germanic languages developed into V2 languages. This means that the finite verb gets

---

[28] Kroch and Taylor (2000) and Pintzuk and Taylor (2006) have demonstrated in detail that a solution in terms of *extraposition* (= movement to the right) or scrambling (= movement to the left) cannot be entirely correct. First, there are clearly non-extraposable items that nevertheless appear in *postverbal* positions, and, on the other hand, there are *preverbal* items that would not scramble (or have properties incompatible with movement). This is a predictable situation under the third-type hypothesis. Since it is the verb that 'moves', there are pre- and postverbal *base* positions for non-verbal items.

[29] Without any exception, all Germanic OV languages admit order variation in the verbal cluster, and, without any exception, no Germanic VO language admits order variation for the verbs and auxiliaries in the clause. The explanation is this (see Haider 2010a, ch.7): OV languages obligatorily cluster the verbs, and if the given language allows/requires moving the verb in any context, it will also have word-order variation in the cluster. Asiatic OV languages do not move verbs. Hence there is no variation in the verbal cluster in Japanese or Korean.

assigned to a unique, derived position in the clause. In sum, these three sources contribute to a complex set of conditions that determine the surface verb position. Eliminating one of these sources is a means of overall complexity reduction. Fixed headedness (as opposed to flexible headedness) eliminates many of the hard-to-trace, structurally ambiguous patterns.[30]

Let us briefly turn now to the *excessive-movement hypothesis* (Roberts 1997), based on Kayne's antisymmetry idea. In Kayne's (1994) view, human languages are basically SVO.[31] If the SVO patterns do not show at the surface, they are assumed to be masked by syntactic movement processes that operate on the SVO structure and distort it. With the 'universal-VO' axiom, it is obvious that present-day English must be the result of having lost all masking effects of its Old English OV appearance. Apparently, the diachronic changes eventually have successfully unveiled the genuine SVO structure.

This is not only a controversial view in general (see the final chapter on the alleged universality of VO), but is diachronically implausible, too. In the Indo-European language family, none of the predecessor languages is an SVO language. The crucial question is not why English has turned into SVO. The criterion of success for the universal SVO hypothesis is this question: what was it that turned the old Indo-European languages into non-SVO languages? Needless to emphasize that we lack any evidence that an Indo-European language has ever changed from a strict SVO language into a non-SVO language. This has been emphasized already by Kiparsky (1996), who points out that 'OV commonly changes to VO but the converse does not happen'. Why should non-SVO languages exist at all?

What we see is SVO as the result of a late development of at least two subfamilies (Germanic, Romance) of Indo-European languages. Roberts (1997)

---

[30] Here is an illustration of the indeterminacy of the antecedent–gap relations for the verbs in a Type III V2 language (i), and for a VO language with the V2-property (ii). The numbers are the number of potential alternative trace positions:

(i) V2+third-type potential (trace) positions of V_{FIN} (and a non-finite V):

XP V_{FIN} YP ZP	3
XP Aux_{FIN} V YP	3+2
XP Aux_{FIN} YP V	3
XP Aux_{FIN} YP V ZP	3+2

(ii) V2+fixed potential (trace) positions of V_{FIN} and V:

XP V_{FIN} YP ZP	1	(VO) or 1 (OV)
XP Aux_{FIN} V YP	1+1	(VO)
XP Aux_{FIN} YP V	1	(OV)
***		

In the rigid system (ii), the trace position is determined, in the Type III + V2 system there are several alternative positions.

[31] From the mediaeval time until the nineteenth century, the universal model language was Latin. Today it is English, or at least languages that are SVO.

provides a sophisticated technical account of what kind of syntactic machinery is necessary for capturing all the non-SVO properties of Old English.[32] Whether this machinery exists, and whether it could justly be said to be part of the Old English grammar, are open questions at best. The coverage of the diverse patterns is technically easy, given the technical richness of the syntactic machinery provided by Kayne's model (viz. any kind of movement to the left). The real problem is not full coverage but independent evidence. It is hard to see what kind of data might falsify such an account at all. The machinery seems to be flexible enough to cover any setting.[33] Hence, given the massive counter-evidence from OV languages, the explanatory power is little as long as the theory that is employed is not solidly grounded (see the final chapter).

Second, the characterization of OE in terms of the universal SVO hypothesis is based on a set of properties, each reconstructed as an *independent* feature-based property of the grammar. This amounts to a system with an extremely high degree of freedom for potential alternative settings. Consequently, when there is a system space with a number of independent system vectors, the stochastic universal behind the second law of thermodynamics will guarantee that the system space will gradually become populated by grammars,[34] each of which occupies an admissible position in the overall system space. Each grammar will differ in at least one of the admissible independent system vectors.

What remains unclear under these circumstances is the cross-linguistically *uniform* result of individual development paths that converged into the uniform SVO properties of the respective languages in the Germanic family. Under the excessive-movement hypothesis, it is an accident that presently there is a uniform VO group and a uniform OV group. The picture predicted by the massive-movement thesis is not one with a clear-cut syntactic grouping but one of family resemblances: for each feature there are some languages that share the setting, and others that do not share it. The result should be a network of family resemblances, and not the complementarity situation of two clear-cut groups of languages in terms of their syntactic complementary properties.

---

[32] This is the massive movement machinery: all kinds of phrases may move to the left (e.g. arguments, non-arguments, lexical phrases, functional phrases); the remnant VP may move to the left; particles may move, too.

[33] It would allow, for instance, the non-existent setting [[V O] Aux]. A special constraint (*FoF*) is needed for a structure immediately ruled out by the BBC.

[34] The second law of thermodynamics – 'In a closed system, entropy accumulates' – is a law on the information quality of closed systems in general. The degree of order (predictability) decreases. This is so because of the high degree of freedom for transitions from the present state of the system into one of many alternative states. In our case, this principle of dissipation would entail that almost any option finds a chance for implementation, eventually.

In sum, neither the competing-grammar model nor the excessive-movement attempt are likely to produce the empirically cogent and theoretically adequate insight into the determinants of grammar change that led to the present-day opposition of OV and VO languages in the Germanic language family.

An open-parameter hypothesis would have been the right kind of idea from the beginning, but its implementation suffered from the inadequate theory inventory in those days. The failure was unavoidable, given the theoretical inventory that was provided by grammar theory in the nineties. There is one crucial area of parameterization that, at that time, was still beyond the horizon. This crucial point is the parameterization of *head* placement in complex lexical phrases in interaction with a universal constraint on the phrasal architecture: only the combination of the BBC (universal left-bound merger) plus parameterized headedness provides a new vantage point for understanding the diversity of head positions across the admissible types. Its natural system space comprises the two traditional types (OV and VO) and, crucially, a third type. This is the missing type in the previous accounts. If OE and the other old Germanic languages are indeed languages of this type, it is not surprising that previous accounts were bound to fail, since they tried to squeeze these languages into a system space that did not contain the required type of grammar, namely the grammar of a language of the third type.

Let us readdress the question raised above. Is it merely accidental that the change from the third-type language Latin to the Romance successor languages yielded only strict VO languages, but no OV languages? The answer is this: only if the change from flexible to rigid directionality coincides with a second change, namely the change into fronting the finite verb (i.e. the V2-property), is OV a possible outcome. The V2-property makes the change of the third type compatible with VO and also with OV as alternative results, both with fixed directionality. The Germanic split is the joint result of a change towards *rigid directionality* and a change towards *V2*. The V2-property makes the change of the third type compatible with VO and also with OV as a result state. Hence, only in the context of the developing V2-property could the split into VO vs. OV happen. This is easy to see: in each sentence with a finite main verb, the trace position can be reconstructed either in the OV or in the VO order *without any consequences* for the surface order.

The Romance situation, on the other hand, is the joint result of creolization,[35] as an external drift, plus an internal drift, resulting from the loss of a

---

[35] Creole languages are VO languages. The majority of Romance languages developed outside the Latin-speaking territory, from Portugal in the far west to Romania in the east. Only the Italian dialects are the successor languages on the original Roman territory.

morphological tense system and the change to analytic tense formation. The rise of analytic tenses complicated the verb syntax because of the rise of Aux-V structures. The avoidance of centre-embedded VPs produced Aux-V patterns with Aux fronting, and these are patterns that invite the grammaticalization of VO, since economy invites base-generating these patterns. The result is a VO structure.

5.6. It's a long way to OV/VO

The development from the third-type grammar of an old Germanic language to the modern strictly directional types and the concomitant bifurcation of the development in the two predictable instantiations (OV, VO) has been a development over many generations of language users. It was by no means accomplished in the so-called old period. It extended in the middle period:[36] Middle High German was still a language with flexible directionality for the verb, whence the testimony of Yiddish.

Prell (2003: 245) described it this way: 'In a Middle High German declarative, the finite verb is in second position (V2) on principle, like in modern German; in a [C-]$_{HH}$ -introduced embedded clause, it is not necessarily in final position but merely in a position not as early as the V2 position ... After 1250, the absolute clause-final position occurs in 65% of all [C-]$_{HH}$-introduced embedded sentences.'[37] The crucial point is that nominal objects may follow the verb in such clauses (Prell 2003: 246). The non-finite verb optionally precedes nominal objects, as expected for the third type:

(24)　　So wirt dir [*vergeben* von got *din missetat*]
　　　　thus is you [forgiven by god your misdeed]　(Hoffmann's sermon collection)

From the point of view of an explanatory reconstruction of the changes, the crucial question is this: what is it that made the languages all converge to the same type eventually? In other words, why has the development in the languages of each present-day subtype been converging on the same subtype? What was it that, apparently independently, guided speakers of early Middle English and early Middle Icelandic over generations on their way to a strict VO language, namely a language with a fixed, rather than a flexible valuation of

---

[36] For Middle Dutch, see e.g. Blom (2002).
[37] Original version: 'Im mhd. Aussagesatz steht das finite Verb wie im Nhd. prinzipiell an zweiter Stelle (V2), im eingeleiteten Nebensatz jedoch *nicht unbedingt an letzter*, sondern lediglich später als an zweiter Stelle. [...] Die absolute Endstellung tritt nach 1250 in über 65% aller eingeleiteten Nebensätze auf.'

the directionality parameter for verbal heads? An analogous question calls for an adequate answer in languages of the OV type, as, for instance, in the transition from Middle Dutch or Middle High German to modern Dutch and modern German, respectively.

Obviously, there must have been a period in which the innovative variety and the old variety of the grammar could co-exist, and there must have been grammatical properties that served as a momentum for a persistent drift, in the sense of Sapir (1921), that brought about a gradual preponderance in the direction of the respective type (OV, VO). Without having identified the drift-generating factor, we have not understood the sustainable processes of grammatical change.

The most likely source for such a driving force is the *coincidence of three independent* factors that are superimposed in the distribution of verbs. One factor is the variation in the distribution of verbs inherent to the third type. The second factor is verb movement by V-second. The third factor is the variation of verb order in the verb cluster in languages that move verbs (see second factor). Clustering is an option in the third type since it becomes obligatory once the head-final variant is chosen. This highly complex set of verb-order possibilities lent itself to a complexity-reducing change. The change was the change from the un(der)specified to the specified directionality for verbal heads. This reduced the variation pool for verb-order variation.

Note that it is predictable that the directionality property invited the change. The other two factors could not be touched without more dramatic changes. Variation in the cluster could only be banned by giving up V-movement. However, this would contradict the V2-property. So, elimination of V-movement in the cluster would entail the elimination of V2. The V2-property is the least likely candidate since it affects finite verbs only. It is the variation space inherent to the third type that can be reduced without affecting other areas of grammar if directionality is fixed. This is equivalent to a change from the third type to either OV or VO.

Why is it the directionality of the verbs that is vulnerable for change and not the directionality of other categories? The reason is this: only verbs are involved in *two* categories of *directional* licensing relations. On the one hand, a verb licenses nominal complements by *nominal case*, and on the other hand, verbs license complements of the same category by '*verbal case*',[38] that is, the

---

[38] The term 'verbale Rektion' (verbal government) was introduced by Bech (1955) in analogy to the government of nouns. A verb governs case for nouns and it governs 'verbal case' ('Statusform') for verbs.

morpho-syntactically coded selection restrictions (infinitival form, participle, VP and its functional extensions).

In VO languages, the verbs are serialized according to the directionality parameter without exception. There is no other order variant since for each verb there is only one directionality option for the selection of its complement, indicated by arrows in (25).

(25)   Surely, you [$_{VP}$ must → [$_{VP}$ have → [$_{VP}$ been → [$_{VP}$ joking]]]]

Assume that a change has successfully started, that is, that there is a subset of speakers whose grammar (but not necessarily their output) differs from the grammar(s) of the majority. This is the beginning of a period of co-existence of two grammars.[39]

Let us look at the *area of reanalysis* now, that is, the area of data that are compatible with both grammars, the old and the new. It is this area that enables and nourishes change that starts with the co-existence of old and new. (26) illustrates the simplest and arguably most frequent distribution types (at most two verbs, at most two arguments), with *head-initial* as the new setting:

(26)   a. YP V$_{FIN}$ XP YP Aux$_{FIN}$ V   old and new
        b. C° XP Aux V, C° XP V Aux   old
        c. C° XP Aux V   new (and old)
        d. C° YP XP V Aux, C° YP Aux XP V, C° YP Aux V XP, etc.   old
        e. C° YP Aux V XP (C° XP Aux V YP)   new (and old)
        f. YP Aux$_{FIN}$ V XP, YP Aux$_{FIN}$ XP V   old
        g. YP Aux$_{FIN}$ V XP   new (and old)

It is evident that the new grammar produces a subset of the serializations of the old grammar. This is true for the head-initial variant, shown in (26), as well as for the head-final variant. The change is not disruptive, it is merely reductive. As the change goes on, there is less variation available.

Let us make an educated guess as to what might have been involved in shifting the weights either towards VO or towards OV. There must have been an attractive property of grammar that covered a subset of patterns and therefore was instantiated and could serve as an attractor for other properties. Here is the guess: VO is the outcome if the reanalysis re-grammaticalizes the beginning of the midfield, and OV will be the result if the reanalysis does this with the rear part of the midfield.

A reanalysis in terms of VO will be supported by a high frequency of (26a,c,e,g). The order in brackets in (26e) is both an old and a new order, if this

---

[39] Change most likely happens when two groups are segregated, of course. But segregation is not the most frequent trigger of language change.

language has CP-internal V-second, as in the modern Scandinavian languages (see Vikner 1995; Haider, Olsen and Vikner 1995: 6).

Danish is representative of the Scandinavian situation: in embedded complement clauses of a large class of verbs the matrix word order is licit (27b), despite the presence of an overt complementizer (which is obligatory). In German, CP-internal V2 is ungrammatical (27c). Embedded V2-clauses occur with the same class of verb, but not with a complementizer.

(27)   a. Peter said *(that) [never before] *had* he read such a good article
        b. Peter sagde *(at) [aldrig før] *havde* han læst sådan en god artikel   Danish
           Peter said (that) [never before] *had* he read such a good article
        c. Peter sagte *(dass) [nie zuvor] *hätte* er so einen guten Artikel gelesen
           Peter said (that) [never before] *had* he such a good article read   German

A drift towards OV arguably starts from a preference for the patterns in (28), all of which are fully compatible with the third type, too.

(28)   a. C° YP (XP) Aux V; C° YP (XP) V Aux
        b. C° YP Aux_{FIN} XP V
        c. XP Aux_{FIN} V; YP Aux_{FIN} XP V

The variation in (28a) is a variation in the verbal cluster as a consequence of the V-final option. The fronting of an auxiliary in (28b) is available in OV languages, as the examples from German (29) testify. The very same patterns in VO are either base-generated ones or result from CP-internal V2. (28c) is the V2-pattern.

It is the prevalence of the patterns in (28), or the patterns (26c,e,g), that will work as a constant drift factor in favour of a grammaticalization of head-*final* or head-*initial* directionality, respectively. This is the covert split. It is not yet overt since the patterns (28) or (26c,e,g) are each a proper subset of the third-type patterns. The new, covert, change will merely have an effect on the frequency of certain types. The high frequency of the patterns in (28), or, in another community, the higher frequency of the patterns (26c,e,g) will favour the grammaticalization of a rigid directionality in language acquisition.

Given sufficient overlap between the patterns of the third type, the OV patterns and the VO patterns, and given the absence of normative institutions (like obligatory schooling, writing norms, wide distribution of printed material) it is likely that these three dialects could co-exist for a long time.

The examples in (29) show that even in an OV language such as German and in its dialectal varieties, auxiliaries may precede the non-finite verbs and even objects. This gives rise to serializations that are well formed in the covert OV and the covert VO dialect (29d).

(29) a. dass er für ihn nicht *hatte* die Firma am Leben *halten* wollen[40]   German
       that he for him not *had* the company at life *keep* wanted
     b. Man *hätte* (halt) *müssen* die Polizei *verständigen*[41]   German dialectal
       one had (PART) *been-obliged-to* the police *call*
     c. das si am Grendel *wöt* sine verlore chlause *zruggeh*[42]   Swiss German
       that she to-the Grendel *wanted* his lost claw *return*
     d. dass er hatte die Firma wollen halten am Leben   (experimental)

The example in (29d) sounds like a hybrid of German and Dutch word-order patterns, but it would be acceptable as a Swiss German pattern. The verbs are in a VO-like order, but not clustering. They are fronted, like in the German construction (29a). Patterns like this are well formed both in the OV and in the VO dialects (and of course in the third type), but they receive a different structural analysis in each type.

Philologists, too, have realized that the variation in verb order deserves specific attention. Prell (2003: 245) writes:

> Another important difference between Middle High German and modern German is the fact that in an embedded clause with several verbs the relative order of verbs is not rigidly determined in MHG. Here, too, the modern order (non-finite verb before finite verb) is already dominant with a percentage between 68% and 75% per half a century. The inverse order in adjacent or distant position may occur at any time, however.[43]

The following data from Prell (2003: 245) from the *Mühlhausener Reichsrechtsbuch* and from a collection of sermons illustrate the point.

(30) a. hivte ist der vroliche tak *daz* vnser herre **wollte**$_{wanted}$ **varn**$_{go}$ ze ierl'm. vn die mrter liden vmbe alle die mennischen die er **heilen**$_{heal}$ **wollte**$_{wanted}$.
       [Kuppitsch'sche Predigtsammlung = Kuppitsch's homily collection]
     b. Hinach is beschribin *daz* ein iclich man hi zv mvlhusen in die richis stat **sal**$_{shall}$ vride$_{peace}$ **habi**$_{have}$ in simmi huz

---

[40] Quotation from: Thomas Mann, *Buddenbrooks. Verfall einer Familie*.

[41] This is a very frequent pattern in the Viennese vernacular: the non-finite modal may be fronted across objects and adverbials, but crucially it is not fronted as far as the finite verb. This is easy to verify since pronouns in the Wackernagel area *precede* the fronted modal, as for instance the reflexive pronoun in (i):

   (i) Er *hätt'* sich *müssen* wärmere Socken anziehen.
       'he had himself been-obliged-to warmer stockings wear'

[42] Schwytzerdytsch (Swiss German), from Wurmbrand's (2006) collection of data.

[43] 'Ein weiterer wichtiger Unterschied zum Nhd. besteht darin, dass im *mehrteiligen Verbalkomplex* im mhd. Nebensatz die Abfolge der Verbformen nicht fest geregelt ist. Auch hier dominiert bereits die nhd. Stellung (Infinitum vor Finitum) mit Werten zwischen 68 und 75% pro Jahrhunderthälfte, die umgekehrte Abfolge einschließlich der Distanzstellung der Verbformen ist aber auch jederzeit erwartbar.'

(30a) documents the variation within a single sentence with two conjoined embedded clauses. The first clause has the 'Dutch order' with the finite modal preceding the main verb (*wollte varn* – wanted travel), while the second conjunct has the 'German order' with the main verb preceding the modal (*heilen wollte* – heal wanted). In (30b) the finite modal precedes and an object intervenes between it and the clause-final verb, followed by an extraposed PP.

Let me summarize the two alternative pathways that gradually led to OV and VO, respectively. In the dialect that became the mother of Germanic VO, the preferred verb patterns were those with the verb(s) fronted (much like in modern-day Swiss German). This strongly enhanced the superficial compatibility between these patterns and genuine VO patterns. In the dialectal mother of OV, the preferred option was reordering in the cluster variant (much like present-day German IPP).

In each of these two mother dialects, the set of third-type patterns was large and varied, though with different preferences. Each of the preferred sets contained a subset of patterns that simultaneously belonged to an intersection set with OV and VO patterns, respectively. It is this large intersection set that made it possible to reduce the complexity of third-type verbal patterns in the period when V2 – an independent source of V-redistribution – got grammaticalized.

5.7   Summary

The modern Germanic languages (with the exception of Yiddish) are all languages with a fixed directionality of heads. As for the VP, there is a group with strictly head-*initial* directionality (Germanic VO languages) and a group with head-*final* directionality for V° and A° (Germanic OV languages). This situation is the result of a change that went on for generations. The common ancestor language was neither OV nor VO; it belongs to the third type. In this type, the directionality of the verbal heads is un(der)specified. This means that it admits the aggregate of VO and OV serializations plus a third pattern, with the verb in between its objects.

The primary change is the change from 'un(der)specified' (or flexible) to 'specified'. The implementation of this change implies a decision on the concrete value of directionality. This choice is a matter of chance. It is not determined. Either of the two options is feasible. In this situation it is expected that both options find their implementation. Since the options are incompatible, the result is the split into two groups, with one of the two available variants as the new core grammar.

At first, this split was not strongly manifest, since the outputs of the two grammars were weakly equivalent for a big enough set of utterances, simply because one could easily avoid optional variants of the old setting that were incompatible with the new one. In that way, the two grammars geared a gradual drift. The end point is the steady OV and VO setting, respectively. For OV, the parallel development of the V2-property was instrumental since it made any main clause with a single verb compatible with either VO or OV or Type III.

What is still missing is a systematic, cross-linguistic investigation of the correlations between the serialization patterns of verbs and objects on the one hand and the serialization patterns of verbs and (quasi-)auxiliaries on the other hand, in as great a detail as has been done for English. These investigations are needed for the differentiated factorization of the superimposed factors of verbal serialization. Except for Old English, the well-analyzed data basis for theoretic modelling is still small. Ideally, we would like to have for each Germanic language as thoroughly analyzed and assessed a picture as we have now for Old and Middle English, thanks to the cooperation of philologists and theoreticians, and thanks to the incarnation of these diverse competences even in an individual's professional competences (see Fischer *et al.* 2000 and the core literature cited there).

Appendix 5.1   A checklist of syntactic correlates of OV and VO, and the third type

What correlates directly with VO?

- Base position of the (non-finite) verb precedes the (nominal) object arguments: [V Obj Obj]$_{VP}$ – *[Obj V Obj]$_{VP}$ – *[Obj Obj V]$_{VP}$
- The relative order of the arguments is invariable ('fixed' word order)
- The particle of a particle verb is *postverbal* and possibly stranded at distance
- Structurally unique, functional subject position, and therefore
- Obligatory structural expletive required for subjectless constructions
- Aux + V order, without any order variation among the auxiliaries
- No compact serialization of auxiliaries (adverbs intervening between non-finite auxiliaries and verbs)[44]
- *Edge effect* (Haider 2004b): head of a preceding modifier phrase (adverbial or attributive AP) must be adjacent (Haider 2005)
- *Strict order* between auxiliaries and main verb: AUX-V.

---

[44] Norwegian seems to be exceptional with respect to compactness. According to Nilsen (2003), it does not tolerate adverbials between a sequence of auxiliaries. However, Norwegian does not show any properties of OV Germanic clustering (verb-order variation, clause union effects, cluster topicalization). See Thráinsson (2010) for the interaction of verb and adverb positions in Scandinavian languages.

What correlates directly with OV?

- (Non-finite) verbs follow their nominal arguments in the VP-internal base position (except for heavy NP-shift): [Obj Obj V]$_{VP}$ – *[Obj V Obj]$_{VP}$ – *[V Obj Obj]$_{VP}$
- The relative order of the arguments is variable ('free' word order = scrambling) if the arguments are marked distinctly
- The particle of a particle verb is *pre*verbal (unless it has been stranded by V-fronting)
- No structurally unique, functional subject position, and therefore
- No structurally triggered subject expletives
- Verbal clustering with compactness in the cluster
- Variation in the relative order of the main verbs, auxiliaries and quasi-auxiliaries[45]
- No edge effect
- *V + Aux* order, with *variation* (if the language is a language with verb movement).

What correlates directly with the third *type (OV and OVO and VO)?*

- (Non-finite) verb positions appear to be *variable* relative to their (nominal) objects
- In addition to the OV and VO order there is also an O – V – O order, viz. [… [$_{VP}$ object$_{nominal}$ [V object$_{nominal}$]]][46]
- The order of arguments *before* the VP-internal V-position is variable ('free' word order = scrambling), like in OV, unless verbs have moved to *functional* positions and the arguments are placed in the respective spec, like in Hungarian (Kiss 2002)

---

[45] This statement is to cover both the variation in the verbal cluster (as e.g. in Dutch) as well as the alternative orders in which the fronted auxiliary or quasi-auxiliary leaves the cluster (as e.g. in German IPP/Ersatzinfinitiv-constructions).

[46] Here is a set of Slavic examples: (a) and (b) illustrate the intermediate position of the verb (in combination with wh-movement out of the first object, as an indicator that the first object is not in a spec position). The order variation in (c) is the same as in Yiddish.

  a. Jaki Iwan samochód *kupił* swoje jżonie?   Polish
     which Iwan car bought his sister   'which car did Iwan buy his sister'
  b. Kakuju Ivan mašinu *kupil* svoej žene?   Russian
     which Iwan car bought his sister
  c. čto Maša *pokazyvaet* Petru svoj dom – … Petru *pokazyvaet* svoj dom – … Petru svoj dom *pokazyvaet*
     that Mary shows Peter her house

- Special structural subject position only if the VO pattern is instantiated, and in this case an expletive is mandatory, too. So, the expletive appears to be optional cross-structurally
- Both an Aux – V order and a V – Aux order is admitted for finite as well as for non-finite Aux, in adjacent or non-adjacent positions (preceding or following an object)
- Verbal clustering is optionally available since clustering depends on the choice of head-final option right through the whole VP
- The wealth of word-order variants is utilized by information structuring. In descriptions of these languages, information structuring categories (focus and background, given and new, topic and comment, theme and rheme) are typically presented as the primary *syntactic* word-order determinants, although they are but the beneficiaries of the large syntactic construction space. Word-order variability is not determined by information structure; it is exploited for information structure distinctions.

Appendix 5.2 Why [[V O] Aux] orders do not exist and the *FoF* constraint is covered by the BBC

The fact described by the *FoF* constraint has been derived from the BBC,[47] avant la lettre, namely in Haider (1997d, §2). The exclusion of the *FoF* pattern immediately follows from the BBC (see also Chapter 3 and Haider 2010a: ch. 2).

The idea that the order (1d) could exist, which the *FoF* constraint strives to rule out, is misguided. It grows on an empirically insufficiently informed, inadequate conception of a simplified order parameter for the VP and its functional extensions: the VP and the head of its dominating functional projection do not have a free variation space provided by a serialization parameterization that would allow this order. (Non-lexical) *functional* heads are *never* permitted to *follow* their complement (see the discussion in Haider 1993: ch. 3, §3.4 and 2010a: chs.1 and 2). This immediately rules out (1c) and (1d). A sister of

---

[47] The alleged need for an *FoF* constraint (*FoF* = final-over-final) is defended, for instance, in Biberauer, Holmberg and Roberts (2009): 'For all heads $\{\alpha, \beta, ..\}$ on a single projection line, if α is a head-initial phrase and β is a phrase immediately dominating α, then β must be head-initial. If α is a head-final phrase, and β is a phrase immediately dominating α then β can be head-initial or head-final.'

a node of an extended projection that precedes is a flat violation of the BBC.[48] That's all.

But why do syntacticians (e.g. Bibérauer, Holmberg and Roberts 2009) think that (1c) and a fortiori (1d) could or should exist? The answer seems to be straightforward. They apparently think in a strongly VO-biased manner, and they do not adequately consider the massive counterevidence for (1c) in OV (see Haider 1993 and 2010a: chs.1 and 2). The misinterpretation is based on the simplified juxtaposition of potential structure patterns, namely (1a) vs. (1c).

(1)   a. [Aux [V O]]   e.g. English (and VO in general)
        b. [Aux [O V]]   e.g. German (in IPP constructions)
        c. [[O V] Aux]   *non-existent* (customarily confounded with 1e)
        d. [[V O] Aux]   *non-existent*
        e. [O [V Aux]]   VP with a *verbal cluster*   German, Dutch
        f. [O [Aux V]]   VP with a verbal cluster   Dutch, German IPP

Here is a single, robust, clear piece of evidence against (1c). If (1c) existed, (2a) would have to exist as well. (2a) is a structure with an intervening element between the VP and the finite auxiliary that follows. This would be the counterpart of (2b) in the OV setting, as an option for extending (1a). (2a) does not exist. In VO, however, there is solid evidence for the structure (2b), and it comes from these *interveners*.

This is the type of evidence usually put forth in introductory lessons in English syntax in order to convey the insight to the students that in English, a finite auxiliary has to be raised across an adverbial or a negation particle. For OV languages, the complete *absence* of this kind of evidence from interveners is constantly ignored by proponents of (1c). The onus of proof is on their side, of course, when they assume that a finite verb raises to the right. The null hypothesis is that things are as they appear to be, namely that the auxiliary stays in its VP-internal position. In German, there are possible interveners, namely any material that is postverbal in the VP. The resulting order (2a), however, remains robustly deviant (2d).

(2)   a. *O V *XP* Aux
        b. Aux *XP* V O

---

[48] *Basic Branching Constraint* (BBC): 'Projection-internal branching nodes of the (functionally or lexically extended) projection line *follow* their sister node.' In other words, lexical projections and their functional extensions are structured as in (i) but not as in (ii):

(i) … […]]   (ii) … [[[…] …]

c. The auxiliary [is [*clearly* ᵥₚ[separated from the VP]]]
d. *dass hier nicht [die VP [getrennt werden *vom Auxiliar*]] kann
   that here not the VP separated get from-the auxiliary can
e. [Getrennt werden *vom Auxiliar*]ᵥₚ kann hier die VP nicht
   separated get from-the auxiliary   can here the VP not
f. dass hier die VP nicht [getrennt werden (**vom Auxiliar*)]ᵥₚ kann
   that here the VP not separated be (from the auxiliary) can

The pattern (2a) is ungrammatical, as (2d) illustrates, and it is ungrammatical despite the fact that this very order is in principle licit for a VP, as the topicalized variant in (2e) shows. It is ungrammatical because a VP cannot be a sister of a selecting V° in OV. It would be a left sister, and this is excluded by the BBC (if the stacked VPs are construed as lexically extended projections) or by a constraint against centre embedding (on the level of UG).

Both the big VP as well as the inner VP (2e) can be topicalized. Reconstruction of the fronted VP into its base position would yield an ungrammatical order, however (2f). The reason for this paradoxical situation has been clarified, too (Haider 2010a: ch.7, verb clustering). OV languages obligatorily cluster the verbs in order to avoid stacked and thereby centre-embedded head-final projections. Clustering is the mandatory grammatical alternative.

Here are illustrations for the grammatical patterns in (1) for OV, viz. (1b,e,f). (1b) is well attested in German, but ungrammatical in Dutch. In Dutch, the verbs always form a cluster and a verb is not allowed to leave the cluster except for V2. In German, the IPP construction has verbs fronted out of the cluster, as the intervener property demonstrates (Haider 2010a: 291):

(3) a. dass er für ihn nicht *hatte* die Firma am Leben halten wollen   German
        that he for him not *had* the company alive keep want-INF
     b. *dat hij graag *wilde* kraanvogels fotograferen   Dutch
        that he with-delight wanted cranes photograph-INF   (ANS 1984: 949)

An IPP construction like in (3a)[49] is a token of the pattern type (1b). Examples for the clause-final orders (1e,f) are listed in (4):

(4) a. weil man nichts [verstehen wollen *wird*]ᵥₑᵣbₐₗ ₑₗᵤₛₜₑᵣ   German
        since one nothing comprehend want shall
     b. weil man nichts [verstehen *wird* wollen]ᵥₑᵣbₐₗ ₑₗᵤₛₜₑᵣ
     c. weil man nichts [*wird* [verstehen wollen]]ᵥₑᵣbₐₗ ₑₗᵤₛₜₑᵣ
     d. [Verstehen wollen] wird man nichts
     e. dat men niets [begrepen heeft] / [heeft begrepen]ᵥₑᵣbₐₗ ₑₗᵤₛₜₑᵣ   Dutch

[49] The example sentence is an excerpt from Thomas Mann's novel *Buddenbrooks. Verfall einer Familie*. See Askedal (1986) for this and other examples with the same kind of verb order, which he gathered from corpora.

that one nothing comprehended has / has comprehended
- f. dat men niets [*zal* begrepen hebben] _{verbal cluster}
that one nothing shall comprehended have
- g. dat men niets [begrepen *zal* hebben]_{verbal cluster}
preferred in Belgium (ANS 1984: 1,069)
- h. dat men niets [*zal* hebben begrepen]_{verbal cluster}
preferred in the Netherlands (ANS 1984: 1,069)

Obviously, the distribution of verbs in the cluster of a simple clause could not be captured by the simple assumption that a VP followed by a functional head attracts the verbal head, neither in Dutch nor in German (for details, see Haider 2010a: ch.7). This assumption would be weakly equivalent only for the pattern (4a) and the first variant in (4e).

Let us recapitulate: OV languages cluster their verbs clause-finally, and, in addition, OV languages with V-movement, like the Germanic languages, in contrast to East Asian OV languages with inert verbs, produce *order variations* within the cluster. This yields at least the following serialization patterns:

(5) a. ... O V Aux
     b. ... O Aux V
     c. ... Aux O V
     d. XP Aux$_{FIN}$ O V   (V2-property)

This set of serialization patterns gets considerably enlarged when the 'third-type' property is active. Note that the third type comprises the OV properties as a subset. Yiddish provides insights as to what kind of serialization patterns arise as third-type patterns (6a,b):

(6) a. ... Aux O V O
     b. ... V Aux (O) O
     c. ... Aux V (O) O

Finally, the third type also admits the strictly head-initial (VO) instantiation (6c). Taken together, this is the wealth of serialization patterns to be expected in a third-type language. If, in addition, the third-type language is a V-movement language (V2 language), the resulting patterns tend to get difficult to trace in processing, whence the latent drive towards changing this situation. This drive has 'spared' Yiddish, mainly because of the fact that its neighbouring languages (in a multilingual linguistic environment) are third-type languages, too, but without the V2-property. Thus, the drive has become fully operative only in the development of the majority of Germanic languages.

6 Adverbial positions in VO and in OV

6.1 Overview and introduction

This chapter will explicate and assess the immediate implications of the BBC (Basic Branching Constraint) and PDI (Principle of Directional Identification) model for the grammar of adverbials.[1] The topics to be covered are as follows:

(i) the BBC and PDI-geared structural constraints that determine *admissible structural positions* for adverbials (adjoined or embedded) in OV and VO, respectively
(ii) the *interface condition* for adverbs (syntax–semantic interface) that guides order and position (*closure principle*)
(iii) the apparently conflicting evidence from post- vs. preverbal adverbials
(iv) the comparative evaluation of competing accounts for the BBC-guided modelling of the syntax of adverbials (viz. Spec-F analyses for adverbials or adjunction analyses that tolerate adjunction on the right-hand side).

The BBC-constrained syntax plus a cross-linguistically *uniform* set of conditions for admissible adverb positions interact and produce cross-linguistically *different* patterns of distribution and construal for adverbials. The patterns strongly correlate with the OV/VO partitioning, that is, the canonical position of the head in the phrase structure. On the one hand, the *tighter* organization of the head-initial VP restricts the availability of phrase-internal positions,[2] and on the other hand, the low versus high position of the head in OV and

---

[1] This chapter draws on, updates and connects previously published work: Haider (1996, 2000a, 2002, 2004b).
[2] Compactness as a consequence of the shell structure rules out VP-internal adverbials in VO that intervene between the head and a nominal object or between nominal objects.

VO, respectively, influences the scope-dependent settings of adverb placement. This is particularly evident, but insufficiently appreciated, for the positioning of the negation particle for sentence negation (see §6.2.1).

In sum, the BBC and PDI are directly or indirectly responsible for an intricate set of differences between OV and VO organization of phrase structure. They will be discussed in Section 6.2:

- Admissibility of low positions for 'high' adverbials in OV but not in VO
- *Misidentified superiority* effects for 'higher-type' wh-adverbials in VO
- *Compactness* of head-initial VPs excludes VP-internal adverb positions in VO
- The *edge effect* is VO specific and rules out pre-VP phrasal adverbials
- *Expanded scope* domains in OV (due to clustering combined with clause union).

Section 6.3 briefly deals with the syntax–semantics interface. Adverbs are semantically integrated as modifiers of the phrase they are merged with. Semantic type requirements determine the relative order and a constraint (*closure principle*) guarantees strict incrementality in terms of type progression.

Section 6.4 confronts a presently widely accepted account with substantial counterevidence from OV. This account assigns adverbials to spec positions of adverbial functional heads. It will be shown that this approach misses relevant empirical generalizations especially for OV clauses. Due to their concentration on VO patterns, the proponents unfortunately fail to appreciate the great 'collateral damage' of this attempt for OV that destroys the empirical adequacy of the enterprise in general.

Section 6.5 readdresses recalcitrant data from the post-VP area. First, evidence from VP-fronting invites structure assignments that are in conflict with evidence from dependency relations and coordination. Second, order preferences for postverbal adverbials mirror the preverbal order and invite an interpretation in terms of adjunction to the right or unmotivated roll-up operations. Adjunction of adverbials to the right, if correct, would curtail the domain of BBC, however. Roll-up accounts, on the other hand, are ad hoc and insufficient. Hence, a reappraisal of this evidence seems to be in order.

6.2 Structural availability of positions for adverbials

6.2.1 Admissibility of low positions for 'high' adverbials in OV but not in VO

In head-final VPs, the canonical position of the verb is at the bottom of the phrase.[3] Hence, any position within the VP preceding the verb necessarily c-commands it. In VO, on the other hand, the canonical position is the advanced position in the shell structure. An immediate effect of this difference is the following: any item that must c-command the canonical position of the verb must precede the VP in VO. In OV, however, this item may be placed in a VP-internal position. A clear instance of this situation is the distribution of sentence negation. Dahl (1979) emphasizes a tendency for the negation particle to occur *close* to the finite element. As documented in Dryer (1988, 2011) and Ouhalla (1991), in VSO, negation is typically preverbal. In SVO, negation is preverbal unless the finite verb is fronted. In OV, negation is close to the verb, either preverbal or suffixed to the verb. Characteristic patterns are listed in (1):

(1) a. [Neg [VSO]]   e.g. Malagasy
     b. [S [Neg [VO]]]   e.g. continental Scandinavian languages[4]
     c. [S V_i [Neg [e_i O]]]   e.g. French
     d. [S O Neg V]   e.g. German
     e. [S O V+Neg]   e.g. Japanese

Semantically, sentence negation needs to c-command the element that situates the event variable. This is the tensed element. So, the negation particle must c-command the tensed verb (or its trace in the canonical position). In VO, this entails a pre-VP position for the negation particle, as confirmed by English or French or the Scandinavian languages. In OV, however, *any* position within the VP is a position c-commanding the tensed verb (or its trace) since it occupies the foot position of the VP. Hence, in OV languages, the negation particle is typically close to the verb, following the objects, as in (2).

(2) a. Da hat$_i$ wer was *nicht* kapiert e$_i$
        There has someone something *not* grasped

---

[3] The 'canonical' position is the lowest position in which the verb is well formed as a syntactic item in surface structure. Crucially, a lower position in the shell structure in VO is not a canonical position.
[4] This applies to embedded clauses. In main clauses the finite verb is fronted to the 'V2'-position.

b. Kapiert$_j$ hat$_i$ wer was nicht e$_j$ e$_i$
c. [Nicht kapiert] hat$_i$ wer was e$_i$
no sentence negation; constituent negation

The objects in (2) are intentionally chosen as indefinites, for a simple reason. They do not scramble. Analyses have been proposed that generalize the VO pattern and claim a universal pre-VP position for negation. If the negation in (2) were in a pre-VP position, the indefinites would be in scrambled positions preceding the VP. But first, there is no evidence for scrambling, and second, the analysis inappropriately overgeneralizes a VO-type pattern to the OV type. (2c) would be ill formed with *nicht* (not) as sentence negation since it cannot c-command the finite verb. So, (2c) would have to be expanded as in (3), as a typical expansion for a constituent negation.

(3) [Nicht kapiert] hat er es, sondern nur auswendig gelernt
not understood has he it, but only rote learned

What is appropriate for negation in OV is appropriate for 'higher' adverbials as well. VP-internal sentence adverbials are ill formed in a VO language like English, but not in German, as the web-sampled examples in (4) illustrate.

(4) a. Da wir unser Geld *leider* nicht selbst drucken können
since we our money unfortunately not ourselves print can
b. Da wollten uns HSBC und die Lloyds-Bank unser Geld *leider* nicht wechseln
here would us HSBC and the Lloyds-bank our money not change
c. Auch wenn man selbst das Geld *glücklicherweise* nicht benötigt
also if one oneself the money fortunately not needs

The grammatical reason for this OV/VO difference is the same as for negation. Sentence adverbials denote propositional attitudes. Hence the adverbial must c-command the proposition-situating element, and this is again the finite verb (or one of its projections). And again, a sentence adverbial in a topicalized V-projection (5a) is ill placed, because the finite verb would not be in its domain.

(5) a. ??[Leider gewonnen] hat das Match die falsche Mannschaft
unfortunately won has the match the wrong team
b. [Gewonnen] hat das Match leider die falsche Mannschaft
won has the match unfortunately the wrong team

Of course, a sentence adverbial may precede arguments in German (5b), but the point is this: only in an OV language, but not in a VO language, may sentence adverbials occur in VP-internal positions.

6.2.2 Misidentified superiority effects for 'higher-order' wh-adverbials in VO

It is an uncontroversial fact that in multiple wh-constructions, adverbial wh-elements behave differently in VO and OV, depending on the semantic type. Wh-elements that range over semantically higher-order[5] type entities must not remain *in situ*:

(6) a. Who(m) did you contact when/where/*why/*how/*how frequently?
 b. Wen hast Du wann/wo/weshalb/wie/wie oft kontaktient?
 who have you when/where/why/how/how often contacted

It is a fact, too, that the contrast illustrated in (6a) is absent in OV (6b). The constraints that rule out *why* and *how* in (6a) are *VO-specific* restrictions and do not hold for OV languages (7). Here are two examples (7a,b), a German one out of more than several thousand that are easily located by a search engine,[6] and one that is representative of Japanese. When the second wh-element is a subject, VO languages are at a loss, since the wh-subject must not remain *in situ* either (7d).

(7) a. *Wer* hat es *weshalb* getan?
 who has it why done
 b. Dare-ga *naze* soko-ni itta no? Japanese (Saito 1994: 195)
 who-NOM *why* there-to went Q-PRT
 c. *Who did it why?
 d. *Why did who do it?

What is wrong with *why* and *how* in (6a)? The difference between a VO structure as in (6a) and an OV structure as in (6b) is obvious. In the former, the *in situ* adverbial wh-elements are postverbal; in the latter case, however, they precede the canonical position of the finite verb. Crucially, they must not be postverbal in VO. The have to c-command the (head of the) VP. But, a preverbal position is independently ruled out for *in situ* wh-adverbials (8).

(8) Who(m) did you *when/*where/*why/*how contact?

In VO, adverbial wh-items cannot occur between VP-internal nominal arguments. The head-initial VP is necessarily compact, that is, it does not provide room for intervening adverbials (or scrambled phrases). This is a consequence

---

[5] 'Higher order' refers to the kind of denotation category (i.e. semantic type) a phrase is semantically assigned to. 'Higher types' are types that are more complex than the type of an *individual entity* ('type *e*'). Szabolcsi and Zwarts (1993) pointed out that *why* and *how* range over higher types (properties, propositions) while wh-items like *when* and *where* range over individual entities (locations, points of time).

[6] As for the second candidate of a higher-order adverbial, namely 'how': *wer es wie* ... (who it how ...) is more frequent ($> 4 \times 10^6$) than *wie es wer* ... (how it who ...) ($> 7 \times 10^5$), but there is no denying that both orders are grammatical.

of the shell structure of complex head-*initial* projections, induced by the 'conflicting' demands of universal merger to the left and the precedence of the head in head-initial settings. So, if the wh-item is not fronted, only the clause-final position is accessible (6a). But this position is too low. Wh-items of a higher type must c-command the canonical position of the finite verb.

As for the *subject-in-situ* deviance (7d), the grammar-theoretic details of the OV/VO correlation are explicated in due detail in Haider (2010a: ch. 3, §3.4). The gist is this: in a head-*final* VP, the subject demonstrably remains in its VP-internal position, and in addition, the projection is demonstrably not compact. In an SVO clause structure, however, a VP-internal subject would fail to be in the same domain of the verbal head as the objects, since it precedes the head, but the objects follow. So, a preverbal *functional* head is enlisted and the subject moves to the spec position. A wh-element in a spec position is an operator, and must be interpreted as an independent wh-operator. But, as an *in situ* wh-element, it is dependent and cannot be interpreted as a wh-operator in the very position it occupies. This rules out *in situ* wh-subjects in VO languages.

In the Generative literature, starting with Chomsky (1973), the English contrasts in (6a) and the grammatical ban against wh-subjects *in situ*, have been (mis) identified as instances of *superiority*, and later as violations of a 'shortest-move' requirement. Data from OV languages of the kind that have been brought to attention in Haider (1986) are clear enough signals for a reappraisal of the narrow view emanating from the exclusive focus on VO patterns.

Manner adverbials are placed low in the VP, close to the verb,[7] in German, and so is the manner-wh-item *wie*:

(9) a. Würdest Du Mädchen Fußball *anders/besser* erklären?
 would you girls soccer differently/better explain
 b. *Wem*$_i$ würdest du e$_i$ Fußball *wie* erklären?
 whom would you soccer how explain
 c. *Wie*$_i$ würdest du *wem* Fußball e$_i$ erklären?
 how would you whom soccer explain

Obviously, the base position of one of the two items in the sentences (9b,c) must be closer to the spec position. So, if a shortest-move condition (or superiority) were indeed operative, either (9b) or (9c) ought to be deviant, which is not the case. On the other hand, in VO languages, there is a clear contrast in

---

[7] 'Closeness to the verb' is a general property of *manner adverbials*, and not an indifferent VO property:

(i) *He must *completely* have misunderstood it
(ii) He must have *completely* misunderstood it

acceptability between the pattern corresponding to (9b) and (9c). Consequently, it is the headedness difference that matters, that is, the structural difference between a head-initial and a head-final structure. In OV, also, a low position in the VP c-commands the head of the VP. This is the essential difference that accounts for the OV/VO contrast in this area of grammar.

6.2.3 Compactness *of head-initial VPs excludes VP-internal adverb positions in VO*

In English head-initial VPs, a verb and its nominal complement must not be separated by intervening items, such as, for instance, adverbials. This is a PDI effect for head-initial phrases. An intervener – an adverbial or a scrambled phrase – destroys the *minimality* relation.

(10)   a.   *analyse *carefully* problems
            b.   Probleme *sorgfältig* analysieren
                problems carefully analyse

In (11a), the verb would not *minimally* c-command the object (as required by the PDI), because of the intervening adverbial. In German (11b), however, any argument position is within the canonical directionality domain of the verb or a projection of the verb. This guarantees minimal c-command in the canonical direction.

(11)   a.   [analyse$_i$ [*carefully* [e$_i$ problems]]]$_{VP}$
            b.   [Probleme [*sorgfältig* [analysieren]]]$_{VP}$

This explains Stowell's (1981: 113) adjacency requirement for the verb and its nominal object. It was formulated as a restriction on case assignment. Assigner and assignee were required to be string-adjacent. Why this should hold only for OV but not for VO remained unclear in those days. What appears to be an adjacency restriction is in fact a consequence of the PDI in head-initial settings only. German or Dutch is particularly instructive in this respect since the VP is head-final while the NP is head-initial:

(12)   a.   Fische *in Zeitungen* einwickeln$_{V°}$ - in Zeitungen Fische einwickeln
                fish in newspaper in-wrap   - in newspapers fish in-wrap
            b.   das Einwickeln$_{N°}$ von Fischen/der Fische *in Zeitungen*
                the in-wrap(ing) of fish/the fish$_{GEN}$ in newspapers
            c.   *das Einwickeln *in Zeitungen* von Fischen/der Fische
                the in-wrap(ing) in newspapers of fish/the fish$_{GEN}$
            d.   *wrap [in newspapers] fish

The German NP (12b,c) is as compact as the English VP and the English NP. They are all head-initial. The head-final VP (12a) is not compact because it is head-final.

6.2.4 The edge effect *occurs only with VO structures and rules out pre-VP adverbials*

The following set of data (13) illustrates an *edge effect* typical for adjunction to head-*initial* projections. For the evaluation of competing theoretical accounts it is important to keep in mind that the edge effect is caused by (not yet fully understood) properties of head-*initial* structures:[8]

(13)   a. He has [(*much more*) carefully (*than anyone else)] analysed it
        b. He has [(*much less*) often (**than I (thought)*))] rehearsed it
        c. Er hat es [*sehr viel* sorfältiger *als jeder andere*] analysiert
           he has it [much more carefully then anyone else] analysed   (= a)
        d. Er hat es [*viel weniger* oft *als ich (dachte)*] geprobt
           he has it [much less often than I (thought)] rehearsed   (= b)
        e. als niemand *luider (dan Jan)* kan roepen
           if no one louder (than Jan) can shout   Dutch
        f. omdat ik het *vel sneller (dan Jan (denkt))* in een zakje kan pakken
           since I it much faster (than Jan (thinks)) in a bag can pack

Descriptively, the edge effect is the result of a constraint against post-head material in between the head of the adjunct and the phrase it is adjoined to. Material on the left of the adjunct is allowed but not on the right-hand side of the adverbial head. Note that Bouchard's (1995) constraint is not an *adjacency* constraint between the head of the VP and the head of the adverbial phrase, respectively, as (14) illustrates:

(14)   Surely, he has [(more) *often* (*than anyone else)] *rudely* criticized her

The edge effect of adverbials should be seen in parallel with the *edge effect of attributes* in the N-projection. The examples in (15) are counterparts to (14). Note that there is an edge effect for *prenominal* attributes in German but not for *preverbal* adverbials, since NPs are head-initial but VPs are head-final projections. Hence, the edge effect is not a language-specific phenomenon but a projection-specific one: it is safe to conclude that it is a side effect of adjunction to head-initial projections. Only adjunction to head-*initial* targets is subject to this effect. Adjunction to head-final targets shows no edge effects. The structural difference is obvious. For head-final phrases, the adjunction site is within the directionality domain of the head of the

---

[8] Bouchard (1995: 409) claims that preverbal adverbials in English or French are head-adjoined to the verbal head. This cannot be entirely correct since the adverbial may be modified, as the examples show, which turns them into *phrasal* heads. What he wants to cover by head–head adjunction is covered better by the edge effect.

target. Adjuncts to head-initial phrases are outside the directional domain of identification.

(15) a. eine [viel größere (*als ich dachte*)] Summe
'a much bigger (*than I thought) sum'
b. ein [unzufriedener (**damit*)] Syntaktiker
'an unsatisfied (*it-with) syntactician'
c. ein [viel schöneres (*als ich dachte)] (neues) Haus
'a [much-more beautiful (*than I thought)] (new) house'

The theoretical relevance of the edge-effect phenomena is obvious: edge effects are unknown for phrases in *spec positions*, as, for example, phrases in Spec-C or Spec-I. So, an adjunction analysis of adverbials is compatible with an edge effect, but a Spec-F analysis clearly is not.[9] This is a cross-linguistically robust fact and damaging for Spec-F analysis of adverbs.

As for the precise grammatical causality of the edge effect, it is not fully understood yet. The head of the adjunct behaves as if it would take the modified phrase (VP for adverbials and NP for prenominal attributes) as its immediate *complement*. Under the standard assumptions of lexically selected complementation (i.e. head–argument relation), adverbials would be *modifiers* of the VP and not elements that take the VP as complement. Lexical complementation corresponds to functor–argument relations of type-changing functional application. On the other hand, adverbials need to be semantically integrated. The characterization of semantic types in terms of categorial grammar invites an interpretation that comes close to complementation:[10] adverbials are *generalized* functors, having no specific, lexically specified complementation requirements. As type-conserving functors

---

[9] Note that the ban against clauses and *PPs* as preverbal adverbials (that is adverbials between the position of the finite auxiliary and the left edge of the VP) is also an aspect of the edge effect because clauses and PPs are left-headed. So their complement blocks adjacency between the phrasal head and the point of attachment: (i) He has *often/twice* challenged it. (ii) He has *five times* *(*more often*) challenged it. (iii) *He has *at every occasion* challenged it. (iv) *He has *whenever it was possible* challenged it. Note: in (iii) and (iv), the phrasal head is not a final head, whence the deviance.

[10] Take, for instance, (i) as the type of a transitive verb, and (ii) as an adverbial modifying a transitive verb (phrase). In terms of functional application (iii), the modifying adverbial is a function from the type of a transitive verb (phrase) it modifies to the identical type. The corresponding syntactic structure is given in (iv). So, the syntactic complementation corresponds to the functor–argument relation on the semantic side.

(i) $<e, <e,t>>$
(ii) $< <e, <e,t>>, <e, <e,t>> >$
(iii) Functional application: $f [< <e, <e,t>>, <e, <e,t>> >, <e, <e,t>>] = <e, <e,t>>$
(iv) $[_{VP} \text{Adv} [_{VP} V° ...]]$

('modifiers'), they map whatever type they are modifying onto the same type. Nevertheless, there is the same kind of functor–argument relation for both kinds of functors.

The difference between OV and VO, viz. the absence of the edge effect in OV, reflects the influence of the opposite directionality of the heads. In OV, the preverbal adjunct is within the directionality domain of the head; in VO it is not. Hence, a *preceding* adjunct is not directionally identified in VO. Instead, the pre-head adjuncts exploit the abstract complementation mechanism as a licensing device: adverbials as semantic functors are (generalized, lexically not individually specified) complement-takers.[11] In OV, they do so as well, but they are independently licensed syntactically by means of directional identification, hence the edge effect does not show; in VO, it shows.

On the one hand, the edge effect is a robust correlate of modifiers in head-initial (as opposed to head-final) contexts. As such, it is crucial (counter-) evidence for analyses that place adverbials in spec positions. Spec positions do not display an edge effect.

On the other hand, the edge effect blocks complex pre-VP adverbial phrases, since in VO these would be head-initial, and therefore they inevitably would conflict with the edge effect if they are complex, since the head could not precede the lexical complement and simultaneously be adjacent to the host phrase. This is particularly easy to see with pre-NP modifiers, that is, adnominal attributes:

(16)   a. Some students are [talented for syntax]$_{AP}$
        b. Einige Studenten sind [talentiert für Syntax]
        c. ein [talentierter (*für Syntax)] Student
           a [talented (*for syntax)] student
        d. ein [(für Syntax) talentierter] Student

The English and the German NP are head-initial. Hence the edge effect is found with attributes in both languages. In German, the AP is head-final (16d). So, the edge effect blocks APs with extraposed PPs. In English, any complement of an adjective follows the head and therefore there is no room for a lexical complement.

German shares the edge effect with English for NP modifiers, since NPs are head-initial, and it differs from English for AP- and VP-modifiers, since APs and VPs are head-final in German.

---

[11] This tends to be overlooked. The predicate–argument relation (for heads and their arguments) is not the *only* functor–argument relation. Modification is a functor–argument relation, too, but of a different type (not 'e' type but 'higher type').

(17) a. [häufiger (als andere) krank]$_{AP}$
often-er than others ill
b. [häufiger (als andere) erkranken]$_{VP}$
often-er than others fall-ill
c. [more often (*than others) ill]$_{AP}$
d. [more often (*than others) fall ill]$_{VP}$

Let me emphasize once more that these phenomena show beyond reasonable doubt that we are dealing with properties of particular phrase structures and not with holistic properties of languages. It is not a holistic property whether a language allows scrambling or not, or whether it displays the edge effect or not. It is a property of the head-directionality of phrase structures in a given language. If languages are of *mixed* directionality, they will be 'mixed' with respect to the properties that correlate with one directionality value but not with the other. The Germanic OV languages are languages of mixed directionality; the Germanic VO languages are languages of homogeneous directionality, whence the particular differences.

6.2.5 Expanded scope domains in OV (due to verb-clustering-triggered clause union)

An essential difference between a head-initial organization and a head-final one is verb clustering. Verbal clusters (18b) obligatorily replace structures that would otherwise consist of stacked VPs or IPs (18a). This is UG's centre-embedding prevention by which parser-unfriendly recursively left-branching structures get blocked. In VO, these stacks are parser friendly since they are always right-branching. For a number of detailed empirical arguments for (18b) and against (18a) the reader is referred to Haider (2010a: ch. 7, §§7.2 and 7.5).

(18) a. *[[[XP V]$_{VP}$ V]$_{VP}$ V]$_{VP}$
b. [XP [[V V] V]$_{VC}$]$_{VP}$ verbal cluster in OV
c. [V [V [V XP]]]$_{VP}$ stacked VP in VO
d. [V [IP [to [V XP]]]]$_{VP}$ VP-IP stack in VO

In German (and in any other Germanic OV language), verbal clusters obligatorily replace those constructions that in English involve stacked VPs or IPs. But even full clause control constructions (19a,c) have a verb cluster construction as a free alternative (19b,c).

(19) a. dass uns [PRO den$_{ACC}$ Urlaub zu genießen] nicht erlaubt wurde
that us$_{DAT}$ [the vacation$_{ACC}$ to enjoy] not permitted was
b. [Zu genießen erlaubt] wurde uns der$_{NOM}$ Urlaub nicht
[to enjoy permitted] was us the vacation$_{NOM}$ not

c. dass uns den$_{ACC}$/der$_{NOM}$ Urlaub zu genießen erlaubt wurde
     that us the$_{ACC}$/the$_{NOM}$ vacation to enjoy permitted was

(19b) is the verbal cluster counterpart of the clausal embedding in (19a). Topicalization of the cluster forces the cluster construction, of course, and this is reflected in the change of the case of the object. In (19a), the object of the infinitival clause is the object of an embedded clause. In (19b), the object is the object of the verbal cluster in a simple sentence. Hence the object surfaces with subject case when the clause is passivized. Since the two options are string identical for (19c), it appears as if the case of the object argument varies between Accusative and Nominative. It does not. (19c) simply is structurally ambiguous between a clausal and a clustering infinitival construction.

Scope data (and numerous independent properties listed in Haider (2010a)) tell us that the construction of the counterparts of English raising verbs is a clause union construction and not a construction with an embedded functional projection ('I'P). In the latter case, the functional constituent would be a c-command domain and constrain the scope of negation. The data tell a different story, however, as illustrated by (20) and (21):

(20)   dass mir Syntaktiker diesen Umstand *nicht* zu würdigen scheinen
        that me$_{DAT}$ syntacticians this circumstance not to appreciate seem
        'it does *not* seem to me that syntacticians appreciate this circumstance'
        'it seems to me that syntacticians do *not* appreciate this circumstance'

In (21a), the negation is sentence negation. Hence the finite verb must be in its scope. Only in the cluster construction does negation c-command the cluster and it thereby c-commands the canonical position of the finite verb. In (21b), sentence negation is implemented by means of the negative indefinite object. Here, too, the wide-scope reading testifies that the object c-commands the matrix verb. In (21c), an intervener, viz. the information structure particle *ja*, forces the clausal structure for the infinitive construction, and, as predicted, the scope of the negative is the embedded clause only.

(21)   a. obwohl wer Fragen *nicht* zu beantworten vermochte/beabsichtigte
                                                              (wide scope)
           although someone questions not to answer able-was/intended
        b. obwohl wer *keine Frage* zu beantworten vermochte/beabsichtigte
                                                              (wide scope)
           although someone no questions to answer able-was/intended
        c. obwohl wer [keine Frage zu beantworten] ja vermochte/beabsichtige
                                                              (narrow scope)
           although someone [no questions to answer] PRT able-was/intended

As expected, the scope properties of adverbials are exact parallels of the scope properties of negation. In clause union constructions, an adverbial has scope over the matrix verb. In the clausal embedding variant, the scope is constrained by the clause boundaries of the embedded clause. Hence, the frequency adverbial in (22a) has narrow scope. The intervening particle *ja* indicates that there is no cluster and that therefore the infinitive is clausal. The infinitival clause is the scope domain of the adverbial. Topicalization of the verbs (22b) is a means of enforcing the cluster construction, and consequently the adverbial gets matrix scope. (22c), finally, is compatible with each of the two structures, and consequently the adverbial has a narrow- or a wide-scope reading, depending on the respective structure assignment.

(22)   a. dass man Eltern [Kinder *mitunter* anzulügen] ja geraten hat
                                                                                    (narrow scope only)
         that one parents$_{DAT}$ [children$_{ACC}$ sometimes to-lie-to] PRT advised has
    b. [Anzulügen geraten] hat man Eltern$_{DAT}$ Kinder$_{ACC}$ *mitunter*
                                                                                    (wide scope only)
         [to-lie-to advised] has one parents children$_{ACC}$ sometimes
    c. dass man Eltern Kinder *mitunter* anzulügen geraten hat
                                                                               (wide or narrow scope)
         that one parents children *sometimes* to-lie-to advised has

6.3   At the semantics interface

6.3.1   *Syntactic identification and semantic integration*

Typically, adverbials are not *selected*. So, there must be an identification mechanism other than selection that is operative and gears compositional semantics. Selected items have a selector that provides argument slots. Functional application is a means of merging the selector with the selected item semantically. In syntax, the argument is a complement of the selector.

For adjuncts, there is no selector and no selected item. Hence the mechanism for functor–argument relations would not apply. In this situation, grammar provides two different measures. One is known from secondary predicates (23a) and one from adjuncts (23b). In (23a), the adjective is semantically integrated as a 'secondary' predicate, that is, as a freely merged item that relates to an already integrated item in the clause. In (23b,c), the adjective is marked for its adverbial function (by *-ly*) and is integrated as a modifier of what is denoted by the VP. (23d) is the ad*nominal* counterpart of ad*verbial* modification.

(23)   a. He ate the steak *raw*
    b. He *quickly* ate the steak

    c. He ate the steak *quickly*
    d. the *raw* steak

'Integration' is the semantic side; 'identification' is the syntactic side. In head-final phrases (OV), preverbal modifiers are identified by the verb (as non-arguments) standardly, that is, as elements within the directional domain of identification. In head-initial phrases, however, pre-head adjuncts are outside the directionality domain of identification. Hence their *syntactic* identification requires extra measures. Theory provides in principle at least two mechanisms. One is the spec–head configuration. An item is placed into a spec position and the head is the identifier (by abstract spec–head 'agreement'). The alternative mechanism is the generalized complementation mechanism. The item to be merged is merged as a complement-taking phrase that takes the phrase it is merged with as its syntactic complement.

For adverbials, the spec-head approach, as worked out by Cinque (1999), is widely accepted. This approach appears to be adequate because it covers (a substantive part of) the empirical situation in VO languages. In the following section (§6.4) it will be argued that OV languages show that the spec-head approach is not an empirically adequate way of modelling the grammar of adverbials. Even in VO languages, there is robust but neglected counterevidence, namely the edge effect. If preverbal adverbials are phrases in a spec position, then an edge effect cannot arise, contrary to the facts. Unfortunately, the advocates of the spec-head approach have not yet taken up the challenge that these data provide.

If the spec mechanism is inadequate, the theory provides a second road to identification, namely either abstract complementation or secondary predication. For adverbials, a complement relation is not lexically coded (in terms of the argument structure of the head), but it is syntactically *applied* and semantically *accepted*. In other words, the given syntactic structure is sanctioned by a well-formed semantic compositional integration. This approach is a reinterpretation of the standard adjunct analysis for adverbials. Preverbal adjuncts are operators on verbal denotations. Their abstract complement is their domain of integration.

This leaves postverbal adjuncts as the residual class of adverbials to be dealt with. Again, there are theoretical alternatives. They could be treated as right-adjoined adjuncts or as embedded phrases. In Section 6.5, data discussed by Pesetsky (1995) and others will be reappraised. He claimed that movement data tell us that postverbal adjuncts are right-adjoined while binding data show that they are embedded. As a consequence, he suggests a dual-structure assignment. I shall argue that postverbal adverbials are embedded and that the movement data do not show what they are deemed to show. As a consequence, postverbal adverbials are handled like secondary predicates. They are predicated of verbal denotations. This happens only for adverbials in the 'extraposition' area since this is an area in the clause in which predication relations are the general identification mechanism.

The domain of semantic integration of an undisplaced preverbal adverbial is its c-command domain. Hence, the semantic type of the c-command domain must match the semantic type requirement of the adverbial for integration.

6.3.2 Adjunct integration and semantic closure

Syntactic structure provides *positions* for adverbials, and semantic integration determines the kind of semantic *domain* that is appropriate for the given adverbial function. The position of an adverbial is well formed if the semantic type of the c-command domain matches the semantic type requirement for its domain, that is, if the given c-command domain is compatible with the required type domain. Bouchard (1995: 408) chose the following formulation: 'The meaning of an adverb determines what nodes it can attach to and modify, hence what position it can appear in.'[12]

In detailed comparative studies based on German, English and French, Frey and Pittner (1998, 1999), who propose an adjunction analysis for adverbials, and Frey (2003) provide ample evidence for their claim that there are distinct c-command domains for adverbials according to their semantic function: frame and domain adverbials are higher than sentence adverbials (e.g. propositional attitude type), which c-command the base positions of event-related adverbials (e.g. time, cause). These adverbials minimally c-command the minimal complete A-projection of the verbal head. Event internal adverbials (e.g. locative, instrumental) are in the minimal c-command domain of the argument they relate to. Process adverbials minimally c-command the verb. For elements of the same type class, the relative order is free. Other orders are analyzed as scrambling derivatives. A structurally fine-grained grid for preverbal adverbials is part of Cinque's Spec-F approach, too.

In either implementation, there is a kind of unsolved chicken and egg problem concerning the interface question: is the structural position of an adverbial inherently semantically typed, or is the structural position a function of

---

[12] Bouchard (1995: 409) distinguishes three type classes: V-projection adverbs (e.g. manner), sentential adverbs (frequency, time, etc.) and E-projection adverbs (expressing a point of view).

matching the semantic type requirement of an adverbial with a given syntactic context?

In other words: does syntax reserve unique positions for specific adverbial functions or is the surface position of an adverbial just a function of a semantically geared choice out of the potential positions in the syntactic structure of an expression? But, even for the former option, it must be conceded that the relative hierarchy of the structural position for adverbials is ultimately determined by their semantic function. So, the adverbial hierarchy would be coded twice, first by the principles of syntactic structuring and second in the algorithm for the construction of semantic representations. This is an unjustified redundancy. The basic alternative is, in Ernst's (1984, 2002) words, one between a *tight fit* conception (for each semantic function there is unique position) of the interface and a *loose fit* conception (semantic domains are identified with syntactic domains). I shall advocate the latter standpoint.

The *relative* distribution of adverbials with respect to other adverbials reflects an incrementality principle of the syntax-to-semantics mapping (25): adverbials can be sorted according to the subset relations of the semantic domains they modify (24a). The set inclusion relations in semantics correspond to syntactic c-command and domain inclusion relations (24b). The inclusion relations in (24a) are inclusion relations in the interpretation domain: a P-type expression denotes a situated event (in a possible world) which in turn is a specified process/state.

(24) a. Interpretation: proposition (T) ⊃ event (E) ⊃ process/state (P)
      b. Serialization: ['T-related'   ['E-related'   ['P-related']]]

(25) **Interface criterion:**
      Syntactic c-command domains are incrementally mapped onto semantic type domains.[13]

Incremental mapping forbids that a lower, that is, less specified, type is addressed once the mapping procedure has already targeted a higher type. The effect is *domain closure*. The integration of an adverbial A_i at a domain D closes D for any c-commanding adverbial A_j that requires a proper subdomain of D for its integration. Incremental mapping requires that the mapping goes parallel with the syntactic incrementality.

---

[13] If the semantic representation is chosen to be a discourse representation structure (DRS; cf. Kamp and Reyle 1993), the mapping of c-command domains on DRS-domains becomes particularly transparent in notation: 'box-command' relations in DRT are a subset of c-command relations on the syntactic structure.

(26) **Domain closure corollary:** If an adverbial A_i is included in the c-command domain of an adverb A_j, with A_j merged with P_n, and A_i merged with P_m, then the semantic type of P_m must be equal to or 'smaller' than the type of P_n.

Compare, for instance, frame adverbials (T-related) and a *local* adverbial function (E-related). The PP in (27a) is compatible with each of the two construals. (27b) shows that the frame adverbial reading is incompatible with the PP being contained in a (fronted) VP. The very same fronted VP is compatible with a local adverbial reading for the PP it contains (27c).

(27) a. weil er ja *in seinem Büro* ein Diktator gewesen ist
 since he PRT in his office a dictator been has
 b. *[In seinem Büro gewesen] ist er ja ein Diktator
 [in his office been] has he PRT a dictator
 c. [In seinem Büro gewesen] ist er ja letzte Woche nie
 [in his office been] has he PRT last week never

What this shows is that the frame adverbial reading requires a domain that is wider than the domain for a local adverbial reading. The frame adverbial must c-command the finite verb. Semantic domain requirements determine the relative order of adverbials.

(28) a. Er hat ja leider selten gut gespielt
 he has PRT unfortunately rarely well played
 b.*Er hat ja selten leider gut gespielt[14]
 c.*Er hat ja gut selten leider gespielt

Manner is a property of the event denoted by the verb; frequency adverbials quantify over events, and propositional attitudes relate to a proposition. So the semantic domain structure requires a syntactic distribution for these adverbials as sketched in (29).

(29) $[_{Proposition} \cdots [Q_{Events} [_{Event} \cdots V]]]$[15]

Consequently, the order will be: *propositional adverbial* before *frequency adverbial* before *event-modifying* adverbial. Why are (28b) and (28c) deviant, then? Each of the adverbials would have the required semantic domain in its

---

[14] Note that the order in (i) is deviant, unless you pronounce the sentence with a rise and fall accent indicated in (ii), that indicates focus fronting. This accent is a signal for reconstruction. The element with the rising accent is reconstructed into the position after the element with the falling accent (see Haider 2001c).

(i) *Er hat ja gut leider selten gespielt
(ii) Er hat ja /gut leider selten\ gespielt

[15] Q_{events} = quantification over events (frequency adverbials, quantification over locations).

c-command domain as a subdomain. What this shows is that the adverbials are integrated incrementally, that is, they are integrated into exactly the domain they are adjoined at. This is covered by the domain closure corollary (26).

(26) captures the obvious fact that an adverbial A_1 whose domain is smaller than the domain of another adverbial A_2, cannot have the adverbial A_2 in its domain, unless A_1 is moved across A_2 as in (30).

(30)   Gut$_i$ hat er leider selten e$_i$ gespielt
       well has he unfortunately rarely played

On the other hand, the very same adverbial item will receive a different interpretation, depending on the domain it is integrated with, if its semantics permits. This is well known from English, with adverbials that modify a property of the event (manner adverbial) or the proposition (sentence adverbial), depending on the position, as illustrated in (31):

(31)   a. He always *cleverly* avoided the problem
       b. He *cleverly* always avoided the problem
       c. He *cleverly* avoided the problem

In (31a) it is said that he did something in a *clever* manner, and in (31b), *cleverly* is judgemental. It was *clever* that he did something. Domain closure forbids a manner interpretation for the positionally higher adverbial in (31b). (31c) is open for either interpretation, since the linear position of the adverb in (29) is compatible with each of the two domain requirements.

6.4   Spec-F analyses of adverbials? The theory is willing but the evidence is not

In Spec-F analyses, adverbials are assigned to spec positions of adverbial functional projections. Analyses of this type were first proposed by Alexiadou (1994) and subsequently in a more extensive style by Cinque (1999, 2004a). A Spec-F analysis is also implied by Kayne's (1994) antisymmetry proposal, since it excludes adjunction. A cascade of functional projections with silent F-heads on top of the VP accommodates the respective adverbials. Thus, the order of adverbials in a clause is supposed to reflect the nesting of functional projections. Since there must be a separate functional projection for each adverbial whose semantics is identified with the semantic value of the silent functional head, each adverbial gives rise to a separate functional projection.[16]

---

[16] In Newmeyer's (2008: 52) count, Cinque's (1999) model distinguishes 32 different adverbial functional heads in the domain between $C°$ and the VP.

When this hypothesis is put to the test seriously, many of its immediate predictions turn out to be empirically wrong. Let us start with the opacity prediction. If preverbal adverbials are elements in a spec position, phrases preceding them must be in an even higher spec position. These positions are consequently predicted to be opaque for extraction.

(32)   a.   the constraint that it became difficult [to talk about e]
         b.   *the constraint that [*talking about e*] became difficult
         c.   *Which kind of constraints$_i$ did [*talking about e$_i$*] become difficult?
         d.   *Who$_i$ did [to e$_i$] she give it?
         e.   *the spot that/which$_i$ he said [$_{CP}$ [on e$_i$] there will stand a huge tower]

A constituent in a preverbal spec position is an extraction island (see 32b–e). The lack of opacity in OV clauses is flat and undeniable counterevidence for a spec analysis. The subject is in a higher spec position and it is opaque for extraction. Topicalization, as in (32d,e), yields an extraction island, too, in a movement-to-spec analysis or in an adjunction analysis of topicalization.

Adverbials clearly do not induce opacity effects for preceding elements, contrary to the predictions of the Spec-F analysis. The spec position of a sentence adverbial like *leider* (unfortunately) or *angeblich* (allegedly) would be VP-external. Hence, a preceding infinitival clause would have to be opaque for extraction, contrary to the facts (33).

(33)   a.   Wen$_i$ hat man [e$_i$ darüber zu informieren] *leider* verabsäumt?
            whom has one [it-about to inform] *unfortunately* failed
            'whom has one unfortunately failed to inform about it'
         b.   Was$_i$ hat denn [e$_i$ damit zu beweisen] einer *angeblich* versucht?
            what has PRT [it-with to prove] someone allegedly tried?
            'What did allegedly someone try to prove with this?'

Next, the *edge effect* is obviously incompatible with a spec analysis. Specs are positions for complete phrases and do not trigger an edge effect. If intermediate adverbial positions are in spec positions, then there is no way for a constraint on *adjunction* to apply to them. The edge effect described above is crucial evidence against a spec analysis. Uncontroversial examples of spec positions are Spec-I or Spec-C. They do not produce any edge effect.

The spec analysis is silent on the correlation between the edge effect and the headedness of a projection. Interestingly, opacity and edge effect are ignored in current proposals although at least opacity has been part of the standard repertoire of syntactic diagnostics for more than a decade in Generative Grammar (and still should be, of course).

Stacking, and in particular the topicalization of stacked adverbials is an additional problem area for spec analyses. Stacking should be unacceptable.[17] This is easy to see: if every adverbial is paired with a functional head that characterizes its semantic value, there is no way of stacking independent specs, since a stack contains adverbials of different kinds, for instance, temporal, local and conditional adverbials (34).

In terms of an approach that denies adjunction, the topicalized stack of adverbials would be either a non-constituent chunk or it would be a fronted constituent that contains the VP and the adverbial projections above it. In both cases, the structure ought to be ungrammatical:

(34) a. [*Gestern, im Hörsaal, als der Vortrag begann*] hustete er wie verrückt
yesterday, in the lecture room, when the lecture started, coughed he like mad
b. Er hustete *gestern im Hörsaal als der Vortrag begann* wie verrückt
c. [*Morgen, am Strand, wenn die Flut steigt*][wird ....
[tomorrow, at-the beach, when the flood-tide rises] [shall ...

In a Spec-F analysis of adverbials, the sequence of adverbials in (34) does not form a constituent. It is a section of the cascade of functional projections on top of the VP. Of course, it could not be simply clipped out and moved. (34a) would have to be the result of *remnant topicalization*. But this entails non-trivial operations. The VP would have to be raised to a position higher than the adverbials and then the whole sub-tree with the trace of VP is moved. But in this case the opacity problem emerges again. The raised VP would be opaque for extraction. So the VP cannot be raised, but it must be evacuated. In this case, the topicalized phrase contains an empty VP with the traces of the evacuated elements, and in particular the trace of the finite verb. And this is ungrammatical, too, as demonstrated by (35):

(35) a. [Die Zeit angesagt]$_i$ hat er noch nie e$_i$
the time announced has he never ever
b. *[Die Zeit an-e$_j$]$_i$ sagte$_j$ er noch nie e$_i$
the time an-e$_j$] nounced$_j$ he never ever[18]
c. Die Zeit sagte$_j$ er noch nie an-e$_j$
the time nounced$_j$ he never ever an-$_j$

V2 strands the particle of complex verbs with a so-called separable prefix. This is mimicked in the gloss of (35) by separating the verb *an-nounce* etymologically.

---

[17] A 'multiple specs' analysis would not help. Stacked adverbials are not specifiers of the *same* semantic relation. They are semantically heterogeneous.
[18] The gloss mimics the split between a separable prefix and the verb in German: *an+sagen*. lit. *on+say*

The unacceptability of (35b) is evidence for a crossover ungrammaticality: the trace of the fronted verb is not in the c-command domain of the verb in the V2-position, if the VP that contains the trace is (part of) the topicalized constituent.

This state of affairs is crucial also for the following data since it turns them into immediate counterevidence for a Spec-F analysis, too: if the fronted constituent in (36) must be a VP and not a higher functional projection containing a VP, the adverbials in (36) must be VP-internal since there is no functional projection to accommodate them.

(36)   a. [Gewöhnlich dann schon immer bestens präpariert] hatte sich nur einer
          usually then already always best prepared had himself only one
    b. [Wohlweislich immer gut ausgerüstet] hatte man die Mannschaft dafür
          wisely   always well-equipped had one the   crew for it
    c. dass man ja heuer hier *schon öfter* wen *ganz schnell wieder fast ganz* geheilt hat
       that one PRT this-year here already more-often someone very fast again almost completely cured has

Note that the examples in (36) contain only adverbials that Cinque (1999: 35 and 106) lists in the set of adverbials that are located in functional spec positions. The fact that these adverbials participate in VP topicalization (36a,b) and the fact that they are found interspersed with circumstantial adverbials (time, place, instrument, etc.) in (36c) forbid *first*, the drawing of a principled distinction between circumstantial adverbials and 'functional' adverbials, and *second*, the exclusion of circumstantial adverbials from a Spec-F analysis for adverbials.

Finally, the coverage of current Spec-F analyses for adverbials is too narrow. It is a shortcoming of this approach that it is tailored to the structure of the verbal projection and its functional extensions, ignoring that there are other contexts (adverbials in APs, DPs) that need to be covered too. This is not a principled defect, but it rules out proposals that tie the functional cascade of adverbials too narrowly to the functional architecture of the clause. Another shortcoming in the same vein is the inattention to the parallels with adnominal attributes. This includes the order preferences among attributes or adverbials that reflect an interface condition as well as the edge effect. In the Spec-F analysis, the functional head of the adverbial projection is seen as the crucial factor. It is supposed to link the spec-phrase to its semantic function represented by the functional head. A comparison with attribution is revealing in this respect:

(37)   a. die [*gestern* noch richtige] Theorie
       the [*yesterday* still correct] theory

b. Die Theorie war *gestern* noch richtig
the theory was *yesterday* still correct

c. die *gestrigen rechtzeitigen mehrfachen gründlichen* Durchsuchungen der Räume
the (of-)yesterday$_{AGR}$ timely$_{AGR}$ repeated$_{AGR}$ thorough$_{AGR}$ searches of the rooms

d. Man hat die Räume *gestern rechtzeitig mehrfach gründlich* durchsucht
they have the rooms yesterday timely repeatedly thoroughly searched

Let us assume for the sake of demonstration that a time adverbial like *gestern* (= *yesterday*) is in the spec of a functional projection. Then this projection should be part of the structure of (37a) and of (37b). The silent functional head of this projection would be semantically typed and play its role in logical form (LF). In (37c), the iteration of attributes corresponds to the iteration of adverbs within or above a VP (37d). Each of these attributes agrees with the head of the NP and the DP in number, gender and case features. So, if there are functional projections involved, these are functional projections of number, gender or case, but not of adverbial functions. Nevertheless, the order and interpretation is the same.[19] The four sentences in (38) are paraphrasing each other. Note that in (38c,d), attributes and adverbials are mixed.

(38) a. [Die *gestrige* Diskussion] dauerte länger als die *heutige*
[the yesterday$_{AGR}$ discussion] lasted longer than the (of) today$_{AGR}$

b. [Die Diskussion *gestern*] dauerte länger als die *heute*
[the discussion yesterday] lasted longer than the (one) today

c. [Die Diskussion *gestern*] dauerte länger als die *heutige*
[the discussion yesterday] lasted longer than the (one) today$_{AGR}$

d. [Die *gestrige* Diskussion] dauerte länger als die *heute*
[the yesterday$_{AGR}$ discussion] lasted longer than the (one) today

The comparison with adnominal attributes shows at least that the relative order among multiple occurrences of adverbials or attributes is semantically rather than structurally conditioned. There is no evidence that would support a duplication of semantic domain properties with syntactic projection properties. It is sufficient that syntax provides the structural positions and c-command relations for semantics. They are subsequently mapped onto types and type domains by the semantic compositionality algorithms.

---

[19] The parallelism is noted also in Quirk *et al.* (1985: 457n):

a. an apparent enemy – he is apparently an enemy   b. a possible meeting – they will possibly meet
c. a slight disagreement – they slightly disagree   d. the current manager – she is currently the manager.

6.5 Postverbal adverbials – right-adjoined or embedded?

6.5.1 Conflicting data?

In OV structures, adverbs are generally preverbal. They are directionally identified and semantically integrated in their respective domains. In VO structures, adverbials occur preverbally as well as postverbally. It is the postverbal distribution that provides non-trivial challenges for theoretical accounts. The controversial issue is the appropriateness of the answers to the following questions:

    a. What is the *structural position* of a postverbal adverbial? Is it right-adjoined or embedded or stranded by roll-up or …?
    b. What is the empirically adequate account for the *ordering preference* of postverbal adverbials as a *mirror-image order* of preverbal adverbials?

In the traditional view, post-VP adverbials are assumed to be right-adjoined to the VP. If right-adjunction obeys the same incrementality-driven sequencing as left-adjunction, the result is a mirror-image order of postverbal adverbials compared with preverbal ones. So, what is wrong with this apparently straightforward account, which is widely accepted, after all?

First, it is now already well known that right-adjunction produces the wrong c-command configurations for all kinds of c-command-dependent grammatical relations. Second, the mirror-image order is *preferential*, but it is not mandatory. This becomes immediately clear with examples like (39):

(39)   a. He has *now completely* accomplished his mission
          b. *He has *completely now* accomplished his mission[20]
          c. He has accomplished his mission *completely now*
          d. He has accomplished his mission *now completely*

If the postverbal order had to be an exact mirror image of the preverbal order because it is driven by the same process modulo left- or right-adjunction, (39d) would be the mirror image of (39b), and it would have to be just as deviant as (39b), which is obviously not the case.

---

[20] The starring of this sentence is supported by a full-text search on the web: 'completely now de' produces no document, while 'now completely de' offers more than 10^4 sites. 'De' was chosen as a verbal prefix with a sufficiently high token probability. The postverbal distribution was checked with 'it now completely' and 'it completely now' and the search produced 5×10^6 and 3.6×10^4 sites, respectively. Note that the mirror-image order prescribed by grammars is vastly outnumbered by the preverbal order repeated as the postverbal order.

A right-adjunction analysis is inadequate also because it over-generates. It is well known that sentence adverbials cannot occur postverbally (40b) at all.[21]

(40)   a.   They would {*probably/surprisingly/fortunately*} split into several groups
            b.   *They would split {*probably/surprisingly/fortunately*} into several groups

If adverbials were simply right- or left-adjoined to their appropriate projections, as indicated in (41c,d), it should not matter whether they precede or follow the VP, given that the c-command domains of adverbials would be the same on either side of a projection (see 41a,b). Hence, the respective hierarchical configurations would be identical, modulo linearization, on either side.

(41)   a.   They have /*extremely carefully*/ examined the data /*extremely carefully*/
            b.   They /*very often*/ tend to produce misleading accounts /*very often*/
            c.   [$_{XP}$ *Adv* [$_{XP}$ ...]]
            d.   [$_{XP}$ [$_{XP}$ ...] *Adv*]

The various adjunction analyses proposed in the literature differ in the details of the adjunction sites. May (1985) and Kayne (1984) assume postverbal adverbials to be adjoined to the VP. Ernst (1984) claims that postverbal adverbials are VP-internal, but they are structurally superior to the arguments in a binary, left-branching V-projection. In each case, an adverbial is higher in structure than a preceding argument in the same VP. The unavoidable but empirically wrong prediction is this: an argument does not c-command postverbal adverbials and therefore it cannot enter a relation that requires c-command. Binding relations are c-command sensitive and arguments may bind into adverbial phrases. This has been reviewed in detail by Pesetsky (1995: 161), and he summarizes it as 'The farther to the right you go, the lower you are' or 'rightward is downward'. This is exactly what the BBC says.

But, and this is crucial here too, Pesetsky (1995: 230) contrasts the evidence from grammatical dependency relations (quantifier–variable binding, anaphor binding, negative-polarity licensing) and from coordination, with evidence from VP-fronting. VP-fronting seems to presuppose a right-adjunction structure, while for the other cases, embedding in a left-associative structure seems to provide the right kind of structural configuration.

This analysis was introduced by Larson (1988) and taken up by Stroik (1990): they assign postverbal adverbs to more deeply embedded positions in a V-projection (42c).

---

[21] Afterthought constructions with 'comma-intonation' (e.g. *Finally they left*↘, *fortunately*↘) are ignored here. These are juxtaposed adverbials, that is, they form a paratactic construction.

(42)   a. [$_{Vmax}$ [$_{Vmax}$ ...] Adv]
       b. [$_{Vmax}$ [$_{V'}$ [$_{V'}$ $V°$ DP] Adv] Adv]
       c. [$_{Vmax}$ ... [$_{V}°$ Adv]]

The following examples illustrate the conflicting data properties. First, the object may bind an anaphor in the adverbial PP. Hence, the object must c-command the PP. This is evidence for an embedding structure (43b). Second, the very same PP may be stranded by VP-fronting (43c). This seems to be immediate evidence for a right-adjoined position, as in (43d).

(43)   a. He gives them$_i$ a book in the garden on each$_i$ other's birthday
       b. He [gives the book to them$_i$ [in the garden [on each$_i$ other's birthday]]]
       c. and [[give the book to them$_i$] in the garden] he did on each$_i$ other's birthday
       d. He [[[gives the book to them$_i$] in the garden] on each$_i$ other's birthday]

In this contradictory situation, one has to question the validity of the evidence, and to search for independent evidence. At first glance it seems to be a conflict between binding and movement data. Since movement is an operation on phrase structure, one is inclined to interpret this as a strong indication for the presupposed phrase structure. But, coordination is phrase-structure dependent as well, and it is compatible with embedding rather than adjunction, as Pesetsky (1995: 161) illustrates:

(44)   a. Kremer will perform this concerto [in Rio on Tuesday] *and* [in Lund on Sunday]
       b. He gave her [money in Boston] *and* [supplies in New York]

In a right-adjunction structure, coordination would have to slice sequences off from the right edge that do not form a constituent and coordinate them. In an embedding structure, coordinations as in (44) coordinate the bottom part of phrases, and these sub-trees are constituents.

So the conflict is not one of phrase-structure assignment versus binding, but one between evidence from alleged movement and all the other evidence. As Phillips (1999: §2) remarks, 'the most widespread response to constituency conflicts is to question the assumptions about the tests which lead to the contradiction'. For instance, the premise that c-command is at the basis of the binding patterns has been questioned,[22] but this would not help since there are the coordination data as well. What we have to question is the validity of

---

[22] Barss and Lasnik (1986), Jackendoff (1990) and Ernst (1984), to name some authors, propose precedence plus m-command instead of c-command.

VP-fronting as a direct source of evidence for the constituent structure of the source variant. Let us do this.

The movement metaphor is so deeply entrenched that it is hard to step back and have a fresh look at the relevant data. It is commonly taken for granted that a fronted VP, as in (45a) or (45b), is an exact copy of the respective VP in the alleged source construction (45c). Otherwise, the argument that VP-fronting provides information on the 'extraction site' would not be valid.

(45)   a. and [give the book to them in the garden]$_i$ he did e$_i$
         b. and [give the book to them]$_i$ he did [e$_i$ [in the garden]]
         c. and he did [[give the book to them] in the garden]$_{VP}$

Is it true that a fronted VP always is an *exact copy* of the VP in the source variant? In other words, would reconstruction of a fronted VP into the associated trace position always yield a grammatically well-formed structure? The answer is a clear no for German. English does not offer a direct testing ground. Here is evidence from German:

(46)   a. [Warten auf besseres Wetter]$_i$ wird$_j$ er [e$_i$ müssen e$_j$]$_{VC}$
         b. *dass er [warten auf besseres Wetter] müssen wird
         c. [Geld ausgeben das er nicht besitzt]$_i$ wird$_j$ er nicht [e$_i$ können e$_j$]$_{VC}$
         d. *dass er nicht [Geld ausgeben, das er nicht besitzt] können wird

As pointed out in Haider (1990), a topicalized VP cannot be reconstructed when it contains extraposed material. In (46a), a PP is extraposed, and in (46c) it is a relative clause. What this clearly shows is that a *copy theory* of movement cannot be correct. The reason for the contrast in (46a) is easy to understand. A VP in the trace position would not be well formed (46b,d) since the clause-final verbs obligatorily form a verbal cluster. In OV languages, cluster formation replaces an embedded VP. The trace of the fronted VP in (46a,c) is *atomic*. Hence it does not impede cluster formation. For cluster formation, the trace is an atomic empty category of the category V.

German (as well as any other Germanic OV language) provides robust evidence against direct reconstruction or, in other words, against a copy theory of movement. The fronted position may serve as a test site for the well-formedness of a constituent, since this position is open only for a single well-formed constituent in a V2 language. But, the fronted position is neither a direct nor an indirect test site for the structure of the constituent *at the trace* position.

English, being VO, does not provide the opportunity of observing a mismatch of the kind displayed by German. But, there is a similar kind of mismatch even for English. VP-fronting is illicit without an auxiliary preceding the trace position (47a). The expletive auxiliary 'do' in (47b) is syntactically triggered.[23] It is not required when there is no trace, as in (47c). (47d) is ill-formed, unless the expletive auxiliary is focused.

(47)   She declared that she would marry him on a yacht, and ...
  a. * ... [married him on a yacht]$_i$ she e$_i$ indeed
  b. ... [marry him on a yacht]$_i$ she did e$_i$ indeed
  c. ... she married him on a yacht indeed
  d. ... she *did* [marry him on a yacht] indeed

It seems that the apparently paradoxical data that Pesetsky has focused on are merely data for which the mismatch becomes visible also in English. The apparent paradox disappears immediately once we realize that a topicalized VP is what it is, namely a well-formed VP in a derived position, that is, as the antecedent of a trace. The trace is atomic. It is an empty node of the category V:

(48)   a. [...V°]$_i$ he did [e$_i$ [in the garden]]$_{VP}$
       b. [...V°]$_i$ he did [e$_i$ [in the garden] [at new year's evening]]$_{VP}$

Note that the internal details of the fronted VP do not matter. Whatever well-formed VP holds the initial position, it is standardly and obligatorily related to the trace, and the trace becomes the nucleus for merging and projecting a residual VP structure. The paradox disappears, once you accept that an empty category is nothing but an empty category, and not a silent copy of a 'moved' phrase (see also Chapter 9, Appendix 9.2).

Phillips (1999) has suggested a solution in terms of *incremental* structure projection: syntactic structures are built incrementally from left to right, i.e. in the order in which the terminal elements are linearized. So, a constituency test may refer to just those strings that are constituents at the point in the incremental derivation when the test applies. Contradictions between constituency tests can arise only when these tests apply at different stages in the derivation. The following example (49a) is to illustrate how the apparent conflict between the assumption of a right-branching VP and the evidence from VP topicalization, notably the well-formedness of (49b,c), are reconciled under this approach.

(49)   a. He will [give$_i$ books [e$_i$ to them [e$_i$ in the garden [e$_i$ on each other's birthday]]]]
       b. and [give books to them] he did in the garden on each other's birthday
       c. [$_{IP}$ [$_{VP}$ Give books to them] [$_{IP}$ he [$_{I'}$ did #
       d. [$_{IP}$ [$_{VP}$ Give books to them [[$_{IP}$ he [$_{I'}$ did [$_{VP}$ *give books to them* #

---

[23] The fronted VP must not contain the finite verb. 'Do' serves as an expletive auxiliary for the finiteness features.

e. Give books to them he did *give books to them* in the garden on each other's birthday
f. and [give books to them in the garden]]] he did on each other's birthday

In (49a), everything is in place. For (49b), the crucial phases of its derivation are given in (49c–e): (49c) shows the structure at the point in the derivation when the fronted VP-material, the subject and the auxiliary has been built. Note that the fronted VP is a well-formed VP constituent. (49d) is the result of copying the VP into its underlying position, in which theta-role assignment is possible. Finally, in (49e) the stranded PPs are added to, that is structurally integrated into, the reconstructed VP. 'This creates a structure in which the anaphor in the second PP is appropriately c-commanded by its antecedent. It also has the effect of destroying the constituency of the copied VP, but this is unproblematic, because the chain was created by constituent copying at the point at which it was created' (Phillips 1999: §4.2).

Note that the constituency of the copied VP has to be 'destroyed'. In other words, the copy and the structure at the trace position do not match. In English, the necessary restructuring would be string-neutral. For German, this would not work. Hence, the representational account seems to be superior, both to Pesetky's double structuring (cascading vs. layered) and to Phillips's incremental structure-building way out. In the representational account, the trace is an atomic verbal unit that serves as the nucleus for a residual V-projection that may accommodate adverbials.

6.5.2 Right-adjoined or embedded?

In addition to the movement data discussed above, scope data (see Ernst 1984; Pesetsky 1995; Stroik 1996) have been adduced for motivating a VP structure with adjunction to the right. The evidence is not as clear-cut as one would like to have it, however. Let us start with an example discussed by Pesetsky (1995: 233).

(50) a. He plays quartets in foreign countries on weekends
      b. He plays quartets on weekends in foreign countries

He states, conditionally hedged: 'if there is any difference in the scope of modification, the PP to the right has wider scope'. This would accord with 'rightward is upward', but there is another interpretation available as well. Phillips (1999: §4.5) notes that arguments based on sentences like (50) fail to control for an essential intervening factor, namely clause-final focus. He claims that 'once this effect is controlled for, which can be done by adding a third adverbial, we find that the strong right-to-left scope preference seen among the first two adverbials [as in (50)] no longer obtains'.

(51) a. Sue kissed him willingly many times (in front of the boss)
b. He plays quartets in foreign countries on weekends (at the height of the season)

According to Phillips, the reading in (51a) with left-to-right scope is much easier to obtain if there is a third adverbial that follows and bears the stress than without it, although right-to-left scope is still available.[24] And in (51b) the additional, clause-final adverbial cancels the preference for interpreting the playing of quartets in foreign countries as restricted to weekends. If focus were indeed the crucial intervening factor, scope data would no longer be in conflict with the dependency data above.[25] However, Ernst (2002) insists that the focus cases are only a subset of right-to-left scope cases.[26]

Another case of conflict that is fairly easy to eliminate is based on a set of data that led Stroik (1996: 66) to the striking conclusion that *manner* and *reason* adverbials are right-adjoined to the VP and AGR_sP, respectively, while time and location adverbials are VP-internal.[27] His diagnostic tool is *antecedent contained deletion* (ACD):

(52) a. *When* did Mary read Lou everything Bill did   (ambiguous)
b. *Where* did Mary read Lou everything Bill did   (ambiguous)
c. *Why* did Mary read Lou everything Bill did   (unambiguous)
d. *How* did Mary read Lou everything Bill did   (unambiguous)

---

[24] Koster (2000) discusses examples with a narrow domain interpretation of an adverbial in clause-final position. (i) *He saw Bill on his birthday twice* (ex. #30 and #47 of Koster). The preferred reading is 'on his birthday, he saw him twice', and not the wide-scope reading 'it happened twice that he saw him on his birthday'.

[25] What is still left unaccounted for is the order preference. Postverbal adverbials are preferentially ordered time before location, whereas preverbal adverbials tend to come in the inverse order.

[26] According to Ernst, sentences (i) and (ii) are ambiguous. In one reading the clause-final adverbials get wide over the preceding ones, even without focal stress or intonation break

(i) They almost got hit again   (ii) The patrol intentionally returned on Tuesday

However, even if there is the possibility of a wide-scope reading in (i) and (ii), scope follows linear order in the following examples. In (iii) the repetitive *again* has wide scope over the frequency adverbial *every Sunday*, and in (iv), *willingly* outscopes *many times*.

(iii) This year, he will sit *again* in the first row *every Sunday*
(iv) Sue kissed him *willingly many times* in front of the boss

This seems to indicate that for postverbal adverbials, scope relations and order relations cannot be *uniformly* reduced to the particular c-command relations prescribed by an adjunction analysis.

[27] It is striking because of its implication for serialization. The base order for postverbal adverbials should be time/locative before manner, which is not the case (cf. Quirk *et al.* 1985: 565).

The important fact is the difference in readings available for (52a,b), on the one hand, and (52c,d), on the other. Unlike (52a,b), according to Stroik (1996: 57), sentences (52c,d) have no readings in which the wh-adverb modifies both predicates: the *why* adverb in (52c) applies only to Mary's reasons for readings, not to Bill's; and the *how* adverb in (52d) modifies only the matrix verb. This observation may be correct, but the conclusion based on this datum is not compelling: the wh-elements are quantifier-like, the adverbials are not. Their distribution is not identical, as the wh-*in-situ* patterns show (see (54)).

Stroik's (1996: 59) account rests on the ECP effect (Empty Category Principle),[28] on the assumption that the traces of the empty operators construed with *when* and *where* – in a Larson and May (1990) style of QR-analysis of ACD, in which the matrix VP is copied into the empty VP at LF – are VP-internal and thereby head-governed, whereas the traces of *why* and *how* in (52c,d) are VP-external and ungoverned and thus in violation of the ECP.

If Stroik were correct, his ECP account would predict island effects for constituents following manner adverbs but not for time and location adverbs, which is incorrect (53a–c). (53a) is discussed by Aoun *et al.* (1987: 544n), and (53c,d) by Costa (1998: 32f.).

(53) a. *Which woman$_i$ did Ray say *yesterday* [that Kay saw e$_i$]?
      b. Which woman$_i$ did Ray *carefully* communicate [that Kay saw e$_i$]
      c. *Which painter$_i$ did he look *yesterday* [at the pictures of e$_i$]?
      d. Which painter$_i$ did he look *carefully* [at the pictures of e$_i$]?

The contrasts in (53) and especially the grammaticality of (53b) are not expected if the *manner* adverbial is higher in structure than a time or locative adverbial. A clause following a manner adverbial would be equally high or higher in structure and outside the VP, if the preceding adverbial is outside the VP. Hence, (53a,b) are predicted to be opaque for extraction and (53c,d) ought to be well formed.

The contrast in (52) can be easily accounted for without appeal to the ECP. It reflects a constraint on dependency relations for wh-elements that can be observed best with wh-*in-situ* constructions, sometimes misleadingly subsumed under superiority cases.

(54) a. What did he buy *where/when/*why/*how*?
      b. Was hat er *wo/wann/warum/wie* gekauft
         what has he where/when/why/how bought

---

[28] In either version of the ECP, that is, the conjunctive formulation of ECP ('a trace must be antecedent governed *and* head-governed') or in the disjunctive formulation ('a trace must be antecedent governed *or* head-governed').

    c. **Wie* hat er es *warum* gekauft?
       how has he it why bought?

In Haider (1997f, 2000d, 2004a, 2010a: ch.3.4), two conditions are identified: first, wh-adverbials of a higher-type semantics (i.e. reason and manner) cannot depend on each other. This rules out (54c), but allows (54b). Second, higher adverbials must c-command (the trace of) the tensed verb. This rules out (54a), if the manner and reason adverbials are VP-internal, but allows (54b).[29] In the ACD case, the empty operator that binds the wh-trace in the empty VP is dependent on the overt wh-element. But in the case of *why* and *how* this dependency is ruled out for the same reason that rules out (54c), namely the constraints against *in situ* licensing of a higher-order wh-quantifier by a higher-order wh-element in Spec-C.

Stroik's (1996: 61f.) second set of data consists of scope interactions between wh-moved operators and *in situ* quantifiers. In his view, the scope ambiguity of (55a) in contrast with the unambiguity in (55b,c) corroborates the choice of structure he used for the ACD account. If the extraction site of the wh-phrase is in the c-command domain of a quantifier, a scope ambiguity arises: the scope of an operator is its c-command domain. The wh-element c-commands the quantifier in its surface position, but is c-commanded by the quantifier in its base position.[30]

(55)   a. *When/where* did Mary read Lou *everyone's* poem   (ambiguous)
        b. *How/why* did Mary read *everyone* the poem   (unambiguous)
        c. *Whose* poem did Mary read Lou *every day/everywhere*   (unambiguous)

The ambiguity of (55a) and the non-ambiguity of (55c) follow, if (the base position of) the adverbial is c-commanded by the argument. For Stroik, (55b), receives the same explanation, but there is also another possible interpretation for the lack of ambiguity of examples like (55b), discussed in Haider (2004b): higher-order wh-operators are interpreted only in positions that c-command the head of the projection they are applied to. A higher-order wh-element cannot be interpreted in its trace position, if it is too low; hence (55b) is *un*ambiguous. A comparison with German corroborates this assumption.

(56)   a. Welches Problem$_i$ hast du jedem e$_i$ erklärt?   (ambiguous)
        which problem have you everyone explained

---

[29] In a finite V-final clause, the position of the finite verb is the *in situ* position, i.e. the head position of the VP (see Haider (2010a: ch.2) for a detailed argumentation).

[30] This is a paraphrase of Aoun and Li's (1993) scope principle: an operator A may have scope over an operator B iff A c-commands B or an A'-element co-indexed with B. For an extensive assessment in German and improvements, see Frey (1993).

b. Warum$_i$ hast du e$_i$ jedem dieses Problem erklärt? (unambiguous)
   why have you everyone this problem explained
c. Wie$_i$ hast du jedem dieses Problem e$_i$ erklärt? (ambiguous)
   how have you everyone this problem explained
d. Was$_i$ hast du ihr jeden Abend/an jedem Ort e$_i$ erklärt ? (ambiguous)
   what has you her every evening/at every location explained

The crucial fact for the present discussion is (56c). This type of sentence is ambiguous in German. The base position of the adverbial in German c-commands the head of the projection, hence it is a possible position for the semantic evaluation of the wh-adverbial. This position is in the scope of the quantified object, though, whence its wide scope. Semantic evaluation in the fronted position yields wide scope for the wh-element. (56b) is unambiguous, as expected, because the quantified object is lower than the base position of the adverbial. The same situation holds for (56a). In (56d), ambiguity is predicted, since there is a licit position for the adverb c-commanding the object position.

The difference between (56b,c) has a counterpart in English. Stroik (1996: 65) noted the following contrast (57a,b) as support for differentiating the adjunction sites for the two adverbials involved. Obviously, in (57a), the adverbial is not in the scope of negation, but in (57b) it is.

(57) a. Why did he [e$_i$] read no one anything?
      b. *How did he read no one anything [e$_i$]
      c. He [read no one anything *completely*]
      d. He *therefore/*completely* has [read no one anything]

This contrast follows immediately if the base position for a manner adverbial is VP-internal, hence within the scope of negation. Reason adverbials, on the other hand, may occur in higher positions. The square brackets in (57a,b) indicate the trace positions assumed by me. The non-wh versions are illustrated in (57c,d).[31] In sum, despite claims to the contrary, the scope data fall in line with the dependency data discussed above and call for an analysis in which 'to the

---

[31] Quirk *et al.* (1985: 574n) note the following contrast (as an intervention effect of negation):

(i) Casually she greeted the stranger – Casually, she did *not* greet the stranger
(ii) She greeted the stranger casually
(iii) Slowly, the nun walked up the hill – *Slowly, the nun did *not* walk up the hill

The appropriate interpretation for the adverbial in (ii) is manner, but the adverbial in (i) is a subject-related event-modifying one (see Quirk *et al.* 1985: 573). Since the latter interpretation is not available for (iii), the manner interpretation requires a trace in the scope of negation, whence the unacceptability.

right' implies 'towards the bottom of a projection' and not towards the roof of a phrase.

6.5.3 Order preferences

For adverb ordering, it is handbook wisdom that in English, the post-VP order of adverbials (58a) is preferentially the mirror image of the pre-VP order, as illustrated by (59a). According to Quirk et al. (1985: 566) clause-initial adverbials 'tend to be in the reverse order to that observed at E',[32] that is, clause-finally. The German unmarked order for adverbials preceding the verb is given in (58b) and illustrated by (59b). It is representative for Dutch as well. Evidently, (58a) and (58b) are mirror-image sequences.

(58) a. $V°$ – respect < process < space < time   (in VO, as e.g. English)
      b. time < space < process < respect – $V°$ (in OV, as e.g. German, Dutch ...)

(59) a. She has *worked* [$_{respect}$ *on her hobby*] [$_{process}$ *with great care*] [$_{space}$ *in the garden*]
      [$_{time}$ *the whole time*] [$_{time}$ *today*]
      b. Sie hat [$_{time}$ *heute*] [$_{time}$ *die ganze Zeit*] [$_{space}$ *im Garten*] [$_{process}$ *mit großer Sorgfalt*]
      [$_{respect}$ *an ihrem Steckenpferd*] *gearbeitet* (= 59a)

Let me emphasize that the order tendencies are not *mandatory*. In other words, a deviation from the 'neutral' order does not make the clause deviant. It merely influences pragmatic features (*information structure*). This indicates that the order is not *structurally* fixed, but only facilitated by syntactic structure. This contrasts sharply with the fixed order of *arguments* in VO.[33]

The preferred order of extraposed adverbials in German mirrors the order of preverbal adverbials, too, and the pattern is the same as in English, namely 'space < time' for extraposed adverbials.

(60) a. Das Geld wurde gefunden [wo er es versteckt hatte] [noch ehe er es entfernen konnte]
      the money was found [where he had concealed it] [before he could remove it]

---

[32] Note the wording: 'tend to' and not 'have to'.
[33] Compare argument order (i) with adjunct order in (ii) and (iii). If, according to Quirk et al. (1985: 566), the preverbal neutral order is 'time < space', only one of the two orders in (ii) can be the neutral order, and vice versa in (iii). However, there is no contrast in acceptability. The fact that none of the order variants in (ii) and (iii) is deviant is evidence for the non-categorical status of these order patterns.

(i) Men tell women lies vs. *Men tell lies women
(ii) That every year, in China, there... vs. that in China, every year, there...
(iii) ... are born in China every year vs. ... are born every year in China

b. ?Das Geld wurde gefunden [noch ehe er es entfernen konnte] [wo er es versteckt hatte]
   c. Man hat ja berichtet, in allen Tageszeitungen, wie man sich verhalten soll, schon lange vor dem Sommer
      they have PRT reported in every newspaper how one should behave oneself, even long before the summer
   d. ?Man hat ja berichtet, schon lange vor dem Sommer, wie man sich verhalten soll, in allen Tageszeitungen.

The situation in Dutch is parallel. The examples in (61) are taken from Koster (1989: 271). Here, it is the preverbal order preference[34] of adverbials followed by the prepositional object (61a) that is mirrored by the inverse order in (61c).

(61) a. Hij heeft *tijdens de pauze aan zijn vader* gedacht
         he has during the break of his father thought
      b. %Hij heeft *aan zijn vader tijdens de pauze* gedacht
         he has of his father during the break thought
      c. Hij heeft gedacht *aan zijn vader tijdens de pause*
         he has thought of his father during the break

What is it that makes us prefer an inverted order in the postverbal area? It is the very same incrementality of the semantic construction process that determines the preverbal order. In each case there is an intervention effect that blocks integration:

(62) $[_{CP} \ldots Adv_1 \, Adv_2 \, [_{VP} \ldots \ldots Adv_3 \, Adv_4]]$

If the adverb Adv_1 in a structure like (62) requires a lower-type domain than Adv_2, the latter adverb cannot be integrated in the domain of Adv_1. So Adv_2 blocks. On the other hand, if Adv_2 is properly integrated, its type domain is not suitable for Adv_1. Hence Adv_2 blocks in either case – either because it is successfully integrated or because it cannot be integrated successfully.

The preverbal area has robust restrictions that result from direct integration. In the postverbal area, adverbials cannot be integrated as adjoined phrases since there are no appropriate type domains for them to adjoin.[35] They are inte-

---

[34] In Koster (2000, 2001), the '%' ('highly marked order') of Koster (1989: 271) is revised to '*' without mentioning the previous paper. This increased severity is unjustified, given the data (i) and (ii) from a corpus, or (iii) and (iv) from ANS² (1997: 1,337):

(i) om met iedereen tijdens de opnames samen te werken
(ii) om tijdens de opnames met iedereen samen te werken
(iii) Misschien zal vader *morgen aan Jan* een boek geven
(iv) Misschien zal vader *aan Jan morgen* een boek geven.

[35] This would work only if right-adjunction was admitted. But, as argued above, both the evidence and the theory rules out right-adjunction.

grated *like secondary predicates*. Here, incrementality instigates a preference for nested dependencies.

Assume that Adv_3 in (62) is construed with a semantically higher-type domain than Adv_4. In this case, the scan of the already completed structure for the clause would identify a suitable target of predication, namely the very projection that the adverb could be directly integrated with if the adverb preceded this projection. If the scanning is to be economical, it must be incremental. This entails that the adverbial that comes next does not require a new scan but only the continuation of the previous scan. Continuation means higher up in the structure. So, the consequence is clear: the adverb that follows is expected to be an adverbial that targets a higher projection than the preceding one, therefore the unmarked serialization of postverbal adverbials is one in terms of *increasing*-type requirements. Preverbal adverbials must be serialized in terms of *decreasing*-type requirements. The result is a mirror-image serialization pattern.

6.6 Towards an adequate theoretical coverage

The convergent evidence points to the conclusion that preverbal adverbials are *left-adjoined* to their target phrase while postverbal adverbials are *embedded*, rather than right-adjoined. 'Embedded' means that they are in a *lower* position than a preceding phrase-mate. The evidence for embedding (rather than right-adjoining) is diverse and sufficiently reliable. What is still missing, though, is the conclusive theoretic modelling. Embedded adverbials in postverbal positions presuppose a shell structure for the right edge of the VP (both in VO and OV), but we do not yet fully understand the grammatical principles that determine the kind of shell structure necessary for the 'extraposition' area (see Haider 1997d: §3, 2010a: ch.5, §5.3).

Second, postverbal adverbials in VO are of a restricted class. So-called sentence adverbials are deviant in postverbal positions:

(63)   a. He talked gently/*fortunately[36] to Mary
       b. Man hat ja die Kunden höflich/glücklicherweise informiert

In a right-adjunction analysis, pre- and postverbal positions would be equivalent modulo adjunction direction. They could be adjoined to the very same phrase on

---

[36] A web search for 'talked fortunately to' produced a *single* entry, with bracketed 'fortunately': 'I talked (fortunately) to a couple of trusted friends'. 'Allegedly' yielded two entries, each with a bracketed adverbial. 'Talked gently to', on the other hand, produced more than 21,000 entries.

either side. Hence a postverbal sentence adverb would have the same c-command domain as a preverbal one. How does theory predict the asymmetry?

Embedding is a consequence of the BBC. First, the restriction on postverbal adverbials indirectly reflects the semantic domain requirement (viz. incremental closure). Second, embedded adverbials do not have the finite verb in their c-command domain in VO. This excludes adverbials that need to have the tensed element in their domain.

A final comment is due on a radical attempt at unifying adverb positioning, as considered in Cinque (2004a): postverbal adverbials are suggested to be *stranded* preverbal adverbials. They are deemed to be stranded by *iterative roll-up* of their respective sub-constituent:

(64) a. ... [Adv$_1$ [Adv$_2$ [$_{VP}$ V ...]]] ⇨ *roll-up* ⇨ ... [Adv$_1$ [[$_{VP}$ V ...]$_i$ [Adv$_2$ e$_i$]]] ⇨
b. [[[$_{VP}$ V ...]$_i$ [Adv$_2$ e$_i$]]]$_j$ [Adv$_1$ e$_j$]]

In this approach, the mirror-image order of postverbal adverbials is a direct consequence of the derivational roll-up. This is the only advantage, it seems. The disadvantages are many.

First, the VP is predicted to become an *opaque domain* by virtue of roll-up. This is inevitable. The VP is fronted into a spec position that is higher than the original VP position. In this area of phrase structure, phrases in spec positions are opaque for extraction. A VP with postverbal adverbials crucially is not opaque. The prediction is entirely clear, and so is its falsification.

Second, the arguments contained in the VP do not c-command the postverbal adverbials. Hence postverbal adverbials should be on a par with preverbal adverbials with respect to scoping and binding: an object is predicted to be unable to bind or outscope an adverbial. This is obviously a wrong prediction.

Third, if every adverbial is a preverbal adverbial, the edge effect is predicted to hold for the apparently postverbal positions as well. Since they are stranded, they remain in their original preverbal position, and the edge effect ought to apply. This prediction is wrong.[37]

Finally, a trigger for roll-up is missing. Without a trigger theory, the roll-up mechanism is wholly ad hoc. What is it that could make a VP move to a clause-internal higher spec position, and what could make this phrase that contains the moved VP in its spec position move to an even higher clause-internal spec position? The possibility of enlisting an intricate series of shifting operations demonstrates the (redundant) system's potential as a derivational model. The

---

[37] But note that this argument would apply only to the roll-up version of an *adjunction* model. In Cinque's model, adverbials are spec-based, and hence the edge effect is not covered at all.

likelihood that this does *not* model a property of the grammars of natural languages is by far greater than the likelihood that it does. The representational approach is the stronger account. It does not provide derivational loopholes.

6.7 Summary

(1) Adverbs are attached wherever the sentence structure permits. In particular, there is more room in an OV clause than in a VO clause. Mapping constraints of the syntax–semantics interface determine the compatibility of an intended interpretation with a structural site.

(2) Adjunction and embedding are subject to a general structural restriction for projections: projections are right-branching. So, adjunction of integrated items to the right is ruled out. Clause-final adjuncts are embedded.

(3) Adverbials are adjoined or embedded, depending on the relation to the head of the containing phrase: they are adjoined if they precede the head of the containing phrase and embedded if they follow the head of the containing phrase.

(4) The *relative order* of adverbials is a result of semantic integration. Preverbal adverbials are directly integrated. This entails that the type domain of the phrase an adverbial is syntactically adjoined to, and semantically integrated into, meets the semantic type requirement of the adverbial. As a consequence, the strict relative order of preverbal adverbials reflects the incremental integration in decreasing-type domains. Postverbal adjuncts are integrated like secondary predicates. Their order preference is the reflex of an economy effect on incremental integration. The result is a preference for mirror-image patterns. Postverbal serialization tends to mirror the preverbal order.

(5) The structural conditions for postverbal embedding are arguably the same kind of structures as those for extraposed items. What is still missing is a full understanding of the grammatical principles that determine the shell structure of the right edge of a projection that accommodates postverbal adverbials as well as extraposed material.

7 Elements of the third kind – resultative predicates and particles in OV and VO

7.1 Introduction

The main concern of this chapter[1] is the grammar of *secondary predicates* and in particular of *result predication* (including resultative verb and particle combinations) from the perspective of BBC-constrained structures: the positioning of result predicates, including particles, is a diagnostics for basic verb positions and consequently for the evaluation of competing theories of verb positioning. The apparently *variable* positioning of result predicates/particles in (some) VO structures is adequately accounted for in terms of optional stranding in a VP-shell structure. The *obligatory* clause-final *and pre*verbal position in OV is positive evidence for the uniformly incremental organization of a *head*-final VP.

The essence of the chapter is as follows. The serialization patterns of *result predicates* correlate in a predictable manner with the canonical directionality of the head of the VP: in VO languages, result predicates are found potentially in two different postverbal positions, namely V-adjacent or in a distant position. In OV languages, the position of result predicates is invariably preverbal and V-*adjacent*.

The analysis of the implications of the factors that determine the serialization of predicates provides empirical support for a theoretical issue: head-*initial* projections are structurally more complex than head-*final* ones. The grammar of secondary predicates and in particular the grammar of result predicates provide independent evidence for the directionality-dependent differences in the structural architecture of phrases. At the same time this is evidence against VO-based, derivational analyses of head-*final* structures as derivatives of (evacuated) head-initial projections.

---

[1] This chapter shares material with Haider (1997b), though in a significantly revised version.

The *empirical* domain of this chapter is the *comparative* syntax of secondary predicates in Germanic languages. This area of comparative grammar has not attracted as much attention as the syntax of heads, complements, arguments and adjuncts. It provides valuable insights, though, into the syntactically epiphenomenal differences of the VO/OV parameterization.

The chapter is organized as follows: after an introduction to the crucial properties of result vs. depictive predicates in Section 7.2, the comparative data are briefly described in Section 7.3. Section 7.4 recapitulates and amends the theoretical background for the theoretical coverage of the descriptive results gained in the preceding sections. The amendment concerns the formation of result predicates.

7.2 Result predication vs. depictive predicates

7.2.1 Syntactic characteristics of result predication

Predicates with a result interpretation (*R-predicates*) differ from predicates with a depictive interpretation (*D-predicates*) in at least three respects.[2] *First*, R-predicates are exclusively construed with the 'unmarked' structural argument (cf. Simpson 1983; Haider 1985), that is, with either the accusative object or the unaccusative subject. Other potential antecedents are ruled out, namely subjects of transitive verbs, inherently case-marked arguments, like Dative and Genitive in German, as well as prepositional objects.

(1)   a. He chased the horse tired
            (depictive: ambiguous; resultative: unambiguous)
    b. Er hetzte das Pferd müde   German
            (depictive: ambiguous; resultative: unambiguous)
       he chased the horse tired
    c. The horse^i was chased tired^i
            (depictive or resultative)
    d. He shot (*at) him^i dead^i
            (depictive or resultative; not resultative with antecedent in PP)
    e. Dieser Arzt^j untersucht (Patienten^i) nur unbekleidet$^{i/j}$
       this doctor examines (patients) only undressed

In the depictive construal of 'tired' in (1a), either he or the horse is tired. In the resultative interpretation, it is only the horse that gets tired as the result of being chased, and not the person referred to by the subject. (1e) shows that a secondary predicate in the *depictive* reading may be construed with a transitive

---

[2] For a detailed survey of the syntax of secondary predication in English see, for instance, Winkler (1994, 1996).

subject. The data in (2) illustrate the constraint against construal with an *inherently case-marked* DP.

(2) a. Etwas verdrießt mich zu Tode   German
   something vexes me$_{ACC}$ to death
   b. *Etwas nützt/schadet mir$_{DAT}$ zu Tode
   something serves/harms me to death

The contrast between (2a) and (2b) follows from the constraint against construal with an *inherently* case-marked object. Examples of result constructions with a genitive object are hard to find because the class of these verbs is so small that it does not contain a semantically suitable verb.[3]

Second, a *result* predicate, unlike a depictive predicate (1e), requires an *explicit* antecedent (cf. Carrier and Randall 1992: 215). An implicit argument would not suffice, neither in German nor in English (3a,b). German and English differ in causative constructions, however. In this kind of resultative construction, the causee may be implicit in German (3d), but not in English (3c):

(3) a. They ran *(the pavement) *thin*
   b. Sie hämmerten *(alles) *flach*
      they hammered (everything) flat
   c. Alcohol makes *(people) *drunk*
   d. Alkohol macht (einen) *betrunken*
      alcohol makes (one(self)) drunk

Depictive predicates may be used without an explicit target of predication (see also (1e)):

(4) a. Diese Untersuchung wird nur *nüchtern* durchgeführt
      this examination is only fasting done
      'For this examination, one has to be fasting'
   b. Ein Aktfotograf^j fotografiert (Models^i) nicht unbedingt *nackt* $^{i/j}$
      a (nude-)photographer photographs (models) not necessarily nude

Third, the *distribution* of R-predicates and D-predicates is clearly different. There are R-predicates, but no D-predicates, that may be placed between the verb and the direct object (4a,e). The alternation between the V-adjacent position and the distant position parallels the distribution of particles with resultative particle–verb combinations, as in (5).

(4) a. The joggers ran *thin* the pavement
   b. The joggers ran the pavement *thin*
   c. *The joggers reached *tired* the winning post

---

[3] An experimental example would be: *Er hat sich der Angreifer$_{GEN}$ zu Tode erwehrt (= he warded the aggressors off to (their) death).

d. The joggers reached the winning post *tired*
e. She not only cut *to pieces/to size/to ribbons* the army of Amazons, but ...
f. She not only cut the army of Amazons *to pieces/to size/to ribbons*, but ...
g. *The president cut *in distress* the budget
h. The president cut the budget in distress

(5) a. They cut *down/to size* the tree
 b. They cut the tree *down/to size*

The discussion in the literature has reached the point at which the complex-predicate analysis (see Larson 1988; Neeleman and Weerman 1993; Winkler 1994: ch.2, §2.4; Koch and Rosengren 1995; Neeleman 1995; Neeleman and van de Koot 2002) turns out to be observationally and descriptively the most adequate account.[4] According to these accounts, the result predicate and the verb form a syntactic unit. This unit functions as a complex predicate (see Grimshaw and Mester 1988; Ritter and Rosen 1993; Ackema 1995; Neeleman 1995 on theta-merging and complex predicate formation), the head components of which may share an argument, as in (6b).

The head-chain in (6a–c) is the chain of the head-V in a VP-shell structure. In English, the result predicate may be stranded in the course of V-fronting or it may travel with the verb. In the latter case, the result is the V-adjacent position of the predicate as in (4a,e). In (7a), the intransitive variant of the verb *drink*, combined with the PP, forms a complex transitive predicate with the external argument of the PP as the direct object.[5] In (6b), the internal argument of the verb and the external one of the adjectival predicate are identified as the internal argument of the complex predicate. In (6c), the argument that the verb and the adjective share is the single argument of the complex predicate, hence it raises to the functional subject position.

(6) a. She cut$_i$ the cloth [e$_i$ [to ribbons]]
 b. She raced$_i$ the horse [e$_i$ [sweaty]]
 c. The lake$_j$ [froze$_i$ [e$_j$ [e$_i$ [solid]]]]   (complex-predicate analysis)
 d. The lake$_j$ [froze [e$_j$ [solid]]]   (small-clause analysis)

The *small-clause analysis* (6d) as an alternative account has turned out to be hard to maintain for OV languages such as German or Dutch, as argued in sufficient detail by Neeleman (1995), for instance. The complex-predicate

---

[4] In Larson's treatment, a complex predicate may project to V′, whereas Neeleman assumes complex predicates to consist of head-level elements only. I will follow Neeleman and consider V-adjacent *resultative PP*s as in (4a,e) licit only if they are lexicalized, that is, if they form an idiomatic, complex lexical entry with the verb: 'cut to pieces' vs. 'cut to twelve pieces'.

[5] Palmer (1974: 236) provides the following example: 'It brings *to light* the facts'.

analysis plus the shell structure of complex VPs with head movement is sufficient for an empirically adequate account, even in cases like the following. In these examples, the verb is intransitive and the secondary predicate introduces the object argument. At first sight, this seems to be a clear case for treating the predicate and its argument as a minimal syntactic unit, that is, as a 'small clause', but the first impression is deceptive (see §7.2.2).

(7) a. She *drank* the glass *empty* in one single sip
 b. She *drank* him *under* the table
 c. She *laughed* *(herself) *silly*
 d. dass sie das Glas in einem einzigen Zug *leer trank*
  that she the glass in a single sip empty drank
 e. dass sie ihn *unter den Tisch trank*
  that she him under the table drank
 f. dass sie *(sich) *dumm und dämlich lachte*
  that she (herself) silly and stupid laughed

Particularly instructive are (7c,f). Here, a reflexive serves as the syntactic target of predication and as a transmitter of the predicated property to its binder, the transitive subject. Direct predication to the subject cannot apply since a transitive subject is excluded (see the discussion above).[6]

(8) a. [$_{VP}$ laugh [herself silly]$_{S.CL}$]   small-clause analysis
 b. [$_{VP}$ [sich dumm] $_{S.CL}$ lachen]
 c. [$_{VP}$ laugh$_i$ [herself [e$_i$ silly]$_{C.PR}$]]   complex-predicate analysis
 d. [$_{VP}$ sich [dumm lachen]$_{C.PR}$]

7.2.2 Where the small-clause analysis fails

A small-clause analysis appears to be appealing at first glance, but it does not stand the test when examined thoroughly. Here are four areas of evidence in favour of the complex-predicate analysis: topicalization, c-command-sensitive relations (scope), word formation and pied-piping. In each of these cases, the predictions based on the small-clause analysis (8a,b) turn out to be wrong, whereas the structure of (8c,d) predicts the properties correctly.

---

[6] The constraint on result predication that rules out *transitive* subjects as targets apparently does not apply to *compounding*, as in the case of Chinese V–V compounding discussed by Li (1990). The compound verbs allow for a result reading that relates to the transitive subject of the base of the compound (i). Arguably, a phonetically silent reflexive bridges the relation to the target of result predication in this case.

 (i) Ta qi-lei-le neipi ma
  'he ride-tired$_{ASP}$ that horse' – He rode that horse (and as a result *he/it* got) tired (Li 1990: 177)
 (ii) Ta ku-zou-le henduo keren
  'he cry-leave$_{ASP}$ many guest' – He cried (so much that) many guests left (Li 1990: 189).

A small clause would be an independent syntactic constituent and a complement of the verb. Complements of the verb may be topicalized. Topicalized 'small clauses' are ungrammatical (9a,c). *Topicalization* of a complex predicate is well formed, however (9b,d).

(9) a. *[Ihn tot]$_{S.CL}$ hat sie geschossen
him dead has she shot
b. [Tot geschossen]$_{C.PR}$ hat sie ihn
dead shot has she him
c. *[Sich krank] $_{S.CL}$ hat sie gearbeitet[7]
herself ill has she worked
d. [Krank gearbeitet]$_{C.PR}$ hat sie sich
ill worked has she herself

Second, let us check the *c-command relations*. The subject of the small clause would not c-command anything outside the small clause. The object argument of the complex predicate, however, c-commands the complex predicate. The prediction of the complex-predicate analysis is correct. A negated object has wide scope over the finite verb. The small-clause analysis would have to invoke obligatory raising in order to protect the analysis against this kind of counterevidence.

(10) a. dass sie [nichts in Stücke]$_{S.CL}$ gehauen hat
that she nothing in pieces cut has
'It is *not* the case that she has cut anything to pieces'
b. dass sie nichts [in Stücke gehauen hat]$_{C.PR}$

What these data show is that there is no small-clause structure in surface structure. This has been acknowledged by Hoekstra (1988). He suggests a derivational analysis that starts with a small clause. Then the subject is raised to the object position of the verb, and the small-clause predicate is raised and forms a complex predicate with the verb. So, the analysis combines a small-clause structure as input with a complex-predicate structure as output. The following piece of evidence, however, is incompatible with a derived complex predicate. If a complex predicate is input to a word-formation process it must be a base structure. Word formation is not fed by syntactic derivations.

Word-formation data clearly show that a verb and a result predicate form a unit that is small enough for word-formation processes to apply to it. In the

---

[7] Note that the deviance is not caused by the reflexive not being c-commanded by its antecedent. Topicalized phrases are bound under reconstruction:

[Stolz auf sich^i] war er^i nie besonders]
proud of himself was he never particularly.

complex-predicate analysis, the verb and the result predicate form a syntactic cluster when both are X°-categories, that is, when the result predicate is a simple lexeme. The cluster is a head-to-head adjunction structure and therefore a structurally licit input for a word-formation rule. This evidence, especially the nominalized infinitive formed on the basis of a verb cluster, is not available in VO languages since cluster formation is an OV property (see Haider 2010a: ch.7, §7.2).

(11)   a. [schön färben]$_{V°}$ – das *Schönfärben* von Skandalen – ein *Schönfärber*
          nice stain   – the nice-stain(ing) of scandals   – a nice-stainer (= eulogist)
    b. [tot schlagen] – das *Tot*schlagen von Fliegen   – ein *Tot*schläger
          the dead slay   – the dead slay(ing) of flies   – a deadslayer (= man slayer)
    c. [rein waschen] – das *Rein*waschen von Geld[8] – ein Geld*rein*wäscher
          clean wash   – the clean wash(ing) of money   – a money clean washer

The small-clause analysis is at loss with this phenomenon. First, the predicate in a small clause is phrasal. Second, it is embedded. So it is in no way accessible for joining it with a verb for purposes of word formation. Note that a syntactic process of predicate-to-verb raising would not help. The result is the result of a derivation, and syntactically derived structures do not qualify as input for word formation. The essential quality of this phenomenon is its *unconstrained productivity*: any combination of a result predicate and a verb yields an action nominalization, provided both items are X°-level categories.

Fourth, the small-clause predicate may be *pied-piped* by the verb, even if it is complex. The pattern in (12a,b) is characteristic of verbs with resultative particles, but it is licit even for predicates that are more complex than X°, as long as they do not contain individually referring items.[9]

---

[8] You should not be distracted by the fact that there is a process of compounding in English that independently produces individual compounds such as 'the cleanwashing'. What is essential is the fact that VO languages (such as English) lack a *systematic* pairing of resultative+verb complexes and their nominalizations. Here is an example:

  (i) to shoot dead – *the deadshooting of ... (zero hits in a web search)
  (ii) tot schießen – das Totschießen von ... (2,800 hits in a web search)
  (iii) to make ready – *the readymaking of ... (3 hits; 'make it ready': 1,620,000 hits)
  (iv) fertig stellen – das Fertigstellen von ... (21,000 hits)

[9] 'The Third [army] *cut to pieces* the Nazi forces in the Saar-Palatinate region' (*NY Times*, obituary for Gen. Patton, 22 December 1945); 'He *cut to pieces* the incense altars that were above them' (Bible, new international version, 2 Chronicles 34: 4); 'Josiah *smashed to pieces* the stone

(12) a. cut/tear/rip *to size /to pieces /to ribbons* the letter
      b. *cut/tear/rip* the letter *to size /to pieces /to ribbons*

This variation is predicted under the complex-predicate analysis for any VO language that either strands or pied-pipes particles or minor predicates. For a small-clause analysis, the V-adjacent position of the result predicates (12a) is unexpected. Its derivation requires ad hoc means. (13a) is the intransitive variant of 'cut', and (13b) the transitive one, with the small clause. There is no obvious reason for a derivational step that would change this structure and yield the observed order.

(13) a. cut [the letter to ribbons]$_{S.CL}$ (intransitive 'cut')
      b. cut the letter^i [PRO^i to ribbons] $_{S.CL}$ (transitive 'cut')

For the complex-predicate analysis, the V-adjacent order is a predictable option for those languages that either pied-pipe or strand in the shell structure of the VP. (14a) is the stranding variant; (14b) is the pied-piping variant. Pied-piping is restricted to 'small' PPs consisting of the preposition and a non-referring noun. Full phrases would destroy the head-chaining format of the verb in the shell structure since they could not be merged with the verb in such a way that the result still counts as a licit (complex) head.

(14) a. cut$_i$ [the letter [e$_i$ *to ribbons/open/out*]]
      b. [[cut *out/open/to ribbons*]$_i$ [the letter e$_i$]]

Independent evidence for the pied-piping analysis comes from coordination data observed by Taraldsen (2000: 101). The following contrast is expected and explained under the complex-predicate analysis.

(15) a. She let [the cat *in*] and [the dog *out*]
      b. *She [let *in* the cat and [*out* the dog]

(15a) is an 'across-the-board' coordination structure, with coordinated sub-VPs (16a). The corresponding structure for (15b) is ill formed, since the second conjunct does not match (16b).

(16) a. She let$_i$ [[the cat e$_i$ *in*] and [the dog e$_i$ *out*]]
      b. *She [let in]$_i$ [[the cat e$_i$] and [[e*$_j$ out]$_i$ the dog e$_i$]]

A point in favour of the small-clause analysis seems to come from the distribution of adverbials, as in (17). The adverbial precedes the predicate of the small clause. The complex-predicate analysis would not tolerate an adverbial intervening between the (trace of the) verb and the result predicate:

pillars they worshiped' (2 Kings 23: 14–24); 'and *slashed to ribbons* the royal army on the coast' (*NY Post*, 31 October 1948, on the Seven-Day War).

(17) a. cut it *carefully* to size
b. cut it to size *carefully*
c. cut it *deliberately* to pieces
d. cut it to pieces *deliberately*

This point does not count, however. The result predicate in (17) is a (non-referential) minimal PP, and as a PP it is extraposable.[10] That extraposition is operative in (17a,c) receives support from the contrast in (18). Adjectivals do not extrapose.

(18) a. set them *free* deliberately
b. *set them deliberately *free*
c. paint it *black* by mistake
f. *paint it by mistake *black*
e. dye it *purple* on purpose
f. *dye it on purpose *purple*

In sum, the small-clause analysis is not compelling, and the onus of the proof rests on the side who claims a small-clause analysis to be superior to a complex-predicate analysis.

7.3 A brief cross-linguistic survey

The following survey shows that the distributional properties in English are paralleled by the distributional properties of result predicates in those Scandinavian languages that allow stranding for particles.[11] These languages either pied-pipe or strand result predicates. As a consequence, both particles and result predicates are found in a verb-adjacent or in a stranding position.

The relative order of the object and an (R-)particle partitions the Scandinavian languages into three sets. Norwegian, like English, allows both the V-adjacent position and the position after the object. In Swedish only the V-adjacent position is grammatical, while in Danish the V-adjacent position is ruled out. It is important to note that the pattern of distribution for R-predicates (in the form

---

[10] In OV, resultative PPs are not extraposable. Extraposition would change the directionality domain in OV, but not in VO. This accounts for the different behaviour of result PPs with respect to extraposition in VO and OV, respectively.

[11] Gratefully, I acknowledge the support of informants: Sten Vikner (Danish), Britt Dalen Laux (Norwegian), Inger Rosengren (Swedish), and for Icelandic, Halldór Ármann Sigurdsson, Höskuldur Thráinsson and Matthew Whelpton provided data. The Dutch examples have been checked by Angelina van Gaal (Antwerp).

of minor PPs, adverbs[12] and adjectives[13]) parallels the distribution of particles (for particles see also Svenonius (1996) and (2003)).

(19) V – object – predicate
    a. They cut the meat to pieces
    b. at de skar kjøtet i biter   Norwegian
    c. at de skar kødet i småstykker   Danish
    d. *att de skar köttet sönder   Swedish
        'That they cut the meat smashed'

(20) V – predicate – object
    a. They cut to pieces the meat
    b. at de skar i biter kjøtet   Norwegian
    c. *at de skar i småstykker kødet   Danish
    d. att de skar sönder köttet   Swedish

(21) V – object – particle
    a. He threw the carpet out
    b. at han kastet matten ut   Norwegian
    c. at han smed tæppet ud   Danish
    d. *att han kastade mattan bort   Swedish

(22) V – particle – object
    a. He threw out the carpet
    b. at han kastet ut matten   Norwegian
    c. *at han smed ud tæppet   Danish
    d. att han kastade bort mattan   Swedish

For R-predicates and particles in German and Dutch, only the V-adjacent position is grammatical. These elements may be stranded by V-movement in the clause-final position. They do not scramble. Fronting of an R-predicate would be possible only under internal topicalization ('focus movement'), which requires a noticeable accent on the fronted element and on the element

---

[12] For instance: *away* (as in put away), *aside* (as in put aside), *forward* (as in put forward), etc.
[13] The V-adjacent position of an adjectival resultative predicate follows preferences similar to scrambling, at least for English. There are cases in which the adjacent position is judged unacceptable (cf. example (d)), but the unacceptability is in fact caused by the definiteness of the object. It is preferred in the fronted position, a property of definite DPs familiar from scrambling contexts in OV.

  a. I declare open the games of Atlanta   b. She cut short his remarks
  c. We must not cut loose the boat   d. He hammered flat an old coin/ *the metal

The Norwegian informant judged both orders as acceptable in her Norwegian variety:

  e. Han hamret blekket flatt   f. Han hamret flatt blekket
    'he hammered metal-the flat'

preceding the extraction site (as a signal for reconstruction; Haider 2001c, 2010a: 143).

(23)   a.   dass man vielleicht das Fleisch *in Stücke* schnitt   German
           'that one perhaps the meat *to pieces* cut'
      b.   *dass man vielleicht *in Stücke* das Fleisch schnitt
      c.   dat men misschien het vlees *in stukken* snijdt   Dutch
           'that one perhaps the meat to pieces cut'
      d.   *dat men misschien *in stukken* het vlees snijdt

(24)   a.   Er warf den Teppich nicht *weg*   German
           'he threw the carpet not *away*'
      b.   *Er warf *weg* den Teppich nicht
      c.   Hij wierp het tapijt niet *weg*   Dutch
           'he threw the carpet not *away*'
      d.   *Hij wierp *weg* het tapijt niet

German and Dutch represent the OV-pattern. Swedish as a VO system shares a characteristic property, namely the strictly V-adjacent positioning of R-predicates or particles, modulo canonical directionality. This is a consequence of not stranding these predicates.

Icelandic deserves a final remark since it appears to be 'special'. On the one hand, particles are stranded or pied-piped, as the following examples demonstrate (cf. Rögnvaldsson 1982: 60), and pronouns are fronted, whence pied-piping is not applicable (26), just like in English.[14] On the other hand, Icelandic does not pied-pipe adjectival result predicates (27b), as illustrated in (25).[15] A likely source of the deviance of (27b) could be the fact that secondary predicates are clearly inflected in Icelandic. The pied-piped head+head complex would contain two independent matrices with different phi-features. If a head position is restricted so that is must not represent more than one set of agreement-dependent phi-features,[16] this would rule out (27b).

(25)   a. Ég gerði nokkra bíla *upp*   Icelandic
         I fixed some cars up
      b. Ég gerði *upp* nokkra bíla
         I fixed up some cars

---

[14] Kress (1982: 223) notes that reflexives do not pattern like personal pronouns in that respect. They appear V-adjacent or after the object: lyfta sér upp – lift oneself up; rétta upp sér – raise up oneself.

[15] I gratefully acknowledge that this example and its typicality have been confirmed independently by Höskuldur Thráinsson and Matthew Whelpton (personal communication).

[16] The phi-features of clitics are not agreement-dependent, and if they are (viz. for subject-bound reflexives) they are *identical* with the phi-features of the finite verb.

(26) a. Ég gerði hann *upp*
 I fixed it up
 b. *Ég gerði *upp* hann
 I fixed up it

(27) a. Járnsmiðurinn hamraði málminn *flatan* Icelandic
 blacksmith-the hammered metal-the flat
 b. *Járnsmiðurinn hamraði *flatan* málminn

Confirmation of the exceptional status of adjectival predicates comes from the fact that minor PPs are accepted in V-adjacent position in Icelandic.[17] In Norwegian, agreement is optional for V-adjacent adjectives (28d) but obligatory in the distant position (28c), as described in Åfarli 1985: n.8.

(28) a. [Tröllkonur] ætluðu að hrista *í sundur* skipið Icelandic
 troll-women were-going to shake in apart ship-the$_{ACC}$
 'the troll women were going to shake the ship apart'
 b. [Tröllkonur] ætluðu að hrista skipið *í sundur*
 c. Vi vaska golvet rein*t* Norwegian
 We washed the floor clean (obligatory agreement)
 d. Vi vaska rein(*t*) golvet
 We washed clean the floor (optional agreement)

7.4 Consequences for grammar theory

Two consequences will be highlighted briefly. The first issue is the need for closing a gap. The complex-predicate analysis would be incomplete without an explication of theta management in the complex predicate. This becomes particularly obvious for result predicates that apparently contribute an argument and turn an intransitive verb into a transitive format (see the examples in (7)).

The second consequence is the immediate relevance of the data discussed in the previous sections as evidence for a BBC-based account and against an LCA-based approach (linear correspondence axiom, see Kayne (1994)) towards OV. Patterns predicted by the LCA-based model are ungrammatical in OV.

The examples in (29) illustrate the issue to be clarified. The direct object of the verb does not receive the theta relation that the verb would assign to its direct object in the absence of the result predicate. Obviously, in situations that fulfil the truth conditions of (29a) and (29b), respectively, you do not *drink a pot* nor do you *cook your family*.

---

[17] The following example I owe to Matthew Whelpton (p.c.).

(29) a. They *drank* the teapot *empty*
b. Er hat seine Familie *magenkrank gekocht*
he has his family stomach-sick cooked(-for)

The small-clause analysis seems to provide a straightforward account. What appears to be the object of the verb is the subject of the small clause. But this is an incomplete solution. 'Drink' or 'cook' are predicates that do not select a proposition as object and the small clause is propositional. Hence both accounts fail, and they fail on exactly the same issue, namely the c- and s-selection properties of the matrix verb. The small-clause analysis suffers since a verb like 'drink' or 'cook' neither c-selects a clausal argument nor s-selects a proposition. The complex-predicate analysis seems to imply that the direct object of the verbs in (29) is bound to end up in the wrong theta relation to the verb.

Kratzer (2005: 38) has suggested a solution that treats the verb and the result predicate like a serial verb construction. The result interpretation is supplied by an empty *functional* head CAUSE that selects the small clause and attracts the (adjectival) predicate of the small clause.

(30) a. drink [CAUSE [the teapot empty]]
b. [[[die Teekanne leer] CAUSE] trinken]
the teapot empty drink

The formal rendering of this analysis is (31): there is a state s that denotes that a teapot is empty and that an entity e drinks and (thereby) causes the state s.

(31) 〚die Teekanne leertrinken〛 = $\lambda e \, \exists s \, [\text{drink}(e) \, \& \, \text{empty (the teapot)}(s) \, \& \, \text{CAUSE}(s)(e)]$.

The open question is where the functional head CAUSE comes from. The verb 'drink' is merged with the CAUSE-phrase that is its syntactic complement. But 'drink' does not select a proposition as argument.

An alternative is the *complex-predicate analysis*. The result reading comes from a *lexical* change of the argument structure of the verb (conversion into a result verb). As a basis of the complex-predicate analysis, I suggest that we reinterpret Kratzer's account of resultatives and introduce the CAUSE-function by means of a word-formation rule that turns a verb like 'drink' into a resultative verb.

In the complex-predicate analysis, 'drink empty' is a complex predicate, with 'teapot' as its object. The argument role for the object is contributed by 'empty'. In this analysis, the resultative reading for 'empty' is the joint effort of conversion and the semantic composition of *drink & empty* that interprets the complex predicate. Eventually, 'empty' in 'drink empty' plays the same role as *aus* (out) in *aus-trinken* (lit. out-drink):

(32)   a. Ich würde den kleinen Becher sofort *aus*trinken
          I would the small cup immediately out-drink (= drink up)
      b. I would immediately drink *up* the small cup

For resultative particle verbs it is obvious that their semantics is not fully compositional. *Aus* (out) in combination with *trinken* (drink) in (32a) produces the same meaning as 'up' in combination with 'drink' in (32b), although the lexical meaning of *aus* (out) and 'up' is not identical. A small-clause analysis with 'up' or 'out' as the head would produce the wrong semantics. For (32b), the compositional meaning would be this: as a result of my drinking, the resulting state for the cup becomes 'up' (and for the German version (32a), the resulting state of the cup would be 'out').

This indicates that the semantics of a particle–verb combination is lexicalized. In the following example, the particle contributes only the resultative quality. (33a,b) are synonymous. The difference between (33a) and (33b) is a morphological one, namely the difference between a particle verb and a morphologically derived verb (by *er-* prefixation of the verb *rechnen*). Both are resultative predicates.

(33)   a. Man wird das Ergebnis *aus*rechnen
          one shall the result out-calculate
      b. Man wird das Ergebnis *er*rechnen
          one shall the result calculate$_{RES}$

As already noted by Kratzer (2005), a primary resultative verb does not tolerate a secondary result predicate. The secondary predicate *mausetot* (stone-dead) in (34b) can only be interpreted as depictive, not as resultative. The explanation is this: *er-* is a morpheme that signals that the verb gets a resultative reading. This becomes understandable if we assume that the morpheme operates on a resultative role in the argument structure of the verb. This relation is not available for relating it to an external result predicate once it is already bound by the internal element *er-*.

(34)   a. Sie werden *(ihn) *er*schießen
          they will (him$_{ACC}$) shoot-dead
          'They will shoot him dead'
      b. Sie werden ihn (mausetot*$_{RES}$) *er*schießen
          they will him (stone-dead) shoot-dead

(35) spells out the semantic effect of the resultative conversion. (35b) is the compositional result of combining (35a) with the CAUSE formation (35c). The

semantic value is identical with the semantic value Kratzer (2005) assigns to CAUSE as a functional head in clause structure. In her account, the result predicate is assumed to raise to this functional position. Syntactically, there is no direct evidence for the existence of this position, nor for raising of the result predicate.

(35) a. T(drink) = λe_s[action(e) & drink(e)] ('T' = translation function)
 b. T(drink$_{CAUS}$) = $\lambda P_{<st>} \lambda e_s \exists s_s$ [action(e) & drink(e) & P(s) & state(s) & CAUSE(s)(e)]
 c. T([cause]) = $\lambda P_{<st>} \lambda e_s \exists s_s$ [event(e) & state(s) & P(s) & CAUSE(s)(e)]

When a resultative verb of the type (35b) combines with a secondary predicate (36a), the result is a complex predicate. Functional application with the object, e.g. 'teapot', produces the appropriate result (36c).

(36) a. T(empty) = $\lambda x_e \lambda s_s$[state(s) & empty(x)(s)]
 b. T(drink empty) T(teapot)
 c. $\lambda e_s \exists s_s$ [action(e) & drink(e) & state(s) & empty(the teapot)(s) & CAUSE(s)(e)]

Let us review the syntactic side. In German, an adjective (phrase) like 'empty' can be used in at least four different functions in a clause (disregarding the function of adnominal attribute for the moment):

(37) a. Die Höhle klang *leer*[$_{ADV}$]
  the cave echoed emptily
 b. Er stellte die Flasche *leer*[$_{depictive\ pr.}$] zurück
  he put the bottle empty back
 c. Die Flasche war *leer*
  The bottle was empty [$_{depictive\ pr.}$]
 d. Er trank die Flasche$_{ACC}$ *leer*[$_{res.pr.}$]
  he drank the bottle empty

In (37a–c), *leer* does not introduce an argument. In (37d), however, the object is not the argument of the activity verb *trinken* (drink). It is the argument of the complex resultative predicate *leer trinken* (drink empty). This is confirmed by *topicalization*. Although a participle can be topicalized, topicalization is deviant when the participle is part of a complex result predicate.

(38) a. Getrunken wurden die Flaschen$_{NOM}$ (??leer$_{RES}$)
  drunk were the bottles (empty)
 b. Getrunken wurden die Flaschen$_{NOM}$ (??aus)
  drunk were the bottles empty (out) [= up]
 c. Getrunken hat er alle (??unter den$_{ACC}$ Tisch)
  drunk has he all (under the table)
 d. Geworfen hat er die Flaschen (??ins Wasser)
  thrown has he the bottles (into-the water)

The well-formed version is (39), with the complex predicate topicalized as a whole:

(39)   a. (Leer)getrunken wurden die Flaschen$_{NOM}$
             (empty) drunk were the bottles
         b. (Aus)getrunken wurden die Flaschen$_{NOM}$
             drunk (up) were the bottles
         c. (Unter den$_{ACC}$ Tisch) getrunken hat er alle
             (under the table) drunk has he all
         d. (Ins Wasser) geworfen hat er die Flaschen
             (into-the water) thrown has he the bottles

PPs may normally be scrambled or extraposed, but not if they are part of the complex result predicate. They must not be displaced, neither by scrambling (40a,b) nor by extraposition (40c,d). This holds for directional PPs, too, when they are interpreted as resultative (40b,d).

(40)   a. *dass die Flaschen [*unter den Tisch*]$_i$ keiner e$_i$ trinken konnte
             that the bottles (=dumb clucks) [under the table] nobody drink could
         b. *dass die Flaschen [*ins Wasser*]$_i$ jemand e$_i$ geworfen hat
             that the bottles [into-the water] someone thrown has
         c. *dass keiner die Flaschen trinken konnte [*unter den Tisch*]
             that nobody the bottles (=dumb clucks) drink could [under the table]
         d. *dass jemand die Flaschen geworfen hat [*ins Wasser*]
             that someone the bottles thrown has [into-the water]

What is true for German holds for VO languages as well. Svenonius (2003: 350), for example, has pointed out independently that 'Swedish sets the locative PPs apart from the directional PPs and classes the latter with particles.' The grammatical reason is easy to guess: both are resultative. Emonds (1985) and Neeleman (1995) discuss the parallel distribution of adjectival result predicates and particles in English:

(41)   a. We [[threw *out*] and [shredded]] the documents
         b. The children [[cracked *open*] and [ate]] the nuts
         c. We threw the documents *out*
         d. The children cracked the nuts *open*

In OV languages, there is only a single position, namely the V-adjacent, preverbal one.

(42)   a. dass wir die Dokumente *weg*warfen
             that we the documents away-threw
         b. dass wird die Nüsse *flach* drückten
             the we the nuts flat pressed
         b. dass wir die Nüsse *in Stücke* knackten
             that we the nuts into pieces cracked

Note that the PDI-based account proves to be empirically adequate. In a head-initial setting, result predicates and in particular the particles of resultative particle verbs are predicted to follow the verb. Second, in languages that allow for particle stranding, the resultative predicates and particles are predicted to occur either in the V-adjacent position or adjacent to the position of the lower empty verb in a complex V-projection.

In a head-final setting, on the other hand, resultative predicates or particles precede the verb immediately. An LCA-approach (i.e. OV as a derivational continuation of VO) – ceteris paribus – predicts distributions that are robustly deviant in OV:

First, PPs as result predicates are wrongly predicted to stay in their alleged postverbal base position. The result would be an OV clause with an apparently extraposed PP. However, resultative PPs (or particles or adjectives) must not be extraposed. Second, result particles are wrongly predicted to optionally appear post- or preverbally, in stranded or pied-piped position.

7.5 Summary

The following claims have been defended in this chapter:

1. As for result predicates, the order variation in VO languages, and particularly in English and the Scandinavian languages (and its absence in OV) with respect to the verbal head is an immediate consequence of two factors. One factor is the VP-shell structure for head-initial VPs, and the second factor is the option of either stranding or pied-piping. English and the Scandinavian languages display all of the possible combinations: obligatory stranding (as in Danish), or obligatory pied-piping as in Swedish, or both variants, that is, optional stranding or pied-piping (as in English or Norwegian).
2. The analysis proposed for result predication is a complex predicate analysis. An account in terms of a predicate phrase ('small clause') would not allow capturing the systematic cross-linguistically different patterns of distribution straightforwardly.
3. The result predicate in a resultative predicate plus verb construction is selected by the verb as a predicate (not as an argument).

8 Asymmetry in nominal structures – word and phrase structure

8.1 Introduction

The canonical directionality of heads in German and other Germanic OV languages is not uniform. N° and P° (and all functional heads) are phrase-*initial*, V° and A° are phrase-final. The *word structure* is head-final, too. In this chapter, three structural issues of nominal structures will be highlighted, all of which are BBC-geared.

First, constraints on noun–noun *compounding* are shown to provide evidence for the grasp of the BBC on *word structure* in general and on compounding in particular. In other words, the BBC does not only constrain phrase structure but word structure too. As a result, compounding is productive only with head-final compounds, as in Germanic languages, but it is highly constrained for head-*initial* compounding, as evidenced by Romance languages.

Second, the productive conversion of infinitival V° into N° in *deverbal nominalizations* (i.e. nominalized infinitival verbs) offers an upfront window to the direct comparison of complex head-*final* structures (VPs) with complex head-*initial* structures (NPs) within the same language. It will turn out that German noun phrases share structural constraints with English head-*initial* structures (especially VP and NP) and differ clearly from the properties of head-*final* phrases (VP in German). NPs are *compact, strictly ordered* and show the expected *edge effect* just like English VPs (and NPs, of course). Thus, *compactness* and the unavailability of *scrambling* is not a holistic property of a language. It is the unavoidable by-product of head-*initial* phrase structuring that is predictably absent in head-final structure.

Third, the *nominalization of infinitives* does not apply only to single verbs but to *whole verbal clusters*. This fact provides immediate independent and supporting evidence for the theoretic modelling of verbal clusters as base-generated head-to-head adjunction constituents headed by a V° node. Only in this analysis – and not in the mainstream approach of syntactically dismantling full VPs – may a verbal cluster serve as input to a word-formation process such as V°-to-N° conversion. Derivational accounts would predict that a verbal cluster – being the result of syntactic processes – cannot feed word-formation operations. Thus, the cluster analysis defended in Haider (2010a: 335–8) is also supported by the properties of cluster nominalization (Haider 2010a: 321).

8.2 Nominal compounds with head-final vs. head-initial word structure

8.2.1 Why are there no head-initial recursive compounds?

Phrase structure is *right*-branching; word structure is *right*-branching, too. Suffixes determine the word category, prefixes do not. In other words, category-changing affixes are suffixes, not prefixes. This is a direct reflex of the fact that the head is the nucleus of merger, and that merger is subject to the BBC. This is the first of three claims in this chapter, based mainly on a comparison between head-final and head-initial compounding.[1]

As a consequence of the BBC, a morpheme merged with the head in a word structure is merged as a preceding element, not as an element that follows the head. The head may be a word-formation affix (derivational suffix) or a free lexeme. In the latter case, the result of merger with another free lexeme is called a compound.

Compounding is a word-formation device offered by most, if not all, languages. A cross-linguistic comparison of compounding structures reveals a uniform constraint: the word structure of complex compounds is asymmetric, namely right-branching. *Recursive*[2] compounding structures are head-final structures. If there is head-initial compounding, as in Romance languages, the complexity of nominal compounds is constrained to the trivial size of a *two-member* compound. This is the topic of this section, namely, the quest for a principled answer to this headedness-dependent complexity restriction. The answer is framed in terms of a general restriction on structure building and headedness, that is, in terms of the BBC.

---

[1] This section draws on Haider (2001b).
[2] Let us call a compound 'recursive' if it is the output of an *iteratively* applied morphologically productive and semantically transparent rule of compounding. Its formation starts with two atomic elements. This is the output and simultaneously the input for the next application of compounding, and so on. Semantically, the head of the initial compound is the semantic head of the whole complex compound. Note that *lexicalization* is a process that overrules any recursive structure. In other words, lexicalized compounds are treated as single words whose originally complex word structure is merely an etymological property.

The first part of this chapter is organized as follows: in subsection 8.2.2, the patterns of head-final compounding (in German) are compared with the restricted possibilities of head-initial compounding in Romance languages in order to corroborate the empirical justification for the complexity constraint mentioned above. In subsection 8.2.3, the theoretical background for structure constraints is introduced. It serves as the frame of reference for deriving the specific constraint on head-initial compounding. In subsection 8.2.4, the specific constraint for compounding is shown to follow from the general structure-building constraint developed in the preceding subsection, and the account presented here is compared with alternative approaches to structure-building constraints in general and to the compounding constraint in particular.

8.2.2   Head-final vs. head-initial compounds

The descriptive generalization for the data under investigation is straightforward: *recursive* compounds are head-*final*. Consistently head-*initial* compounds are non-recursive and hence are only *two*-member compounds.[3] This is illustrated in (1a) and (1b). What this contrast amounts to is a ban against recursion on the right side of a compound, that is, merger on the side disallowed by the BBC.

(1)   a. [X [Y [Z]]]   – baby cat fish; Babykatzenfisch (German)
      b. [[[Z] Y] *X]   – poisson chat (*bébé)[4]

The English compound *cat fish* can be augmented by compounding it with *baby*, and the resulting complex compound could be merged with the compound *deep sea*, resulting in *deep sea baby cat fish*. These compounds are

---

[3] Instances of apparent three-member compounds are two-member compounds of words that are lexicalized compounds themselves, as in [[*air port*] *security*]. This is not a three-member compound but a two-member compound, whose first member is a compound again). Two of the three items are treated as a single item, that is, a lexicalized word. The prediction is: novel compounds consisting of simple compounded items are constrained to the trivial size of two: [N N]$_N$

[4] Delfitto *et al.* (2008) illustrates the ban on recursion with *Italian* examples:

(i)   pesce zebra   – zebra fish   (ii) *pesce zebra spada   – sword zebra fish
      fish zebra
(ii) pesce spade   – sword fish   (iii) *pesce spade zebra   – zebra sword fish
      fish sword

A *Spanish* example from Piera (1995) is:

*perro policía mascot – mascot police dog
dog police mascot

head-final: the final noun determines the category and the hyperonym semantics of the compound. The French compound in (1b), the verbatim equivalent of the English compound (1a) modulo headedness, is head-initial: the initial noun determines the category and the semantic basis modified by the compounded element. Augmenting the basic two-member compound with an additional member on its right is unacceptable: the restricting element follows the base noun in the simple compound, but adding a second restricting element is ruled out. This is the restriction on recursion that distinguishes head-initial and head-final compounding. This very restriction will be shown to be responsible for the general unproductivity of head-initial nominal compounding. Examples of the limited set of French, Spanish and Italian nominal compounds are given in (2a–c), respectively.

(2)   a. café filtre (filter coffee), oiseau mouche (*bird fly* = humming bird), timbre-poste (postage stamp), roi soleil (sun king)
        b. hombre lobo (wolf man), hombre rana (frog man), lavaplatos (dishwasher), niño modelo (model boy), abre latas (can opener)
        c. capo familia (family head), pesce cani (*fish dogs* = shark), spremi-agrumi (fruit-press), porta-lettere (mail carrier)
        (cf. Dressler 1988: 148f.; Katamba 1993: 316f.; Piera 1995)

As for German, the possibility of forming excessively complex compounds is known as a playground of linguistic creativity, but also as a much-exploited source for the nomenclature of law matters.[5] A medium-sized (non-recursive) example is (3):

(3)   [[[[Arbeits vertrags] rechts] anpassungs] *gesetz*]
        work   contract regulation adjustment law
        'adjustment law for the regulation of work contracts'

Since compounding may take compounds as inputs, the parsing of a compound may result in various possible alternative structure assignments. A morphology demo-parser fed with the example (4a), correctly computed the parses (4b) and (4c). (4c) is the correct parse of (4a) in its actual usage, whereas (4b) is a possible structure for (4a) that is not utilized in present-day German:

---

[5] Lawmakers are notoriously productive compounders in German-speaking countries. The following example is the title of a law initiative of the federal state parliament of Mecklenburg-Vorpommern (19 January 2000), and a testament to the productivity of compounding in German: *Rinderkennzeichnungs- und Rindfleischetikettierungsüberwachungsaufgabenübertragungsgesetz.* The second conjunct consists of sixteen morphemes that are combined into seven nominals (see: http://mv.juris.de/mv/RkReUeAUeG_MV_rahmen.htm, accessed 5 September 2011).

(4) a. Altersteilzeitrente
 b. [[Alters teil] [zeit [rente]]]
    old-age part temporary pension
 c. [Alters [[teil zeit] rente]]
    old-age part-time pension

The structure (4c) is the recursive structure of a complex compound whose compositional structure is formed by recursively adding nominal elements to the nominal base. One nominal element is a compound itself (viz. *teilzeit* – part-time). In fact, there are many more possible bracketings for (4a) since any two contiguous nouns may form a compound.

For the sake of demonstration: here is a five-piece *recursive* nominal compound structure with atomic members that is recursively built up in (5a–d):

(5) a. [N + N]: Garten*zwerg* – garden gnome
 b. [N + [N+N]]: Plastikgarten*zwerg* – plastic garden gnome
 c. [N + [N + [N+N]]]: Riesenplastikgarten*zwerg* – giant plastic garden gnome
 d. [N + [N + [N + [N+N]]]]: Importriesenplastikgarten*zwerg* – import giant plastic garden gnome

The interpretation of a complex (recursive) compound such as (5d) follows a general semantic hierarchy of restrictive predication.[6] The order of stacked attributive APs follows the same pattern as in the compounds in (5), namely *source > evaluation > size > substance*:

(6) a. ein [importierter [wunderschöner [hölzerner [Gartenzwerg]]]]
    an imported   wonderful   wooden   garden gnome
 b.??ein hölzerner importierter wunderschöner Gartenzwerg
    a wooden   imported   wonderful   garden gnome

The question wanting a principled answer is this: is there a principled reason why the mirror-image structure of (1a), namely (1b), does not occur in compounding? In other words: why is there no language with recursive compounding in a head-initial structure? In such a language, compounds would have the mirror-image structure of the German compounds. We would, for instance, expect to find (7) instead of (5d), with the same meaning as (5d):

(7) *[[[[N+N] + N] + N] + N] – 'gnome garden plastic giant import'

The answer is implied by the BBC. Word structure is structure resulting from merger. These structures are constrained by the BBC. Hence recursive compounds are predicted to be right-branching.

---

[6] 'Root compound' =$_{def.}$ compound without *syntactic* dependency relations between members of the compound.

8.2.3 On deriving the branching direction of recursive compounds

In the preceding section, *recursive* nominal compounds have been shown to be right-branching, as in (8a): the noun merged with the base of the compound is attached on the *left* side of the base, and not on the right-hand side (8b). Note, that this does *not* entail that there are no compounds with a structure [[N N] N]. What it does entail is that in this structure, the [N N]-complex is not the *base* of the compound. It is a compound noun merged with the base on its right, as in [[*compound formation*] *rule*]. A *compound formation rule* is semantically a 'rule', and not a 'formation' nor a 'compound'.

This fact and the absence of complex left-branching structures as in (8b) would follow immediately if the BBC applied not only to syntactic phrase structure but also to word structure. The BBC admits (8a) and extensions of (8a) with compound elements to the left, as in (5c,d): in each case, the respective complex bases in the structure of the compound are branching nodes to the *right* of their sister node: the base noun, and each of its extensions, is to the *right* of its merged sister.

(8)

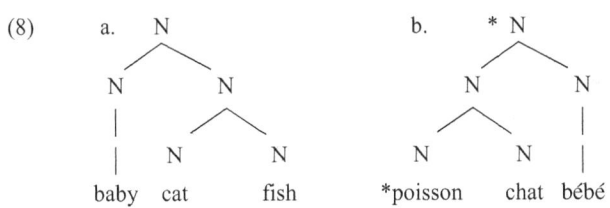

Head-initial compounds, however, are limited to the trivial size of two-member compounds for a simple reason: a two-member compound is the only compound structure without embedded branching nodes. The single branching node is the top node. So, this is the only structure that meets both conditions: it is head-initial but it does *not violate* the BBC. Any extension of this trivial structure leads to a violation of the BBC. Recursive compounding of *poisson chat* with another noun to its right turns the node of the complex base of the compound into a *left* sister node and thereby incurs a violation of the BBC. If, however, the base of the compound is merged with a noun to its left, the resulting compound is not head-initial. Hence we conclude: if the BBC applies to the word structure of compounds, the restriction against complex head-*initial* compounds, as exemplified in Romance languages, follows. Does this generalization prove valid in a cross-linguistic perspective, too? Here is independent evidence from Vietnamese.

Hoeksema (1992), based on data like those in (9) and (10) from Van Chình (1970), conjectures that headedness (head-final, head-initial) is parametric in compounding, just like in phrase structuring. Compounds as in (9b) and (9c) are obviously challenges for the BBC-based account presented in this section.

(9)   a. nhà-máy   – *house*-engine   (= factory)
       b. nhà-máy-loc   – $house_N$-$engine_N$-$filtrate_V$ (= refinery)
       c. nhà-máy-loc-dau   – *house*-engine-filtrate-oil   (= oil refinery)

In addition to head-initial compounds, Vietnamese also has a large class of so-called Sino-Vietnamese compounds. According to Van Chình, these compounds have been calqued from Chinese in parts or in their entirety. These compounds have the Chinese structure, which is head-final (10).

(10)   a. ngu *vi*   – language *unit*   (= morpheme)
        b. [[ngu vi] *hoc*]   – language unit *study*   (= morphology)
        c. [ap [chien *luoc*]]   – village fight *plan*   (= strategy)

Examples like (11c) are the result of combining two lexicalized Sino-Vietnamese compound in the 'Vietnamese' style. The result is a head-initial N–N compound, whose two nominal parts are lexicalized head-final compounds.

(11)   a. giáo *su*   – teach *master*   (= teacher)
        b. dai *hoc*   – great *study*   (= university)
        c. $[[\text{giáo su}]_N \, [\text{dai hoc}]_N]_N$ (= university professor)

Lexicalization is likely to be the key for answering the challenge of examples like (9b,c) for the BBC. (9b,c) would be ruled out as recursive compounds. But they are not recursive. They are nominal compounds of lexicalized compound nouns. This is easy to see for the particular case of (9a). 'Engine-house' or the German counterpart *Maschinenhaus* would be a licit compound in English and German, respectively, but its compositional meaning would not be 'factory' but merely 'house for/with engines'. Second, the term for 'refinery' consists of two elements, namely 'house' and 'filtering engine'. This shows most clearly that (9a) is not a recursive compound consisting of atomic elements only. Third, the term for 'refinery' (9b) is semantically not compositional, hence it must be lexicalized. Therefore the combination with another element ('oil') does not violate the recursion generalization.

The fact that these nouns are complex does not matter as long as this complexity is not the result of a productive, stepwise word-formation process. As long as the complexity is 'historical' in the sense of a *lexicalized* item that was once the result of productive word formation but in synchronic grammar is treated as a lexical unit. Conclusive counterevidence from Vietnamese (or any

Asymmetry in nominal structures 197

other language) would be this: recursive compounds of atomic elements with a strictly compositional meaning and a left-branching structure.

It is worth emphasizing at this point once more that the BBC applied to word structure does not blindly rule out complex left-branching morphological structures. What is ruled out are *recursive* structures with the head (in a constituent) on a left branch:

(12) a. *[α [α Wα Wβ] Wδ]
     b. [β [α W Affα] Affβ]
     c. *[α [α W Affα] Affβ]

The structure (12a) is the already familiar compound structure that violates the BBC. (12b) illustrates a complex word structure with two affixal heads of distinct categories: a word W is affixed with a suffix of category α, resulting in a formation of category α. This complex formation is again affixed with a suffix, but of category β. So, the result is of category β. Hence, each constituent is a different two-member constituent. So, the BBC is not at stake since this is not a case of recursive merger.

A structure ruled out by the BBC is (12c). The head of the whole expression is part of a left-branch constituent. This is in violation of the BBC, because there is a branching node on the projection line of Affα that is to the *left* of its sister node. This is the constituent [α W Affα], dominated by the recursive node α. Its sister node is Affβ. The consequence of subsuming word structure to the domain of application of the BBC is a welcome generalization for derivational affixation:

(13) Generalization: word structure is right-branching (for the immediately merged items)

Note that 'right-branching' applies to nodes on the projection line. (13) does not apply to two-member expressions, whence the possibility of the Romance compounding pattern. It applies when a projection is needed. (14) illustrates the point once more.

(14a) is a small-sized recursive compound: a bench for the garden made of wood. (14a') is not recursive. It is a two-member compound, whose left compound element is a recursive compound itself. (14b,c) show that prefixes behave like modifiers and may be iterated.

(14) a. [Holz [garten bank]]   a'. [[Holz [garten bank]] bein]
        wood garden bench   wood garden bench leg
     b. [Ur [ur [großmutter]
        great great grandmother
     c. [anti [anti [anti missile]]]   c'. re-re-distribute; un-un-do

d. [[[lead-er]ship]qualities]
e. [[[Obama's dog's] tail] waggle]

The word structure of (14d) is left-branching throughout, as the many initial brackets betray. But, this is in accordance with the BBC, of course. Each pair is a separate item. There is no recursion step involved; hence there is no extending projection line. Only in that case would the BBC be at stake. Each bracket is the result of a different word-formation step. This is a situation like a left-branching syntactic structure as in (14e).

8.2.4 Alternative accounts

8.2.4.1 A ban against word-internal inflection?

In the present account, the low productivity of *head-initial* compounding is a consequence of the highly limited output structure of the compounding rule. A syntactic N-projection (15b) is used instead of a word-formation option (15a). The syntactic device that is obligatory for complex structures is therefore also an option for the simple cases in which a compound could be used:

(15)   a. porta contenitori (*altomare)
        carry-container   high-sea
        '(high sea) container carrier'
    b. porta contenitori d'altomare
       container carrier of/for high-sea

Groseclose (1998) suggested that the restriction against complex head-initial compounds in Romance might be due to the fact that inflection is marked on the head, that is, on the *first* element of the compound:

(16)   a. hombre rana – frog man
    b. hombre*s* rana – frog men

The very fact that there are compounds like (16b) is evidence against the blocking effect of inflection: (16b) is an example of compound-internal inflection.[7] So, it is unclear how merging (16b) with another noun could be forbidden. A ban against word-internal inflection would rule out (16b) right away. (16b)

---

[7] Montermini (2008) illustrates with corpora counts (numbers in brackets) that in many cases, a conflict between having to inflect the base and preferring inflection at the end of a word is 'solved' by inflecting both nouns in the compound (for plural): e.g. donna-prete (she-priest) – donne-prete (70) vs. donne-preti (2); porta-finestra (window frame) – porte-finestra (74) vs. porte-finestre (1,149); frase-chiave (key word) – frasi-chiave (372) vs. frasi-chiavi (14). Interestingly, there is no case in which only the final noun (and not the base noun) would be inflected. This is a clear indication that the actual word structure is not neglected or overruled.

is good evidence for the morphological reality of word structure, however: compounding does not delete word boundaries.

8.2.4.2 Linearization as a function of asymmetric c-command?

In Kayne's (1994) theory and the work building on it, linearization is characterized as a function of asymmetric c-command. Head-initial projections are head-initial underlyingly, whereas head-final structures are derived. This is a consequence of the basic axiom of this theory, the *linear correspondence axiom* (LCA).[8] It postulates that phrase structures are built in such a way that the linear order of terminals is completely determined by asymmetric c-command relations in the syntactic structure. In the specific implementation of Kayne (1994), asymmetric c-command is axiomatically mapped on *precedence*: if an element X occurs in a position that asymmetrically c-commands an element Y, X must precede Y in the linear order. In particular, the head precedes the complement and the adjoined spec precedes both. Head-final structures are taken to be the result of XP-movement applied to the complements of head-initial projections. The basic building unit of a syntactic structure is (17). Head-final structures must be analyzed as basically head-initial, whose post-head elements have been moved to pre-head spec positions by movements postulated just for gaining this result.

(17)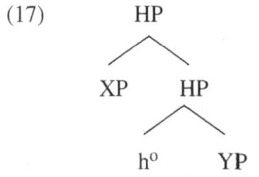

XP: spec position, h° = head, YP: complement position.
Note: The spec position is an *adjoined* position.

The crucial difference between the BBC approach and Kayne's LCA approach is easy to characterize: in Kayne's perspective, all structures are *head-initial*, that is, the head precedes the complement. Head-final structures are derived by *moving* the *complement* to the *left*. In the BBC account, on the other hand, the *head-final* structure is basic. Head-initial structures are derived by *head movement* to the *left*. In the BBC system, the axiomatic part is the BBC. The axiomatic part in Kayne's system is the *precedence* property in the

---

[8] Linear correspondence axiom (LCA): d(A) is a linear order of T, for a given phrase marker P, with T the set of terminals and A the maximal set of ordered pairs <X_j, Y_j>, such that for each j, X_j asymmetrically c-commands Y_j (Kayne 1994: 5f.).

mapping function. For a detailed empirical comparison, see Haider (2000b) and the final chapter.

Word structure is an independent testing ground for evaluating the relative adequacy of these alternative approaches to structural asymmetry. The successful applicability of the BBC has been demonstrated above. What are the predictions of the LCA system in the present context of word structure?

Here are some LCA-based predictions: first, head-final word structures must be derived from head-initial ones (see Roeper *et al.* (2002) as a representative approach). Second, head-initial compounds are predicted to be less complex than head-final ones. As illustrated in (18a), a suffixal head has to be merged on the left-hand side of its complement. So, the complement must be moved to spec in order to derive the desired surface order. Things become slightly more complex, though, when, as in a case like (18b), a compound serves as the head of a complex word structure (cf. 18c).

(18)   a. $[\text{-ation}_N \text{ [form]}] \rightarrow [\text{form}_i \text{ [-ation}_N \text{ [e}_i\text{]]]}$
          b. $[\text{formation}_N \text{ [word]}] \rightarrow [\text{word}_i \text{ [formation}_N \text{ [e}_i\text{]]]}$
          c. $[\text{word}_i \text{ [formation}_N \text{ [e}_i\text{]]]} = [\text{word}_i \text{ [[form}_j \text{ [-ation}_N \text{ [e}_j\text{]]]]}_N \text{ [e}_i\text{]]}$

First, the parts of the complex head 'formation' do not asymmetrically c-command the complement 'word' in (18c) because they do not c-command it at all. Second, the head and the complement are sisters, hence they c-command each other and there is no asymmetric c-command relation. So the requirement that linearization be determined by structure is not fulfilled. Moving the complement to the spec position is a means of arriving at a well-formed asymmetric structure that determines a linearization for the terminal elements of the structure: the spec position asymmetrically c-commands the rest. However, it is not at all evident that word structure provides or involves a spec–head–complement structure, nor is it evident that it is a domain of filler–gap relation (viz. movement).

Keyser and Roeper (1992) suggested a slightly different solution. They postulate an abstract clitic position[9] instead of the trace in (18a–c), for the sake of breaking the symmetry within compounds. A compound is not assigned the straightforward structure (19a), but an 'antisymmetric' structure (19b), by virtue of the empty complement, that is, the empty 'abstract clitic' (ACP).

(19)   a. $[\text{word}_N \text{ structure}_N]_N$
          b. $[\text{word}_N \text{ [structure}_N \text{ ACP]}_N]_N$

---

[9] 'Abstract clitic hypothesis': in English, each of the lexical categories (N, V, A, P) can have the abstract clitic position (ACP) as its complement.

According to Keyser and Roeper (1992), (19b) is nevertheless derived from a head-initial base structure in which 'word' originates in the ACP position and gets moved to the pre-head position. But, if we grant this analysis for the sake of discussion, the word structure of head-*initial* compounds is hard, if not impossible, to derive. The base structure of *café filtre* (cf. 2a) is predicted to be mapped onto a word structure that yields the incorrect *filtre café* as the surface order.

Roeper and Snyder, who discuss only French, and who are perhaps not aware of the fact that the French situation holds for Romance languages in general (see Italian, Spanish, etc.), declare French an exception: French is assumed to simply lack the ACP, and 'creating a new endocentric, root compound is comparable to inventing a novel morpheme' [sic!].

Obviously, the existence of these compounds is a crucial testing ground for the success of the LCA – and the BBC approach towards word structure. The BBC predicts that head-initial compounds are restricted to the trivial case of two-member compounds. The LCA predicts either that there are no head-initial compounds at all (because the complement is always moved to a spec position in order to arrive at an asymmetric c-command structure), or, as Roeper and Snyder (2005) assume, that head-initial compounds do not have a word structure (see quote in the preceding paragraph). Actually, the LCA theory should predict that head-initial compounds are the ideal compounds, since they are 'born' in the head–complement order, and the constraint against recursion should follow from the 'precedence' axiom: asymmetric c-command is mapped on precedence, hence merger on the right-hand side is ruled out. But the base structure is symmetric and so its symmetry must be broken by turning it into a structure in which one member of a compound asymmetrically c-commands the other member.

Consequently, the LCA approach predicts that there is a lot of movement even in the domain of lexical word structure, without providing any evidence that there is indeed movement. In sum, the empirical evidence seems to be in favour of the BBC, and the onus of proof lies on the side of the advocates of an antisymmetry axiom.

A final issue to be raised in this context is the applicability of the spec vs. complement distinction (as for the empty clitic hypothesis) for the nominal compounds discussed under (5) above. The semantic relations in the word structures in (5) correspond to the semantic relations between the head and its *attributes* in a noun phrase, and not to the relation between the head and its complements. A compound like (20a) is ambiguous between a relational reading (20c) and an attributive one (20b):

(20) a. Riesenarbeit (giant-work)
b. riesige Arbeit – gigantic work
c. Arbeit von Riesen – work of giants

The semantic contribution of the first noun in the compound (20a) can be either interpreted as in (20b) or as in (20c). The latter interpretation could be justly associated with a structure in which the first noun figures as a complement of the base noun, given that elements with argument-like relations are licensed as complements. For the attributive reading, however, the assignment of the first member of the compound to a spec position seems to be more adequate than to a complement position. But the assignment of a rigid spec–head–complement structure to compounds might be inadequate since the locality restrictions it would impose are too strict.

In (21), the noun with a complement relation to the head of the compound ends up higher in the word structure than the noun with a kind of adverbial relation. This is unexpected since in head-initial structures complements are assumed to stay closer to the head than adverbials.

(21) a. [Güter [bahn [transport]]]   b. ??/?[Bahn [güter [transport]]]
goods train transport   train goods transport
transport of goods by (means of) train
c. [Pelztier [käfig [haltung]]]   d. ??/?[Käfig [pelztier[haltung]]][10]
fur-animals cage keeping   cage fur-animal keeping
keeping of fur animals in cages

The order in the compounds (21a,c) follows the unmarked word order in the VP (22a) and in nominalizations (22b) in German:

(22) a. [$_{VP}$ Pelztiere [in Käfigen halten]]   b. [$_{NP}$ Käfighaltung [von Pelztieren]]
fur-animals in cages keep   cagekeeping of fur-animals
keep fur-animals in cages

In English, a compound of the type (21a,c) or a nominalization of the type (22b) is ungrammatical: the argument relation must be instantiated closer to the base than the adjunct-relation. A theory that derives the head-final structure from a head-initial one therefore seems to miss an important point: according to the LCA approach, head-final compounds in English should be isomorphic

---

[10] This pattern is not generally excluded, though, as the following structure illustrates:

Freiland-hühner-haltung = open-air chicken keeping (keeping chickens in open air, rather than in cages). This structure alternates with the structure (21d). On the other hand, *Kinder-land-verschickung* (children countryside transfer; i.e. the transfer of children to the countryside) has no other variant: *Land-kinder-verschickung* would not be a variant, but a different compound. It could only mean 'transfer of children who are from the countryside'.

with head-final compounds in German, simply because they are instances of an identical structure-building device. But, as a matter of fact, they are different, and the difference goes parallel with some of the syntactic differences between an OV language such as English and a VO language such as German. The mirror-image order of (22a) is ungrammatical in English, and so is the corresponding order in the nominal compound.

The BBC is not committed to the categorial typing of positions in the right-branching structure. All it requires is that a recursive structure be right-branching. Although it is not enforced, it is not surprising either that the order by which a phrasal structure is linearized (cf. 22a) is the same order in which the elements in word structure are linearized (21c).

8.2.5   Summary of Section 8.2

This section defends a simple claim: recursive compounds in languages with productive compounding are head-final. A head-final, recursive compound like the following German *[Riesen[eis[skulptur]]]* (giant-ice-sculpture) does not have mirror-image counterparts (i.e. head-*initial* recursive compounds) in any other language.

Head-*initial* compounds cannot be expanded recursively. There is no language in which the word-by-word translation of the above compound would be *[[[Skulptur] eis] riesen]*, that is, a mirror image of the head-final linearization. This constraint is derived from a general constraint on structure building that applies both to phrase structure and to word structure. Recursive compounding with a head-initial base would produce right-branching word structures, but this type of structure is not admitted by the BBC.

8.3   German NP structure in comparison to German VP structure

In German, any infinitival verb can be converted into a noun. This is called infinitival nominalization. Nominalization is the effect of the word-formation process called conversion, that is, it is merely the exchange of the category label V° with N°. Therefore, simply combine an infinitival form with a neuter definite article and you have a DP (23).

(23)   a. das *Schreiben* und das *Lesen*
         the write$_{INF}$ and the read$_{INF}$
         'the writing and the reading'
    b. das Übersetzen dieser Bücher$_{GEN}$ / von diesen Büchern$_{DAT}$
         the translate$_{INF}$ these books / of these books
         'the translating of these books'

The positive signal for an NP structure is the fact that the direct object of the nominalized verb (24a) appears as a post-nominal object of the noun, namely as a genitive DP (23b) or a PP headed by *von* (23b). A deverbal noun inherits only the arguments of the verb that are not marked for a lexical case (Dative, verbal Genitive), since a noun (in contrast to a verb or an adjective) cannot license Accusative (24b) or a lexical case as *verbal* Dative (24d) or Genitive (24e).

(24)   a. [diese Bücher lesen]$_{VP}$
           these books read
      b. *lesen diese Bücher
           read these books
      c. das Unterstützen/die Unterstützung der Eltern$_{GEN}$
           the support/the supporting (of) the parents
      d. *das Helfen/die Hilfe den Eltern$_{DAT}$
           the help/the helping the parents
      e. *das Gedenken des Kriegsendes$_{GEN}$
           The remember(ing) the end of the war

Unterstützen is a transitive verb; hence (24c) is well formed, with the adnominal Genitive for the object argument. 'Help' is intransitive. Its dative object is not transferred into the NP structure (24d). A verb like *gedenken* in (24e) is one of the few verbs in German that selects a genitival object. Its nominalization, however, does not tolerate the lexical Genitive of a verb as object. This fact indicates that the adnominal Genitive is a *structural* realization of case; it is the subject/object case of the verb that corresponds to Nominative/Accusative in the VP (see Haider 2010a: ch.6).

The nominalized infinitive as the head of an NP must not be confused either with nominal incorporation (25a,b) as in compounding, or with phrasal nominalization, that is, VPs converted to NPs (25c,d):

(25)   a. das [Gedankenlesen]$_{N°}$
           the mind-reading
      b. das [Steinewerfen]$_{N°}$
           the stone-hurling
      c. [das [sich dauernd über irgendetwas beschweren]$_{VP}$]$_{DP}$
           the REFL constantly over something complain
           'the constant complaining of something'
      d. dein [unvorsichtiges [bei Rot ohne Schauen über die Straße laufen]$_{VP}$]$_{DP}$
           your careless at red (light) without looking across the street run
           'your careless running across the street at red traffic light'

The clear difference between genuine nominalizations as heads of NPs and incorporated nouns in deverbal compounds on the one hand, and VPs as complements of determiners on the other hand, is easy to recognize. Nominalizations display the structure of NPs, with the direct object of the verb realized as the genitival, *post-head* complement of the noun.

Nominalized infinitives as heads of plain NPs (23b) are the focus of this subsection because they are head-initial, while the VP is head-final. These NPs (like any complex NP in German and in the other Germanic OV languages) share the syntactic properties of head-initial phrases, hitherto illustrated by head-initial VPs in VO languages, namely *compactness* and *strict word order*, with an *edge effect* for adjuncts, as will be demonstrated succinctly:

(26)   a. [Decken an Obdachlose (*kostenlos*) verteilen]   (not compact)
           blankets to homeless (for free) distribute
       b. [an Obdachlose$_i$ Decken e$_i$ (kostenlos) verteilen]   (scrambling)
           to homeless blankets (for free) distribute
       c. an Obdachlose öfter (*als erwartet war*) Decken verteilen (no edge effect)
           to homeless more-often (than expected was) distribute

The VP is head-final, hence it is expected that it is not compact, that it admits scrambling and that there is no edge effect constraining adjuncts adjoined to a verbal (sub-)projection. The inverse holds for NPs in general and NPs with a nominalized infinitive as head, in particular.

A temporal adverbial is licit in an NP (27b), but not between the head and the object (27a). Analogously, scrambling, as in (27c), would produce an intervener that disrupts the proper identification relation (PDI). Finally, adnominal adjuncts display the expected edge effect (27d).

(27)   a. das Verteilen (**im Winter*) von Decken an Obdachlose   (compact)
           the distribut(ing) (during winter) of blankets to homeless
       b. der Urlaub im Winter
           the vacation in winter
       c. das Verteilen an Obdachlose$_i$??von/*der$_{GEN}$ Decken e$_i$ (no scrambling)
           the distribut(ing) to homeless of/the blankets
       d. das [so häufige (**wie nötig*) [Verteilen von Decken]$_{NP}$]$_{NP}$ (edge effect)
           the as often (as necessary) distribut(ing) of blankets

Note that the acceptability of (27c) improves for the PP *von Decken* compared with the genitive DP. The reason is obvious: PPs may extrapose. The order in (27c) may result either from scrambling the PP *an Obdachlose* or from extraposing the PP *von Decken*. Since DPs do not extrapose, the variant with the Genitive is completely deviant. Apparently, the object PP *von Decken* does not extrapose freely, otherwise (27c) would have to be completely acceptable with the two PPs, as, for instance, with the PPs in (28a,b), in analogy to the order variation between PPs in an English VP (28c).

(28) a. das Sprechen über Bäume mit Gärtnern
the speak(ing) about trees with gardeners
b. das Sprechen mit Gärtnern über Bäume
the speak(ing) with gardeners about trees
c. speak about trees with gardeners – speak with gardeners about trees

Independent evidence for extraposition as the differentiating moment in (27c) comes from the parallels with PP extraposition in VPs. First, an extraposed *von*-PP that codes an argument (29a) is degraded in acceptance in comparison to an extraposed adverbial *von*-PP (29b). This parallels the behaviour of the argumental *von*-PP in NPs (29d).

(29) a. ?[Gelöst [von Politikern]]$_{VP}$ wurden keine Probleme
solved [by politicians] were no problems
b. [Gelöst [von der Verankerung]]$_{VP}$ wurde keine Boje
separated [from the anchorage] was no buoy
c. das Lösen *von Problemen* mit Gewalt
the solving$_{INF}$ of problems by force
d. ??das Lösen mit Gewalt *von Problemen*
the solving$_{INF}$ by force of problems

Second, the acceptability of the extraposition variant improves further in heavy-NP-shift contexts as in (30d) compared with (30b).

(30) a. das Verwandeln *von Blei* in Gold
the transforming$_{INF}$ of lead into gold
b. ??das Verwandeln in Gold *von Blei*
the transforming$_{INF}$ into gold of lead
d. das Verwandeln von allem, was er mit Händen anfasste, in Gold
the transforming$_{INF}$ [of everything that he with hands touched] into gold
e. ?das Verwandeln in Gold [von allem, was er mit Händen anfasste]
the transforming$_{INF}$ into gold [of everything that he with hands touched]

Third, binding data that require a c-command relation between binder and bindee confirm that the extraposed *von*-PP is in a lower position in the phrase (see Haider 2010a: ch.5).

(31) a. das Festhalten jedes^i Politikers an seinem^i Job
the clinging$_{INF}$ (of) every politician$_{GEN}$ to his job
b. das Festhalten [von jedem^i Politiker]^i an seinem^i Job
the clinging$_{INF}$ [of every politician] to his job
c. das Festhalten an seinem*^{i} Job [von jedem^i Politiker]^i
the clinging$_{INF}$ to his job [of every politician]

What the above discussion demonstrates is this: as expected, NPs compared with VPs headed by the same (nominalized) verb differ in the predicted ways.

NPs obey the syntactic constraints of head-initial phrases, and VPs display the greater syntactic freedom of head-final phrases. NPs are compact and therefore do not allow scrambling, VPs do.

Example (32) briefly illustrates the *edge effect* for head-initial phrases (Haider 2010a: 194). The head of the phrase adjoined to a head-initial phrase must be adjacent to the target phrase:

(32)   a. the [[proud$_{A°}$ (*of his children)]$_{AP}$ [father]$_{NP}$]$_{NP}$
        b. das [häufigere$_{A°}$ (*als nötig)]$_{AP}$ Impfen der Kinder]$_{NP}$]$_{NP}$
        c. [[more often$_{ADV°}$ (*than it is necessary)] [vaccinate children]$_{VP}$]$_{VP}$
        d. [Kinder [[viel häufiger (als nötig ist)] impfen]$_{VP}$]$_{VP}$

The source of this effect is the lack of directional identification. An adjunct pre-adjoined to a head-initial phrase is not in the directional identification domain of the head of the target phrase. Hence, the head of the adjunct must combine with the target phrase by means of the head–complement relation.

The head of the adjunct, however, cannot select the complement as an argument. It selects it as a *structural* complement and thereby gets structurally integrated. Semantically, in the absence of lexical complement selection, the adjunct is treated as a modifier and not as an argument-selecting domain. As a modifier it combines with a phrase of a suitable type and yields a phrase of the same semantic type.

(33)   a. [$_{NP}$ [A° [$_{NP}$ N° …]$_{NP}$]]   e.g. *new arguments on NP structure*
        b. [$_{NP}$ [A° [$_{NP}$ [A° [$_{NP}$ N° …]$_{NP}$]]]] e.g. *unproven new arguments on NP structure*

Adjacency is the consequence of the structural complement relation. Intervening material to the right of the head of the adjunct would block complement selection between the head of the adjunct and the structurally selected target phrase. The post-head phrases themselves would be in a complement relation to the head.

8.4   The nominalization of verbal clusters

It is a fact of German (and other OV languages as well)[11] that nominalization does not only apply to single verbs but also to verbal clusters. The size

---

[11] As for instance Dutch:
    (i) Het [*laten zien*] van problemen (… *let see* …)
    (ii) Denk aan de traditie van het [*moeten laten zien*] van het witte doekje met rode vlekken aan familieleden als bewijs dat de vrouw in kwestie maagd is gebleven (… the tradition of the [*must$_{INF}$ let see*] …).

is constrained only by the processing capacities. Here are some illustrative samples:[12]

(34)   a. Das *Verabreichen* von Alkohol an Jugendliche
the administer(ing) of alcohol to adolescents
b. Das *Verabreichen helfen* von Alkohol an Jugendliche
the *administer help*(ing) of alcohol to adolescents
c. Das *Verabreichen helfen sehen* von Alkohol an Jugendliche
d. Das *Verabreichen helfen sehen lassen* von Alkohol an Jugendliche
e. Das *Verabreichen helfen sehen lassen müssen* von Alkohol an Jugendliche
the *administer help see let need*(ing) of alcohol to juveniles
'the *obligation* to *let* (s.one) *see* (s.one) *helping administer* alcohol to adolescents'

It is a fact, too, that this kind of *recursive* cluster nominalization is unavailable for head-initial structures (Haider 2009: 87), as illustrated by (35a,b). Note the difference with (35c). This is not a cluster nominalization, as the intervening object indicates, but merely a VP selected by a nominal determiner.

In English, the gerund construction is illicit with tense auxiliaries (35a), but in German, the tense auxiliary is part of the verbal cluster and therefore occurs in cluster nominalizations:

(35)   a. *the having understood of positions vs. das *Verstanden haben* von Positionen[13]
b. *the letting see drop of glasses vs. das *Fallen sehen lassen* der/von Gläser/n
c. [This [letting deadlines expire]$_{VP}$]$_{NP}$ gives the department a bad name.

But even for VO languages, there is an option of quasi-cluster formation, namely a V+V combination, examples of which (36) can be found on the web:

Bartos (2004: 404) first discussed the phenomenon in Hungarian. The Hungarian order in the nominalized cluster is strictly head-final. Hungarian is a Type III language and therefore has OV as one of its options (see Chapter 3, §3.4 and Chapter 5).

[12] I gratefully acknowledge the spontaneous creativity of the audience of my lecture at the University of Bochum, 14 July 2011, who provided me with numerous cluster nominalizations consisting of up to five infinitives, such as:

das Baden-gehen-lassen-sehen-müssen einer so maroden Firma
[the bathing$_{INF}$-go-let-see-must$_{INF}$] (of) a sick company

Baden-gehen has the idiomatic reading 'drowning as a consequence of bathing'. Combined with *lassen* (let) it means: 'let perish, let go bankrupt'. The approximate translation is the nominalized version of 'to have to see (someone) let(ing) a sick company go bankrupt'.

[13] Here is a sample from the web: Um miteinander kreativ (mit-) gestalten zu können, braucht jeder innerlich *das Verstanden-haben* von so vielen momentanen Positionen, wie Personen beteiligt sind.

(36) a. Obama has called for the *letting expire* of the tax cuts for the top 2 pct.
 b. The '*letting drop*' of the scientist's name Richard K. ...

Genuine cluster formation in OV is recursive; the VO quasi-cluster nominalization is restricted to the trivial size of V+V coupling. The necessary recursion step for real clusters would be a step in the branching direction excluded by the BBC. A recursive V° cluster is ruled out just like a recursive compound is ruled out in N-compounding (see §8.2 above).

Let us turn now briefly to the theoretical impact of the cluster nominalization phenomenon. It provides straightforward evidence for deciding between competing theories of modelling verb clustering in OV languages (see Haider 2010a: ch.7, §7.5 for details).

Verbal clusters are feeding infinitival nominalization. This is a word-formation process. In particular, it is a conversion process that maps an item of lexical category V° into an item of category N°. This mapping transfers that portion of the argument grid that is compatible with the resulting category. For the V-to-N conversion this means that *lexically cased* A-positions are not transferred to the nominal A-structure. The change from V° to N° involves a change of the canonical directionality of identification, too. It is this very property that makes the nominalized verbs easily identifiable in German. Their objects follow. Objects of verbs precede.

Word-formation processes operate on X°-structures. Hence, if verbal clusters are feeding a word-formation process (namely deverbal nominalization) they must be of category V°. This is the argument. Presently, the only account that is compatible with this phenomenon is the base-generation approach discussed in Haider (2010a: 335). Both a V-raising and a VP-evacuation account, as contemplated in Wurmbrand (2006), are bound to fail (not only with respect to cluster formation; see Haider 2010a: 325).

Here is the reason in brief: in both accounts, clustering effects are modelled as results of complex syntactic derivations. However, the output of a syntactic derivation is never a possible input to word-formation processes. So, these accounts predict that OV and VO systems do not differ in cluster nominalizations, but they obviously do. (37) confronts the three types of structural analysis (for details see Haider 2010a: ch.7, §7.5):

(37) a. dass man das Buch [[übersetzen$_{V°}$ lassen$_{V°}$]$_{V°}$ muss]$_{V°}$ (base-generated)
 that one the book translate let must
 'that one must let translate the book'
 b. dass man das Buch$_i$ [[[e$_i$ übersetzen]$_{VP}$ lassen]$_{VP}$ muss]$_{VP}$
                                                                (by VP evacuation)
 c. dass man [[[das Buch e$_i$]$_{VP}$ e$_j$]$_{VP}$ [übersetzen$_i$ lassen]$_j$ muss]$_V$°
                                                                (by V-raising)

The VP in (37b) cannot be turned into the *head* of noun phrase, obviously. The cluster in (37c), which is derived by iterative V-raising plus adjunction of the raised item(s) to the higher verb, is a product of verb movement and does not exist independently. Hence it cannot serve as input for a word-formation process either. In sum, the derivational accounts fail to capture the generalization that verbal clusters in head-final structures, but not those in head-initial structures, may feed word-formation processes.

8.5 Summary

The structure of complex nominal expressions is instructive in several respects. First, nominal compounds may be head-final or head-initial, such as in Romance. In the latter case they are subject to restrictions that become understandable as effects of the grasp of the BBC on word structure.

Second, nominalized infinitives shed light on two issues of the OV/VO debate. On the one hand, the nearly minimal-pair situation of VPs and NPs with a deverbal head provides immediate insights into the syntactic restrictions that correlate with headedness: e.g. compactness, word-order rigidity and edge effect. On the other hand, the comparison makes clear beyond any reasonable doubt that these properties are not holistic properties attributable to specific languages. They are properties of head-initial vs. head-final *phrases*, respectively. Hence, they may be present within the same language, in correlation with headedness. Thus, NP and VP structures in languages with mixed headedness (e.g. Afrikaans, Dutch, Frisian, German) differ exactly along these parameters.

Third, the fact that nominalization applies to verb clusters is immediate counterevidence to any account that derives verb clusters from stacked full VPs by whatever syntactic process. Such accounts fail to cover the data from cluster nominalization and thereby miss an essential generalization.

9 BBC or LCA? – fact finding and evaluation

9.1 Background

The agenda of the final chapter is the comparative evaluation of the role of asymmetry and linearization in two competing approaches: BBC (basic branching constraint) (Haider 1992) vs. LCA (linear correspondence axiom) (Kayne 1994). It is a comparison of competing conceptions of the relation between an *input/output property* at the phonetic form (PF) interface, namely *linearity*, and a *computational property*, namely the *structural organization* of syntactic representations. And moreover, these are *complementary* conceptions as to the basic syntactic process that relates the cross-linguistically apparently diverse structural architectures (viz. head-*final* and head-*initial* structures).

In the BBC model, the basic quality that relates and distinguishes OV and VO[1] is *head positioning* (viz. the make-up of the shell structures of complex head-initial phrases, or the partial shell formation in the Type III structures). In the LCA model, however, the basic tool is *phrasal* movement. SVO is taken as axiomatic and OV is derived from the axiomatic VO structure by means of massive movement of *non-head* constituents.

Given the fact that the two models employ complementary grammatical tools, viz. *head*-chaining vs. *phrasal* movement, it should not be overly difficult to identify and empirically falsify or 'verify' relevant predictions of each model. Since the two models cannot both be fully right, at least one of them must be eventually identifiable as empirically more adequate and consequently also theoretically superior.

In the BBC perspective, grammar is a cognitive algorithm for mapping *linear arrays* (strings) onto hierarchically organized *box-in-box structures* (= phrase structures) and vice versa; in other words, grammar is conceived of as a *string-to-structure* or *structure-to-string mapping algorithm*. The fact that

---

[1] Here, 'VO' is meant to cover both SVO and VSO, abstracting away from the final destination of the verbal heads that start out in a head-initial V-projection, and also the V-movement in the 'third type'.

utterances look like *linear concatenations* of terminals is primarily an interface property (the phonetic channel provides only a single, linear, dimension, and its only degrees of freedom are *precede* and *follow*).[2]

From the perspective of the mapping algorithm, the basic asymmetry of phrase structures – *No left-branching projection!*[3] – is understandable as the UG-determined parser friendliness of grammars (see Chapter 2), which is a result of adaptation by cognitive selection in the cognitive co-evolution of grammars and language processing. The crucial gain of this type of structuring is the simultaneous applicability of bottom-up (= data-driven) and top-down (= grammar-driven) processes, since the earlier (= left) element in a phrase is always the higher one. 'OV' and 'VO' are just the effects of the alternatively admissible directionality factors, given the string property of linguistic expressions and the universal phrase-structure constraints. Technically, these data structures are optimal for a *left-corner parser* (see Phillips 1995, 2003).

The mainstream stance in grammar theory of the Generative camp favours a different, opposed view, namely a *structure-on-structure mapping algorithm*. Grammar is regarded as an algorithm for *generating* structures, successively mapping them onto other structures in the course of the derivation, and linearizing them ('spell-out'). Grammar is not primarily seen as a *direct* PF-to-structure-to-SF ('semantic form') mapping algorithm, but rather as a *generation algorithm* that takes lexical items as input ('numerations') and generates a series of representations with specific PF and SF properties. This approach, despite its popularity, is neglecting and therefore missing a crucial objective, both on empirical as well as on theoretical grounds. It neglects the undeniable fact that a grammar is put to use as a mapping algorithm, and that the conditions of use are part of the cognitive selection environment that shaped the grammars in the course of their cognitive evolution.[4]

It is reasonable to take for granted that grammars have the core properties they have because the brain provides effective processing routines (as the neuro-cognitive substrate that is reflected by and compiled in UG) for the unique properties of linguistic expressions characterized by these grammars.

---

[2] This characterization applies to the organization of morpho-lexical terminals. This does not exclude that there are other tiers, for other information qualities (e.g. intonation contours). But, crucially, for the morpho-lexical terminals, there is only a single dimension, namely the dimension of the time course of the utterance. This is a linear dimension.

[3] In the *merger* terminology of Chomsky's Minimalist Program, this reads as follows: merger in a given projection is to the left.

[4] Here are examples of structural parsing theories with principles that favour right-branching structures: late closure (Frazier 1987), recency (Gibson 1991), connect bottom-up (Stabler 1994), low attachment (Abney 1989).

In other words, it is entirely *un*reasonable to maintain that grammars might primarily hamper the processing routines by insisting on structures and relations that are hard to process or even intractable for the human brain's processing capacities.

Let me very briefly point out two aspects of language processing that clearly favour a *string-to-structure mapping* perspective over a *generation and linearization* view.[5]

9.1.1   Language acquisition (feasibility)

L1 acquisition presupposes a 'mapping algorithm', not a 'generation algorithm': what the child is confronted with are linear arrays, whose structures and regularities the child has to detect. UG ought to support the child in identifying the core grammar properties of the string-to-structure mapping properties of the language the child is confronted with, otherwise the task will be beyond the child's capacities.

A mapping algorithm is tractable for the child, a production algorithm is not. The latter is not tractable because it *starts* with *a hidden step* (viz. with the generation process on the speaker's side) and produces the overt product (linearization). The mapping algorithm, however, starts with the *public part* (the linearization) and yields the hidden quality (the phrase structure). Since in a production grammar, the start is hidden, the non-deterministic derivational history of expressions in a production grammar makes it impossible for the child to identify the language-specific initial state. S/he could do so only by constant analytic step-by-step backtracking (*reverse engineering*), which is intractable (even with strong UG support), however, since a UG-compatible core grammar is not narrowly deterministic. UG, as is well known, must allow for considerable cross-linguistic variation, which – see the OV/VO debate – is characterized as the effect of complex derivational relations. How could the child find out the *language-specific* settings, if they are hidden in a non-deterministic derivational algorithm? By testing and retesting?

It is highly unlikely for a child to proceed in a *testing mode* that continuously fixes and re-fixes several interacting parameters in order to determine what is the momentarily optimal fine-tuning for a given input language. This would

---

[5] Much of the attractiveness of the generation and linearization approach, in my opinion, rests on its fascinating system complexity. It is much more entertaining than a simple string-to-structure mapping algorithm because it allows one to devise and solve intriguing puzzles of possible derivational interactions of rules under various conditions of application. What I doubt is that the human language faculty is algebraic, that is, a *derivational* puzzle-solving algorithm. I prefer the conjecture that it is geometric, that is, a *gestalt mapping* algorithm.

presuppose a highly effective, domain-general capacity of executive control and crypto-analytic supervision, which is unavailable to a child's brain. Even professional linguists have been struggling with this task for decades. A child is unaware of the problem and accomplishes the task within months or a few years.

Generative (viz. structure-generation) models give rise to a *learning paradox* which does not arise in a mapping model (Haider 1999): in order to know what the structure of a given input is, you have to generate it (and compare its spell-out with the input), but in order to be able to generate it, you must know what the structure is, that is, you must have learned how to fix the various open parameters that apply to the given structure. This in turn presupposes that the learning process crucially involves a comparison process: generate the alternative structures and compare them and find out which one is the adequate one. If the structures (as in the case of phrase structures) involve more than one parameter, the multidimensional parametric system space of alternatives soon becomes too complex and intractable for any human learner.[6] The direct mapping model (BBC-based) does not suffer from this paradox, evidently. The learner locally compares direct mapping alternatives rather than complex alternative derivations that produce the mapping as their output.

9.1.2 Processing efficiency (economy of usage)

Efficiency involves the economic employment of limited resources. What is the limited resource in language processing? It is the processing time in the *comprehension* process, that is, the time for processing the structure of a given string when parsing it. It is not the time for the *production* (generation) of a string. In principle, I could allow myself as much time as I need for generating an utterance. But when I am engaged in processing the ongoing discourse, I have to be finished with an utterance when the following utterance reaches my brain. So the efficient system is one with *mapping* efficiency rather than *production* efficiency (see Haider 1997e).[7] The generation-algorithm approach has

---

[6] Note that the appeal to the 'invisible guiding hand' of UG would not help. It is precisely the variation space admitted by UG that is the problem for the learner. The learner cannot know in advance that (s)he is exposed to a VO or OV or third-type language, with or without V_{FIN}-movement, for instance.

[7] A production system such as the Minimalist Program is of no advantage for the production process either, ironically: it starts with a lexical choice ('numeration'), but when it is going to assemble the pieces, it takes off from the 'wrong' side, namely the bottom. Imagine me as a speaker of German, who is planning a medium-length utterance. I cannot utter the first word until the whole sentence has been generated bottom up, if production is grammar based, and the grammar is organized like the MP wants to have it. The first word is the top item, but generation

no direct way of optimizing the receptive side. This side is not a respected part of the system. The string-to-structure mapping, on the other hand, provides a natural system property. Effectiveness is enhanced by gestalt properties of pattern-matching procedures. Patterns are compiled into *complex gestalt properties*. For the generation approach, compiling would amount to a packaging of derivations. A packaged derivation is cognitively intractable; a complex gestalt property, however, is still in a direct and continuous relation to the string properties of terminals.

Once one abandons the generation-algorithm bias, the LCA-based system loses its major attractive quality of imposing structural restrictions on the derivation of a structure suitable for the given linearization. In fact, the LCA merely serves as a *benchmark condition* for production grammars. The benchmark condition is that a grammar must guarantee a particular function, namely the unique mapping of structures onto linearizations. The benchmark is checked at the PF interface: does the given representation meet the LCA requirement? LCA-compatible grammars are grammars that are organized such that their outputs meet the LCA. Assuming LCA as a principle of UG is like postulating 'I expect a grammar to organize the data structures in such a way that this guarantees the property I require to hold, namely a unique mapping of structure to linearization, based on asymmetric c-command.'

Note that the LCA as a benchmark condition is a *global* well-formedness condition rather than a principle of phrase-structure generation ('transderivational constraint'): if a given representation cannot obey the LCA (e.g. a head that merges with several complements simultaneously), a movement operation has to be applied and the grammar has to enable this by providing a functional projection to accommodate the moved item (see Kayne 1994: 30, on the small-clause structure of double-object constructions).

From the string-to-structure mapping perspective, it is not evident why one should adopt the LCA as an axiom from the beginning. The mapping function[8] it is meant to cover is crucial only in a generation perspective, but not in a string-to-structure mapping perspective, since the inverse of the LCA – *Generate a structure, starting from a linearization!* – remains just one of the many one-to-many mappings[9] embodied by grammars.

---

starts at the bottom. The inevitable but wrong prediction is this: every speaker knows the very last word of the utterance already when (s)he starts with the very first word.

[8] For every structure there is a unique linearization the structure is mapped on to.

[9] For a given linearization there may be more than one LCA-compatible structure (simply because it may involve empty positions that are not visible/audible for linearization).

That the LCA allows deriving restrictions for generating phrase structures that previously had to be simply postulated is not enough justification, though. It must be shown that the restrictions plus the implications of the model are empirically adequate. In the following sections, the focus will be set on empirical issues that play an essential role in evaluating the relative success of the LCA approach in comparison with a BBC-based account.

9.2 Verification versus falsification

An obvious and crucial testing ground for the empirical adequacy of an LCA-account compared to a BBC-based account of the OV/VO distinction is the empirical success of the given model in explaining the contrasting aspects of grammars. The crucial question that calls for an answer is this: how straightforward or how recalcitrant do the numerous, apparently independent structure properties of closely related languages fit into the respective theoretic model?

It is not unfair to underscore that the applicability of the LCA approach benefits to a significant extent from its high degree of derivational *flexibility*.[10] In system-internal terms, it is free and costless to move to the left as many phrases as one deems necessary and thereby introduce as many functional layers as one needs as landing sites, as long as the result obeys the LCA – if one does not hesitate to flatly disrespect Ockham's razor as a maxim of scientific work (and the obligation for providing independent evidence for each of these hypothetical derivational steps).

From the point of view of theory evaluation, most applications of the LCA merely pursue a *verification* approach. You simply show that the system is able to produce a reasonable output after a series of derivation steps. But it is well known that the fact that a model is flexible enough to capture a given phenomenon (or a subset of phenomena) does not prove the model to be empirically adequate and correct. It is a truism of the theory of science that verification is not the decisive step. The decisive test for a theory is demonstrating its merits under thorough falsification trials.

What is crucially underrepresented in the LCA literature is this scientific obedience to thorough *falsification testing*: what are the main empirical predictions and how successfully does the proposed system deal with them? The problems are less conspicuous for VO languages, the favourite demonstration

---

[10] Flexibility is greatly enhanced when – as is the case – the LCA environment is combined with the Minimalist Program's abundant toolkit: *overt and covert movement, covert lowering, remnant movement, roll-up movement, strong or weak features, overt or covert checking of features*, etc.

area for the LCA model. For OV languages, however, the problem areas are numerous and easy to identify (see section 9.4, on comparative counter-evidence). The literature has proliferated many affirmative contributions (e.g. Zwart 1996; Haegeman 2001; DiSciullo 2003), but no systematic accounts of the potentially falsifying empirical evidence, with few exceptions, as, for instance, Haider (2000b). Answers are still missing in Kayne (2005), where essential LCA-saving derivational procedures are extrapolated for Japanese, but the paper stops short of justifying the adequacy of these postulated measures on the basis of independent evidence from Japanese. It is not enough to merely point out a way through a maze if one cannot plausibly make sure that it eventually leads out of the maze rather than deeper into it.

9.3 Theoretical shortfalls

This section lists obvious areas of actually or potentially falsifying evidence for an LCA approach. A prominent problem for the LCA system is the *missing trigger theory*. There is no general account of a reasonable *trigger* in the derivational continuation from VO to OV, that is, a trigger for turning an otherwise well-formed VO base structure into an OV structure. In the LCA perspective, an OV language appears to be an unexpected and puzzling distortion of a well-behaved VO system. If the OV structure is indeed derived from an underlying VO organization, this is the primary question: why should a well-formed VO structure be further transformed into an OV arrangement by starting a machinery of massive derivational dislocations and evacuations? Why are *not all* languages VX languages, if UG allegedly is so strongly VO-biased? Why did non-VO languages not change into VO languages in the preceding millennia of diachronic changes, given the alleged system pressure towards VO?

The lack of a *trigger theory* is a serious shortfall of the LCA model.[11] In the absence of a trigger theory for movement, the LCA theory simply postulates that natural languages are head-initial languages. But there are OV languages. So, if the OV order is the result of derivationally transformed head-initial projections, this transformation must be triggered. Moreover, the trigger in the LCA system must be a *global* one because it indiscriminately affects all elements in a superficially head-final structure, independent of their category

---

[11] Note that a *trigger theory* is not identical with a set of guesses as to what particular features might be useful candidates for the unknown trigger of the respective individual movement process. A trigger theory is an essential part of the theoretical account. It must follow from principles of the theory as an integral part and it must be empirically adequate, of course.

and grammatical function: arguments, attributes (including relative clauses), adverbials, particles, (secondary) predicates and so on.

Holmberg (2000) proposes *c-selection* (i.e. strict sub-categorization) as the parametric locus for the global trigger of the respective movement types. In his view, the basic difference between OV and VO languages is reducible to a difference in terms of checking c-selection features: in OV languages, c-selection features are to be checked by phrasal movement, but in VO languages they are checked by head movement. As he himself acknowledges, this fails to account for the serialization of non-sub-categorized elements, such as PP adverbials, adverbial clauses, secondary predicates, extraposed relative clauses and so on, without the help of additional non-standard assumptions.

What is equally problematic for Holmberg's proposal is the existence of mixed language types, such as, for instance, German and Dutch: N°, most P° and all functional projections are head-initial; V°- and A°-projections are head-final. If the trigger is framed as a computational property of the different implementation of a feature-checking mechanism, parameterization in terms of category subclasses would amount to a language-internal parameterization at the computational level, and not at the level of lexical properties. This raises additional questions as to how plausible and insightful this account would be. In addition, Holmberg's proposal remains open on all the particular empirical issues that are raised against an account that takes head-initial structures as a starting point for deriving head-final ones (see below).

The really tough task for devising a triggering scenario is the *mixed-bag characteristics* of the elements that have to be made to move when turning a basic VO structure into an OV structure. The set of elements to be moved out of the VP is completely inhomogeneous. The LCA simply requires moving *any* elements whatsoever out of the head-initial phrase that is to be turned into an apparent head-final structure. This leaves hardly any room for a grammatical feature that could be made responsible for the distribution of the elements that are allegedly moved in order to arrive at a consistent OV linearization. But it would be just begging the question if one invented a 'kick out' feature as a feature of the head that makes the phrase-internal elements flee their place of origin and move to the left just in order to produce the impression that the head is a phrase-final head. Presently, the model operates as if there was an *expulsion feature*, without admitting it, though.

The mixed-bag problem could be circumvented, as proposed in Kayne (1998: 134), if the clause-final position of the verb was the result of V-movement out of the VP, followed by remnant VP-fronting across the moved V. This, however, is equally problematic, though for different reasons. As pointed out in

Haider (2010a: ch.2), there is diverse, robust and recalcitrant counterevidence for a proposal that assigns the (clause-final finite) verb to a functional head position. Second, invoking clause-internal remnant VP-fronting would overgenerate excessively (see the discussion on the distribution of particles and on opacity of extraction, below).

9.4 Comparative (counter)evidence

Let me repeat: in the LCA model, OV is derived from a structure that is basically VO. Postverbal material is fronted to preverbal positions and even the emptied VP may be moved subsequently, if necessary. Hence, if OV contains VO as a derivationally transformed core, *ceteris paribus*, OV is predicted to embody VO properties (that is, at least the subset that is unaffected by the derivational changes) plus a derivational fringe benefit.

For the sake of concreteness, let me take Icelandic and German as representatives of Germanic VO and OV languages, respectively. A comparison of Icelandic and German is a most advantageous testing ground for competing grammar-theoretic accounts on the relations between 'VO' and 'OV'. Icelandic is consistently head-initial (VO), whereas German is head-final in the [+v]-projections, that is, for VP and AP. The two languages differ with respect to headedness (OV vs. VO in the narrow construal of OV/VO) but their morpho-syntactic systems of verbal and nominal inflection are similar to an extent that guarantees a broad enough common background for identifying the specific effects of the different headedness options. Moreover, German and Icelandic are historically closely related members of the same language family, and they share the Germanic V2-property.

In the LCA account, German would turn out as a particular derivational continuation of the generation of Icelandic structures. So, German is predicted to be derivationally more complex than Icelandic. In the BBC approach, however, Icelandic and German structures are the result of implementing opposite directionality values for identification. Here, Icelandic is predicted to be the structurally more complex language since it not only requires VP-shells, but also a functional projection for the subject, because of its head-initial V-projection. Let us therefore look out for straightforward predictions based on contrasts and similarities between Icelandic and German in particular,[12] and the *mixed-bag problem* in general (see also Haider 2000b). Consider the following German

---

[12] This section is largely based on a more detailed account of the pertinent phenomena presented in Haider (2005).

example. The four underlined items are obligatorily postverbal in VO (1b), and hence they would have to be fronted somehow, given the LCA premises on deriving OV from VO.

(1) a. dass ja keiner <u>diese Dinge</u> heutzutage <u>Syntaktikern</u> <u>auf ihr Brot</u> <u>schmieren</u> muß
that nobody$_{NOM}$ PRT these things$_{ACC}$ these-days syntacticians$_{DAT}$ on their bread butter must
b. that nobody must butter syntactians these things on their bread these days

The four items in (1a) consist of two objects, a PP interpreted as a directional predicate and the main verb. The objects may come in any order, relative to each other or to the subject. This fact makes it unlikely that they target special licensing positions for nominal arguments, e.g. for the purpose of functional checking of case. PP arguments are optionally pre- or postverbal in German, that is, they appear in the midfield or in an extraposed position. Case licensing as a trigger for fronting would fail in this case as an explanation for the preverbal PP positioning since PPs are not assigned case. Analogously, preverbal infinitival argument clauses in German are a puzzle for a case-based (or nominal-feature-based) trigger theory.

The PP in (1) is a directional PP. This is a sub-instance of result predicates. Result predicates are obligatorily preverbal in OV, regardless of their syntactic category. This separates result PPs from PP objects. Only the latter are extraposable in German and in Dutch.

Finally, the verb (or the emptied VP containing only the verb) must have been inverted. Three grammatical categories (DP, PP, VP), three grammatical functions (argument, secondary predicate, main verb (phrase)), three different triggers for a uniform result? Technically, this is no problem. We could simply postulate an 'expulsion feature' with the property that it cannot be checked within the licensing phrase. So, the DPs, the PP and the VP must leave their original home position.

Obviously, this would be entirely ad hoc, even if it worked somehow. However, grammar theory is not practical engineering. It strives to become an empirical science. For science it does not matter whether an idea 'works' somehow. The idea must be shown to be empirically adequate and superior to all presently known alternative accounts.

For an *engineering* problem there may exist many diverse and mutually incompatible solutions. Each one may be a viable solution in itself, though. However, if there appear to exist several incompatible solutions for a problem in *science*, at most one of them has the chance of being (close to) the 'right' one. If there is a competing theory, you have to show why yours fares better, and if there is none, you have to investigate and check possible alternatives. There are empirical obstacles for any interesting theory, but your particular solution will be uninteresting and ad hoc, as long as you merely propose ancillary assumptions but do not present solid independent evidence for the assumptions that are needed for protecting your central assumptions. It is not prejudiced if one states that thoroughgoing, uncompromising empirical testing of its consequences has not been a key part of the biography of the by now already teenaging LCA theory.

Under the BBC approach, the difference between (1a) and (1b) is predicted and follows from the opposite licensing directionality: in OV, the arguments have to precede. In (S)VO, the subject precedes, the objects follow, due to the different licensing relations (lexical, functional). The main verb precedes the auxiliary in OV, unless the auxiliary is fronted. Finally, result predicates are selected by a governing verb (see Chapter 7) and thus they precede in OV, and they follow in VO. A simple, single fact of grammar covers the distribution of the four elements in (1a) and (1b), respectively, without any ad hoc excuses and hand waving.

Let us now enter the German–Icelandic fact-finding mission. The following non-exhaustive list of OV/VO-dependent properties will be discussed in the given order since they highlight essential differences between a BBC-based account and an LCA approach:

(1) functional subject position and EPP-effects
(2) quirky subjects
(3) opacity for extraction
(4) scrambling versus object shift
(5) particle–verb order (even in the case of verbs that do not move)
(6) stacked VPs vs. V-clustering
(7) participle agreement
(8) word structure
(9) diachronic history of VO and OV
(10) verb clustering and verb-order variation.

First, the *obligatory functional* subject position is the hallmark of SVO clause structures. In OV, the subject is VP-internal and it remains VP-internal. Since it is within the directionality domain of the head, just like any other argument of the head, it does not need an external functional licenser. As a consequence, there are no robust subject–object asymmetries in German (or any other OV language) that would compare to grammatical subject–object asymmetry contrasts in English or in other Germanic VO languages.

Generative Grammar has not put forth an interesting answer to the fact that VO clauses have obligatory functional subject positions. Instead, an Extended

Projection Principle (EPP) feature is postulated that allegedly needs to be checked by a functional head and something in its spec. This is merely begging the question. In plain English, the answer reads as follows: the grammatical property is as it is because there is a grammatical feature that produces this property. This merely shifts the problem to feature theory and urges paraphrasing the question: why should grammars contain such a particular feature? The theory itself does not provide an explanation. This situation would be acceptable as long as the property covered by the assumed feature is empirically valid. Its validity is improbable at least, given the cross-linguistic counterevidence.

OV languages do not have obligatory functional subject positions. The uninteresting answer would be that they do not possess the EPP feature. Again, this ignores a crucial question, namely: is the presence/absence of an EPP feature an independent property? If it is, we ought to see OV languages with and without the EPP property and we should see VO languages with and without the EPP property.[13] This is not the case, and therefore the feature story loses explanatory force because of the weakness of its narrowly circular formulation.

OV languages do not implement obligatory functional subject positions and therefore they do not need obligatory expletives if the obligatory functional subject position cannot be lexicalized.[14] The fact that VO needs a functional licenser for the subject is a VO property. The OV situation is the unmarked situation: all arguments are structurally equal. They are projected into phrase structure within their VP. They are licensed there and therefore they stay there. In SVO, the subject is the only VP-internal argument that is not in the directionality domain of the verbal head. Hence, it needs an external, functional licenser. This is the causality of the otherwise unexplained EPP property. BBC and PDI explain the difference, LCA does not. It wrongly predicts EPP for OV as well.

Second, under the LCA approach, German makes available the grammatical 'ingredients' for the *quirky subject* phenomenon. However, there is no quirky subject phenomenon in German. Icelandic admits quirky subjects, German does not. Given the parallel situation in German (viz. availability of VP-internal nominative licensing and the availability of inherent morphological case marking),

---

[13] See Biberauer and Roberts (2005) for an EPP-based discussion of diachronic developments in English.

[14] In Scandinavian languages, *intransitive* verbs may be passivized, and there is an obligatory expletive. Modern English, for instance, does not have a suitable candidate for a dummy subject and therefore intransitive verbs cannot be passivized: 'There' must be associated with a postverbal DP, and 'it' is either a lexically selected quasi-argument or it is associated with an extraposed clause. There is no independent dummy element available.

German should/could have quirky subjects too, says the LCA account. Both languages allow VP-internal Nominatives and both languages have morphological Datives. The functional subject position is not reserved for checking Nominative and therefore it is able to accommodate the highest-ranking DP of the VP. If the highest-ranking argument happens to be an inherently cased argument (e.g. in the passive of intransitive verbs with a dative object, or in a clause with an unaccusative dative-nominative verb), the result should be a quirky subject construction, with the oblique DP in the subject position and the Nominative in the VP-internal position, as in Icelandic.

German and Icelandic would just differ with respect to the postverbal occurrence of arguments in Icelandic. In German, these would be fronted to preverbal positions. But the candidate for the functional subject position would be the same, given that German and Icelandic both have verb classes with an oblique argument as the highest-ranking argument.

The BBC theory predicts a different outcome: Icelandic employs a functional subject position, because the highest VP-internal argument – the argument in the preverbal VP-spec position – is not identified by the verbal head. So it needs a functional identifier, which in turn is associated with a functional spec position. This position determines the structural subject qualities.

In a head-final VP, all arguments are within the directionally restricted domain of the verbal head, since all positions homogeneously precede the verb. The corresponding construction in German is not a quirky subject construction but a VP with an oblique argument as the leftmost argument in the neutral word order, with a nominative argument following (if there is one). There is no structural head-room for a quirky subject construction in an OV language.

Third, for OV, the LCA approach inevitably and wrongly predicts the same kind of structure-triggered *opacity effects* as in VO. The conditions on extraction domains make a difference for pre- vs. postverbal arguments in VO. The preverbal ones are opaque for extraction in English and other VO languages (see also Haider 2010a: ch.1, observation 8). What constrains extraction out of the subject as the only preverbal argument in VO is bound to constrain extraction from any preverbal argument in OV. This empirical generalization is the robust result of more than a decade of research in conditions of extraction domains at the end of the last century. The prediction is false for OV, obviously:

(2) a. He said that [eating eels] is fun
 b. *What$_i$ did he say that [eating e$_i$] is fun?
 c. *What$_i$ did he say that [eating e$_i$] he dislikes?
 d. What$_i$ did he say that he dislikes eating e$_i$?
 e. *Whom$_i$ would [to have dinner with e$_i$] please you more?

f. Mit wem$_i$ hätte denn [e$_i$ speisen zu dürfen] dich mehr gefreut?
with whom had PRT [dine to be-allowed] you$_{ACC}$ more pleased
g. Wen$_i$ hat [damit e$_i$ zu konfrontieren] keiner versucht?
whom has [it-with to confront] nobody tried
h. Was$_i$ hat sich [ihr e$_i$ zu schenken] Fritz denn vorgenommen?
what has himself [her to present] Fritz PRT decided
'What did Fritz decide to present her?'

In English, preverbal positions are opaque for extractions. In (2b,e), it is the subject position, in (2c) is a fronted object phrase. In German, none of these preverbal sites are opaque. This is a flat contradiction for the LCA account, since in this account the preverbal positions in OV are structurally of the same kind as in VO. In the BBC model, however, the prediction is clear and supported by the facts. In OV, preverbal positions are in the directionality domain of the verb; in VO, preverbal positions are *not* in the directionality domain. This accounts for the opacity contrast.

Opacity conditions were the primary concern of syntactic research in the nineteen eighties and these investigations produced reliable descriptive generalizations. Today, this area has fallen victim to a kind of neglect syndrome. Neither the LCA system nor the Minimalist Program has fully integrated the findings of the eighties.

But this is not the real problem. The crucial problem is that the facts are as they are, and that the LCA system predicts opacity effects where there are none. In an OV language, any preverbal argument phrase is predicted to be as opaque as any preverbal argument phrase in VO. This is an unavoidable prediction since the positions targeted by the fronted argument phrases in OV are the same kind of positions as the subject position in VO and positions preceding the subject position.

Fourth, *scrambling* is problematic for the LCA account. It is predicted for OV and for German in particular by the BBC-based account, however. And scrambling is ruled out for Icelandic (and for VO in general) in the BBC system. Both Icelandic and German show word-order variation for arguments. In German this is referred to as *scrambling*, the Icelandic phenomenon is referred to as *object shift*. The crucial differentiating properties are these: scrambling *permutes* arguments whereas object shift strictly *conserves* the relative order of arguments, and object shift presupposes an empty left edge of the VP (Holmberg 1999; Haider 2010a: 159), but scrambling is independent of this restriction. If German was just a derivational continuation of Icelandic, the contrast seems to be accidental. In other words, the contrast could equally well be even the inverse, with Icelandic as a scrambling language and German as an object-shifting one. From the BBC point of view, the prediction is straightforward: scrambling is possible only in a head-final environment. It is internal merger-by-adjunction to the VP *within* its domain of identification. In a head-initial VP, adjunction to the left would leave the domain of identification and thus produce a different outcome, and adjunction to the right is banned by the BBC anyway.

Moreover, the LCA theory predicts scrambled phrases to become opaque for extraction, which is contrary to the facts. In an LCA perspective, scrambled phrases are phrases moved to preverbal spec positions. Hence, they are expected to display the behaviour of phrases in preverbal spec positions just like an English subject. In particular, these phrases are predicted to be opaque for extraction just as preverbal subjects are. This is not the case, however. It is uncontroversial that scrambled clauses do not become opaque in German (Haider 2010:155).

Fifth, *particle–verb order* (even in the case of immoveable verbs) is an excellent testing ground for the opposing theories, since the LCA approach needs to invoke particle movement for deriving the preverbal particle position in OV. Normally, if the particle of a particle verb is not V-adjacent, this indicates that the particle is stranded. Languages such as German and Dutch clearly show that functional particles (i.e. particles without truth-conditional semantic content) are inert.[15] They are only found in V-adjacent positions.

Vikner (2001: 37) formulates a descriptive generalization: 'In the Germanic OV languages, particle verbs whose particles are postverbal under V2 (separate) nevertheless always have preverbal particles in non-V2 contexts, whereas in the Germanic VO-languages, particle verbs whose particles have to be stranded under V2 never have preverbal particles in non-V2 contexts.' If particles could move, that is, move to the left, they ought to occur in the midfield in OV languages or in preverbal positions in the VO languages. This is not the case, however.

Hence, if particles do not move, how do they end up in a preverbal position? And why is there no OV language with postverbal particles? They could surface in preverbal position only if the verb could move to the right, but this is excluded, both in the LCA as well as under the BBC, since there is no head-final functional projection to accommodate the verb. So, in the LCA account a syntactic process of *particle fronting* must be invoked, or else a particle would never appear in a preverbal position (Kayne 1998: 136). But once you assume particle fronting for deriving the OV order, you allow this rule

---

[15] This is true also for 'cluster creepers', that is, stranded particles within the verbal cluster in Dutch. This is the result of V-movement to the right (V-cliticization), and not the result of particle movement (see Haider 2003).

in principle also for VO. It becomes part of the grammatical toolkit, and you could not discriminate VO languages. Of course, there is no VO language with preverbal particles, but the LCA theory would admit it.

The BBC predicts the preverbal position of particles in OV (and for word structure both in VO and OV): if the lexical head of a c-projection is head-final, the dependants of this verbal head must precede; if it is head-initial, the dependants must follow. The LCA system, on the other hand, does not provide a straightforward account. It is bound to assume an ad hoc measure, namely particle movement, and this measure over-generates.

A second aspect of particle constructions is the fact that VO languages may differ as to whether they permit stranding. Danish obligatorily strands, Swedish does not strand at all; English, Icelandic and Norwegian allow both stranding or pied-piping of the particle. However, crucially, there is no Germanic OV language that allows a particle position that is not V-adjacent, and the particles are invariably preverbal. If OV resulted from VO, there should exist a stranding OV language with postverbal particles. Note that this argument rests on the assumption that OV is the result of VP evacuation. But an account in terms of *remnant VP-fronting* would not work either.

Remnant VP-fronting as a vehicle of particle movement is doomed to fail too. It is a fact that remnant VP topicalization must not pied-pipe a stranded particle. This is easy to check with a fronted remnant VP and a stranded particle in German. Take the particle verb *auffallen* – 'attract one's attention' (lit. up-fall). If the LCA account of preverbal particles in VO is based on remnant VP-movement, it would incorrectly allow (3a). This structure shares the basic configuration with the alleged remnant VP-fronting that is necessary for producing preverbal particles: first, the verb is fronted, stranding the particle. Then the VP with the particle is fronted.

(3)   a.   *[Mir auf-e$_i$]$_{VP}$ fiel$_i$ das nicht
          (to) me up fell this not ['up fall' = come to one's mind]
          'It did not come to my mind' (= I did not notice it)
    b.   [Mir aufgefallen]$_{VP}$ ist das nicht
          (to) me up-fallen is this not

As (3a) shows, particle stranding in a fronted VP is not allowed. This is the consequence of a crossing violation. A phrase that contains a trace is fronted across the antecedent of the trace. Thus, the trace of the verb in the fronted remnant VP is not properly bound. This is true for (3a) and analogously for (4), that is, for the hypothetical derivational vehicle that is to produce particle fronting.

(4)   dass mir etwas [$_{VP}$ auf-e$_i$ ...]$_j$ fiel$_i$ e$_j$
                                     [beware: this structure is expository only]

The **sixth** region of contrasting data is *verb clustering* in OV (see Haider 2010a: ch.7). In languages with head-*initial* VPs, verbs that select a VP are projected/merged into stacked VPs (5a). In languages with head-*final* VPs, they are merged in clusters (5b). Stacked head-*initial* VPs are right-branching structures. Stacked head-*final* VPs would be left-branching (5c). This violates the BBC. VO languages stack VPs, OV language cluster the verbs. Why should this be so?

The bracketing in (5c) already reveals the crucial factor. For (5c), the parser would have to guess how many brackets to open; in (5a), the parser encounters the head of the topmost VP first, with the maximal projection of the head as the immediately dominating node. Clustering (5b) reduces the indeterminacy for the parser to the *local* environment of a single V-projection. Clustering is UG's contribution to parser friendliness of complex head-final structures.[16]

(5)   a.   [$_{VP}$ V$_1$ [$_{VP}$ V$_2$ [$_{VP}$ V$_3$ ...]]]   head-initial
       b.   [$_{VP}$ ... [$_{V°}$ [$_{V°}$ V$_3$ V$_2$] V$_1$]]   head-final
       c.   *[$_{VP}$ [$_{VP}$ [$_{VP}$ ... V$_3$] V$_2$] V$_1$]   head-final

Icelandic verbs, like those in English and the other Scandinavian languages, do not cluster, neither with auxiliaries nor with other verbs. Why do German and Dutch verbs cluster? The answer has to be sought in the headedness difference again: the constraint against left-branching (extended) projections does not only rule out structures with head-*final functional* heads (see Appendix 5.1 in Ch. 5) but also *lexically* extended head-final V-projections,[17] that is, V° selecting VPs as its *left-hand* complement.

For the LCA, the mirror-image order of auxiliary sequences in German and the clustering property in general are unexpected. Moreover, the core problem is the *compactness* of the cluster: the verbs in the cluster do not tolerate non-verbal, intervening material (except particles; these I consider as part of a complex verbal lexical entry). This property is not captured by movement analyses (e.g. remnant VP-fronting, as suggested by Koopman and Szabolcsi

---

[16] It is presupposed here that the structures provided by the core grammar (as a function of UG) are parser friendly, given that UG and parsing developed in a process of cognitive co-evolution (see Haider 2003). The data-to-parser fit is optimal if the parser – a left-corner parser – can simultaneously operate bottom up and top down, that is, with continuous data processing (bottom up) plus grammar guidance (top-down information on possible structures). This is implemented best with right-branching projection structures.

[17] 'Lexical extension of a VP' refers to verbal elements that contribute to the aspectual, modal, epistemic or other semantic modifications of a VP by selecting the respective VP as complement. In German and Dutch, these verbs are obligatorily clustering. In addition, a large subclass of control verb is clustering optionally.

2000), except for a head-to-head adjunction analysis (Zwart 1993). He primarily analyzed Dutch, and advocates a V-raising approach in which the auxiliary order is derived by iterative head-to-head adjunction (cf. Zwart 1993: §2.4). Even if it is possible to derive the order by means of the devices suggested by Zwart, the theoretical and empirical soundness remains to be demonstrated.

First, it is unclear why clustering is found only in OV but not in VO languages. Zwart's (1993) movement account would work in VO as well as in OV. The BBC provides a principled answer, the LCA apparently not. Second, the BBC provides an answer to the specific variations within the cluster, and in particular the contrast between German and Dutch in this respect. In the LCA framework, which starts from a VO organization of auxiliary verb sequences, the inversion of this order is a disturbing factor, and the variation in the inverted sequences is even more disturbing. In the absence of a reasonable trigger theory, the head-to-head adjunction proposal (actually a revival of Arnold Evers' original verb-raising idea) remains an ad hoc feature of the model.

Third, *clause union phenomena* provide robust evidence that the crucial aspect of clustering is not so much the formation of a verb cluster by means of head-to-head adjunction, but, as already acknowledged in Evers (1975), the crucial aspect is the lack of the VP- or functional complement structure, which provoked Evers to resort to a pruning operation. Head movement would not destroy the stacked VP or IP structure. Nevertheless, the available evidence points to the absence of these remnants of an infinitival clause structure (see the list of sixteen properties in Haider 2010a: 311–13). Here, the LCA model is at a loss, on principled grounds, because it predicts the conservation of clause-internal structures, on the one hand, and has no answer for the question as to why this structure is absent, on the other hand, giving rise to numerous clause union phenomena. Movement would not destroy these structures, but the diverse evidence is incompatible with them.

The clustering analysis is extensively explicated in Haider (2010a: ch.7). Here, a single piece of evidence may suffice as representative,[18] namely *rigorous compactness* as a sign of clustering. Another piece of evidence has been discussed in Chapter 4, namely cluster nominalization.

(6)   a.   dass er was zu sehen war [gesehen *wird* haben]$_{cluster}$
                that he what to see was seen shall have
                'that he shall have seen what was to be seen'

---

[18] In Chapters 1 and 8, the availability of cluster nominalization has already been mentioned as a specific piece of evidence for the V°-category of the cluster, consisting of head-to-head adjoined verbs.

b. [Gesehen, was zu sehen war]$_{VP}$ *wird* er haben
c. *dass er [*gesehen* was zu sehen war] *wird haben*
   that he [seen what to see was] shall have
d. dass er gesehen wird haben [was zu sehen war]

The specific cluster variant (6a) has the finite verb in between the non-finite verbs. In a derivational analysis, the participle in (6a) would be the right edge of the deepest VP. This VP is a possible target of extraposition, as illustrated by the topicalized VP with extraposition (6b). Hence, (6c) should be a well-formed order if the participle is projecting a VP, but it is not. In the clustering analysis, the three verbs in (6a) are elements of a verbal cluster. This immediately rules out a word order as in (6c). In a derivational analysis, a clause with three verbs would start with three VPs, and these VPs could not be done away with. Koopman and Szabolcsi (2000) are fully aware of the problem of over-generating. The set of filters they propose are a last-resort measure for taming the derivational machinery (see also the discussion of verb-order variation in the cluster below, under 'tenth').

Seventh, predicative adjectives agree in VO, but not in OV. The OV languages German, Frisian, Dutch and Yiddish have inflected *attributive* adjectives, but *un*inflected *predicative* adjectives, whereas those VO languages that have inflected attributive adjectives (that is, all the Scandinavian languages and all the Romance ones) *also* have inflected predicative adjectives.

The fact that none of the present-day Germanic OV languages has adjective agreement for predicative adjectives is surprising in the LCA model, but not in the BBC system. Only if OV was the derivational continuation of VO would this entail the agreement relations like in VO. Neither A-movement (e.g. NP-movement in passive) nor A'-movement (e.g. topicalization or wh-movement) destroys previously established agreement relations.

The crucial difference that is responsible for the contrast seems to be the following: in VO, the subject of the predicative adjective needs an external licenser since its pre-adjectival, AP-internal subject position is not in the canonical directionality domain of the head. In OV, however, the subject argument in the predicative AP is in the canonical domain of the head. In VO, licensing is implemented in terms of a functional head, and this head is lexicalized with the copula. The copula enters an agreement relation with the subject, and selects the AP as complement.

(7) a. VO: [DP$_i$ [Copula [$_{AP}$ e$_i$ A°]]]
            (as in: *It$_i$ is [e$_i$ green]* vs. in: *paint [it green]*)
     b. OV: [[$_{AP}$ DP [A° Copula]]]

In OV, the copula and the adjectival head (optionally) form a head–head cluster. This is predicted by the BBC. The copula should not select the AP just like an auxiliary cannot select a VP in OV. It is functional selection, and the phrase would be a functional extension of the AP. Hence the AP would end up as a left sister in an extended projection. This is avoided.

In VO, however, the AP is a full-fledged complement. It is this difference in structure that prevents agreement in the OV type. In this type, the adjective is part of the cluster, and the cluster is the complex head of the VP. So, there is only a single candidate for agreement, and this is the copula. In VO, the subject agrees with the copula, and moreover, it is in a relation to the AP-subject position. Therefore, if the adjective is able to agree, it may agree as the head of a separate projection.

The situation for participle agreement in Romance languages such as French, Italian or Old Spanish is instructive in this respect. In active sentences, the perfect participle is in an agreement relation with the object if the object is fronted (by wh-movement or by cliticization). The resulting configuration is analogous to (7a): a DP is fronted to a functional position and thereby leaves the phrase it was born in. Consequently, in a derivational analysis of OV, predicative adjectives should agree in OV languages just like in VO, given the massive movement of phrases to the left. The antecedent of the predicative adjective would be in a higher spec position.

What these contrasts tell us is that the LCA owes us an explanation, whereas the BBC model is compatible with this set of differences. In fact, they support the principled difference between an OV and a VO set-up of clause structure.

Eighth, *word structure* contradicts the LCA and confirms the BBC. The latter predicts merger to the left (see Chapter 8). The former predicts a left-headed structure. It is an undeniable fact that word structure in the vast majority of languages is right-headed, both morphologically as well as semantically. Suffixes determine the category, prefixes don't, as in the German example (8a,b):

(8) a. Fett$_{N°}$ → [fett-*en*$_{V°}$]$_{V°}$ → [*ent*-fetten]$_{V°}$ → [Entfett-ung$_{N°}$]$_{N°}$
      fat   fatt*en*   *de*-grease   de-greas*ing*
    → [Voll [Entfett-ung$_{N°}$]$_{N°}$]$_{N°}$
    full de-greasing
  b. white$_{A°}$ → whit-*en*$_{V°}$ → re-whiten$_{V°}$ → re-whiten-*ing*$_{N°}$

The BBC is a UG property and constrains the make-up of recursively built structures. Hence, it will apply both to phrase structure and to word structure. It requires merger to the left. Merger to the left produces head-final structures.

This is what we see in word structure (see Chapter 8). Word structure is the pure reflex of the BBC since in English or German word structuring there is no directionality parameter involved.

The LCA account predicts a universal spec–head–complement structure.[19] This covers all kinds of structures, and presumably it is to cover word structure, too. Hence (9a) should have the order (9b), since *radar* is clearly the object of *detecting*, nominalized in the form *detector*.

(9)   a.   [radar-[detector]]
        b.   detector-radar   (with 'detector' as the semantic base)

Roeper and Snyder (2005) accept the implications of the LCA account and consequently postulate movement operations as in (10a,b), without independent evidence, though. What they seem to overlook, for instance, is the fact that in word formation, children do not produce the kind of variation they produce in phrase structuring, namely a variation between OV and VO patterns. This apparent variation is in fact an independent, third-type option, resulting from an unfixed directionality value (see also the ninth property, below).[20] From a BBC point of view this is predicted: when there is no movement, there is no variation. Word structure is not a domain of movement. Roeper and Snyder (2005), however, accept the LCA dogma that the head-final organization of word structure is a derivational result of a head-initial base structure.

(10)   a.   hold pen   → [pen$_i$ [hold e$_i$]]
         b.   [er [pen$_i$ [hold e$_i$]] → [[pen$_i$ [hold e$_i$]$_j$ er [e$_j$]]

Although it is not immediately evident that a simple 'penholder' has as rich a structure and derivational history as the one suggested in (10b), Roeper and Snyder (2005) do not say what kind of evidence might have convinced them that (10b) is really more than a forced ad hoc analysis for those who want to maintain the LCA against the evidence of word structure. For a BBC account of the word structure, see the discussion of compounding in Chapter 4.

---

[19] Recall that Kayne (1994) and Chomsky (1995) have advanced the following claims:
     a. Any movement rule is universally left-bound.
     b. Complex structures are represented in the form of Specifier–Head–Complement.

[20] Karl (2010) studied the acquisition of nominal compounds [N$_1$ N$_2$], with N$_2$ being the base, as deverbal noun, and an N$_1$ in an object relation (e.g. *nut cracker*). It turned out that children at the age of 3–4 already use the correct order. The percentage of mistakes with the inverted order was very small and correlated significantly with X – V – O order in the elicitation sentence.

Ninth, the LCA and the BBC model differ in their prediction of *diachronic changes* within the Germanic (and also in the Romance) language family in particular. This is the topic of Chapter 5.

The present discussions of OV and VO tend to downplay the existence of languages that exhibit both VO and OV surface orders simultaneously, plus orders that do not occur in VO or in OV (see Chapter 3, §3.5 and Chapter 5). Examples of this type of language are historic variants of Germanic languages, such as Old Icelandic (e.g. Rögnvaldsson 1996; Hróarsdóttir 2000) and Old English (e.g. Pintzuk 1991), as well as a present-day Germanic specimen, namely Yiddish.[21]

(11)   a. [XP [YP [ZP V°]]]   OV
       b. [XP [$V_i°$ [YP [$V_i°$ ZP]]]]   VO
       c. { [XP [YP [ZP V°]]], [XP [YP [V° ZP]]], [XP [$V_i°$ [YP [$V_i°$ ZP]]]] }
                                                                                  Type III

The OV and the VO option are the result of merger with either the value *left* or *right*, just like in (11a) and (11b). The third possibility is the result of *adjustable* (or underspecified) directionality, that is, the possibility of switching the directionality in the course of merging. The second variant in (11c) starts out with *directionality value = right*,[22] licensing a complement to the right, and then the value switches to *left*, proceeding in an OV manner.

The implication for diachronic syntax is this: if the historic variants of Germanic languages are viewed from this perspective, the development of the Germanic languages is much easier to understand. The basic change has been one from an *adjustable* (i.e. underspecified) headedness value to a *rigid* one. The rigid directionality allows either of two values. The choice of the value is in principle free. One branch of Germanic languages fixed it in the OV way (West Germanic), the other in the VO way (North Germanic). So, two very similar languages in terms of their morpho-syntactic make-up, namely Icelandic and German, ended up in different systems by accident. The accident is the choice of the directionality value when giving up the adjustability option.

The BBC model provides the right kind of tool for capturing these developments, namely the directionality parameter of licensing by a lexical head. In

---

[21] Slavic languages should be listed in this group as well, and Hungarian also. Since the descriptive tools of typologists are not accurate enough for capturing the differences, the list of Type III languages is likely to be approximately as long as the list of OV or VO languages.

[22] Note that this is the only available possibility. Obviously, structure building could not start in the OV style and switch to VO.

the LCA model, the West Germanic OV languages would have to be filed as continuations of a VO system that is still conserved in the North Germanic VO languages.

This is not what diachronic studies tell us. There is no indication that in the attested history of Germanic languages the predecessors of OV languages had previously been VO. The known facts support the BBC-based account: the modern Germanic languages with their OV/VO split are continuations of a predecessor language. This language resembled the only surviving Germanic 'Type III' language, namely Yiddish, in a crucial respect, that is, the apparently variable pre- and postverbal order of nominal arguments. In the BBC model, this is the option you get if the directionality parameter is underspecified. Fixing the parameter value yields two possible outcomes, namely strict head-final or strict head-initial projections. And, moreover, the direction of the attested drift towards OV and VO is in accordance with the degrees of freedom the model offers for diachronic change.

Tenth, and finally, OV and VO robustly differ with respect to V–V(P) dependencies. In VO languages, the relative order of auxiliaries, quasi-auxiliaries and verbs is *invariant*. In VO languages with V-movement, verb-order variation is common and typical. In all Germanic OV languages there is verb-order variation, and this variation does not contribute anything to semantics or pragmatics. It is entirely optional:

(12)   a. dass er es *lesen müssen wird*$_{FIN}$ */lesen wird*$_{FIN}$ *müssen / wird*$_{FIN}$ *lesen müssen*
that he it read must shall /read shall must /shall read must
    b. dat hij niets *gezien kan*$_{FIN}$ *hebben / kan*$_{FIN}$ *gezien hebben / kan*$_{FIN}$ *hebben gezien*   Dutch (ANS 1984: 1,069)
that he nothing seen can have / can seen have / can have seen

The first variant in (12a), namely *lesen müssen wird* has a fully inverted counterpart in Dutch, namely *zal moeten lezen*, whose order is congruent with English 'shall have-to read'. Koopman and Szabolcsi (2000) suggested a simple account: VO, as in English, is the base configuration (13a). Then the object is fronted (13b). The other variants are the result of VP-fronting (13c) to a spec position in between the two auxiliary positions or in front of the two auxiliaries (13d).

(13)   a. dat hij [*kan*$_{FIN}$ [*hebben* [*gezien* niets]]]   LCA base order
        b. dat hij niets$_i$ *kan*$_{FIN}$ *hebben gezien* e$_i$ object shift
        c. dat hij niets kann [$_{VP}$ gezien e$_i$]$_j$ hebben e$_j$ VP shift
        d. dat hij niets [$_{VP}$ gezien e$_i$]$_j$ kann hebben e$_j$ VP shift
        e. *dat hij niets [[$_{VP}$ gezien e$_i$]$_j$ hebben e$_j$]$_k$ kann e$_k$ VP shift

The *first* remarkable aspect of this analysis is that it massively over-generates. The authors admit this, but they are content with proposing a set of filters for eliminating the over-generated variants. The reason for massive over-generating is this: first, the verbal cluster in Dutch is compact. No non-verbal material must intervene between the verbs in the cluster, except for a verbal particle. The VP, however, may pied-pipe (extraposed) material. This would produce interveners. Second, the very VP-fronting option needed for (13d) produces the order (13e), which is ungrammatical in Dutch. It is a possible German order, however, and therefore it could not be excluded on principled grounds.

The *second* remarkable aspect is the complete absence of independent evidence. There is not the slightest evidence that a VP has moved in these constructions, and there is no reason why it should have moved. The analysis is ad hoc and it makes the order variation properties appear ad hoc too. It is motivated by theory-internal considerations only, wilfully elevating the VO order property to the level of an unquestioned but unfounded axiom.

In the BBC-based approach, clustering in OV and its absence in VO is predictable: head-*final* complementation produces centre-embedded V-projections (14a). A grammar with clustering in OV is a parser-friendly grammar. Clustering reduces centre embedding and confines the domain of left-branching to the local domain of the verbal cluster (14b). The variations of word order in the cluster are partial (or full) 'repairs' of the left-branching cluster structure (see Haider 2010a: ch.7, §7.5):

(14)   a. ... $[_{VP} [_{VP} [_{VP} ... V_1] V_2] V_3]$
         b. ... $[_{VP} ... [[[V_1] V_2] V_3]$ German cluster variant
         c. ... $[_{VP} ... [V_3 [V_2 [V_1]]]$ Dutch cluster variant

In the BBC-based approach, clustering is not a bizarre property but the immediate outcome of the head-final option for V-projections. Clustering is not a Germanic peculiarity but holds for OV languages in general. In languages without V-movement, such as Japanese or Korean, it has no linearization effect and hence it tends to be overlooked (see Haider 2010a: 324 and the literature cited there).

9.5   Ockham's razor, epicycles and (im)perfect systems

Is the LCA- or the BBC-based system closer to the ideal of a minimal, necessary and sufficient set of conditions for an at least descriptively adequate account of the relation between head-initial and head-final structures?

Empirical success or failure is only one side of the coin. As every scientist implicitly knows, and as Duhem and Quine established on philosophical grounds,[23] you always can mend, bend and expand your system in order to cover or block off problematic evidence. So, there is no final and definite way of falsifying a theory. All one can do is point out what kind of data are problematic for a given version. The more diverse and widespread the varieties of counterevidence are, or become, the greater is the likelihood that the theoretical premises a system is based on are inappropriate. Having discussed empirical issues, let us turn now briefly to theoretical considerations.

A distinctive area of theory comparison is a comparison in terms of the overall system properties. Is the system *elegant, economic*, and *heuristically* productive? Here, Ockham's razor as a principle of theoretical economy has its place.[24] It applies to several aspects:

- economy of the inventory
- economy of the combinatorics (i.e. structuring and derivational processes)
- relation to the null hypothesis.

The merits of the LCA and the BBC models clearly differ with respect to the various parameters of evaluation. Let me start with the inventory. The LCA system claims to work without a *directionality* parameter (Kayne 1994: 132). This is true in a literal sense, since directionality is not used as a primitive feature of the system. It seems, however, that this is merely a terminological difference. In fact, *directionality* is a primitive element of the LCA system, too. It is necessary for symmetry breaking: the LCA (Kayne 1994: 5–6) merely requires that the grammar provide a means of mapping asymmetric c-command relations into linearization relations. This mapping can be grammatically implemented in various ways, however. The structures in (15) are obviously different structures, but they share the same asymmetric c-command relations and therefore they are each mapped onto the same linearization relation: the

---

[23] According to the 'Duhem–Quine thesis', the holistic nature of scientific theories makes the rejection of a *particular* hypothesis as a consequence of counterevidence virtually inconclusive: one can always retain the hypothesis at hand by making *appropriate adjustments* elsewhere in the system. Theories tend to be rescued by modifications (of their *periphery*) in order to protect the *core* against the very counterevidence (Lakatos 1977).

[24] William of Ockham (*c.* 1285–1347): 'Non sunt multiplicanda entia praeter necessitatem' [You must not introduce a (theoretical) entity without (having shown its) necessity]. Or, in the words of Georg Christoph Lichtenberg (1742–99), who inverted Hamlet's sigh ('There are more things in heaven and earth, Horatio, than are dreamt of in your philosophy'): 'There are even more things in our philosophy that do not occur anywhere between heaven and earth.'

item that asymmetrically c-commands is linearized in a relation R with respect to the item that it c-commands. R could be 'precede', as Kayne postulates (15), or 'follow'. So, a decision on directionality is at stake on the *linearization* side, and on the *structure* side, too. The LCA system is *inherently* parametric. The *hidden* parameter is the linearization relation (*precede* or *follow*).

(15) a. [A [B [C [D]]]] → A – B – C – D (or D – C – B – A)
 b. [[[[D [C [B [A] → A – B – C – D (or D – C – B – A)
 c. [A [B [[D] C]]] → A – B – C – D (or D – C – B – A)
 d. [A [B [[D] C]]] → A – B – C – D (or D – C – B – A)
 e. etc.

Directionality covers the essential degree of freedom for the PF representations: PF representations are one-dimensional (i.e. with the single ordering relation: precede vs. follow). This is a necessary consequence of the coding of complex linguistic representations as *sequences*. Since complex expressions cannot be produced instantly, they must be sequenced on the time axis, either as a stream of sounds or a stream of gestures (in sign languages).

The degree of freedom for the single dimension of a string is *before* and *after*. Algorithmic parameterization, on the other hand, would become intractable if it started from the PF side. But it must start from the PF side when it unfolds the syntactic structure of a string. So, there is no continuous relation between the organization of the string in terms of *before* and *after* and the algorithmic feature that is responsible for deriving a head-final organization from a head-initial one by means of derivational processes.

Therefore, the question 'Should the theory contain a directionality feature as a primitive?' should be answered with *yes*, if one is pleased by the idea that the way grammars manage linguistic data structures is in a continuous relation with the properties of the data structures at the interfaces. In other words, if one thinks that our brain employs effective and efficient processing algorithms for transforming objects with one specific property (namely strings with precede/follow as their inherent order relation) into objects with another specific property (namely phrases as hierarchically organized box-in-box structures), one should not be surprised to see that a core property of one set of objects (namely precede/follow) maps directly onto a core property of the other set (directional identification in a structure). Here comes the essential difference.

If, on the other hand, the mapping of structures onto PF is a *stepwise derivational process* (= algebraic model), it would not matter at all whether a structure had a linear order or not. In the latter case, each one of the different bracketings in (15a–d) is an instantiation of one and the same structure, with its notational variants. If, however, the mapping is a *direct pattern-matching process* (= geometric model), the linearization of the structure matters. Only (15a) can be mapped directly on 'A<B<C<D'.

The BBC model is a *geometric* one, the LCA model is *algebraic*. This is a neuro- and psycholinguistically testable difference, and it is a relevant aspect for the comparative evaluation: the BBC model embodies a *direct* matching between structure and linearization; the LCA model defines a global constraint for grammars: A grammar is licit only if it 'somehow' manages to guarantee that phrase structure is antisymmetric, in order to get it uniquely mapped onto linearizations. The direct approach by the BBC, on the other hand, is evidently the stronger theory as it provides fewer degrees of freedom for the bridging relations between syntactic structure and linearization.

Let us now turn to the algorithmic quality of the theory in the characterization of OV vs. VO. The LCA model is a system that characterizes the OV properties as the result of a derivationally *more complex* grammar. For the BBC system, on the other hand, OV structures are *less complex* than VO structures (because the latter, but not the former, need shells plus a functional projection for the subject). Given the massive derivational efforts needed for turning VO into OV,[25] Ockham's razor simply says: give me good reasons for the extra derivational apparatus and show me that it really is at work. The extra machinery is necessary if you cannot plausibly do without it, and it is at work if you can show us several immediate and independent effects of this apparatus in the data properties.

A system that achieves the same result (namely providing insight into the principal relations that differentiate OV and VO, and characterizing them as alternative options within the same system potential) without an excessive and hitherto largely unmotivated (see: lack of a trigger theory) derivational machinery is the BBC model.

What is a reasonable *null hypothesis* with respect to OV versus VO, you should ask yourself. 'OV' and 'VO' refer to different phrasal organizations, but the difference is not haphazard. 'OV' and 'VO' are dependent variables, and the dependency rests on factors that correspondingly partition the system space provided by UG for the phrasal architecture.

At least two possibilities have to be acknowledged and checked: the dependency may be an *opposition*, with OV and VO as alternative outcomes,

---

[25] Heavy syntactic traffic to the left is not limited to the derivation of an OV structure. Even for VO grammars, Kayne (1998) employs Neg phrase preposing (p.135), Neg° raising (p.152), raising of *not* (p. 153), VP-preposing (p.135), particle preposing (p.136, 143), predicate raising (p.138), *only*-phrase preposing (p.146), raising of *only* (p.150) and direct object preposing (p.162).

or, and this is the more restricted hypothesis, the dependency may be a case of an *inclusion* relation, with one state as the more specific variant of the other. The LCA proposes the specific inclusion relation, the BBC holds an opposition relation. In the light of the arguments developed in this volume, the inclusion hypothesis appears to be insufficiently grounded and unlikely to be appropriate. The more adequate model is one that characterizes OV and VO as alternative (parametric) options within the *same* system space of UG.

Let me finally briefly highlight a well-known problem of dealing with *economy and perfection* on the level of theory design.[26] It is the desire of most theorists to reduce the observed complexities to complexities in the output of an elegant and parsimonious system (of *virtual necessity*). Perfection, however, does not guarantee explanatory success. The history of science offers numerous examples of elegant and complex systems whose only defect was that they turned out to be empirically wrong. Unfortunately, nature had not bothered instantiating them.

A case in point readily comes to mind from the history of astronomy. It was possible to maintain a simple, easy-to-understand, wrong idea for quite some time (approximately from the time of Apollonius of Perga at the end of the third century BC until Kepler's days). The leading idea, which has turned out to be empirically wrong after all, was the idea that celestial bodies move on geometrically minimal and perfect trajectories, namely circles. This restricts the degree of freedom for movement to a single parameter. It is the strongest constraint on possible movements.

Only 'planets' (Greek for 'rovers') appeared to be exceptional, but their exceptionality was explained away as a *complexity effect*: like other celestial bodies, planets were thought to move on circles, but unlike other celestial bodies, the centre of the respective circle moves on a circle (the so-called *deferent*), too (whose centre may again move on a circle, and so on). In other words, this system was a system with a highly restricted theory of movement (movement on circles only), and with a simple derivational component for integrating the actual movement of planets (namely *epicycles*, that is, circles on circles on circles ...). How can we assure ourselves that the massive movements in the LCA-based accounts are not epicycles? The answer is obvious. Provide

---

[26] 'Universal grammar is perfectly designed, that is, it contains nothing more than what follows from our best guesses regarding conceptual, biological, physical necessity' (Boeckx 2006: 4). Pinker and Jackendoff (2005: 227) justly emphasize: 'The overall claim that language is "perfect" or "optimal" is a personal view of how language ought to be characterized rather than an empirical discovery about the way language is.'

positive and independent empirical results for the numerous implications, like Copernicus, Kepler and others did in astronomy.[27]

Without sufficient independent evidence for the derivational complexity invoked by the LCA system for OV, the need for massive derivational rearrangements on the way to OV raises the suspicion that this is just the epicycle part of an allegedly minimalist and elegant grammar theory. Its design may be elegant, minimal and sophisticated, but the way it models the facts may nevertheless be inadequate, simply because the linguistic products of a domain-specific mental capacity do not fit into this very model.

With the idea of perfection, linguists in the vicinity of the Minimalist Program have revived a scholastic kind of reasoning that had been given up with the idealist concepts of the eighteenth century. It is the *argument from perfection*: a property is postulated and declared as existing simply because its absence would make the system less perfect than one would like to have it. This is an argument known from mediaeval debates on metaphysical matters but its value in empirical domains is nil. Inferences from an alleged quality of 'perfection' (Roberts 2000) are simply irrelevant in empirical domains. *Perfection is a property of a platonic object like a calculus, but not of grammar as a mental capacity embodied in a neuro-biologically evolved organ.*[28] Even if a grammar might resemble a calculus in important aspects, it is obvious that it is an indirect product of *biological* and *cognitive* evolution. Evolution is tinkering and by no means perfect. 'In reality, evolution is a blind process, with absolutely no guarantee of perfection' (Kinsella and Marcus 2009: 187). What is true for biological evolution is equally true for cognitive evolution. It is extremely unlikely that a grammar could be a perfect system on the one hand and on the other hand a product of an organ, namely the human brain, whose capacities and operative qualities are the result of biological and cognitive evolution (see Haider 2011, for examples of grammatical inconsistencies).

---

[27] The social biotope of Generative Grammar apparently instigates ambitions for becoming a linguistic Copernicus, if not Newton, more than the desire to come close to a respected linguistic Regiomontanus or Brahe. The average syntactician's desire for innovating or revolutionizing a present variant of a theory usually prevails over the apparently less impressive attempt of carefully assessing a generalization over a relevant database.

[28] Those who claim that a grammar is the result of a perfect UG must firmly close their eyes and ears when being confronted with English as a specimen of an evidently imperfect instantiation: no passive of intransitive verbs, although all Germanic languages have it; movement of finite auxiliaries, but not of finite main verbs (in V1 and V2 patterns), which lead to a patch-up construction ('do-support'), and no other (Germanic) language enjoys this exception; no morpho-syntactic marker for infinitive and as a consequence an exceptional class of verbs that cannot be used in infinitival constructions (i.e. modals). These are but a few examples of properties that are much closer to tinkering than to perfection (see Haider 2010a: 9).

A grammar may be a highly adaptive system for the purposes for which it is employed, but this is a property of selection (on the biological, neuro-cognitive and cognitive level) and not of striving for perfection. The argument from perfection uses 'perfection' as a *teleological* quality: in order to be/become *perfect* a grammar must have the properties $P_1 \ldots P_i \ldots P_n$, hence UG must guarantee the properties $P_{1\text{-}n}$. This metaphysical conception of grammar theory I do not want to adopt. It is clearly idealist in all but name; it is the contemporary version of linguistic idealism of the eighteenth century. Science is orthogonal to idealism, and I prefer linguistics to develop into a science.

Appendix 9.1 On hyper-derivational syntax and the scientific conduct of grammar theory

The Minimalist Program and the LCA programme are strongly (if not hyper-) derivational. Their major syntactic tool is massive overt as well as covert 'movement',[29] plus the devices for taming these hyperactive 'animals'. The evidence, however, comes only from properties of the *output* of the assumed mental counterpart of the machinery, and in particular from introspective judgements on, and eclectic informant consent to, these expressions. The aim of these theories apparently is not so much a model of a domain-specific capacity of human brains but rather a demonstration of the algorithmic properties of a system that produces these properties. The relation between the properties of the algorithm and the properties of the processing brain is one of *weak* generative *equivalence* between the derivational apparatus on the one hand and whatever mental system there is that is operative in the human brain on the other.

It cannot be more than *weakly* equivalent because these approaches are linguistic ones, that is, they investigate the properties of the *output* but not of the system itself that is embodied in a human brain as a cognitive and neuro-cognitive entity. This objection had already been raised by W. V. O. Quine (1960, 1970) in the early days of the Generative program (see also Stich 1979; Fraser 2000). Chomsky's (1968) answer to this challenge was suggestive but not entirely appropriate: you can find out many things about the sun without having visited the star physically. But this is clearly not the essential point.

---

[29] 'Overt' vs. 'covert' movement is a weird and wonderful concept. It suggests a kind of eyewitness-like direct perception ('overt') contrasting with a highly indirect perception. 'Covert movement' means that phrases are not where they appear to be, and you cannot *perceive* where they have gone to. It is only the *smile* of a ph(r)ase that you see (cf. Alice's Cheshire cat), but 'in reality' the ph(r)ase has disappeared and gone away. Entertaining, but difficult to prove conclusively as an empirically testable reality.

A scientist who wants to test a hypothesis about what is going on in the interior of the sun is of course unable to run an experiment on or inside this star. But the analogy with solar research is inappropriate. The crucial difference is this: the scientist has a model at his disposal whose *components* have been tested and experimentally assessed under immediate control in the lab. Linguistics has neither an animal model nor a reliable background theory from the (cognitive) neuro-sciences.[30]

Theoreticians of these two related camps (MP, LCA) do not investigate (or say how to investigate) whether there is any empirical evidence for the psycholinguistic or neuro-cognitive reality of some (implications) of the general postulates (e.g. for the cascades of processes for overt or covert structure-on-structure mapping operations). It is speculative, in the best sense. It is hypothetical. But this is not enough for the modelling of an empirical object. It is not enough to model the output somehow, but forget about the fact that the capacities you study are put to use under real-time conditions. They have a history in cognitive evolution. They are embodied in a brain with a biological evolution that vastly outdates the time span since humans have existed (c. 6×10^6 years have passed since the split into the *homo* and the *pan* branch). How can you be sure that the human mind uses a specific *derivational* machinery, as long as you have not shown that there is some piece of conclusive experimental evidence? The probability that your initial speculative bold guess on such a complex matter is right is indistinguishably near or equal to zero and not near or equal to 1, of course.

Until the nineteen nineties, grammar theory had to treat the language faculty as a black box that could not be accessed directly. But since then, experimental psycho- and neuro-linguistics have built viable access paths for observing brain activities. It is not completely inaccessible any more. Here is a conclusion from Haider (2009: 96–97):

> The self-understanding of linguists as members of the scientific community of the cognitive sciences sharply contrasts with the established working traditions. If linguistics is to be grounded as a branch of science, grammar theory will have to give up its 'splendid isolation' with respect to the experimental camps in psycho- and neuro-linguistics and in psychology. The theoreticians must acknowledge that the practice that proved successful in the pioneering phase of the past decades, namely introspection and eclectic feed-back from informants, has reached its limits.

---

[30] We do not have the slightest idea of what kind of 'software' is running on the brain's 'wetware' and what kind is excluded.

If they do not actively seek the cooperation with experimental research, it is at least their responsibility to clearly point out what are empirically testable implications of their model. It is not enough to present novel and bold hypotheses and embed them into a set of assumptions that is complex enough to make an experimenting linguist immediately resign.

Note, importantly, that the preceding paragraphs are not meant as a *revival* of the *'psychological reality'* debate of the seventies (as in Devitt 2006, countered by Slezak 2009). It is just a plea for improving the quality of data assessment (beyond introspection and eclectic informant consent) with means provided by today's psycholinguistic methods of experimenting.

It is beyond reasonable doubt that the old-fashioned reliance on introspection and informant inquiries produces unreliable results (see Haider 2009 and 2011); note in particular the discussion of the exemplary case of the incoherent judgements for Dutch wh-*in-situ* on p.79 of the former).[31] The problem is simple: 'crystal clear', run-of-the-mill data are handled by every theory variant somehow. If you want to discriminate among the competing variants, you have to resort to more *peripheral* issues for which the variants diverge. But more often than not, the judgements become peripheral, too. Data assessment is indispensable, like in any empirical discipline. What is crucially missing in linguistics is a mutually agreed and obeyed standard of data evaluation, as, for instance, in psychology. Data assessment by self-observation (introspection) and eclectic informant consent would be far from meeting these standards in the neighbouring disciplines in cognitive science. Psychology has made its way since Wundt's (1888, 1901) initiatives, but linguistics still goes with Delbrück's time (1901) in its predilection for mere introspection as the primary source of data.[32]

But even if we disregard the problems on the data side, the *theory testing* side is underdeveloped as well. The LCA model (and the Minimalist Program) is a highly flexible tool,[33] and in fact it invites overly flexible, and highly complex, implementations of syntactic analyses. Let me demonstrate this with an

---

[31] Incoherent set of judgements of twenty-two native Dutch syntacticians on wh-*in-situ* data from Dutch.

[32] 1901 was the year of the very first debate on psycholinguistics and grammar theory: Wundt (1901: 17–18) had argued that linguistics would greatly benefit from psychological insights, but Delbrück (1901) refused this offer: it would be of no help for a linguist who is struggling to reconstruct grammar change if he had to consult Herbart's associative psychology or Wundt's volitionistic theory for explanatory assistance.

[33] You may, if you wish, derive *any order* of elements, even if you strictly obey the rules of the game: move everything to the left, and make sure that your landing position is always in a spec–head–complement configuration. For the rest you are in principle free.

example. Assume, counterfactually, just for the sake of demonstration, that English is basically OV, and that this would be so because languages are universally OV.[34] With this premise, English would leap into its derivational maze with an initial structure like Japanese (1a).

Next, the LCA enters the grammatical saloon and insists on asymmetric c-command for all items that need to be serialized. So, (1a) must undergo some derivational procedures that guarantee this outcome, namely movement of at least one of the two sister items in (1a). One of the two sister constituents has to move out, either the verb, or the object, or maybe both.

(1) a. $[O\ V°]_{VP}$ — starting point
     b. $[V°_i\ [O\ e_i]]_{FP}$ — the verb moves to a head position,[35] *or*
     c. $[O_i\ [e_i\ V°]]_{FP}$ — the object moves to spec, *and*
     d. $[[e_i\ V°]\ [[O_i\ e_j]]]_{FP}$ — the emptied VP is fronted to a spec position ('roll-up')

Having exemplified the ingredients for a simple case, we move on to a more entertaining case, viz. a verb with two objects:

(2) a. $[IO\ [O\ V°]]_{VP}$ — starting point
     b. $[V°_i\ [IO\ [O\ e_i\ ]]]_{FP}$ — the verb moves to a head position, *or*
     c. $[IO_j\ [O_i\ [\ e_j\ e_i\ V°]]]_{FP}$ — the objects move to specs, *and*
     d. $[[e_j\ e_i\ V°]_k\ [[IO_j\ [O_i\ e_k]]]]_{FP}$ — the emptied VP is fronted to a spec position ('roll-up')

Note that the OV/VO surface order would depend only on fronting the VP in (1d) and (2d) versus (1b) and (1c), in the case of a surface OV order. This scenario gets close to the results of the BBC approach, with an essential difference, though. In the latter approach, the object positions in a head-final VP and in a head-initial VP are VP-*internal*. In the derivations sketched above, any argument position is VP-external at the derivational end point.

This implementation of VO produces the same surface orders as the implementation of VO in Kayne's original conception. Which one is right? This is an empirical question, of course. The answer does not come from the inspection of the output. The output is the same, as far as linearization is concerned. The answer comes from testing the various implications of each of the two competing *structural* analyses. This would also be the answer to the central question

---

[34] Here is a plausible-sounding reason for this hypothetical axiom: they are OV because the construction process starts with the head that is merged stepwise with its argument phrases. Fukui and Takano (1998) assume the order complement-before-head as basic. As for English and Dutch, the idea of the universality of OV has found a (part-time) advocate in Koster (1988).

[35] *FP* is a cover variable for any kind of functional projection.

of this chapter, namely: what is the better model for understanding the properties of an OV language, an LCA- or a BBC-based one? Derive the implications and see which is right!

Moreover, the onus of proof for the empirical adequacy of an LCA-based massive-movement approach towards OV is on the side of the proponents. One of the clear but clearly wrong predictions is the opacity prediction.

Preverbal arguments in OV are claimed to be in positions of the same kind as preverbal arguments in VO, viz. in spec positions of functional heads preceding the VP. The same kind of conditions that make subject phrases and phrases that precede the subject opaque for extraction in VO will make any preverbal argument phrase in OV opaque for extractions, too.

This is a grand prediction, and languages could easily be this way. Unfortunately, natural languages are not this way. Hence the prediction is wrong, and the theory that produced this prediction is wrong, too. It clearly cannot be fully right.

In sum, there is still an unsound imbalance between theoretical creativity and experimental rigidity in grammar research. It is time for a change. Linguistics prides itself as a discipline with scientific standards but disregards the need for, and the outcomes of, an experimental discipline (experimental psycho- and neuro-linguistics) that would plainly put to test the numerous platonic objects of the theoreticians on the one hand, and confront the theoretician with its own findings that call for a theoretical modelling on the other.

Every mature branch of science has a theory camp and an experimenting camp. Linguistics has an experimental camp but theory-developing people largely ignore and marginalize the results of the experimenting groups. Enthrallingly, this has not been recognized as a serious deficit yet. For psychology, Wundt's (1888) plea for thorough experimental checks of theoretical claims (based on introspection) was the starting point of present-day psychology. Linguistics still suffers from the introspectionist heritage that was given up in psychology already at the end of the nineteenth century. If linguistics does not seriously take up the experimental programme, it will sooner or later and deservedly get marginalized in the family of cognitive sciences.

Appendix 9.2   Linearization is not a (series of) spell-out snapshot(s)

In the Minimalist Program, linearization has become a piecemeal by-product of structure generation. In the Chomskyan view, linear order is characterized as a snapshot through a language-specific, cross-linguistically adjustable inspection window on the order of terminals at a given stage of *structure generation*.

For a more recent modification, Fox and Pesetsky (2005) suggested regarding spell-out not as a single snapshot but as a series of snapshots taken through a sequence of windows, each looking at a different spell-out domain, e.g. VP, DP and CP (roughly corresponding to *phases*).[36]

They claim a principle of *order preservation* that is to constrain the mapping between syntax and phonology when movements take place. Once established at the end of a given spell-out domain, this very linear order is not changed any more in a derivation. When the derivation reaches a spell-out domain S, spell-out applies and the terminals get linearized. When a new spell-out domain S' is completed, spell-out linearizes the new material while preserving the information produced by previous applications of spell-out. Thus, spell-out is strictly incremental. It *adds* new material to the linearization already established at the previous spell-out domains and thereby constrains movement.

As a consequence, only movement of an element X from the *edge* position of a spell-out domain D to a position in a higher spell-out domain is licit, since only in this case would the moved item continue to precede the elements that it precedes in D (and conversely for rightward movement).

Movement from a phase-internal position that skips the edge is illicit since the ordering statements established in the phase are inconsistent with the ones established after movement. Suppose the derivation has created the spell-out domain S in (1), with the given linearization:

(1)   [$_S$ X Y Z]

Subsequently, Y moves to the left, up into the next spell-out domain, as in (2). As a consequence, the linearization information in (1) and the linearization information in (2) are contradicting: in its original spell-out domain S in (1), Y is linearized after X, but in (2), Y precedes S, and therefore it also precedes X. Consequently, before undergoing further movement, Y must first move to the edge of S.

(2)   *[$_{S'}$ ...Y$_i$ ... [$_S$ X e$_i$ Z]

Movement from a non-edge position is licit only if the previously established linearization is not disrupted. Y can move from the non-edge position in (1) only if X moves as well and X and Y preserve their original order in the higher spell-out domain.

---

[36] It is not only a series of snapshots; they must match, in addition. How this is to be guaranteed, they do not say. Apparently, grammar theory must provide a snapshot comparison file and a checking mechanism that certifies what they call 'order preservation'.

The database for the proposal is small, as usual: Scandinavian object shift, Scandinavian preverbal negated quantifiers and (a non-problem with) scrambling, exemplified with Korean data. In Korean, like in German, scrambling may separate a DP and a quantifier associated with it, as in (4a). The counterpart of (3b) is not well formed in Korean. For Korean a stranding analysis for the dissociated quantifier has been motivated.

(3)   a. dass *die Bilder*$_i$ keiner e$_i$ *alle vier* gesehen hat
           that the pictures nobody all four seen has
           'that nobody saw each of the four the pictures'
    b. dass *die Kinder*$_i$ das Bild (e$_i$) *alle* vier angefasst haben
           that the children the picture all four touched have

The null hypothesis for (3b) is clearly this: the order of the arguments in (3b) is congruent with the base order. Hence a base structure is projected. If in the base structure, the DP and the quantifier must be adjacent, then (3b) is simply ill formed because of the distant quantifier. The distant quantifier itself does not trigger an analysis for (3b) in which both DPs are recognized as scrambled, since scrambling is non-string-vacuous (see the argumentation in Haider 2010a: 185–7). In German, the quantifier expression and the DP do not necessarily form a constituent; otherwise they would make a well-formed Spec-C phrase (4b). Hence, it must not come as a surprise that (3b) is well formed in German, but not in Korean, if in this language, the quantifier is a constituent of the nominal expression.

(4)   a. *Die Männer* haben *alle zwei* den Raum verlassen
           the men have all two the room left
    b. */??[*Die Männer alle zwei*] haben den Raum verlassen
           [the men all two] have the room left

A more challenging case for the order conservation principle is extraposition in a fronted constituent in V2 languages that would be ill formed in the base position. The phenomenon was first brought to attention in Haider (1990). A VP is a site for extraposition. This can be clearly demonstrated with a topicalized VP. In (5a), the PP is extraposed. In the non-extraposed version, the PP precedes the verbal head *gesprochen* ('spoken').

(5)   a. [Gesprochen mit dem Zimmermädchen]$_i$ würde er nicht e$_i$ haben
           [spoken with the room maid] would he not have
    b. *dass er nicht [gesprochen *mit dem Zimmermädchen*] haben würde
           that he not [spoke with the room maid] have would
    c. dass er nicht *mit dem Zimmermädchen* gesprochen haben würde
           that he not with the room maid spoken have would
    d. dass er nicht gesprochen haben würde *mit dem Zimmermädchen*
           that he not spoken have would with the room maid

The crucial point is this: the VP in (5a) cannot and must not be reconstructed, since in the base order extraposition targeting an embedded VP is ill formed, because of obligatory cluster formation. The well-formed extraposition version is 5(d). (5a) is well formed, but it is obviously ruled out by cyclic spell-out: in the base structure, extraposition is impossible (5b). The correctly extraposed version (5d) cannot be the base for VP-fronting with the extraposed PP. So, there is no way for deriving (5a).

Assume you start with the base order of the lowest VP 'mit dem Zimmermädchen gesprochen haben' as in (5c). In this phase, you must not extrapose; otherwise you derive (5b). But if you topicalize the VP, you cannot extrapose any more. The PP in (5a) is representative of any extraposable constituent, as, for instance, a relative clause (6a) or a wh-clause (6b):

(6)   a. [Das Buch lesen, das ich ihr empfohlen habe]$_i$ würde$_j$ sie nicht e$_i$ wollen e$_j$
            [The book read, that I her recommended have] would she not want
     b. [Gefragt, wo sie wohne]$_i$ würde$_j$ er nicht e$_i$ haben e$_j$
            [asked, where she lived] would he not have

Note that (5b) and (6) are disastrous for a *copy theory* of movement, too. In each case, the copy is ill formed because of the illicit extraposition site in the would-be base position. The well-formed order would not match the fronted phrase.

German and other V2 languages with VP topicalization are not the only source of this kind of non-compliant data. English offers exactly the same kind of constellation, with preverbal adverbial phrases in combination with the edge effect:

(7)   a. Everyone has much faster [(*than his competitors*) [reached his destination]$_{VP}$]$_{VP}$
     b. [How much faster *than his competitors*]$_i$ has everyone [e$_i$ [reached his destination]]?

(7a) illustrates the edge effect for adjuncts of head-initial phrases. In this case it is an adjunct of the VP. The edge effect is absent in the *spec* position (7b), of course. What is the point of departure for the fronted adverbial in (7b)? It is ungrammatical in the pre-VP position, because of the edge effect. So, it could be generated at the end of the VP (8), but then it would have to move to the left edge of the VP before it could leave this VP, according to Fox and Pesetsky's order preservation restriction. But the left edge is accessible only for the adverbial phrase *without* its post-head material, because of the restriction perceived as the edge effect in (7a):

(8)   Everyone has *much faster* reached his destination *than anyone else*

Note that the puzzle is identical with the puzzle for extraposition in a topicalized VP. For a sketch of a solution of these puzzles consult Chapter 6, §6.2.4, and be aware that the puzzle is a puzzle only for derivational accounts, but not for representational approaches.

A *representational* account of this kind of derivational problem is sketched in Haider (2010a: §7.7.1): the topicalized constituent is a (not necessarily maximal) V-projection. It is related to an empty category in the base position. The empty category is not structured or layered, but atomic. It gets assigned the semantic content of its antecedent (but not its shape, since it remains atomic) and it's not yet discharged part of the argument structure. Its syntactic shape is that of an atomic empty element of category V. So, it matches the cluster requirements. Any element in the verbal cluster is an atomic element of the category V.

The phrase in the derived position (i.e. the topicalized V-projection) must be a well-formed phrase. Crucially however, this does not imply that it can be embedded in any other position in its given, well-formed shape. Since an OV clause structure does not allow stacked VPs (but only V-clustering), the topicalized VP could not be reconstructed into the position of the empty category (i.e. the so-called 'trace') in the verbal cluster. From a representational point of view, this is unproblematic; from a derivational point of view, it is detrimental.

The very same considerations apply to (7a). The fronted complex adverbial phrase is related to its atomic trace marking the base position. This position 're-imports' the semantic interpretation of the fronted phrase (basically as a 'how', with semantic modifications), but syntactically it is atomic.

Let me finish by emphasizing once more the surprisingly underestimated role allotted to *linearization* in the Minimalist Program. Imagine the non-trivial problems for the L1 learning brain. If the MP was right, linearizations would not be predictive of the structure of a given expression until you have managed to determine which window position the given spell-out snapshot belongs to. I have not the slightest clue how a learner could possibly solve this intractable problem. The problem is intractable because of the obvious indeterminacy of the linearization-to-structure relation for an L1 learner in this situation.

Before you can determine the structure of an expression, you have to find out the language-specific 'window positions', but before you can find out the window positions, you have to determine the given structure in order to be able to determine the corresponding window position. An innate tractability device would have to be really prophetic. It would have to anticipate the specific syntactic properties of the language that the brain is going to acquire.

This is a nasty paradox for L1 acquisition, if the world is like the MP wants to have it. It seems that cracking the Enigma code was as demanding for Turing as cracking the 'window code' would be for a child. Fortunately, the child does not have to rely on 'Turingeries' and is able to solve its task without crypto-analytical methods. The task becomes achievable once you accept that there are no windows, but only a single orifice, namely the mouth that spells out the linearization at what is customarily called the surface structure level.

Bibliography

Abney, Steven P. (1989) 'A computational model of human parsing', *Journal of Psycholinguistic Research* 18: 129–44.
Abney, Steven P. and Mark Johnson (1991) 'Memory requirements and local ambiguities of parsing strategies', *Journal of Psycholinguistic Research* 20: 233–50.
Ackema, Peter (1995) *Syntax Below Zero*, Ph.D. dissertation, Utrecht University.
Åfarli, Tor A. (1985) 'Norwegian verb particle constructions as causative constructions', *Nordic Journal of Linguistics* 8: 75–98.
—— (1992) *The Syntax of Norwegian Passive Constructions*, Amsterdam: Benjamins.
Alexiadou, Artemis (1994) *Issues in the Syntax of Adverbs*, Ph.D. dissertation, University of Potsdam.
Alexiadou, Artemis and Elena Anagnostopoulou (1998) 'Parametrizing Agr: word order, verb movement and EPP-checking', *Natural Language and Linguistic Theory* 16(3): 491–539.
Andersen, Henning (1973) 'Abductive and deductive change' *Language* 49: 765–93.
ANS (1984) *Algemene Nederlandse Spraakkunst*, see Geerts *et al.*
ANS² (1997) = second, revised edition of ANS (two volumes), see Haeseryn *et al.*
Aoun, Joseph, Norbert Hornstein, David Lightfoot and Amy Weinberg (1987) 'Two types of locality', *Linguistic Inquiry* 18: 537–77.
Aoun, Joseph and Yen-Hui Audrey Li (1993) 'Scope and constituency', *Linguistic Inquiry* 20: 141–72.
Askedal, John Ole (1986) 'Über Stellungsfelder und Satztypen im Deutschen', *Deutsche Sprache* 3: 193–223.
Baker, Mark C. (1988) *Incorporation – A Theory of Grammatical Function Changing*, University of Chicago Press.
—— (1991) 'On the relation of serialization to verb extension' in Claire Lefèbre (ed.) *Serial Verbs*, Amsterdam: John Benjamins, pp. 79–102.
—— (2003) 'Linguistic differences and language design', *Trends in Cognitive Sciences* 7(8): 349–53.
Barss, Andrew and Howard Lasnik (1986) 'A note on anaphora and double-objects', *Linguistic Inquiry* 17: 347–54.
Bartos, Huba (2004) 'Verbal complexes and morpho-syntactic merger' in Katalin É. Kiss and Henk van Riemsdijk (eds.) *Verb Clusters: A Study of Hungarian, German, and Dutch*, Amsterdam/Philadelphia: John Benjamins, pp. 395–415.
Bayer, Josef (1998) 'Final complementizers in hybrid languages', *Journal of Linguistics* 35: 233–71.

(2001) 'Two grammars in one: sentential complements and complementizers in Bengali and other South Asian languages' in Peri Bhaskararao and Karumuri V. Subbarao (eds.) *The Yearbook of South Asian Languages: Tokyo Symposium on South Asian Languages – Contact, Convergence and Typology*, New Delhi: Sage Publications, pp. 11–36.

Bech, Gunnar (1955) *Studien über das deutsche verbum infinitum*, Copenhagen: Munksgaard, Tübingen: Niemeyer. [Second unchanged edition (1983), introduced by Cathrine Fabricius-Hansen.]

Berthold Delbrück (1901) *Grundfragen der Sprachforschung*, Strassburg: Trübner.

Berwick, Robert C., Paul Pietroski, Beracah Yankama and Noam Chomsky (2011) 'Poverty of the stimulus revisited', *Cognitive Science* 35: 1,207–42.

Biberauer, Theresa, Anders Holmberg and Ian Roberts (2009) 'Linearization and the architecture of grammar: a view from the final-over-final constraint' in Vincenzo Moscati and E. Servidio (eds.) *StiL – Studies in Linguistics (Proceedings of XXXV Incontro di Grammatica Generativa)*, pp. 78–91.

Biberauer, Theresa and Ian Roberts (2005) 'Changing EPP-parameters in the history of English: accounting for variation and change', *English Language and Linguistics* 9: 5–46.

Bierwisch, Manfred (2000) 'Evolutionstheorie und Linguistik – Drei Probleme' in Klaus Richter (ed.) *Evolutionstheorie und Geisteswissenschaften*, University of Erfurt: Acta Academia Scientiarum 5, pp. 129–89.

Blom, Corrien (2002) 'Word order in Middle Dutch: the interpretation of different types of data', *Linguistics in the Netherlands 2002*: 13–24.

Boeckx, Cedric (2006) *Linguistic Minimalism*, Oxford University Press.

Bonet, Eulàlia (1990) 'Subjects in Catalan', *MIT Working Papers in Linguistics* 13: 1–26.

Bouchard, Denis (1995) *The Semantics of Syntax*, University of Chicago Press.

Carrier, Jill and Janet Randall: (1992) 'The argument structure and syntactic structure of resultatives', *Linguistic Inquiry* 23: 173–235.

Chomsky, Noam (1968) *Language and Mind*, New York: Harcourt Brace Jovanovich.

(1973) 'Conditions on transformations' in Steven Anderson and Paul Kiparsky (eds.) *A Festschrift for Morris Halle*, New York: Holt, Rinehart and Winston, pp. 232–86.

(1975) *Reflections on Language*, New York: Pantheon.

(1981) *Lectures on Government and Binding*, Dordrecht: Foris.

(1982) *Some Concepts and Consequences of the Theory of Government and Binding*, Cambridge, MA: MIT Press.

(1992) 'A minimalist program for linguistic theory', *MIT Occasional Papers in Linguistics*, 1, Cambridge, MA: MIT.

(1995) *The Minimalist Program*, Cambridge, MA: MIT Press.

(2008) 'On phases' in Robert Freidin, Carlos P. Otero and Maria Luisa Zubizarreta (eds.) *Foundational Issues in Linguistic Theory. Essays in Honor of Jean-Roger Vergnaud*, Cambridge, MA: MIT Press, pp. 133–66.

Cinque, Guglielmo (1999) *Adverbs and Functional Heads: A Cross-Linguistic Perspective*, Oxford University Press.

(2004a) 'Issues in adverbial syntax', *Lingua* 114: 683–710.
(2004b) 'Restructuring and functional structure' in Adriana Belletti (ed.) *Structures and Beyond: The Cartography of Syntactic Structures*, vol. III, Oxford University Press, pp. 132–91.
Citko, Barbara (2011) *Symmetry in Syntax: Merge, Move and Label* (Cambridge Studies in Linguistics), Cambridge University Press.
Colarusso, John (1979) 'Rightward movement, question formation and the nature of transformational processes: the Circassian case', *Papiere zur Linguistik* 21: 27–73.
Corver, Norbert (1997) 'The internal syntax of the Dutch extended adjectival projection', *Natural Language and Linguistic Theory* 15: 289–368.
Corver, Norbert and Henk C. van Riemsdijk (1997) 'The position of the head and the domain of scrambling' in Bohumil Palek (ed.) *Typology: Prototypes, Item Orderings and Universals*, Prague: The Carolinum Press, pp. 57–90.
Costa, João (1998) *Word Order Variation: A Constrained Approach*, The Hague: Holland Academic Graphics.
Croft, William (2009) 'Language use and the evolution of languages' in Kenny Smith and Philippe Binder (eds.) *The Language Phenomenon*, Berlin: Springer.
Dahl, Östen (1979) 'Typology of sentence negation', *Linguistics* 17: 79–106.
Darwin, Charles (1871) *The Descent of Man, and Selection in Relation with Sex*, London: John Murray, Albemarle Street.
Deacon, Terrence W. (1997) *The Symbolic Species: The Co-evolution of Language and the Brain*, New York: Norton.
Dehé, Nicole (2002) *Particle Verbs in English*, Amsterdam: Benjamins.
Delbrück, Berthold (1901) Grundfragen der Sprachforschung, Straßburg: Trübner.
Delfitto, Denis, Antonio Fábregas and Chiara Melloni (2008) *Compounding at the Interfaces*, unpublished ms., University of Verona and CASTL, University of Tromsö.
Dennet, Daniel C. (2002) 'The new replicators' in Mark Pagel (ed.) *The Encyclopedia of Evolution*, vol. I, Oxford University Press, pp. E83–E92.
Devitt, Michael (2006) *Ignorance of Language*, Oxford: Clarendon Press.
Diesing, Molly (1997) 'Yiddish VP order and the typology of object movement in Germanic', *Natural Language and Linguistic Theory* 15: 369–427.
den Dikken, Marcel (1992) *Particles*, doctoral dissertation, University of Leiden [published 1995 Oxford University Press].
DiSciullo, Anna Maria (ed.) (2003) *Asymmetry in Grammar*, 2 vols, Amsterdam: Benjamins.
Donohue, Mark and Søren Wichmann (2009) *External Pressure Prompts Language Change: A Polynesian Case Study*, ms., Monash University and MPI for Evolutionary Anthropology, Leipzig.
Downing, Bruce (1978) 'Some universals of relative clause structure' in Joseph Greenberg (ed.) *Universals of Human Language*, vol. IV: *Syntax*, Stanford University Press, pp. 375–418.
Dressler, Wolfgang U. (1988) 'Preferences vs. strict universals in morphology: word-based rules' in Michael Hammond and Michael Noonan (eds.) *Theoretical Morphology. Approaches in Modern Linguistics*, New York: Academic Press, pp. 143–54.

Dryer, Matthew, S. (1988) 'Universals of negative position' in Michael Hammond, Edith Moravcsik and Jessica Wirth (eds.) *Studies in Syntactic Typology*, Amsterdam: Benjamins, pp. 93–124.

(2009) 'The branching direction theory of word order correlations revisited' in Sergio Scalise, Elisabetta Magni and Antonietta Bisetto (eds.) *Universals of Language Today* (Studies in Natural Language and Linguistic Theory 76), Berlin: Springer, pp. 185–207.

(2011) 'Position of negative morpheme with respect to subject, object, and verb' in Matthew S. Dryer and Martin Haspelmath (eds.) *The World Atlas of Language Structures Online*, Munich: Max Planck Digital Library, chapter 144. Available online: wals.info/chapter/144 (last accessed on 2 July 2012).

Edelman, Gerald M. (1998) 'Building a picture of the brain', *Dædalus* 127: 37–69.

Emonds, Joseph (1985) *A Unified Theory of Syntactic Categories*, Dordrecht, Foris.

Ernst, Thomas (1984) *Towards an Integrated Theory of Adverb Positions in English*, Ph.D. dissertation, Indiana University Linguistics Club, Bloomington, Indiana.

(2002) *The Syntax of Adjuncts*, Cambridge University Press.

Evers, Arnold (1975) *The Transformational Cycle in Dutch and German*, doctoral dissertation, University of Utrecht (distributed by the Indiana University Linguistics Club, Bloomington, Indiana).

Falk, Cecilia (1990) 'On double-object constructions', *Working Papers in Scandinavian Syntax* 46: 53–100.

Fischer, Olga, Ans van Kemenade, Willem Koopman and Wim van der Wurff (2000) *The Syntax of Early English*, Cambridge University Press.

Fortmann, Christian (2007) 'Bewegungsresistente Verben', *Zeitschrift für Sprachwissenschaft* 26: 1–40.

Fox, Danny and David Pesetsky (2005) 'Cyclic linearization of syntactic structure', *Theoretical Linguistics* 31: 1–45.

Fraser, Bruce (2000) *Syntax, Semantics, and the Justification of Linguistic Methodology: An Investigation into the Source and Nature of the Disagreement Between Noam Chomsky and W. V. O. Quine*, dissertation, Graduate School of Arts and Sciences, Boston University.

Frazier, Lyn (1985) 'Syntactic complexity' in David Dowty, Lauri Karttunen and Arnold Zwicky (eds.) *Natural Language Parsing: Psychological, Computational and Theoretical Perspectives*, Cambridge University Press, pp.129–89.

(1987) 'Sentence processing: a tutorial review' in Max Coltheart (ed.) *Attention and Performance XII: The Psychology of Reading*, Hillsdale, NJ: Lawrence Erlbaum Associates, pp. 559–86.

Frey, Werner (1993) *Syntaktische Bedingungen für die semantische Interpretation* (Studia Grammatica 35), Berlin: Akademie Verlag.

(2003) 'Syntactic conditions on adjunct classes' in Ewald Lang, Claudia Maienborn and Cathrine Fabricius-Hansen (eds.) *Modifying Adjuncts*, Berlin: Mouton de Gruyter, pp. 163–209.

Frey, Werner and Karin Pittner (1998) 'Zur Positionierung von Adverbialen', *Linguistische Berichte* 176: 489–534.

(1999) 'Adverbialpositionen im Deutsch-Englischen Vergleich' in Monika Doherty (ed.) *Sprachspezifische Aspekte der Informationsverarbeitung* (Studia Grammatica 47), Berlin: Akademie Verlag, pp. 14–40.
Fukui, Naoki and Yuji Takano (1998) 'Symmetry in syntax: merge and demerge', *Journal of East Asian Linguistics* 7: 27–86.
Geerts, Guido, Walter Haeseryn, Jaap de Rooij and Maarten C. van den Toorn (1984) *Algemene Nederlandse Spraakkunst*, Groningen: Wolters-Noordhoff.
Geilfuß, Jochen (1991) 'Jiddisch als SOV-Sprache', *Zeitschrift für Sprachwissenschaft* 9: 170–83.
Gibson, Edward (1991) *A Computational Theory of Human Language Processing: Memory Limitations and Processing Breakdown*, Ph.D. thesis, Carnegie Mellon University, Pittsburg.
Grimshaw, Jane and Armin Mester (1988) 'Light verbs and theta-marking', *Linguistic Inquiry* 19: 205–32.
Groseclose, Mike (1998) 'Formation of compounds in Spanish and German', paper presented at GLAC 4 Conference, Ohio State University, 19 April 1998.
Haegeman, Liliane (2001) 'Antisymmetry and verb-final order in West Flemish', *Journal of Comparative Germanic Linguistics* 3: 207–32.
Haeseryn, Walter, J. de Rooij, Guido Geerts, Jaap de Rooij and Maarten C. van den Toorn (1997) *Algemene Nederlandse Spraakkunst* (tweede geheel herziene druk), Groningen/Deurne: Martinus Nijhoff/Wolters Plantyn.
Haider, Hubert (1985) 'The case of German' in Jindrich Toman (ed.) *Studies in German Grammar*, Dordrecht: Foris, pp. 65–101.
(1986) 'Affect alpha', *Linguistic Inquiry* 17: 113–26.
(1990) 'Topicalization and other puzzles of German syntax' in Günther Grewendorf and Wolfgang Sternefeld (eds.) *Scrambling and Barriers*, Amsterdam: Benjamins, pp. 93–112.
(1991) 'Die menschliche Sprachfähigkeit – exaptiv und kognitiv opak', *Kognitionswissenschaft* 2: 11–26.
(1992) 'Branching and discharge', *Working Papers of the SFB 340*, #23, Univ. Stuttgart and Tübingen and IBM Heidelberg [reprinted in Peter Coopmans, Martin Everaert and Jane Grimshaw (eds.) (2000) *Lexical Specification and Insertion*, Amsterdam: Benjamins, pp. 135–64].
(1993) *Deutsche Syntax, generativ – Vorstudien zur Theorie einer projektiven Grammatik*, Tübingen: Narr.
(1995a) 'Downright down to the right' in Uli Lutz and Jürgen Pafel (eds.) *On Extraction and Extraposition in German*, Amsterdam: Benjamins, pp. 145–271.
(1995b) 'The basic branching conjecture', *Studies on Phrase Structure and Economy. Working Papers of the SFB 340* (University of Stuttgart, University of Tübingen and IBM Heidelberg) 70: 3–31.
(1996) 'Wenn die Semantik arbeitet – und die Syntax sie gewähren läßt' in Gisela Harras and Manfred Bierwisch (eds.) *Wenn die Semantik arbeitet*, Tübingen: Niemeyer, pp. 7–27.
(1997a) 'Extraposition' in Dorothee Beerman, David LeBlanc and Henk van Riemsdijk (eds.) *Rightward Movement*, Amsterdam: Benjamins, pp. 115–51.

(1997b) 'Precedence among predicates', *The Journal of Comparative Germanic Linguistics* 1: 3–41.
(1997c) 'Scrambling – locality, economy, and directionality' in Shigeo Tonoike (ed.) *Scrambling*, Tokyo: Kurosio Publishers (Linguistics Workshop Series 5), pp. 61–91.
(1997d) 'Typological implications of a directionality constraint on projections' in Artemis Alexiadou and Tracy A. Hall (eds.) *Studies on Universal Grammar and Typological Variation*, Amsterdam: Benjamins (Linguistics Today 13), pp. 17–33.
(1997e) 'Economy in syntax is projective economy' in Chris Wilder, Hans-Martin Gaertner and Manfred Bierwisch (eds.) *The Role of Economy Principles in Linguistic Theory*, (Studia Grammatica 40) Berlin: Akademie Verlag, pp. 205–26.
(1997f) 'Towards a superior account of superiority', *Working Papers of the Sonderforschungsbereich* 340 (Univ. of Stuttgart, Univ. of Tübingen, IBM Heidelberg) 76: 327–9.
(1998) 'Form follows function fails – as a direct explanation for properties of grammars' in Paul Weingartner, Gerhard Schurz and Georg Dorn (eds.) *The Role of Pragmatics in Contemporary Philosophy*, Vienna: Hölder-Pichler-Tempsky, pp. 92–108.
(1999) 'On the survival of the fittest grammar (theory)', *Zeitschrift für Sprachwissenschaft* 18: 216–18.
(2000a) 'Adverb placement – convergence of structure and licensing', *Theoretical Linguistics* 26: 95–134.
(2000b) 'OV is more basic than VO' in Peter Svenonius (ed.) *The Derivation of VO and OV*, Amsterdam: Benjamins, pp. 45–67.
(2000c) 'The license to license' in Eric Reuland (ed.) *Argument and Case: Explaining Burzio's Generalization*, Amsterdam: Benjamins, pp. 31–54.
(2000d) 'Towards a superior account of superiority' in Uli Lutz, Gereon Müller and Arnim von Stechow (eds.) *Wh-scope Marking*, Amsterdam: Benjamins, pp. 231–48.
(2001a) 'Not every why has a wherefore – notes on the relation between form and function' in Walter Bisang (ed.) *Aspects of Typology and Universals*, Berlin: Akademie Verlag, pp. 37–52.
(2001b) 'Why are there no complex head-initial compounds?' in Chris Schaner-Wolles, John Rennison and Friedrich Neubart (eds.) *Naturally!*, Turin: Rosenberg and Sellier, pp. 165–74.
(2001c) 'Prosodic signals for reconstructing the basic item order. On the interplay between structure and prosody' in Bohumil Palek and Osamu Fujimura (eds.) *Item Order: Its Variety and Linguistic and Phonetic Consequences*, Proceedings of LP 2000, Prague: The Karolinum Press, pp. 347–66.
(2002) 'Adverbials at the syntax–semantics interface' in Hans Kamp and Uwe Reyle (eds.) *How We Say WHEN It Happens*, Tübingen: Niemeyer, pp. 53–70.
(2003) 'V-clustering and clause union: causes and effects' in Pieter Seuren and Gerard Kempen (eds.) *Verb Constructions in German and Dutch*, Amsterdam: Benjamins, pp. 91–126.

(2004a) 'The superiority conspiracy' in Arthur Stepanov, Gisbert Fanselow and Ralf Vogel (eds.) *The Minimal Link Condition*, Berlin: Mouton de Gruyter, pp. 147–75.

(2004b) 'Pre and postverbal adverbials in VO and OV', *Lingua* 114(6): 779–807.

(2005) 'How to turn German into Icelandic – and derive the VO – OV contrasts', *The Journal of Comparative Germanic Linguistics* 8: 1–53.

(2009) 'The thin line between facts and fiction' in Sam Featherston and Susanne Winkler (eds.) *The Fruits of Empirical Linguistics*, vol. I: *Process*, Berlin: de Gruyter, pp. 75–102.

(2010a) *The Syntax of German*, Cambridge University Press.

(2010b) 'Wie wurde Deutsch OV? Zur diachronen Dynamik eines Strukturparameters der germanischen Sprachen' in Arne Ziegler (ed.) *Historische Textgrammatik und Historische Syntax des Deutschen – Traditionen, Innovationen, Perspektiven*, Berlin: de Gruyter, pp. 11–32.

(2011) 'Grammatische Illusionen, lokal wohlgeformt, global deviant', *Zeitschrift für Sprachwissenschaft* 30(2): 223–57.

(forthcoming) 'Cognitive evolution – why language systems are society-based and usage-friendly adaptations of robust, autonomous, structural systems', in Aria Adli, Marco García García and Göz kanfmann (eds.) *System, Usage, and Society*. Berlin and New York: de Gruyter.

Haider, Hubert, Sue Olsen and Sten Vikner (eds.) (1995) *Studies in Comparative Germanic Syntax*, Dordrecht: Kluwer.

Haider, Hubert and Inger Rosengren (1998) *Scrambling*, (Sprache und Pragmatik 49) Lund: Germanistisches Institut, University of Lund.

(2003) 'Scrambling – non-triggered chain formation in OV languages', *Journal of Germanic Linguistics* 15: 203–67.

Haider, Hubert and Luka Szucsich (forthcoming) 'Scrambling and V-positioning in Slavic languages – exceptionally VO or regular T3?' in Kristine Bentzen, Roland Hinterhoelzl, Augustin Speyer and Luka Szucsich (eds.) *Word order variation and typology*. Berlin: De Guyter.

Han, Chung-Hye, Jeffrey Lidz and Julien Musolino (2007) 'V-Raising and grammar competition in Korean: evidence from negation and quantifier scope', *Linguistic Inquiry* 38: 1–47.

Hawkins, John A. (1994) *A Performance Theory of Order and Constituency*, Cambridge University Press.

Herslund, Michael (1986) 'The double-object construction in Danish' in Lars Hellan and Kirsti Koch-Christensen (eds.) *Topics in Scandinavian Syntax*, Dordrecht: Reidel, pp. 125–47.

Hoeksema, Jack (1992) 'The head parameter in morphology and syntax' in Dicky G. Gilbers and S. Looyenga (eds.) *Language and Cognition* II (Yearbook of the research group for linguistic theory and knowledge representation of the University of Groningen), Groningen: De Passage, pp. 119–32.

Hoekstra, Teun (1988) 'Small clause results', *Lingua* 74: 101–39.

Höhle, Tilman N. (1991) *Projektionsstufen bei V-Projektionen*, unpublished ms., University of Tübingen.

Hoji, Hajime (1985) *Logical Form Constraints and Configurational Structures in Japanese*, Ph.D. dissertation, University of Washington.

Holmberg, Anders (1999) 'Remarks on Holmberg's Generalization', *Studia Linguistica* 53(1): 1–39.
  (2000) 'Deriving OV order in Finnish' in Peter Svenonius (ed.) *The Derivation of VO and OV*, Oxford University Press, pp. 123–52.
  (2012) 'Verb second' in Tibor Kiss and Artemis Alexiadou (eds.) *Syntax: An International Handbook of Contemporary Research* (HSK Series), 2nd edition, Berlin: Walter de Gruyter.
Holmberg, Anders and Christer Platzack (1995) *The Role of Inflection in Scandinavian Syntax*, Oxford University Press.
Horvath, Julia and Tal Siloni (2002) 'Against the little-v hypothesis', *Rivista di Grammatica Generativa* 27: 107–22.
Hróarsdóttir, Thorbjörg (2000) *Word Order Change in Icelandic. From OV to VO*, Amsterdam: Benjamins.
Huang, James C.-T. (1982) *Logical Relations in Chinese and the Theory of Grammar*, doctoral dissertation, MIT.
Jackendoff, Ray (1990) 'On Larson's account of the double-object construction', *Linguistic Inquiry* 21: 427–56.
Jacobson, Pauline (1987) 'Phrase structure, grammatical relations, and discontinuous constituents' in Geoffrey J. Huck and Almerindo E. Ojeda (eds.) *Discontinuous Constituency* (Syntax and Semantics 20), New York: Academic Press, pp. 27–69.
Kamp, Hans and Uwe Reyle (1993) *From Discourse to Logic*, Dordrecht: Kluwer.
Karl, Susanne (2010) *Erwerb deverbaler Rektionskomposita*, Master's thesis, Dept. of Linguistics, University of Salzburg.
Katamba, Francis (1993) *Morphology*, London: Macmillan.
Kayne, Richard S. (1984) *Connectedness and Binary Branching*, Dordrecht: Foris.
  (1994) *The Antisymmetry of Syntax*, Cambridge, MA: MIT Press.
  (1998) 'Overt vs. covert movement', *Syntax* 1: 128–91.
  (2005) 'Antisymmetry and Japanese' in Richard Kayne *Movement and Silence*, Oxford University Press, pp. 215–40.
Kenstowicz, Michael (1987) 'The phonology and syntax of wh-expressions in Tagale', *Phonology Yearbook* 4: 229–41.
Keyser, Samuel J. and Tom Roeper (1992) 'Re: the abstract clitic hypothesis' *Linguistic Inquiry* 23: 89–125.
Kinsella, Anna R. and Gary F. Marcus (2009) 'Evolution, perfection, and theories of language', *Biolinguistics* 3(2–3): 186–212.
Kiparsky, Paul (1996) 'The shift to head-initial VP in Germanic' in Höskuldur Thráinsson, Samuel Epstein and Steve Peter (eds.) *Studies in Comparative Germanic Syntax II*, Dordrecht: Kluwer, pp. 140–79.
Kiss, Katalin É. (2002) *The Syntax of Hungarian*, Cambridge University Press.
Koch, Wolfgang and Inger Rosengren (1995) 'Secondary predication', *Sprache und Grammatik* 35, Lund: University of Lund.
Koopman, Hilda (1984) *The Syntax of Verbs*, Dordrecht: Foris.
Koopman, Hilda and Anna Szabolcsi (2000) *Verbal Complexes*, Cambridge, MA: MIT Press.
Koster, Jan (1988) *The Residual SOV Structure of English*, ms., University of Groningen.

(1989) 'Left–right asymmetries in the Dutch complementizer system' in Dany Jaspers, Wim Klosters, Yvan Putsys and Pieter Seuren (eds.) *Sentential Complementation and the Lexicon*, Dordrecht: Foris, pp. 171–82.

(2000) 'Pied piping and the word orders of English and Dutch' in Masako Hirotani, A. Coetzee, N. Hall and J.-Y. Kim (Hg.), *Proceedings of the NELS 30*, GLSA, Amherst, pp. 415–26.

(2001) 'Mirror symmetry in Dutch' in Marc van Oostendorp and Elena Anagnostopoulou (eds.) *Grammar in Progress: Articles Presented at the 20th Anniversary of the Comparison of Grammatical Models Group in Tilburg*. Available online: www.meertens.knaw.nl/books/progressingrammar/ (last accessed 3 July 2012).

Kratzer, Angelika (2005) 'Building resultatives' in Claudia Maienborn and Angelika Wöllstein (eds.) *Event Arguments: Foundations and Applications*, Tübingen: Niemeyer, pp. 177–212.

Kress, Bruno (1982) *Isländische Grammatik*, Munich: Hueber.

Kroch, Anthony S. (1994) 'Morphosyntactic variation' in CLS 30/2: *Papers from the 30th Regional Meeting of the Chicago Linguistic Society*, vol. II: *The Parasession on Variation in Linguistic Theory*, pp. 180–201.

Kroch, Anthony. S. and Ann Taylor (2000) 'Verb-complement order in Middle English' in Susan Pintzuk, G. Tsoulas and A. Warner (eds.) *Diachronic Syntax: Models and Mechanisms*, Oxford University Press, pp. 132–63.

Kural, Murat (1997) 'Postverbal constituents in Turkish and the Linear Correspondence Axiom', *Linguistic Inquiry* 28: 498–519.

Lakatos, Imre (1977) *The Methodology of Scientific Research Programmes: Philosophical Papers Volume 1*, Cambridge University Press.

Larson, Richard (1988) 'On the double-object construction', *Linguistic Inquiry* 19: 335–91.

(1990) 'Double-objects revisited: reply to Jackendoff', *Linguistic Inquiry* 21: 589–632.

Larson, Richard and Robert May (1990) 'Antecedent containment or vacuous movement: reply to Baltin', *Linguistic Inquiry* 21: 103–22.

Li, Yafei (1990) 'On V–V compounds in Chinese', *Natural Language and Linguistic Theory* 8: 177–207.

Liao, Wei-wen (2011) *The Symmetry of Syntactic Relations*, unpubl. Ph.D. dissertation, University of Southern California.

Lightfoot, David (1999) *The Development of Language: Acquisition, Change and Evolution*, Malden, MA: Basil Blackwell.

Mahajan, Anoop (1997) 'Toward a unified theory of scrambling' in Norbert Corver and Henk C. van Riemsdijk (eds.) *Studies on Scrambling*, Berlin: Mouton de Gruyter, pp. 301–30.

May, Robert (1985) *Logical Form*, Cambridge, MA: MIT Press.

Mayr, Ernst (1991) *One Long Argument*, Cambridge University Press.

McCawley, James and K. Momoi (1986) 'The constituent structure of *-te* complements' in Shige-Yuki Kuroda (ed.) *Working Papers from the First SDF Workshop in Japanese Syntax*, La Jolla, Dept. of Linguistics, UC San Diego, pp. 97–116.

McCloskey, James (1991) 'Clause structure, ellipsis and proper government in Irish', *Lingua* 85: 259–302.

(2005) 'Predicates and heads in Irish clausal syntax' in Andrew Carnie, Heidi Harley and Sheila Ann Dooley (eds.) *Verb First: On the Syntax of Verb-Initial Languages*, Amsterdam: John Benjamins, pp. 155–74.

Monachesi, Paola (1999) *A Lexical Approach to Italian Cliticization* (CSLI Lecture Notes 84), Stanford, CA: CSLI Publications.

Montermini, Fabio (2008) 'La composition en italien dans un cadre de morphologie lexematique' in Dany Amiot (ed.) *La composition dans une perspective typologique*, Arras: Artois Presses Université, pp. 161–87.

Neeleman, Ad (1995) 'Complex predicates in Dutch and English' in Hubert Haider, Sue Olsen and Sten Vikner (eds.) *Studies in Comparative Germanic Syntax*, Dordrecht: Kluwer, pp. 219–40.

Neeleman, Ad and Hans van de Koot (2002) 'Bare resultatives', *The Journal of Comparative Germanic Linguistics* 6(1): 1–52.

Neeleman, Ad and Fred Weerman (1993) 'The balance between syntax and morphology: Dutch particles and resultatives', *Natural Language and Linguistic Theory* 11: 433–75.

Newmeyer, Frederick J. (2001) 'Where is functional explanation?' in Mary Andronis, Christopher Ball, Heidi Elston and Sylvain Neuvel (eds.) *Papers from the Thirty-Seventh Meeting of the Chicago Linguistic Society. Part 2: The Panels*, Chicago Linguistic Society, pp. 99–122.

(2008) 'Universals in syntax', *The Linguistic Review* 25: 35–82.

Nilsen, Øystein (2003) *Eliminating Positions: Syntax and Semantics of Sentential Modification*, Ph.D. dissertation, University of Utrecht.

Ordóñez, Francisco (1997) *Word Order and Clause Structure in Spanish and Other Romance Languages*, Ph.D. dissertation, CUNY Graduate Center, New York.

Ouhalla, Jamal (1991) *Functional Categories and Parametric Variation*, London: Routledge.

Palmer, Frank R. (1974) *The English Verb*, London: Longman.

Pesetsky, David (1995) *Zero Syntax. Experiencers and Cascades*. Cambridge, MA: MIT Press.

Phillips, Colin (1995) 'Right association in parsing and grammar', *MIT Working Papers in Linguistics* (Papers on Language Processing and Acquisition), 26: 37–93.

(1999) *Linear Order and Constituency*, ms., University of Delaware (revised version 2003 in *Linguistic Inquiry*).

(2003) 'Linear order and constituency', *Linguistic Inquiry* 34: 37–90.

Piera, Carlos (1995) 'On compounding in English and Spanish' in Hector Campos and Paula Kempchinsky (eds.) *Evolution and Revolution in Linguistics. Essays in Honor of Carlos Otero*, Washington, DC: Georgetown University Press, pp. 302–15.

Pinker, Steven and Ray Jackendoff (2005) 'The faculty of language: what's special about it?', *Cognition* 95: 201–36.

Pintzuk, Susan (1991) *Phrase Structures in Competition: Variation and Change in Old English Word Order*, Ph.D. dissertation, University of Pennsylvania, Philadelphia.

(1999) *Phrase Structures in Competition: Variation and Change in Old English Word Order*, New York: Garland (revised and expanded version of Pintzuk (1991)).
  (2002) 'Verb–object order in Old English: variation as grammatical competition' in David Lightfoot (ed.) *Syntactic Effects of Morphological Change*, Oxford University Press, pp. 276–99.
Pintzuk, Susan and Ann Taylor (2006) 'The loss of OV order in the history of English' in Ans van Kemenade and B. Los (eds.) *The Handbook of the History of English*, Oxford: Blackwell, pp. 249–78.
Prell, Heinz Peter (2003) 'Typologische Aspekte der Mittelhochdeutschen Prosasyntax. Der Elementarsatz und die Nominalphrase' in Anja Lobenstein-Reichmann and Oskar Reichmann (eds.) *Neue historische Grammatiken*, Tübingen: Niemeyer, pp. 241–56.
Quine, Willard V. O. (1960) *Word and Object*, Cambridge, MA: MIT Press.
  (1970) 'Methodological reflections on current linguistic theory', *Synthese* 21 and 22: 386–98.
Quirk, Randolph, Sidney Greenbaum, Geoffrey Leech and Jan Svartvik (1985) *A Comprehensive Grammar of the English Language*, London: Longman.
Resnik, Philip (1992) 'Left-corner parsing and psychological plausibility' in *Proceedings of Coling* 92, pp. 191–7.
Ritter, Elizabeth and Sara Thomas Rosen (1993) 'Deriving causation', *Natural Language and Linguistic Theory* 11: 519–55.
Rizzi, Luigi (1982) *Issues in Italian Syntax*, Dordrecht: Foris.
  (1990) *Relativized Minimality*, Cambridge, MA: MIT Press.
Roberts, Ian (1997) 'Restructuring, head movement and locality', *Linguistic Inquiry* 28: 423–60.
  (2000) 'Caricaturing dissent', *Natural Language and Linguistic Theory* 18: 849–57.
Roeper, Thomas and William Snyder (2005) 'Language learnability and the forms of recursion' in Anna Maria DiSciullo and Roberto Delmonte (eds.) *UG and External Systems: Language, Brain and Computation*, Amsterdam: John Benjamins, pp. 155–69.
Roeper, Thomas, William Snyder and Kazuko Hiramatsu (2002) 'Learnability in a Minimalist framework: root compounds, merger, and the syntax–morphology interface' in Inge Lasser (ed.) *The Process of Language Acquisition*, Frankfurt (Proceedings of the 1999 GALA Conference), Frankfurt am Main: Peter Lang.
Rögnvaldsson, Eiríkur (1982) *Um orðaröð og færslur í íslensku*, Master's thesis, Reykjavik: University of Iceland. [Published 1990 as vol. II of *Málfræðirannsóknir*, Málvísindastofnum Háskóla Íslands, Reykjavík.]
  (1996) 'Word order variation in Old Icelandic', *Working Papers in Scandinavian Syntax* 58: 55–86.
Saito, Mamoru (1994) 'Additional wh-effects and the adjunction site theory', *Journal of East Asian Linguistics* 3: 195–240.
Saito, Mamoru and Naoki Fukui (1998) 'Order in phrase structure and movement', *Linguistic Inquiry* 29: 439–74.
Sapir, Edward (1921) *Language*, New York: Harcourt, Brace.
Schallert, Oliver (2006) *Hybride OV/VO Systeme und syntaktischer Wandel zu OV und VO in den germanischen Sprachen*, Master's thesis, FB Linguistik, University of Salzburg.

Schneider, David Andrew (1999) *Parsing and Incrementality*, Ph.D. dissertation, University of Delaware, Newark.
Sells, Peter (1990) 'VP in Japanese: evidence from -te complements' in Hajime Hoji (ed.) *Japanese Korean Linguistics*, Stanford, CA: CSLI Publications, pp. 319–33.
Simpson, Jane (1983) 'Resultatives' in Lorraine Levin, Malka Rappaport and Annie Zaenen (eds.) *Papers in Lexical-Functional Grammar*, Bloomington, IN: Indiana University Linguistics Club, pp. 143–57.
Singh, Uday N. (1980) 'Bole: an unresolved problem in Bengali Syntax', *Indian Linguistics* 41: 188–95.
Slezak, Peter (2009) 'Linguistic explanation and psychological reality', *Croatian Journal of Philosophy* 9: 3–21.
Speas, Margaret (1990) *Phrase Structure in Natural Language*, Dordrecht: Kluwer.
Stabler, Edward P. (1991) 'Avoid the pedestrian's paradox' in Robert C. Berwick (ed.) *Principle-based Parsing: Computation and Psycholinguistics*, Dordrecht, Boston: Kluwer Academic Publishers, pp. 199–237.
  (1994) 'The finite connectivity of linguistic structure' in Charles Clifton Jr., Lyn Frazier and Keith Rayner (eds.) *Perspectives on Sentence Processing*, Hillsdale, NJ: Lawrence Erlbaum Associates, pp. 303–36.
Stepanov, Arthur and Wei-Tien Dylan Tsai (2008) 'Cartography and licensing of wh-adjuncts: a cross-linguistic perspective', *Natural Language and Linguistic Theory* 26(3): 589–638.
Stich, Stephen (1979) 'Between Chomskyan rationalism and Popperian empiricism', *British Journal for the Philosophy of Science* 30(4): 329–47.
Stowell, Tim (1981) *Origins of Phrase Structure*, Ph.D. dissertation, MIT, Cambridge, MA.
Stroik, Thomas (1990) 'Adverbs as V-sisters', *Linguistic Inquiry* 21: 654–61.
  (1996) *Minimalism, Scope, and VP Structure*, Thousand Oaks, CA: Sage Publications.
Svenonius, Peter (1996) 'The optionality of the verb–particle construction', *Working Papers in Scandinavian Syntax* 57: 47–75.
  (2003) 'Swedish particles and directional prepositions' in Lars-Olof Delsing, Cecilia Falk, Gunlög Josefsson and Halldór Ármann Sigurdsson (eds.) *Grammar in Focus: Festschrift for Christer Platzack*, University of Lund, Dept. of Scandinavian Studies, pp. 343–51.
Szabolcsi, Anna and Frans Zwarts (1993) 'Weak islands and an algebraic semantics for scope-taking', *Natural Language Semantics* 1: 235–85.
Taraldsen, Knut Tarald (2000) 'V-movement and VP-movement in derivations leading to VO-order' in Peter, Svenonius (ed.) *The Derivation of VO and OV*, Amsterdam: Benjamins, pp. 97–122.
Thráinsson, Höskuldur (2010) 'Predictable and unpredictable sources of variable verb and adverb placement in Scandinavian', *Lingua* 120: 1,062–88.
Travis, Lisa (1984) *Parameters and Effects of Word Order Variation*, Ph.D. dissertation, MIT.
  (1989) 'Parameters of phrase structure' in Mark R. Baltin and Anthony S. Kroch (eds.) *Alternative Conceptions of Phrase Structure*, University of Chicago Press, pp. 263–79.
Trips, Carola (2001) *From OV to VO in Early Middle English*, Amsterdam: Benjamins.

Tuller, Laurie (1992) 'The syntax of postverbal focus constructions in Chadic', *Natural Language and Linguistic Theory* 10: 303–34.
Van Chình, Tru'o'ng (1970) *Structure de la langue vietnamienne*, Paris: Imprimerie nationale librairie orientaliste Paul Geuthner.
Van Kemenade, Ans (1987) *Syntactic Case and Morphological Case in the History of English*, Cambridge, MA: MIT Press.
Vikner, Sten (1995) *Verb Movement and Expletive Subjects in the Germanic Languages*, Oxford University Press.
   (2001) *Verb Movement Variation in German and Optimality Theory*, tenure thesis (*Habilitationsschrift*), University of Tübingen. Available online: www.hum.au.dk/engelsk/engsv/papers/viknhabi.pdf (last accessed 3 July 2012).
Wilson, John and Alison Henry (1995) 'Parameter setting within socially realistic linguistics', *Language in Society* 27: 1–21.
Winkler, Susanne (1994) *Secondary Predication in English: A Syntactic and Focus-Theoretic Approach*, Ph.D. dissertation, University of Tübingen.
   (1996) *Focus and Secondary Predication*, Berlin: Mouton de Gruyter.
Wundt, Wilhelm (1888) 'Selbstbeobachtung und innere Wahrnehmung', *Philosophische Studien* 4: 292–309.
   (1901) *Sprachgeschichte und Sprachpsychologie. Mit Rücksicht auf B. Delbrücks 'Grundfragen der Sprachforschung'*, Leipzig: Engelmann.
Wurmbrand, Susi (2006) 'Verb clusters, verb raising, and restructuring' in Martin Everaert and Henk van Riemsdijk (eds.) *Syncom* (The Blackwell Companion to Syntax), Chapter 75, Oxford: Blackwell, pp. 227–341.
Yatsushiro, Kazuko (2000) 'VP-internal scrambling', *Arbeitspapiere des Sonderforschungsbereichs 340*, #160, University of Stuttgart, University of Tübingen, IBM Heidelberg.
Zaenen, A., J. Maling and H. Thráinsson (1985) 'Case and grammatical functions: the Icelandic passive', *Natural Language and Linguistic Theory* 3: 441–83.
Zwart, C. Jan-Wouter (1993) *Dutch Syntax: A Minimalist Approach*, doctoral dissertation, Groningen University.
   (1996) *Morphosyntax of Verb Movement: A Minimalist Approach to the Syntax of Dutch*, Dordrecht: Kluwer.
   (1997) 'The Germanic SOV languages and the Universal Base Hypothesis' in Liliane Haegeman (ed.) *The New Comparative Syntax*, London: Longman, pp. 246–67.

Index

adaptive design, 34, 39
adjacency, 13, 14, 51, 107, 142, 143, 144
Afrikaans, 62, 98, 210
antisymmetry, 201, 257

Bengali, 71, 73, 251, 260

centre-embedded, 16, 92, 96, 120, 134, 234
Circassian, 83, 252
clause union, 91, 130, 137, 146, 147, 148, 228
closure principle, 136, 137
compactness, xiv, 11, 12, 15, 16, 57, 62, 107, 110, 111, 130, 131, 190, 205, 210, 227, 228
competing-grammar hypothesis, 116, 117
complex-predicate analysis, 176, 177, 178, 179, 180, 181, 184, 185, 189
compound noun, recursive, 196, 197, 203, 209
Croatian, 60

Danish, 6, 41, 42, 43, 97, 127, 181, 182, 189, 226, 256
Darwinian, 20, 39
depictive predicates, 174
deverbal nominalization, 209
directional identification, 41, 87, 100, 145, 207, 236
directionality parameter, 4, 41, 63, 64, 94, 101, 125, 126, 231, 232, 233, 235
domain closure, 151, 153
double object, 2, 15, 40, 41, 46, 49, 56, 57, 108, 215, 256, 258

edge effect, 11, 12, 13, 14, 36, 60, 79, 94, 95, 130, 131, 137, 143, 144, 145, 146, 149, 154, 156, 171, 190, 205, 247
endocentric, 9, 27, 30, 31, 49, 105, 201
EPP property, 10, 109
EPP feature, 222

evolution, cognitive, 7, 8, 20, 21, 23, 24, 26, 32, 34, 35, 38, 212, 239, 241
expanded scope, 137, 146
extraposition by movement, 68, 70, 82

falsification, 171, 216,
Faroese, 97, 98, 109
French, 13, 21, 61, 97, 101, 117, 138, 143, 150, 193, 201, 230
Frisian, 62, 98, 210, 229
functional head, clause-final, 71, 73, 76, 80, 81
functional subject position, 10, 11, 12, 62, 64, 90, 109, 110, 130, 131, 176, 221, 222, 223
functionalist, 25, 32, 33, 34, 35, 38

head-initial compounding, 14, 190, 191, 192, 198
head-to-head adjunctions, 17
heavy NP, 43, 104, 131
higher order, 140, 166
Hungarian, 16, 105, 131, 208, 232, 250, 253
hyper-derivational, 240

Icelandic, 12, 15, 42, 43, 56, 63, 89, 97, 98, 99, 108, 112, 113, 117, 120, 124, 181, 183, 184, 219, 221, 222, 223, 224, 226, 227, 232, 256, 257, 260
idiom formation, 54
infinitival construction, 16, 62, 77, 93, 95, 96, 97, 101, 109, 126, 147, 148, 154, 190, 203, 209, 220, 228, 239
information structure, 132, 147, 168
interface condition, 136, 156
IPP, xvii, 129, 131, 133, 134
Irish, 89
Italian, 35, 44, 78, 79, 83, 92, 123, 192, 193, 201, 230, 258, 260

Japanese, 15, 34, 42, 75, 84, 88, 91, 93, 120, 138, 140, 217, 234, 243, 256, 257, 258, 260

Kashmiri, 2
Korean, 88, 91, 93, 120, 234, 246, 256, 260

language acquisition, 8, 9, 33, 101, 114, 117, 127
left-corner parser, 8, 25, 212, 227
lexical C°, 68, 72, 73
lexical complementizer, 72
lexical functional head, 68, 69, 71, 81, 95

Malagasy, 138
Middle High German, 103, 124, 125, 128
minimal mutual c-command, 12, 64
Minimalist Program, 17, 18, 48, 53, 55, 212, 214, 216, 224, 239, 240, 242, 244, 248, 251

nominalization, 17, 45, 179, 190, 202, 203, 204, 207, 208, 209, 210, 228
North Germanic, 98, 232, 233
Norwegian, 15, 56, 88, 97, 108, 130, 181, 182, 184, 189, 226, 250

Ockham's razor, 216, 235, 237
Old English, 99, 112, 119, 121, 122, 130, 232, 259
Old High German, 99, 112, 113
opacity effect, 82, 154, 223, 224
opaque for extraction, 59, 154, 155, 165, 171, 223, 225, 244

parser friendliness, 25, 26, 212, 227
particle stranding, 57, 108, 226
particles, postverbal, 112, 225, 226
particles, preverbal, 225, 226
particle–verb order, 104, 221, 225
PDI, 4, 7, 9, 10, 11, 12, 55, 89, 94, 142, 205
Polish, 44, 59, 60, 61, 131
postverbal adverbials, 136, 137, 150, 158, 159, 164, 170, 171, 172, 256

quirky subject, 12, 63, 89, 222, 223

relative clause, 35, 83, 84, 161, 247, 252
result predication, 173, 174, 177, 189
right-adjoined, 149, 158, 160, 164, 170

right-associative, 26, 27, 28, 29, 30, 31, 37, 38, 39, 40, 41, 42, 47, 63, 67, 70, 84, 94
Romansh, 2
Russian, 58, 59, 60, 131

scope domain, 14, 79, 148
secondary predicate, 174, 177, 186, 187, 220
sentence adverbial, 139, 153, 154
sentence negation, 85, 137, 138, 139, 147, 252
Serbian, 60
serialization pattern, 112, 170
Slavic language, 58, 105
small-clause analysis, 176, 177, 178, 179, 180, 181, 185, 186
stacked VP, 134, 146, 221, 227, 228, 248
string-to-structure, 25, 34, 93, 211, 213, 215
structure generation, 215, 244
superiority, 28, 42, 49, 137, 140, 141, 165, 255, 256
Swedish, 42, 43, 97, 181, 182, 183, 188, 189, 226, 261
symmetry breaking, 2, 5, 11, 20, 40, 61, 235

Tangale, 82, 83
third-type language, 102, 123, 135, 214
transderivational constraint, 215
Turkish, 82, 84, 85, 86, 258

*V – O – Aux, 118, 119
V2-property, 66, 97, 98, 101, 102, 117, 123, 125, 130, 135, 219
verb-order variation, 16, 67, 91, 115, 125, 130, 221, 229, 233
Vietnamese, 195, 196
V-movement, 2, 16, 48, 51, 66, 67, 73, 78, 79, 80, 83, 84, 91, 107, 125, 135, 182, 211, 218, 233, 234, 261
VP-shell, 29
VP topicalization, 80, 162, 226
V-to-'I', 68, 69, 78, 80
V-to-C, 76, 77, 79

wh-movement, 59, 66, 74, 75, 82, 83, 131, 229, 230
wh-movement to the right, 83
word-formation process, 17, 57, 178, 191, 196, 203, 209, 210

Yiddish, 97, 100, 102, 103, 104, 105, 111, 119, 124, 129, 131, 135, 229, 232, 233, 252